T0256028

Artificial Intelligence and the Media

# Artificial Intelligence and the Media

Reconsidering Rights and Responsibilities

*Edited by*

Taina Pihlajarinne

*Professor, Faculty of Law, University of Helsinki, Finland*

Anette Alén-Savikko

*University Lecturer, Faculty of Law, University of Helsinki, Finland*

Cheltenham, UK • Northampton, MA, USA

© The Editors and Contributors Severally 2022

All rights reserved. No part of this publication may be reproduced, stored in a retrieval system or transmitted in any form or by any means, electronic, mechanical or photocopying, recording, or otherwise without the prior permission of the publisher.

Published by
Edward Elgar Publishing Limited
The Lypiatts
15 Lansdown Road
Cheltenham
Glos GL50 2JA
UK

Edward Elgar Publishing, Inc.
William Pratt House
9 Dewey Court
Northampton
Massachusetts 01060
USA

A catalogue record for this book
is available from the British Library

This book is available electronically in the **Elgar**online
Law subject collection
http://dx.doi.org/10.4337/9781839109973

ISBN 978 1 83910 996 6 (cased)
ISBN 978 1 83910 997 3 (eBook)

Printed and bound in Great Britain by TJ Books Ltd, Padstow, Cornwall

# Contents

# Contributors

**Anette Alén-Savikko**, University Lecturer, University of Helsinki, Faculty of Law.

**Rosa Maria Ballardini**, Professor, University of Lapland/Faculty of Law, Finland.

**Catalina Goanta**, Assistant Professor, Faculty of Law, Maastricht University, the Netherlands.

**Fabienne Graf**, Research Assistant, School of Law, University of Lucerne, Switzerland.

**Robert van den Hoven van Genderen**, Professor, University of Lapland, Finland and Vrije Universiteit Amsterdam, the Netherlands.

**Päivi Korpisaari**, Professor, Faculty of Law, University of Helsinki, Finland.

**M. R. Leiser**, Assistant Professor, eLaw, Leiden University, the Netherlands.

**Leo Leppänen**, doctoral student, Department of Computer Science, University of Helsinki, Finland.

**Philip M. Napoli**, James R. Shepley Professor of Public Policy, Sanford School of Public Policy, Duke University, USA.

**Inger B. Ørstavik**, Professor, Department of Private Law/Centre for European Law, University of Oslo, Norway.

**Taina Pihlajarinne**, Professor, Faculty of Law, University of Helsinki, Finland.

**Ole-Andreas Rognstad**, Professor, Department of Private Law/Centre for European Law, University of Oslo, Norway

**Gerasimos Spanakis**, Assistant Professor, Faculty of Law and Department of Data Science and Knowledge Engineering, Maastricht University, the Netherlands.

**Alexander Thesleff**, doctoral candidate, Faculty of Law, University of Helsinki, Finland.

**Jingrong Tong**, Senior Lecturer in Digital News Cultures, Department of Journalism Studies, The University of Sheffield, UK.

**Sini Valmari**, MSc in Information Processing Science and MSc in Economics and Business Administration, Finland.

**Juha Vesala**, University Researcher, Faculty of Law, University of Lapland and University of Helsinki, Finland.

# Introduction to *Artificial Intelligence and the Media*

## Taina Pihlajarinne and Anette Alén-Savikko

## 1.    EVOLUTION AND REVOLUTION IN THE AI ERA

The media industry has always been changing in close connection to technological development, whether in terms of the printing press or radio waves. Currently, artificial intelligence (AI) and automation are key drivers in the (r)evolution of the ways in which news and other media content is produced, distributed, and consumed. Increased use of AI and automation in media practices and the underlying technical architecture implies changes to journalistic work and challenges conventional media roles and functions. Nonetheless, the public's right to information should be preserved alongside civil rights, while the idea of journalism still includes (maybe more than ever) expectations of accountability: its task is to serve and answer to the public, to act responsibly.[1]

New technologies are expected to increase efficiency in the newsroom: many routine tasks are apt for automation; consumption patterns become highly measurable, while AI-based content production gains new ground. For their part, online platforms for content-sharing and social networking moderate and curate their catalogue and newsfeed with the help of AI-based solutions. As its 'fuel', the use of AI and automation relies on massive amounts of data, and utilisation of data is becoming an integral part of media practices. This is not without legal and policy implications: First, AI and automation rely on data utilisation. This in turn means reassessing data ownership and intellectual property (IP) rights. Second, AI and algorithmic control are accompanied by issues involving agency and responsibilities, whether in terms of authorship,

---

[1]    Robert G Picard and Victor Pickard, 'Essential Principles for Contemporary Media and Communications Policymaking' (2017) *Reuters Institute for the Study of Journalism* 7, 30–31 http://reutersinstitute.politics.ox.ac.uk/publication/essential -principlescontemporary-media-and-communications-policymaking accessed 23 January 2020.

public interest rationales, or private law liability. These aspects raise fundamental questions about how rights and responsibilities should be reconsidered in the light of incentives for accountable utilisation of AI.

Utilisation of AI affects the media sector in a wide sense, from legacy media to online platforms, including social media sites. Moreover, the changes go deep into the institutional fabric of the media. It is increasingly important to view the media sector from a holistic perspective instead of as separate silos.[2] It is no longer clear-cut where to draw the lines of editorial conduct, while challenges arise both for conventional approaches regarding the role and functions of the media as well as in terms of incentives and conditions for the media to operate in the digital environment and in today's data-driven society.[3] AI and algorithms also pose challenges for editorial decision-making and content production by introducing 'outsiders' to the newsroom and to journalistic practices, such as programmers and developers. At the same time, the public is being exposed to new types of threats and forms of opacity, especially in terms of privacy and algorithmic decision-making. Personal data is increasingly used by the media in order to monitor consumption and customise production, while AI-based solutions are adopted to facilitate content management.

These developments take us back to fundamental questions, such as: what is 'journalism' or 'news'. They also imply a need to revisit basic rationales and justifications of media regulation as well as familiar demands for accountability. Reliance on data makes a case for examining data protection and IP laws. Moreover, use of AI highlights questions of agency, entitlements, and obligations, especially as the human contribution becomes increasingly detached from automated (autonomous) processes and end products. From a legal perspective, this translates into questions of authorship and (among others) private law liability. This edited volume examines the feasibility of principles and concepts as currently applied in the light of incentivising accountability and puts forward alternative solutions. Accountable use of AI reduces negative societal impacts, including those related to harms to privacy and the credibility of journalism as well as overprotection of IP rights, while promoting positive societal impacts, such as efficient and high-quality content production.

---

[2]    Andrew Chadwick, *The Hybrid Media System: Politics and Power* (OUP 2013).
[3]    Philip Michael Napoli, *Audience Evolution: New Technologies and the Transformation of Media Audiences* (Columbia University Press 2011); Chris Peters and Marcel Broersma (eds), *Rethinking Journalism Again: Societal Role and Public Relevance of in a Digital Age* (Routledge 2016); Philip Michael Napoli (ed), *Mediated Communication. Handbooks of Communication Science* (Mouton De Gruyter 2018).

## 2.    REGULATION, RIGHTS AND RESPONSIBILITIES

The legal and policy dimensions are of fundamental importance for the future of the media and journalism. Importantly, investing in and relying on new technologies in the media sector requires some degree of predictability, while policy-makers are in desperate need of evidence-based solutions. At the same time, however, it has become clear that the concept of AI needs to be explained and anchored in journalistic practices so as to enable informed policy and law-making. For their part, regulatory and self-regulatory tools may work as incentives for accountability. Then again, the market for AI-based solutions is developing even as we speak. The role of global online platforms has been questioned not only by legacy media companies but also by legislators. However, these platforms have considerable power in terms of developing media practices and constructing their own rights and responsibilities, for instance in the field of copyright or data protection.[4] There is clearly a need for a more principled approach that draws from ethics and shared societal values.[5] However, conventional principles are seldom applicable as such in the context of AI and automation, but rather require in-depth analysis. Moreover, in many cases, the legislative framework is in a state of flux and lagging behind real-life development. This is true in the case of automated or AI-based content supervision and user data processing by online platforms. Indeed, many policy and legislative solutions have rather operated on a piecemeal basis or have seemed rather uncritically to be drawing from conventional regulatory models and following a one-sided economic logic.[6]

During the finishing stages of this volume, the EU Commission released its draft framework for regulating AI. On 21 April 2021, the Proposal for a Regulation laying down harmonised rules on artificial intelligence (Artificial Intelligence Act)[7] was introduced. Due to the timing of this book, most of the

---

[4]    Jockum Hildén, *The Politics of Datafication: The Influence of Lobbyists on the EU's Data Protection reform and its Consequences for the Legitimacy of the General Data Protection Regulation* (University of Helsinki 2019) http://urn.fi/URN:ISBN:978 -951-51-3410-3 accessed 24 June 2021.

[5]    Picard and Pickard (n 1) 5–10.

[6]    See also Andrej Savin, 'Regulating Internet Platforms in the EU – The Emergence of the "Level Playing Field"' (2018) 34(6) *Computer Law & Security Review* 1215–1231 https://doi.org/10.1016/j.clsr.2018.08.008.

[7]    Commission, 'Proposal for a Regulation of the European Parliament and of the Council laying down rules on artificial intelligence' (Artificial Intelligence Act) and amending certain Union legislative acts COM (2021) 206 final (21 April 2021) https://eur-lex.europa.eu/legal-content/EN/ALL/?uri=CELEX:52021PC0206 accessed 16 May 2021.

authors have not been able to take account of the proposal in their chapters. However, the approaches adopted and connections between this volume and the proposal are briefly touched on here, in Mark Leiser's opening chapter as well as in the Conclusions. The proposal for an Artificial Intelligence Act aims to safeguard a functioning internal market as far as AI systems are concerned, at the same time stressing fundamental rights, trustworthiness, and ethics. The proposal essentially relies on a risk-based approach and aims to establish harmonised rules in the European Union.[8] The proposal identifies and acknowledges both the societal benefits and the new types of risks involved in using AI.[9] This 'duality' is closely similar to the approach of this volume, which tackles both rights and responsibilities in automated media. As far as regulatory tools are concerned, similarly to the core of this volume, the proposal for an Artificial Intelligence Act in the EU claims to offer a 'balanced regulatory approach'.[10]

## 3.     STRUCTURE AND CONTENTS OF THE VOLUME

This volume discusses pressing issues at the intersections of AI, the media, and the law under an umbrella of critically re-examining rights and responsibilities from the perspectives of incentives for accountable utilisation of AI. The volume asks: (1) What do 'AI' and 'accountability' mean in terms of media practices, principles, and power relations? (2) How to address the (r)evolution with informed law and policy in order to incentivise accountable utilisation of AI and reduce negative societal impacts? What kind of solution offers a balanced outcome? Both legislative and ethical solutions related to these themes are analysed. With regard to the Proposal for the Artificial Intelligence Act, this volume may be read both as complementary and as a source of critique. Complementarity takes place especially where the specifics of AI in the media sector are concerned, while critique mainly relates to the more principled or rights-oriented approach that this volume is seeking.

In Part I on 'Journalistic Principles and Artificial Intelligence', the focus is on general legal and policy issues at the intersections of AI and journalism from the perspective of incentives for accountable utilisation of AI in the media. In setting the scene, Leiser discusses journalistic endeavours and the risks of AI, especially from the perspective of some inherent biases that are involved in the utilisation of AI and automation. Leiser sheds light on some inaccuracies and discriminatory features that training data contains or contrib-

---

8     Ibid., 1–3, 7, 12–14.
9     Ibid., 1–3.
10    Ibid., 3.

utes to. In doing so, he also ends up questioning assumptions of objectivity traditionally linked to journalism, data, and AI. Nonetheless, the importance of 'exposure diversity'[11] is acknowledged in the context of AI solutions – a topic of utmost importance in a world filled with disinformation of various sorts.

Alén-Savikko elaborates on the concept of transparency in data and computational journalism, analysing it in terms of both law and ethics. She explores potential 'rights' to identify computer-generated content and to access information about the background data and logics of algorithmic news production. However, transparency proves to be a rather peculiar demand and one which is somewhat difficult to turn into actual practice. These questions go beyond what transparency is as a data protection issue. However, since personal data is involved in the processes around AI systems, it is essential to discuss relevant aspects of European data protection law in the context of automated media.

Korpisaari elaborates on the 'journalistic exemption' in the EU General Data Protection Regulation (GDPR). This also leads to interesting questions about journalism itself.

Part II of this volume, dedicated to 'Trust, Disinformation and Platforms', deals with the role, rights, and obligations of platforms as well as the power relations involved in their operation from the perspective of incentives for accountable utilisation of AI. For their part, Napoli and Graf offer an approach to social media platforms as public trustees. By this, they mean a model familiar in the US broadcasting sector. Napoli and Graf ask whether it could apply to social media so as to offer solutions to the challenges involved in disinformation.

Tong addresses practices of policing content on social media platforms such as Facebook and Twitter by addressing three dilemmas: she addresses trust, freedom of information, and liability and their implications for ethics and law.

Social media recommender systems and their commercial unfairness are addressed by Goanta and Spanakis. As a result of the increase in social media users earning a living with content creation, the underlying power imbalance becomes evident – while lack of transparency in algorithmic operations is apt to make matters worse. This calls for approaches that draw from unfair competition.

In Part III, the topic of 'Remits and Limits of Exclusive Rights' is discussed from the perspective of intellectual property (IP) law. The chapters look at the guiding principles, concepts, and new types of rights in the field of IP law, mainly copyright, as well as limitations to those rights. Exclusive rights are examined from the standpoint of incentivising content production powered by

---

[11]   See also Natali Helberger and Mira Burri, 'Public Service Media and Exposure Diversity' (2015) 9 *International Journal of Communication* 1319–1323.

AI and taking into account societal impacts, such as those related to freedom of information. Part III addresses essential questions related to the incentive function of copyright. This is examined critically in the light of AI-based content production, while the need to rethink legal personality is discussed in the context of creative processes. Thereby, pressing questions of appropriate forms of stimuli and legal status with regard to AI are addressed in the context of the media in particular. Moreover, access to data is discussed as a crucial issue with regard to use of AI in the media sector.

For his part, Rognstad addresses AI and European copyright law in terms of works having to be the results of authors' own intellectual efforts. He contributes to efforts to rethink the current legislative framework in order to make room for AI in content production.

Ballardini and van den Hoven van Genderen explore the question of AI as a legal subject in the specific context of automated media.

For their part, Pihlajarinne, Thesleff, Leppänen, and Valmari analyse some specific problems relating to AI-based journalism in terms of incentives, current copyright doctrines, and problems of overly extensive or mistargeted IP protection.

Vesala discusses the newly introduced EU press publishers' right from the perspective of AI, while particularly targeting the effects of the new right on news production and services powered by AI.

Finally, Ørstavik takes a look at access to data for training of algorithms. She discusses the prospects of IP protection, while joining in the wider policy debate on the role of IP rights as mechanisms of stimuli and control.

## 4.    ABOUT THE TOPIC

The writing of this volume took place in the middle of the global Covid-19 pandemic. If nothing more or less, we have seen not only the importance of the media in our society, but also witnessed the power of recommender systems, coordinated campaigns involving disinformation and many other topics addressed in this volume. The following chapters – although originally not intended by the authors – will now be read through the lens of the glasses that this global experience has placed on our noses.

PART I

Journalistic principles and artificial intelligence

# 1. Bias, journalistic endeavours, and the risks of artificial intelligence

## M. R. Leiser

## 1. INTRODUCTION

We are living in a world of fast-developing technologies enabled by machine-learning systems that analyse structured data to infer the probability of an outcome. To address the legal, ethical, and societal challenges associated with allegations and concerns that machines will soon be able to duplicate and replicate the human mind, artificial intelligence (AI) is presently subjected to significant attention from eager legal researchers and policy makers.[1] Of course, the promoters of AI and its associated uses have a dirty little secret – there is no such thing as 'artificial intelligence'. Rather, AI describes a series of technologies used by humans to do the heavy lifting required in the era of big datasets and computational analytics. Its potential ranges from identifying correlations in datasets indiscernible to the human mind to increasing the efficiency of production across a range of industrial applications.

Increasingly, AI is used in the production of news and other journalistic endeavours.[2] Not only are machine-learning systems perceived to be replacing humans in the 'creative' process, but AI also enables journalists by personalizing, recommending, fact-checking, labelling, and translating vast arrays of user-generated and viral content. The deployment of AI systems for the purpose of personalizing content provides a way for platforms to make recommendations that the platform believes might be beneficial to the user. However, commingled within 'personalization' are recommender systems that

---

[1]  R Girasa, 'Artificial Intelligence as a Disruptive Technology', Springer Science and Business Media LLC, 2020; See also R Sil, A Roy, B Bhushan, A K Mazumdar, 'Artificial Intelligence and Machine Learning based Legal Application: The State-of-the-Art and Future Research Trends' (2019) International Conference on Computing, Communication, and Intelligent Systems.

[2]  For a survey of AI use across European Newsrooms, see A Fanta, 'Putting Europe's Robots on the Map: Automated Journalism in News Agencies' (2017) Reuters Institute Fellowship Paper, 9.

are presented by platforms as a means of helping users identify content that they might find appealing, but in reality boost advertising revenue, and can lead to filter bubbles that reinforce narrow or inaccurate viewpoints. As a result of vast amounts of collected data and complex algorithmic judgements, certain recommendations can effectively reinforce discriminatory beliefs (direct/indirect as well as discrimination by association, and discrimination by perception) and/or encourage harassment and victimization.

AI also has a role to play in investigative journalism to 'extract references to real-world entities, like corporations and people, and start looking for relationships between them, essentially building up context around each entity' in big datasets such as the Panama Papers (13.5 million documents) or the ICIJ's data set of 2.5 million documents relating to the offshore holdings and accounts of over 100,000 entities across four large databases.[3] Its promise lies in its capabilities to do the heavy lifting and analytics of huge amounts of data, freeing journalists to undertake more probing and investigative reporting. AI systems have both an important creative potential and an editorial function in 21st-century journalism. AI can find patterns or flag outlier events for further investigation. The promise of AI also plays an important role in identifying misleading content but can direct people to alternative and better sources of information.

With AI becoming instrumental to our information ecosystem, regulators have undertaken to address an identified normative concern associated with machine-learning systems: both implicit and explicit biases in the training data can lead to discriminatory effects. Accordingly, concepts like 'fairness in machine learning', 'accountability', 'algorithmic transparency' as well as 'explainability' alongside various approaches to 'ethical AI' have preoccupied academia, civil society, and policy makers.[4] Significant critique has also been

---

[3]   Can Artificial Intelligence Like IBM's Watson Do Investigative Journalism?, *Fast Company*, 12 November 2013, available at https://www.fastcompany.com/3021545/can-artificial-intelligence-like-ibms-watson-do-investigative-journalism, accessed 25 February 2021.

[4]   J Burrell, 'How the Machine "thinks": Understanding Opacity in Machine Learning Algorithms' (2016) 3 *Big Data & Society* http://bds.sagepub.com/lookup/doi/10.1177/2053951715622512 accessed 25 February 2021; M Butterworth, 'The ICO and Artificial Intelligence: The Role of Fairness in the GDPR Framework' (2018) 34 *Computer Law & Security Review* 257; https://www.sciencedirect.com/science/article/pii/S026736491830044X accessed 25 February 2021; A Datta, M C Tschantz and A Datta, 'Automated Experiments on Ad Privacy Settings: A Tale of Opacity, Choice, and Discrimination' (2015) *Proceedings on Privacy Enhancing Technologies* 92; N Diakopoulos, 'Algorithmic Accountability: On the Investigation of Black Boxes' (New York: Tow Center for Digital Journalism, Columbia University, 2014) http://towcenter.org/research/algorithmic-accountability-on-the-investigation-of-black

undertaken of AI's role in journalistic creation, moderation, and fact-checking disinformation.[5] This chapter attempts to bridge the gap between the regulatory environment for artificial intelligence in the European Union, on the one side, and its use in journalism on the other. The first section explains how machine-learning systems work. The second section identifies vulnerabilities in the deployment of AI in the newsroom. The third section examines the EU's response to the 'rise and risks of AI', before concluding with a discussion of the responsibilities for newsrooms that deploy automated journalism, fact-checking, content creation, and other forms of AI-generated news.

## 2.    UNDERSTANDING AI AND MACHINE LEARNING SYSTEMS

AI systems are defined as:

> software (and possibly also hardware) systems ..., that, given a complex goal, act in the physical or digital dimension by perceiving their environment through data acquisition, interpreting the collected structured or unstructured data, reasoning on

---

-boxes-2/ accessed 25 February 2021; L Diver and B Schafer, 'Opening the Black Box: Petri Nets and Privacy by Design' (2017) 31 *International Review of Law, Computers & Technology* 68 https://doi-org.ezproxy.is.ed.ac.uk/10.1080/13600869.2017.1275123 accessed 25 February 2021; F Doshi-Velez et al., 'Accountability of AI Under the Law: The Role of Explanation' [2017] arXiv:1711.01134 http://arxiv.org/abs/1711 .01134 accessed 25 February 2021; T Gillespie, 'The Relevance of Algorithms' (2014) 167 *Media Technologies: Essays on Communication, Materiality, and Society*; G Kendall and G Wickham, *Using Foucault's Methods* (London; Thousand Oaks, Calif: Sage Publications, 1999); J A Kroll et al., 'Accountable Algorithms' (Rochester, NY: Social Science Research Network, 2016) SSRN Scholarly Paper ID 2765268; http://papers.ssrn.com/abstract=2765268 accessed 25 February 2021; f Pasquale, *The Black Box Society: The Secret Algorithms That Control Money and Information* (Cambridge: Harvard University Press, 2015); A D Selbst and J Powles, 'Meaningful Information and the Right to Explanation' (2017) 7 *International Data Privacy Law* 233; S Wachter, B Mittelstadt and L Floridi, 'Why a Right to Explanation of Automated Decision-Making Does Not Exist in the General Data Protection Regulation' (2017) 7 *International Data Privacy Law* 76.

    [5]    See, e.g., M Broussard, N Diakopoulos, A L Guzman, R Abebe, M Dupagne, and C-H Chuan, 'Artificial Intelligence and "Journalism"' (2019) 96(3) *Journalism & Mass Communication Quarterly* 673–95; N Diakopoulos, *Automating the News: How Algorithms are Rewriting the Media* (Harvard University Press, 2019); A McStay, *Emotional AI: The Rise of Empathic Media* (Sage, 2018); M Hansen, M Roca-Sales, J M Keegan, and G King, *Artificial Intelligence: Practice and Implications for Journalism* (Academic Commons, Columbia, 2017); On a wide range of aspects of journalistic endeavours, see F Marconi, *Newsmakers: Artificial Intelligence and the Future of Journalism* (Columbia University Press, 2020).

the knowledge, or processing the information, derived from this data and deciding the best action(s) to take to achieve the given goal.[6]

Programmers have developed AI systems using natural language processing to write simple articles such as sports or stock market reports. GPT-3, OpenAI's language generator, can generate endless texts in response to input parameters provided by humans;[7] for example, Tencent's 'Dreamwriter' can write an article in 0.5 seconds and up 300,000 articles a year.[8] Smartphone applications such as Prisma provide their users with an AI-based digital lens to change or ameliorate their photos, while ZAO offers their users an opportunity for creating short deepfake videos with their own faces.[9] Google's AI poetry uses neural network techniques to train its AI system;[10] it then uses an autoencoder to write full sentences.[11] Furthermore, generative Adversarial Networks (GANs) facilitate projects such as fake picture generators or Grover, a fake news generator.[12]

---

[6]   High-Level Expert Group on Artificial Intelligence, High-Level Expert Group on Artificial Intelligence, available at https://ec.europa.eu/digital-single-market/en/news/definition-artificial-intelligence-main-capabilities-and-scientific-disciplines, at 6, accessed 16 February 2021.

[7]   For an example of this, see 'A robot wrote this entire article. Are you scared yet, human?', *The Guardian*, 8 September 2020, available at https://www.theguardian.com/commentisfree/2020/sep/08/robot-wrote-this-article-gpt-3, accessed 16 February 2021.

[8]   For an introductory video of 'Dreamwriter', available at https://v.qq.com/x/page/z071387ge88.html, accessed 16 February 2021.

[9]   For Prisma, see V Savov, 'Prisma will make you fall in love with photo filters all over again', *The Verge*, 19 July 2016, available at https://www.theverge.com/2016/7/19/12222112/prisma-art-photo-app accessed 25 February 2021. For ZAO, see Z Doffman, 'Chinese Deepfake App ZAO goes viral, privacy of millions "at risk"', *Forbes*, available at https://www.forbes.com/sites/zakdoffman/2019/09/02/chinese-best-ever-deepfake-app-zao-sparks-hugefaceapp-such as-privacy-storm/, accessed 16 February 2021.

[10]   Deep learning is a subset of machine-learning. It uses deep neural networks, deep belief networks, recurrent neural networks and/or convolutional neural networks for machine-learning processes: it uses these architectures to model its predictive computational statistics. See, G Ras, M Gerven, and W Haselager, 'Explanation Methods in Deep Learning: Users, Values, Concerns and Challenges', ArXiv 1803.07517 (2018).

[11]   M Burgess, 'Google's AI has written some amazingly mournful poetry', *WIRED*, 16 May 2016, available at https://www.wired.co.uk/article/google-artificial-intelligence-poetry, accessed 16 February 2021.

[12]   T Karras et al., 'Analyzing and Improving the Image Quality of Stylegan', arXiv preprint arXiv:1912.04958 (2019), demonstrations available at https://thispersondoesnotexist.com accessed 25 February 2021. For Grover, see also rowanz, 'Code for Defending Against Neural Fake News', available at https://github.com/rowanz/grover, demonstrations available at https://thisarticledoesnotexist.com accessed 25 February 2021.

Generative AI systems can be divided into two categories: fully autonomous generative AI and co-creative generative AI. The latter is rarer as it involves real-time human–AI interaction during the process. The user and the AI system generate outputs in response to inputs provided by the other party. In traditional decision or prediction systems, outputs are based on a 'handcrafted' model: data is pumped into a handcrafted model of pre-determined algorithms and pre-set parameters. As Leiser and Dechesne state, 'handcrafted systems are those that answer questions directed at classifying items (i.e., predicting discrete values), or predicting continuous values (such as risks, price development, etc.). Humans are left to interpret the outcomes'.[13] However, machine-learning models operate on a set of pure correlations without 'explicit pointers' for humans to interpret. Deep learning is a type of machine learning that uses deep neural networks to train a computer to perform human-like tasks, like recognizing speech or images. Machine-learning systems turn this 'training data' into a model that can predict or classify new data on the basis of patterns distilled from the training data. Private traits and attributes are predictable from the digital records of human behaviour. However, training data does not get stored in the model. This is mostly done by machine-learning algorithms, where the algorithms reconstruct relationships and dependencies between the characteristics in the training data and the target output. The resulting model then contains a 'logic' of the dependency of the output on the input for the given task, which it has derived from the training data. Machine-learning systems will develop capabilities without any way of reverse engineering the data from which the system learned, nor is it possible to fully understand the logic inside the 'black box'.[14]

Most regulatory attention in this space concerns lack of transparency about the logic used in AI systems either trained on personal data or for the purposes of decision-making that has an impact on individuals. For example, in its final report on 'Disinformation and fake news', the UK's Department of Culture, Media and Sport specifically called for the extension of protections of privacy law 'to include models used to make inferences about an individual'.[15]

---

[13]    M R Leiser and F Dechesne, 'Governing Machine-learning Models: Challenging the Personal Data Presumption' (2020) 10(3) *International Data Privacy Law* 187–200.

[14]    'Black box(es)' is a semi-colloquial term used to describe opaque machine-learning models, which are traditionally, although need not be, deep-learning based; See F Pasquale, *The Black Box Society* (Harvard University Press, 2015).

[15]    Department of Culture, Media and Sport, 'Disinformation and "Fake News": Final Report', Eighth Report of Session 2017–19, 18 February 2019 at para 48, available at https://publications.parliament.uk/pa/cm201719/cmselect/cmcumeds/1791/179105.htm#_idTextAn%20chor005, accessed 17 February 2021. See also S Wachter and B Mittelstadt, 'A Right to Reasonable Inferences: Re-thinking Data Protection Law in the Age of Big Data and AI' (2019) *Colum. Bus. L. Rev.*, 494 and L Edwards and

Data Protection Regulators have also issued guidelines about the obligation to provide meaningful information about the logic involved in automated decisions.[16] With concerns that machines are dehumanizing decision-making, both profiling and general automated decision-making *about humans* can only take place when robust legal protections are in place, the principles of data protection are adhered to, and data-subject rights can be upheld.[17] These issues manifest themselves in the general belief that AI challenges the set of legal guarantees put in place in Europe to combat discrimination and ensure equal treatment.[18]

These forms of machine-learning models also play an important role in modern data-driven journalism. AI systems, trained for the purpose of news creation, can search for independent input, and with zero or limited human intervention. These systems can also operate without processing any personal data[19] – the caveat that activates the European Union's data protection regime.[20] An AI system that analyses crime data for hotspots, for example, would not fall under the remit of the GDPR, unless the data subject is identi-

---

M Veale, 'Slave to the Algorithm: Why a Right to an Explanation is Probably not the Remedy you are Looking for' (2017) *Duke & Tech. Rev.*, 16, 18; M E Kaminski, 'The Right to Explanation, Explained' (2019) 34 *Berkeley Tech. LJ* 18.

[16]   Information Commissioner's Office, and the Alan Turing Institute, 'Explaining Decisions Made with AI', available at https://ico.org.uk/media/for-organisations/guide-to-data-protection/key-data-protection-themes/explaining-decisions-made-with-artificial-intelligence-1-0.pdf, accessed 17 February 2021; see also Article 29 Working Party Guidelines on Automated individual decision-making and Profiling for the purposes of Regulation 2016/679, available at https://ec.europa.eu/newsroom/article29/document.cfm?action=display&doc_id=49826, accessed 17 February 2021.

[17]   General Data Protection Regulation, Arts 13–21.

[18]   Algorithmic discrimination in Europe: challenges and opportunities for gender equality and non-discrimination law, available at https://op.europa.eu/en/publication-detail/-/publication/082f1dbc-821d-11eb-9ac9-01aa75ed71a1, accessed 11 June 2021.

[19]   GDPR, Art 4(1).

[20]   Regulation (EU) 2016/679 of the European Parliament and of the Council of 27 April 2016 on the protection of natural persons with regard to the processing of personal data and on the free movement of such data, and repealing Directive 95/46/EC (General Data Protection Regulation) (Text with EEA relevance); Directive (EU) 2016/680 of the European Parliament and of the Council of 27 April 2016 on the protection of natural persons with regard to the processing of personal data by competent authorities for the purposes of the prevention, investigation, detection or prosecution of criminal offences or the execution of criminal penalties, and on the free movement of such data, and repealing Council Framework Decision 2008/977/JHA; Directive 2002/58/EC of the European Parliament and of the Council of 12 July 2002 concerning the processing of personal data and the protection of privacy in the electronic communications sector (Directive on privacy and electronic communications).

fiable.[21] Understandably, much of the work in this area has focused on historical biases that are embedded in the very training data that machine-learning
systems are built on.[22] For example, 'predictive policing' is sold to financially
challenged law enforcement agencies (LEAs) as a 'neutral' method to counteract unconscious biases, yet increasingly deploy data mining techniques to
predict, prevent, and investigate crime.[23] However, research indicates that predictive policing can adversely impact minority and vulnerable communities.
For example, using historical data to assist in deployment can lead to more
arrests for nuisance crimes in neighbourhoods primarily populated by people
of colour. Algorithms employed to help determine criminal sentences in the
USA inadvertently discriminated against African Americans.[24] Not only does
historical data risk discriminatory effects, but data integrity, too. Dörr and
Hollnbuchner posit that missing items can lead to bias in content generation.[25]
These effects are an artefact of the specific technology and will take place
regardless of any measures implemented to mitigate the machine's bias.[26]

## 3.      AI IN THE NEWSROOM

The growing datafication and algorithmicizing of society, the emergence of
the platform economy, the mediatization of everyday life, and growing adop-

---

[21]   This is not without considerable controversy. Some have argued that all informa-
tion could theoretically relate to an individual – see N Purtova, 'The Law of Everything.
Broad Concept of Personal Data and Future of EU Data Protection Law' (2018) 10(1)
*Law, Innovation and Technology* 40–81. However, the very broad concept of personal
data could make the entire data protection regime unmanageable – see B J Koops, 'The
Trouble with European Data Protection Law' (2014) 4(4) *International Data Privacy
Law* 250–261.
[22]   N Mehrabi, F Morstatter, N Saxena, K Lerman and A Galstyan (2019) 'A Survey
on Bias and Fairness in Machine Learning' arXiv preprint arXiv:1908.09635.
[23]   The Correctional Offender Management Profiling for Alternative Sanctions
(COMPAS) algorithm was used to predict the risk ratings of offenders on a scale
from 1–10, with the latter being the highest risk. If the algorithm predicted a lower
score, this helped judges decide whether offenders could go on parole or probation:
see F. Zuiderveen Borgesius, 'Discrimination, Artificial Intelligence, and Algorithmic
Decision-making', 2018 Strasbourg: Council of Europe, Directorate General of
Democracy, at 15 and J Angwin et al., 'Machine Bias: There's Software Used Across
the Country to Predict Future Criminals. And it's Biased Against Blacks' (2016)
*ProPublica* 23 May 2015, available at https://www.propublica.org/article/machine-bias
-risk-assessments-in-criminal-sentencing, accessed 23 February 2021.
[24]   Angwin et al., ibid.
[25]   K N Dörr and K Hollnbuchner, 'Ethical Challenges of Algorithmic Journalism'
(2017) 5(4) *Digital Journalism* 404–419, p 9.
[26]   A D Selbst, 'Disparate Impact in Big Data Policing' (February 25, 2017) 52
*Georgia Law Review* 109.

tion of machine-learning and AI-powered tools and services are transforming both newsrooms and media services. It is not unreasonable to foresee that the practice of journalism would join numerous other disciplines characterized by the ubiquity of interconnected intelligent systems with autonomous capacities. *The New York Times* (NYT) 'Editor' project applies tags to traditionally written news articles.[27] *The Washington Post* (WP) covers financial news and local sports events via various forms of 'automated journalism',[28] a broad term used to describe the use of AI, i.e., software or algorithms, to automatically generate news stories with no contribution by human beings, apart from that of the programmers who developed the algorithm. It covers algorithmic, automated, and robot journalism, and bots that write news. An AI algorithm independently collects and analyses data and then writes a news article.

Because it reduces costs and could broaden its audience and increase its market share, the WP incorporated AI to cover and write simple local stories.[29] *Associated Press, Forbes, The Los Angeles Times*, and *ProPublica* all use various forms of automated journalism.[30] Automated journalism is based on natural language generation (NLG) technology, which generally permits creation of text-based journalism from a dataset consisting of digitally structured data:

> Early examples of the use of NLG technology to automate journalism are mostly confined to relatively short texts in limited domains but are nonetheless impressive in terms of both quality and quantity. The text produced is generally indistinguishable from a text written by human writers and the number of text documents generated substantially exceeds what is possible from manual editorial processes.[31]

---

[27] *Washington Post* PR Blog, 'The Washington Post experiments with automated storytelling to help power 2016 Rio Olympics coverage', available at https://www.washingtonpost.com/pr/wp/2016/08/05/the-washington-post-experiments-with-automated-storytelling-to-help-power-2016-rio-olympics-coverage/, accessed 23 March 2021.

[28] N Martin, 'Did a Robot Write This? How AI Is Impacting Journalism', *Forbes* (Feb 8, 2019), available at https://www.forbes.com/sites/nicolemartin1/2019/02/08/did-a-robot-write-this-how-ai-is-impacting-journalism/?sh=563c1e779575, accessed 23 March 2021; see J Keohane, 'What news-writing bots mean for the future of journalism' (2017) WIRED. February. https://www.wired.com/2017/02/robots-wrote-this-story/ accessed 25 February 2021.

[29] L Moses, 'The Washington Post's robot reporter has published 850 articles in the past year', *DigiDay* (17 Sept 2017), available at https://digiday.com/media/washington-posts-robot-reporter-published-500-articles-last-year/, accessed 23 March 2021.

[30] A Graefe, *Guide to Automated Journalism* (Columbia University Academic Commons, 2016).

[31] D Caswell and K Dörr, 'Automated Journalism 2.0: Event-driven Narratives' (2017) *Journalism Practice* 2.

Of course, crime is a favourite subject of the news media, with crime stories estimated to make up between 12.5 and 40 per cent of local news.[32] Chermak's analysis of six print and three broadcast media organizations revealed that 'print media present nine crime stories a day, on average, and electronic media four crime stories per day'.[33] More recently, Curiel et al.'s social media analysis revealed that an astounding 15 out of every 1,000 tweets were about crime or *fear* of crime.[34] Despite social media suffering from a strong bias towards violent or sexual crimes, little correlation exists between social media messages and crime. Social media is not useful for detecting trends in crime but demonstrates insight into the amounts of *fear* about crime.

Given the cost effectiveness and processing capacity of modern computing, machine-learning is being rapidly deployed across newsrooms.[35] Yet AI systems used in newsrooms are often trained on crime reports. In AI discourse, and especially machine-learning, 'models' are arrived at. The first step is inputting (relevant) data into the machine, the data inputted largely depending on what the machine would be used for or be doing ultimately. Secondly, the machine identifies the relevant patterns, dots, differences, and especially similarities in the data inputted to it. The third stage is model creation. This is based on steps 1 and 2 – basically, the machine develops a model that can be used for a task when data similar to step 1 is inputted, and so on. Machine-learning's predictive analytics is used to analyse historical and 'real-time' data to make predictive decisions in, not only news reporting, but fact-checking the authenticity of an unverifiable news story. As discussed in the previous section, the accuracy of these predictive decisions increases with the amount of data processed, including the training data upon which the AI system is modelled.

AI is already used to facilitate automated reporting of murders and other forms of violent crime. For example, an AI system retrieves homicide data directly from a coroner's office, which in turn generates leads for reporters

---

[32]    J Grosholz and C Kubrin, 'Crime in the News: How Crimes, Offenders and victims are Portrayed in the Media' (2007) 14 *Journal of Criminal Justice and Popular Culture* 59–83.

[33]    S Chermak, 'Crime in the News Media: A Refined Understanding of How Crimes Become News' in G Barak (ed), *Media, Process, and the Social Construction of Crime: Studies in Newsmaking Criminology* (New York: Garland Publishing, 1994), 95–129.

[34]    R P Curiel, S Cresci, C I Muntean, and S Bishop 'Crime and its Fear in Social Media' (2020) *Palgrave Commun* 6, 57 https://doi.org/10.1057/s41599-020-0430-7 accessed 25 February 2021.

[35]    Automated Journalism – AI Applications at New York Times, Reuters, and Other Media Giants, available at https://emerj.com/ai-sector-overviews/automated -journalism-applications/, accessed on 23 February 2021.

to expand with details about the victim's life and family.[36] AI could be used to match details about the deceased's life with details from social media and public registries. Incredibly, this has been touted as an example of automated journalism operating *without bias*,[37] ignoring the numerous instances that data could contain errors and the bias in decision-making by the journalist who chose what to report from the available data, and that any errors in reporting could appear in the training data of other AI systems designed to search for patterns – for example, crime trends.

The outcomes of any machine-learning system will be trained on a data set for the purpose of creating a new output correlating with the set of inputs on its own with zero or limited human intervention. Automated journalism operates by either independently writing and publishing news articles without input from a journalist or by 'cooperating' with a journalist who can be deputized to supervise the process or provide input to improve the article. All methods are dependent upon access to, and availability of the structured data needed to generate news articles. Thus, any simple error in the coroner's reporting could theoretically infect the entire cycle of *news reporting*, undermining the integrity of the system. Worryingly, the use of predictive policing by LEAs could facilitate further unconscious bias in news reporting, which in turn would affect real-world policing, which in turn would affect the outcomes of predictive policing. The general advantages of this method are the speed with which data can be collected and articles written, fewer errors in output, and cost savings. Yet the quality of automated journalism depends on the training data. However, not only is perfect training data never possible, human error, prejudice, and misjudgement can enter into the journalistic lifecycle at multiple points. Consequently, biases are introduced at any point in the news delivery process, from the preliminary stages of data extraction, collection, and pre-processing to the critical phases of news formulation, model building, and reporting (Figure 1.1).

## 4.   AI IN FACT-CHECKING

There are growing efforts by journalists, policy makers, and technology companies towards finding effective, scalable responses to online disinformation and false information. Whether by design or coincidence, false online content

---

[36]   N Lemelshtrich Latar, 'The Robot Journalist in the Age of Social Physics: The End of Human Journalism?' in G Einav (ed), *The New World of Transitioned Media* (New York, 2015), 74.

[37]   M Monti, 'Automated Journalism and Freedom of Information: Ethical and Juridical Problems Related to AI in the Press Field' (2019) *Opinio Juris in Comparatione*, 1.

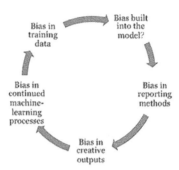

*Figure 1.1    Therein lies the challenge in preventing bias in the newsroom*

appears to exploit a specific conjunction of technological and psychological factors. In a content analysis of 150 fake and real news items, fake news titles were found to be substantially more negative in tone than real news titles.[38] The furore over 'fake news' has exacerbated long-standing concerns about political dishonesty, harmful conspiracy theories, malicious rumours, and deceptive campaigns; for example, online conspiracies about Covid-19 spores emanating from 5-G masts have caused real-world arson attacks,[39] while deceptive campaigns about election integrity incited an insurrection at the US Capitol.[40] Online disinformation is generally understood as intentional dissemination of false and misleading information via the Internet so as to mislead its recipients for politically and financially motivated reasons. Terms like 'fake news', 'disinformation' and 'misinformation' are frequently conflated in the surrounding discourse, but the emerging preference is for using the term 'disinformation' as a descriptor. To avoid infringements of collateral rights, the EU has made a conscious decision to refrain from implementing legislative remedies for online disinformation until such time as self-regulation has been conclusively proven ineffective. Non-state responses within the EU stem primarily from measures like credibility labels, transparency in political advertisements, restrictions on artificial amplification of engagement statistics,

---

[38]    J Paschen, 'Investigating the Emotional Appeal of Fake News Using Artificial Intelligence and Human Contributions' (2019) 29 *Journal of Product & Brand Management* 223–233.

[39]    Sky News, 'Coronavirus: 90 attacks on phone masts reported during UK's lockdown', available at https://news.sky.com/story/coronavirus-90-attacks-on-phone-masts -reported-during-uks-lockdown-11994401, accessed 16 February 2021.

[40]    The QAnon conspiracy theory and a stew of misinformation fuelled the insurrection at the Capitol, available at https://www.insider.com/capitol-riots-qanon-protest -conspiracy-theory-washington-dc-protests-2021-1, accessed 17 February 2021.

and media literacy initiatives implemented by online platform providers. Other non-state responses include fact-checking and other trust-building initiatives from traditional media houses, as well as continued research and awareness campaigns by civil society organizations.

In 2006, Facebook and Instagram started working together with third-party fact-checking organizations and individuals (3PFC) in many countries to ensure that content uploaded by users on the platform is truthful and to avoid dissemination of disinformation. Fact-checkers have to be certified by the International Fact-Checking Network (IFCN). They can mark content as 'true', 'partly true', 'false', 'partly false', 'false title', 'not applicable for evaluation', 'satire', 'hoax', 'opinion' and 'not evaluated'. In December 2019 it was announced that a pilot programme would recruit part-time contracted 'community reviewers' to expedite its fact-checking process. In 2019 Facebook started allowing fact-checkers to check ads and flag them as false. US fact-checkers were also gradually allowed to remove paid ads they thought were false. In 2020, Facebook started belatedly acting against Holocaust deniers, anti-vaxxers, and QAnon, the dangerous movement responsible for many right-wing conspiracies.

Unsurprisingly, AI is increasingly used for detecting fake news, fact-checking, image verification, and video authentication.[41] A natural language processing engine can go through the subject of a story along with the headline, main body text, and the geo-location. Further, AI will find out if other sites are reporting the same facts. In this way, facts are weighed against reputed media sources. Using predictive analytics backed by machine-learning, a website's reputation can be predicted through considering multiple features like domain name and Alexa web rank. When it comes to news items, the headline is key to capturing the attention of the audience. The technology has grown in significance as it tries to understand pages' context without relying on third-party signals.

AI has been instrumental in discovering and flagging fake news headlines by using keyword analytics. A key tool in NLP is a neural network architecture that encodes words to a latent space, decodes to a translation, typo, or classification. The 'neural' part of the architecture learns which words to focus on and for how long.[42] In theory, after these tools are combined, they can train models efficiently and in parallel. However, using these types of AI systems to online fact-check massive amounts of user-generated content either *ex-ante* or *ex-post*, for example, public posts would require an unprecedented amount

---

[41] X Zhou and R Zafarani, 'A Survey of Fake News: Fundamental Theories, Detection Methods, and Opportunities' (2020) 53(5) *ACM Computing Surveys (CSUR)* 1–40.
[42] Available at https://medium.com/@edloginova/attention-in-nlp-734c6fa9d983, accessed 23 February 2021.

of computational power; for example, the BERT natural language processing system uses over 100 million parameters.[43] As well as raising questions about whether platforms are monitoring content, using AI for online fact checking *at scale* would require an exponential increase in computing power relative to linear generation of new content. However, AI might have a role to play at the generative level. Rather than dealing with the burden of content moderation downstream, Facebook uses AI to mitigate creation of fake accounts[44] and to detect word patterns that could indicate fake news.[45] It does not attempt or purport to draw its own conclusions about the accuracy of a story. As it can extract and manipulate information from text, NLP could be instrumental in fact-checking online content.

The same approach cannot be said for checking the *accuracy, trustworthiness*, and *validity* of user-generated content. Nor can NLP address the amplification effect of algorithms designed to make people share and engage with as much content as possible by showing them things they are most likely to be outraged or titillated by. They were not created to filter out what was false or inflammatory. The upstream problem – and the one that is ultimately far more difficult to resolve – is whether it is possible for AI to establish whether an online claim found in user-generated content is true or false,[46] nor is it yet capable of determining what Bernal labels as 'false narratives'.[47] There is also the challenge of identifying misinformation where content may have been deliberately and intentionally fabricated, may or may not be true but is not verifiable, but is produced with the intention of making a profit, and/or pushing a certain ideological or political agenda but is believed by a user to be accurate and shared accordingly. Even using AI to identify and remove inaccurate

---

[43]    Facebook said it 'disabled' 1.2 billion fake accounts in the last three months of 2018 and 2.19 billion in the first quarter of 2019; see 'Fake Facebook Accounts: The Never-ending Battle against Bots', *Phsy Org*, available at https://phys.org/news/2019 -05-fake-facebook-accounts-never-ending-bots.html, accessed 23 February 2021.

[44]    R Lever, 'Fake Facebook accounts: the never-ending battle against bots', *Phys Org* (24 May 2019), available at https://phys.org/news/2019-05-fake-facebook -accounts-never-ending-bots.html#:~:text=Facebook%20says%20its%20artificial %20intelligence,before%20they%20can%20post%20misinformation, accessed 23 March 2021.

[45]    'Facebook is using AI to Remove Fake News', available at https://www.clickatell .com/articles/digital-marketing/facebook-using-ai-remove-fake-news/, accessed 23 February 2021.

[46]    https://www.brookings.edu/research/how-to-deal-with-ai-enabled-dis information/, accessed 16 February 2021.

[47]    P Bernal, 'Facebook: Why Facebook Makes the Fake News Problem Inevitable' (2018) 69 *N Ir Legal Q* 513.

content is debatable: the user would never appreciate the corrective effect, or the social shaming associated with the marketplace of ideas.

The legitimacy of collaborative AI to counter disinformation will largely depend on the perceived impartiality and credibility of participating news organizations.

We have not yet realized the true potential of artificial intelligence in combating fake news. The future needs more sophisticated tools that can harness the power of AI, big data, and machine learning to stop fake news making ripples in the user world. Technically speaking, the main problems associated with automated journalism, in terms of narrative and critical considerations, surround their low quality. Yet the effects of AI and AI systems are not only going to refashion human relationships but redistribute labour and creativity. Accordingly, examination is required of these transformative effects on journalism and news production.

## 5.   REGULATING AI IN THE EUROPEAN UNION

While newsrooms forge ahead with automated journalism and fact-checkers increasingly rely on AI to search for patterns of analysis that indicate deceptive content, the EU has been struggling to come up with a single framework for the regulation of artificial intelligence.[48] The deployment of AI inside institutions traditionally responsible for democratic accountability without the appropriate safeguards and a lack of coherent ethical and legal safeguards raises alarms. Recognizing this problem before the cancer of disinformation metastasizes is a fundamental principle of the responsible AI movement.[49] The AI HLEG expert group42 published its Ethics Guidelines for Trustworthy AI in April 2019.[50] According to the Guidelines, trustworthy AI should meet three criteria throughout the system's entire life cycle:

(1)   lawful – respecting all applicable laws and regulations
(2)   ethical – respecting ethical principles and values
(3)   robust – both from a technical perspective and considering its social environment.[51]

---

[48]   J Black and A D Murray, 'Regulating AI and Machine Learning: Setting the Regulatory Agenda' (2019) 10(3) *European Journal of Law and Technology*.

[49]   Available at https://www.technologyreview.com/2021/03/11/1020600/facebook -responsible-ai-misinformation/, accessed 12 March 2021.

[50]   AI HLEG Ethics Guidelines For Trustworthy AI, available at https://ec.europa .eu/digital-singlemarket/en/news/ethics-guidelines-trustworthy-ai, accessed 27 March 2021.

[51]   Ibid., at 5.

The concept of 'transparency' has been posited as a prerequisite to machine-learning and AI systems to allow one to grasp 'some sense of understanding the mechanism by which the model works'.[52] However, both supporters and critics argue that the very nature of the technology means that complete transparency is an unachievable goal.[53] In the purest sense, every instance of AI trained on personal data would be incompatible with the requirements of Article 5(1)(a) GDPR: personal data cannot be processed in a transparent (and concise) manner in a way that is understandable to the data subject.[54] Thus, transparency gives way to the concept of interpretation, or the process of translation of 'an abstract concept (e.g., a predicted class) into a domain that the human can make sense of'.[55] There can be different levels of understanding depending on a person's age, mental condition, and education so that 'meaningful information about the logic involved'[56] under GDPR rules may vary. Frustratingly, the GDPR does not explicitly provide examples of what level of understanding needs to be explained. Some opine that application of the criteria like 'average person' tests[57] may solve the problem.[58] However, considering protection of personal data as a fundamental right under the EU Charter,[59] such an approach does not exactly mitigate the discriminatory effects that its proponents claim the GDPR is tasked with eliminating.[60] Even the Unfair Commercial Practices Directive provides more protection: if a clearly identifiable group who are particularly vulnerable can be identified,

---

[52]   R Roscher, B Bohn, M F Duarte, J Garcke et al., 'Explainable Machine Learning for Scientific Insights and Discoveries' doi: 10.1109/access.2020.2976199 accessed 27 March 2021, but compare to Y Bathaee 'The Artificial Intelligence Black Box and the Failure of Intent and Causation' (Spring 2018) 31(2) *Harvard Journal of Law & Technology* 906–919, 929.

[53]   Recital 58 GDPR.

[54]   R Roscher et al. (n 52), quoting G Montavon, W Samek and K R Müller, 'Methods for Interpreting and Understanding Deep Neural Networks' (2018) 73 *Digital Signal Processing* 1–15; see also Leiser and Dechesne (n 13).

[55]   Montavon et al., ibid.

[56]   Arts 13(1)(f) 14(1)(g) and 15(1)(h) GDPR.

[57]   Similar to that of the 'average consumer' who is reasonably well informed, and reasonably observant and circumspect, see CJEU in *Severi*, C-446/07, ECLI:EU:C:2009:530, para 61 and the case-law cited.

[58]   See https://www.twobirds.com/~/media/pdfs/gdpr-pdfs/bird--bird--guide-to-the-general-data-protection-regulation.pdf?la=en at 23; https://ico.org.uk/media/for-organi sations/guide-to-the-general-data-protection-regulation-gdpr-1-0.pdf at 103, both accessed 15 October 2021.

[59]   Rec 1 GDPR; see also Art 21(1) EU Charter: Any discrimination based on any ground such as sex, race, colour, ethnic or social origin, genetic features, language, religion or belief, political or any other opinion, membership of a national minority, property, birth, disability, age or sexual orientation shall be prohibited.

[60]   Rec 71 GDPR.

the impact of commercial practice should be assessed from the perspective of the average member of *that group* [emphasis added].[61]

Other efforts in Europe include the European Data Protection Supervisor's (EDPS) recent public consultation on the necessity of a 'digital ethics' framework to address technological developments such as AI and robotics;[62] also, the European Union Agency for Fundamental Rights report on 'Getting the Future Right: Artificial Intelligence and Fundamental Rights'[63] and the Council of Europe's CAHAI Secretariat report 'Towards Regulation of AI Systems: Global perspectives on the development of a legal framework on Artificial Intelligence systems based on the Council of Europe's standards on human rights, democracy and the rule of law'.[64] The Software and Information Industry Association (SIIA) developed its own 'Ethical Principles for Artificial Intelligence and Data Analytics' in late 2017 to help in well-developed ML/AI.[65]

The rapid development of AI technologies has stimulated a variety of responses from the EU to the phenomenon.[66] Its Declaration expressed the

---

[61]   Unfair Commercial Practices Directive 2005/29/EC, Art 5(3).

[62]   https://edps.europa.eu/data-protection/our-work/ethics_en, accessed 23 March 2021.

[63]   https://fra.europa.eu/sites/default/files/fra_uploads/fra-2020-artificial -intelligence_en.pdf, accessed 23 March 2021.

[64]   https://rm.coe.int/prems-107320-gbr-2018-compli-cahai-couv-texte-a4-bat-web/ 1680a0c17a, accessed 23 March 2021.

[65]   https://www.pr.com/press-release/735528 accessed 25 February 2021.

[66]   European Commission. Report on the safety and liability implications of Artificial Intelligence, the Internet of Things and robotics (2020) https://ec.europa.eu/info/ publications/commission-report-safety-and-liability-implications-ai-internet-things -and-robotics-0_en; European Commission. White Paper. On Artificial Intelligence – A European approach to excellence and trust (2020) https://ec.europa.eu/info/sites/ default/files/commission-white-paper-artificial-intelligence-feb2020_en.pdf; European Commission. Liability for Artificial Intelligence and other emerging digital technol- ogies (2019) https://op.europa.eu/en/publication-detail/-/publication/1c5e30be-1197 -11ea-8c1f-01aa75ed71a1/language-en; European Parliament. European Parliament resolution of 12 February 2019 on a comprehensive European industrial policy on artificial intelligence and robotics (2019) https://www.europarl.europa.eu/doceo/ document/TA-8-2019-0081_EN.html; AI HLEG. Ethics Guidelines for Trustworthy AI. (2019);   https://digital-strategy.ec.europa.eu/en/library/ethics-guidelines-trustworthy -ai; AI HLEG. A definition of AI: Main capabilities and scientific disciplines (2019) https://digital-strategy.ec.europa.eu/en/library/definition-artificial-intelligence -main-capabilities-and-scientific-disciplines AI HLEG. Policy and Investment recom- mendations for Trustworthy AI (2019) https://futurium.ec.europa.eu/en/european-ai -alliance/open-library/policy-and-investment-recommendations-trustworthy-artificial -intelligence; Council of Europe. Guidelines on Artificial Intelligence and Data Protection   (2019)   https://rm.coe.int/guidelines-on-artificial-intelligence-and-data -protection/168091f9d8; Council of Europe. Guidelines on the protection of individu-

need for a workable definition of AI and AI systems, for determining ethical guidelines for its use, alongside liability considerations associated with deployment of AI.[67] Its efforts were intended to build a human-centric 'ecosystem of excellence' and 'ecosystem of trust' for industry deployment of AI. The EU eagerly reiterated the importance of investment in terms of both money and data into research and application of AI. Furthermore, the Communication from the Commission called for the EU to 'strengthen fundamental research and make scientific breakthroughs ... facilitate the uptake of AI and the access to data', 'supporting testing and experimentation' and 'encourage the wider availability of privately-held data'.[68] Additionally, the JRC's report 'Artificial Intelligence: A European perspective'[69] provided different accounts of the developing technology alongside possible impacts, examining artificial entities when they involve unique cognitive or behavioural implications. The report stresses that known psychological attributes and systematic biases appear to be further amplified by digital media.[70]

At the precipice of a significant technological development, with concerns about unforeseen harms, and without an emerging winner from the heterogeneity of competing ethical approaches (as well as concerns about favouring ethics in lieu of regulatory intervention backed up by sanctions), the European

---

als with regard to the processing of personal data in a world of big data (2019) https://rm.coe.int/t-pd-2017-1-%20bigdataguidelines-en/16806f06d0; Council of Europe. Report on Artificial Intelligence Artificial Intelligence and Data Protection: Challenges and Possible Remedies (2018) https://rm.coe.int/report-on-artificial-%20intelligence-artificial-intelligence-and-data-pro/16808e6012; EDPB Guidelines 3/2019 on processing of personal data through video devices (2020) https://edpb.europa.eu/our-work-tools/our-documents/guidelines/guidelines-32019-processing-personal-data-through-video_en;.EDPS Opinion 3/2018. EDPS Opinion on online manipulation and personal data. (2018) https://edps.europa.eu/sites/edp/files/publication/18-03-19_online_manipulation_en.pdf; ICO Guidance on the AI auditing framework. Draft guidance for consultation (2020) https://ico.org.uk/about-the-ico/ico-and-stakeholder-consultations/ico-consultation-on-the-draft-ai-auditing-framework-guidance-for-organisations/; EU Science Hub, *'Artificial Intelligence: A European Perspective'*, https://publications.jrc.ec.europa.eu/repository/handle/JRC113826, all accessed 16 February 2021.

[67]  https://ec.europa.eu/jrc/communities/en/node/1286/document/eu-declaration-cooperation-artificial-intelligence accessed 16 February 2021.

[68]  European Commission Brussels, 'Communication from The Commission', 25.4.2018; COM (2018) 237 final; 'Artificial Intelligence for Europe' {SWD (2018) 137 final}.

[69]  S Lewandowsky, L Smillie, D Garcia, R Hertwig, J Weatherall, S Egidy and M Leiser 'Technology and Democracy: Understanding the Influence of Online Technologies on Political Behaviour and Decision-making' Publications Office of the European Union, 2020)available at https://publications.jrc.ec.europa.eu/repository/handle/JRC122023, accessed 11 June 2021.

[70]  Ibid., 45.

Commission introduced a legislative process to address the risks that AI poses to safety and fundamental rights. The proposal for the Regulation of Artificial Intelligence[71] harmonizes rules in a risk-based and 'future-proof' manner to provide predictable and sufficiently clear conditions under which enterprises can develop AI applications and plan their business models, while ensuring that the EU and its Member States maintain control over regulatory standards, so are not forced to adopt and live with standards set by others.

The regulation uses a risk-based approach to regulating AI. Applications with minimal or no risk are permitted without restrictions;[72] high-risk AI is permitted, subject to specific transparency obligations;[73] higher risk applications are permitted, subject to compliance with AI requirements[74] and *ex-ante* conformity assessment;[75] while forms of 'unacceptable AI' (subliminal manipulation; exploiting children or mentally disabled persons; general purpose social scoring; remote biometric identification for law enforcement in publicly accessible spaces (with exceptions)) are deemed unacceptable and prohibited.[76] Recital 68 of the Draft Regulation suggests that 'certain AI systems intended to interact with natural persons or to *generate content*' [italics added] may pose risks of impersonation and deception; therefore, AI-generated content must comply with transparency obligations regardless of whether classified as high risk. Manipulated images, audio, or video content should also contain a disclosure that the content has been artificially created or manipulated by labelling not only the output but the source material.

## 6.   JOURNALISTIC RESPONSIBILITY WHEN USING MACHINE-LEARNING SYSTEMS

Automation bias leads decision makers to assume that quantitative methods are superior to qualitative methods, and to reduce the task at hand to applying

---

[71]   Proposal for a Regulation laying down harmonized rules on artificial intelligence, https://digital-strategy.ec.europa.eu/en/library/proposal-regulation-laying-down -harmonised-rules-artificial-intelligence, accessed 05 June 2021; Communication on Fostering a European approach to Artificial Intelligence, https://digital-strategy .ec.europa.eu/en/library/communication-fostering-european-approach-artificial -intelligence, 05 June 2021.

[72]   Art 69: no mandatory obligations, but possible voluntary codes of conduct for AI with specific transparency requirements.

[73]   Art 52: notify humans that they are interacting with an AI system unless this is evident; notify humans that emotional recognition or biometric categorization systems are applied to them.

[74]   Title III, Ch 2.

[75]   Title III, Annexes II and III; CE marking and Process (Title III, Ch 4, Art 49).

[76]   Title II, Art 5.

the quantitative data available. This undermines and devalues the necessary complex contextualization that human reasoning applies. With trust in legacy media a rather fluid dynamic, and public attitudes to the credibility of social media as a replacement to traditional news outlets, and both legal and political fallout from the use of automated decision making, there is a general attitude among Europeans that the use of AI should be transparent and discernible. A recent Eurobarometer study focusing on AI found that 80 per cent of the representative EU population sample think that they should be informed when a digital service or mobile application uses AI.[77] A recent representative survey probed the German public's attitudes towards use of online AI and use of machine learning to exploit personal data for personalization of services.[78] Attitudes towards personalization were found to be domain-dependent: most people find personalization of political advertising and news sources unacceptable. The degree of moral outrage elicited by reports of immoral acts online has been found to be considerably greater than for encounters in person or in conventional media.[79]

The diffusion between a designer's intention and the actual behaviour of an AI system creates a 'responsibility gap' that is difficult to bridge with traditional notions of responsibility[80] and is subject to ongoing debate (e.g., the EU's recent statement on artificial intelligence by the Group on Ethics in Science and New Technologies).[81] Traditionally, responsibility for any journalistic error would attach to the newsroom through a variety of ethical obligations, regulatory frameworks, and most importantly, tort (defamation/ libel) law. However, autonomous learning machines are fed data sources, learn without supervision, and produce outputs that cannot be predicted. In a normative sense, responsibility means being able to explain actions that you were able to control. Someone will be responsible to the extent that they know the circumstances and facts around decisions that they undertake. Thus, responsibility can be ascribed to a principle of 'control'. AI systems and

---

[77]   EU Barometer Public Opinion, available at https://ec.europa.eu/commfrontoffice/ publicopinion/index.cfm/Survey/getSurveyDetail/%20instruments/STANDARD/ surveyKy/2255, accessed 16 February 2021.

[78]   A Kozyreva, S Herzog, P Lorenz-Spreen, R Hertwig, and S Lewandowsky, 'Artificial Intelligence in Online Environments: Representative Survey of Public Attitudes in Germany' (2020).

[79]   M J Crockett, 'Moral Outrage in the Digital Age' (2017) 1(11) *Nature Human Behaviour* 769–771.

[80]   Lewandowsky et al. (n 69), 45.

[81]   Ibid., referring to the EU's recent statement on artificial intelligence by the Group on Ethics in Science and New Technologies, available at https://op.europa.eu/ en/publication-detail/-/publication/dfebe62e-4ce9-11e8-%09be1d-%2001aa75ed71a1, accessed 23 March 2021.

machine-learning models turn that principle on its head. At present, there are AI systems in newsrooms that are able to decide on a course of action and to act without human intervention. The rules on which they act are not fixed, but are changed during the operation of the AI system, by the system itself. The machine learns and produces a series of actions, where traditional ways of attributing responsibility are not compatible with the control principle. No one has enough control over the machine's actions to be able to assume responsibility for them. These constitute the 'responsibility gap'.

## 7.    EXPLAINABILITY

The second example of explainability refers to the obligation to make the internal logic of AI systems discernible to human beings.[82] This does not require disclosing the inner working of the logic, nor does it equate to algorithmic transparency.[83] The ethos behind explainability lies in distinguishing what input produced what undesired effect in order to justly allocate responsibility for that effect. As they may be asked to explain, any media or news organization using AI should be prepared to explain its workings and rationale and should understand the reasons behind its output. When processing personal data inside an AI system or when personal data appears in the training set, the legal requirements for explainability come from a variety of hard and soft law measures.

Under Article 5(1)(a) GDPR,[84] a media organization that uses an AI system will have to ensure that any personal data be processed in a 'lawful', 'fair' and 'transparent' way. The latter requires that information disclosure be discernible by the data subject whose data is subjected to processing.[85] Analysis of personal information by AI systems could amount to (a) 'processing of personal data', and (b) 'profiling'.[86] Although these provisions keep data subjects abreast as to the 'generalities' of data processing, Articles 13 and 14 provide the legal basis for data subjects to be provided with 'meaningful information about the logic provided' where relevant.[87] The subject of an AI-generated news report could exercise their rights against the media organization if acting

---

[82]    N Gill, P Hall, and N Schmidt 'Proposed Guidelines for the Responsible Use of Explainable Machine Learning' (2020).

[83]    For a detailed account of why this is not feasible, see Leiser and Dechesne (n 13).

[84]    Regulation (EU) 2016/679 on the protection of natural persons with regard to the processing of personal data and on the free movement of such data (General Data Protection Regulation) 2016.

[85]    The 'Transparency Principle'; see also GDPR, Rec 64.

[86]    GDPR, Art 4(2) and (4).

[87]    GDPR, Rec 39, 58 and 60.

as a data controller.[88] The Information Commissioner's Office (ICO), the UK's regulator for data protection, has stressed the need for explainability in the use of AI systems.[89] In this regard, the ICO stresses that explainability is needed, not only for regulatory compliance and system accuracy, but also to ensure that data subjects are informed.[90] Thus, explainability should be interpreted and applied widely. The regulator notes that the approach of institutions to 'explaining [machine-learning]-assisted decisions should be informed by the importance of putting the principles of transparency and accountability into practice, and of paying close attention to context and impact'.[91] It is advised that these require appreciating the:

- purported aim of the modelling;
- type of modelling derived and as implemented;
- variables and/or data to be used in when processing, inclusive of their integrity, validity, and availability;
- data set on which the model is trained;
- purported and literal impact of the model;
- target audience of the explanation;
- required explanation for said audience's intelligibility;
- any other reasonable consideration.

The ICO envisages explainability to be tailored, not only to the relevant intelligence of the audience, but to the context in which the AI system is used; therefore, any machine-learning that uses personal data, including content creation, moderation, and fact-checking, should be explainable, not just to data subjects, but to anyone with a stake in accessing good quality and/or corrective journalism. Because of algorithmic opacity and AI systems' autonomous and ever-evolving learning curve that transforms data into an incomprehensible

---

[88]    The extent of the 'right to an explanation' is hotly contested. For various takes on the extent of the right, see Edwards and Veale (n 15), 16, 18; S Wachter, B Mittelstadt and C Russell, 'Counterfactual Explanations without Opening the Black Box: Automated Decisions and the GDPR' (2018) 31(2) *Harvard Journal of Law & Technology* 841–887; F Doshi-Velez, M Kortz, R Budish, C Bavitz, S Gershman and D O'Brien et al., 'Accountability of AI Under the Law: The Role of Explanation' (2019) Working Draft 1–21; A Selbst and J Powles, 'Meaningful Information and the Right to Explanation' (2017) 7(4) *International Data Privacy Law* 233–243; Wachter, Mittelstadt and Floridi (n 4) 76–99.
[89]    The Information Commissioner's Office (ICO), Guidance on the AI Auditing Framework: Draft Guidance for Consultation (2020); The ICO, Explaining Decisions Made with AI Draft Guidance for Consultation Part 1, 2 and 3 (2019).
[90]    Ibid.
[91]    The Information Commissioner's Office, Explaining Decisions Made with AI Draft Guidance for Consultation Part 2 (2019), 4.

form, along with obscurity in AI decision-making processes, anything less than the evolving legal standard for transparency and procedures for ensuring explainability will likely involve push-back by regulators.

## 8.     DISCLOSURE AND TRANSPARENCY

As AI systems in newsrooms are data hungry and require massive amounts of information, *data transparency* is crucial for building trustworthy AI. Explanations may help ordinary citizens understand how data was processed within an AI system, but this does not amount to the same as disclosure. As Kissinger asserts, 'there is a fundamental problem for democratic decision-making if we rely on a system that is supposedly superior to mere humans but cannot explain its decisions'.[92]

By shining light on what is actually explained, explanations serve as a means to verify the accuracy of the explanation. However, explanations amount to a single branch of transparency.[93] Bloch-Wehba argues that 'true algorithmic transparency goes far beyond an explanation of a challenged action to the individual that is affected'.[94] Transparency is a complex construct that evades simple definitions. It can refer to explainability, interpretability, openness, accessibility, and visibility.[95] Overall transparency encompasses disclosures about the AI system, the logic involved, information about the data, and how that data is used. The European Parliament's Governance Framework for Algorithmic Accountability and Transparency report states:

> transparency may relate to the data, algorithms, goals, outcomes, compliance, influence, and/or usage of automated decision-making systems (i.e., algorithmic systems) and will often require different levels of detail for the general public, regulatory staff, third-party forensic analysts, and researchers.[96]

---

[92]    H Kissinger, 'How the Enlightenment Ends: Philosophically, Intellectually— in Every Way—Human Society Is Unprepared for the Rise of Artificial Intelligence' (2018) *The Atlantic*, available at https://www.theatlantic.com/magazine/archive/2018/ 06/henry-kissinger-ai-could-mean-the-end-of-human-history/559124/, accessed 26 March 2021.

[93]    M Brkan, 'Do Algorithms Rule the World? Algorithmic Decision-making and Data Protection in the Framework of the GDPR and Beyond' (2019) 27(2) *International Journal of Law and Information Technology* 91–121.

[94]    H Bloch-Wehba, 'Access to Algorithms' (2019) 88 *Fordham L. Rev*, 1265.

[95]    H Felzmann, E Fosch-Villaronga, C Lutz and A Tamò-Larrieux, 'Towards Transparency by Design for Artificial Intelligence' (2020) *Science and Engineering Ethics* 1–29.

[96]    A Koene, R Richardson, Y Hatada, H Webb, M Petel, D Reisman, C Machado, J L Violette, and C Clifton, 'A Governance Framework for Algorithmic Accountability and Transparency', 2018. EPRS/2018/STOA/SER/18/002, 2018.

A data processing impact assessment (DPIA) is necessary when *data process-ing* operations are likely to result in a high risk to the rights and freedoms of natural persons. A DPIA is mandatory in cases of the following non-exhaustive activities, characteristic of a majority of AI applications:

- systematic and extensive evaluation of the personal aspects of an individual, including profiling
- processing of sensitive data on a large scale
- systematic monitoring of public areas on a large scale.[97]

If a DPIA discovers that such risk exists and cannot be mitigated, the AI operator is obliged to consult the data protection regulator.[98] The most severe regulatory action against an operator who cannot demonstrate ability to comply is 'temporary or definitive limitation including a ban on processing',[99] but it has certain time limits.[100] The EU Commission has proposed introducing a requirement to undertake an overall AI impact assessment to ensure that any regulatory intervention is proportionate, and distinguishing those being 'high risk' from the remainder. Two cumulative criteria clarify when and how AI should be specified as bearing high risk: (1) a sector where significant risks can be expected to occur; and (2) application in such a manner, when significant risks are likely to occur.[101] In addition to this general category, some types of activity are considered as always bearing high risk, e.g., applications for recruitment and other situations that can have an impact on the rights of workers, use for purposes of remote biometric identification.[102]

## 9.    CONCLUSION

The world is abuzz with the prospects and promises of AI and its ability to process large datasets accurately in order to derive predictive outcomes. Four factors have ensured AI's success as we see today in almost every sector. These include: 'exponential increased computer processor capabilities; emergence of global digital networks; advances in distributed computing (hardware and software); and especially the emergence of Big Data'.[103] The indescribable

---

[97]   Art 35(3) GDPR.
[98]   Rec 84 and Art 35(1) GDPR.
[99]   Art 58(1)(f) GDPR.
[100]  Art 36(2) GDPR.
[101]  Brussels, 19.2.2020 COM(2020) 65 final White Paper On Artificial Intelligence – A European approach to excellence and trust, 17.
[102]  Ibid., 18.
[103]  R Subramanian, 'Emergent AI, Social Robots and the Law: Security, Privacy and Policy Issues' (2017) 26(3) *Journal of International Technology and Information Management* Art. 4; at 84.

amounts of available personal data for fuelling AI, increased processing power and access to cheaper and greater storage capacity have ensured advances in creating ML-models.[104] AI holds great promise and utility for news media and fact-checkers. However, as is widely acknowledged, many machine-learning applications function as 'black-boxes' that have been built using vast amounts of 'historical data'.[105] Predictive profiling offers a unique approach to threat mitigation that begins from the point of view of the aggressor/adversary and is based on an actual adversary's methods of operation, their modus operandi. This method is applicable to securing virtually any environment and to meeting any set of security requirements. The post-crime orientation of criminal justice is increasingly overshadowed by the pre-crime logic of security. Frameworks for preventing crime are not as concerned with gathering evidence, prosecution, conviction, and subsequent punishment as in targeting and managing through disruption, restriction, and incapacitation those individuals and groups considered to be a risk. Using unexplainable, unaccountable, irresponsible AI will end the system of checks and balances. Worryingly, few insights can be derived about the internal logic of AI systems.[106] The absence of understanding the logic behind machine-learning is grave, not only from a journalistic integrity perspective (given the necessity of warranting algorithmic transparency) but also a broader societal perspective.[107]

The consequences of using biased training data in journalistic endeavours that rely on machine-learning is a prime example. Subjects of a news article could face the social stigmatization of being labelled a 'suspect' or even a 'criminal'.[108] Under the present system of checks and balances, the burden of

---

[104] '[I]t is data, in many cases personal data, that fuels these systems, enabling them to learn and become intelligent' (see https://iapp.org/media/pdf/resource_center/ Datatilsynet_AI%20and%20Privacy_Report.pdf, at 5, accessed 15 October 2021).

[105] Wired, Machine Learning and Cognitive Systems: The Next Evolution of Enterprise Intelligence (Part I) (2020), available at https://www.wired.com/insights/ 2014/07/machine-learning-cognitive-systems-next-evolution-enterprise-intelligence -part/, accessed 16 February 2021; Wired, Location Intelligence Gives Businesses a Leg Up Thanks to Real-Time AI (2020), available at https://www.wired.com/ wiredinsider/2019/06/location-intelligence-gives-businesses-leg-thanks-real-time-ai/, accessed 16 February 2021.

[106] J Brownlee, 'What is Deep Learning?' (2019), available at https://machinelearn ingmastery.com/what-is-deep-learning/, accessed 16 February 2021; see also N Gill, P Hall and N Schmidt, *Proposed Guidelines for the Responsible Use of Explainable Machine Learning* (2020).

[107] G Ras, M Gerven and W Haselager, 'Explanation Methods in Deep Learning: Users, Values, Concerns and Challenges' ArXiv 1803.07517 (2018).

[108] G Sinha, 'To Suspect or Not to Suspect: Analysing the Pressure on Banks to be "Policemen"' (2014) 15(1) *Journal of Banking Regulation* 75–86; SAS Institute, What is Next-generation AML? The Fight against Financial Crime Fortified with Robotics,

proof is on the person discriminated against to show that this was the result of (a) bad data and/or (b) an algorithm, and/or an automated decision. This would require a person subjected to a decision to have access to the model used by the newsroom, the training data, and the raw data from, for example, the coroner's office. Therefore, automated journalism and AI systems used in newsrooms are an unchecked power with indeterminable consequences for society. This can lead to further discrimination, catastrophic economic and social losses, as well as loss of reputation and, in some cases, infringement of civil liberties. It is important that everyone affiliated with media production and consumption, including readers, have some kind of understanding of what artificial intelligence actually is and how it operates. This fundamental understanding will not only shape how we use it but enable us to use it in a way that actually serves society, rather than just the technology.

---

Semantic Analysis and Artificial Intelligence (2020) at 8, available at https://www.sas .com/content/dam/SAS/documents/marketing-whitepapers-ebooks/sas-whitepapers/ en/next-generation-aml-110644.pdf, accessed 16 February 2021.

# 2. Transparency in algorithmic journalism: from ethics to law and back

**Anette Alén-Savikko**

## 1. INTRODUCTION: JOURNALISM ON THE MOVE

### 1.1 From Radio Waves to Codes

Technological developments and the media have been intertwined from Gutenberg to radio waves. Indeed, the media have always implied or involved some form of 'artificial' extension of the human senses.[1] As such, computers have been employed in newsrooms since the 1950s, while data-driven forms of journalism have been developing since the 1970s, with computational journalism gaining ground from the 2010s. Currently, the move is towards further automation and utilisation of artificial intelligence (AI), algorithms, and machine learning (ML), among others, both in content production and in managing the consumption side. Algorithmic tools are employed from data collection to content creation and curation.[2] According to an EBU News

---

[1]   Konstantin Nicholas Dörr, 'Mapping the Field of Algorithmic Journalism' (2016) 4 *Digital Journalism* 700; Paul Hodkinson, *Media, Culture, and Society: An Introduction* (2nd edn, Sage 2017) 19; European Broadcasting Union (EBU), 'News Report 2019 – The Next Newsroom: Unlocking the Power of AI for Public Service Journalism' (19 November 2019) 21 www.ebu.ch/publications/strategic/login_only/report/news-report-2019 accessed 13 April 2020.

[2]   Mark Coddington, 'Clarifying Journalism's Quantitative Turn: A Typology for Evaluating Data Journalism, Computational Journalism, and Computer-assisted Reporting' (2015) 3 *Digital Journalism* 331; Nicholas Diakopoulos, 'Enabling Accountability of Algorithmic Media: Transparency as a Constructive and Critical Lens' in Tania Cerquitelli, Daniele Quercia and Frank Pasquale (eds), *Transparent Data Mining for Big and Small Data* (Studies in Big Data, vol 32, Springer, Cham 2017) 26; Mark Coddington, 'Defining and Mapping Data Journalism and Computational Journalism: A Review of Typologies and Themes' in Scott Eldridge II and Bob Franklin (eds), *The Routledge Handbook of Developments in Digital*

Report from 2019, we are witnessing the fourth wave of digitalisation after online, mobile, and social media.[3]

For his part, Coddington has drafted a typology of 'data-driven strain(s) of journalism',[4] that is, various forms of journalism that analyse and present quantitative, or numerical, data. Dating back a few decades already, computer assisted reporting (CAR) brought computing to the newsroom. However, the development has gained new ground and developed new forms with digitalisation and information being available as zeros and ones, as well as increased cooperation among programmers and journalists. Often all forms of data-driven journalism are lumped together, but for analytical purposes there is a need for more detailed categorisation.[5] Then again, terms have also pro-liferated among academics, including labels such as automated or algorithmic journalism and robot journalism, reflecting this rapidly changing field.[6] Then again, the term 'news (ro)bot' is considered inappropriate by some writers.[7] Alongside CAR, Coddington talks about two main forms of quantitative journalism: data journalism and computational journalism. All three forms of journalism are linked to the development of computer science but differ from each other in terms of four dimensions: professional orientation; epistemology; view of the public; and openness. Whereas CAR represents somewhat clearly a traditional professional orientation, combined with a focus on professional expertise and sampling, data journalism is linked to the 'open source' move-ment in the field of software development, thereby implying a more networked and participatory orientation. Data and computational journalism also rely on 'Big Data' rather than sampling. CAR still relied very much on a modernist professional culture favouring opacity rather than opening up its practices, while with open source ideology came transparency in the form of exposing raw data and engaging people. Moreover, whereas CAR viewed its public as passive and fixed, later forms of data-driven journalism rather build on the

*Journalism Studies* (Routledge 2018) 225–236; see also on the importance of geneaol-ogy in the context of AI, Riikka Koulu, 'Human Control over Automation: EU Policy and AI Ethics' (2020) 12(1) *European Journal of Legal Studies* 9, 18.

[3]  European Broadcasting Union (EBU) (n 1) 6–7, 12.

[4]  Coddington, 'Clarifying Journalism's Quantitative turn' (n 2) 331.

[5]  Ibid., 331–333.

[6]  Dörr (n 1) 700; Coddington, 'Defining and Mapping Data Journalism and Computational Journalism' (n 2) 226–227; European Broadcasting Union (EBU) (n 1) 113.

[7]  See e.g., Carl-Gustav Lindén and Hanna Tuulonen (eds), *News Automation: The Rewards, Risks and Realities of 'Machine Journalism'* (World Association of Newspapers and News Publishers, WAN-IFRA 2019) 8; Carl-Gustav Lindén and Laurence Dierickx, 'Robot Journalism: The Damage Done by a Metaphor' (2019) 2 *Unmediated: Journal of Politics and Communication* 152.

notion of an active and fragmented public.[8] Algorithmic journalism may also be viewed as data journalism 'on steroids', that is, journalism gaining new ground and greater processing capacity with AI-based solutions.[9] For its part, content production has benefited from automation and AI tools in pioneering fields with available data and which prioritise speed and accuracy, such as weather reports, sport, finance, and political elections.[10]

Data journalism is widely used as the term for current data-driven journalism, dating back to the millennium shift. Computational journalism may also refer to an overall concept or more specifically to a form of quantitative journalism drawing from computing and computational thinking in information processing. Data journalism and computational journalism are sometimes used as synonyms and both are traced back to the 2010s. These forms of quantitative journalism share many epistemological elements and overlap in some regards but they also differ from each other especially in terms of transparency. Data journalism builds on openness of both its product and its process, alongside source material which may also be public or published following an open source ideology. The public has an opportunity to check all data, thereby promoting democratisation of resources and methodologies. However, in the context of computational journalism, algorithms are not similarly apt for publication.[11]

Together with this 'digital turn' and developments related to automation, many fundamental questions have resurfaced in the media sector, such as what is (quality) journalism, what is journalistic authority and where does it find its basis? At the same time, a redefinition of journalistic practices has emphasised the importance of human creativity instead of accuracy and speed.[12] On the other hand, digitalisation and automation are vested with promises of increased

---

[8]   Coddington, 'Clarifying Journalism's Quantitative Turn' (n 2) 333–343; Coddington, 'Defining and Mapping Data Journalism and Computational Journalism' (n 2) 227–228.

[9]   European Broadcasting Union (EBU) (n 1) 89–91, 113.

[10]   Dörr (n 1) 703; European Broadcasting Union (EBU) (n 1) 63–64, 82–84; Lindén and Tuulonen (n 7) 20, 24.

[11]   Coddington, 'Clarifying Journalism's Quantitative Turn' (n 2) 334–336, 339–341; Coddington, 'Defining and Mapping Data Journalism and Computational Journalism' (n 2) 229–233.

[12]   Arjen van Dalen, 'The Algorithms Behind the Headlines: How Machine-written News Redefines the Core Skills of Human Journalists' (2012) 6 *Journalism Practice* 648; Matt Carlson, 'The Robotic Reporter: Automated Journalism and the Redefinition of Labor, Compositional Forms, and Journalistic Authority' (2015) 3 *Digital Journalism* 416; Andreas Graefe, 'Guide to Automated Journalism' (7 January 2016) www.cjr.org/tow_center_reports/guide_to_automated_journalism.php#status-quo accessed 2 May 2018.

efficiency and enabling human resources to be directed away from routine tasks.[13] Automation thus brings about qualitative and quantitative changes in journalism and in newsroom practices. At the same time, questions of account-ability in the media are more pressing than ever, reaching all the way to data utilisation, AI, and algorithms.[14]

This chapter sheds light on transparency in terms of demands for openness in the media and clarifies the meaning of AI in automated content production. This will be achieved by answering the following questions: what does trans-parency mean for media practices and what forms does it take in algorithmic journalism? First, transparency is elaborated on a general level and in the context of AI. Then, transparency is discussed specifically in the media sector. To that end, a few existing legal rules around transparency are presented. After that, algorithmic journalism is discussed from the perspective of transparency demands, followed by interesting case studies from Finnish self-regulation and ethical guidelines for journalists. Lastly, some concluding remarks are presented with a focus on a rights-based approach to transparency.

## 1.2    The Quest for Transparency

Transparency is currently a general demand on a societal level, having links to democracy, public discussion and accountability. The assumption is that informed decision-making rests on the availability of information, while decisions may also be questioned based on information. Demands for transparency are thus targeted at powerful organisations and institutions, ranging from public sector openness and access to information to corporate 'full disclosure' and transparency reporting.[15] According to Dean, democracy

---

[13]    Tal Montal and Zvi Reich, 'I, Robot. You, Journalist. Who Is the Author? Authorship, Bylines and Full Disclosure in Automated Journalism' (2017) 5 *Digital Journalism* 829; Lindén and Tuulonen (n 7) 5, 9–10.
[14]    Stephanie Craft and Kyle Heim, 'Transparency in Journalism: Meanings, Merits and Risks' in Lee Wilkins and Clifford G Christians (eds), *The Handbook of Mass Media Ethics* (Routledge 2008); Robert G Picard and Victor Pickard, 'Essential Principles for Contemporary Media and Communications Policymaking' (2017) *Reuters Institute for the Study of Journalism* 7–8, 28–31 http://reutersinstitute.politics .ox.ac.uk/publication/essential-principlescontemporary-media-and-communications -policymaking accessed 23 January 2020.
[15]    Jonathan Fox, 'The Uncertain Relationship Between Transparency and Accountability' (2007) 17 *Development in Practice* 663; Christopher Hood, 'Accountability and Transparency: Siamese Twins, Matching Parts, Awkward Couple?' (2010) 33 *West European Politics* 989, 989–993; Fenwick McKelvey, 'Algorithmic Media Need Democratic Methods: Why Publics Matter' (2014) 39 *Canadian Journal of Communication* 597 (referring especially to John Dewey's work); Han Byung-Chul, *The Transparency Society* (Stanford University Press 2015); Brent

and capitalist technoculture meet where publicity – and the need for it – are concerned.[16] However, Berns points out that publicity as a principle is limited in comparison to transparency as 'continuous visibility'.[17] Transparency has a trans-ideological character and strong appeal, as Fox notes, leading to a lack of explicit definition, addressee, and contextual specification. It is demanded by various stakeholders, who attach different meanings to it.[18] Ideally, the method of transparency involves bringing conflicts into the open, making issues visible, and enabling discussion and debate. At the core of transparency lies the idea of openness and explanation, while these are seen as essential requirements for holding somebody accountable for their (in)action(s).[19] Indeed, the causal link between transparency and accountability is a general assumption, so much so that Fox calls the two 'twin principles'.[20] Accountability means responsibility for one's actions, harmful and unlawful conduct, and it is a fundamental building block in a democratic society both for individuals and institutions, including journalism.[21] Accountability, too, lacks precise definitions, but implies at least a limit on abuse of power, the capacity to inquire and demand explanation (or the obligation to provide justification) as well as remedies in terms of sanctions or compensation; this means a soft side and a hard side, according to Fox. Ultimately, accountability always requires intervention by third parties, that is, a reaction to transparency.[22]

---

Mittelstadt, 'Auditing for Transparency in Content Personalization Systems' (2016) 10 *International Journal of Communication* 4991, 4992; Tal Montal and Zvi Reich, 'The Death of the Author, the Rise of the Robo-Journalist: Authorship, Bylines, and Full Disclosure in Automated Journalism' in Scott Eldridge II and Bob Franklin (eds), *The Routledge Handbook of Developments in Digital Journalism Studies* (Routledge 2019). For a detailed account of the development of transparency, see Stefan Larsson and Fredrik Heintz, 'Transparency in Artificial Intelligence' (2020) 9(2) *Internet Policy Review* 3–7.

[16]  Jodi Dean, 'Publicity's Secret' (2001) 29 *Political Theory* 624; Jodi Dean, *Publicity's Secret: How Technoculture Capitalizes on Democracy* (Cornell University Press 2002) 30, 15–46.

[17]  Thomas Berns, 'Not Individuals, Relations: What Transparency Is Really About. A Theory of Algorithmic Governmentality' in Emmanuel Alloa and Dieter Thomä (eds), *Transparency, Society and Subjectivity* (Palgrave Macmillan 2018) 244.

[18]  Fox (n 15) 663–665.

[19]  McKelvey (n 15) 607; Stefan Larsson, 'Sju nyanser av transparens: Om artificiell intelligens och ansvaret för digitala plattformars samhällspåverkan' in Jonas Andersson Schwarz and Stefan Larsson (eds), *Plattformssamhället: Den digitala utvecklingens politik, innovation och reglering* (Fores 2018) 297, 301.

[20]  Fox (n 15) 663.

[21]  McKelvey (n 15); Picard and Pickard (n 14) 7–8, 30–31.

[22]  Fox (n 15) 665–666, 668–669.

However, as Fox points out, the causal link between transparency and accountability may be questioned: if the power of transparency rests on shame, it is insufficient to guide anyone who is shameless. For companies, transparency may even offer what Fox calls 'a market-friendly substitute' for actual sanctions imposed by the authorities. So the question of appropriate conditions for the assumption of causality to work becomes crucial, while the focus has to be on different types of transparency and accountability. Fox talks about 'opaque transparency' (sic!) in which case huge investments may be required to interpret public data and 'clear transparency' that explicitly reveals actual behavior.[23] For her part, Dean talks about publicity's secret: this means that more information and access seem to provide an answer to everything. However, publicity requires secrecy at least in three ways: as a constitutive limit, as a historical background (e.g., the Habermasian public sphere), and as a part of ideological regulation of the invisible and the visible.[24] Similarly, transparency also meets its limits where 'full disclosure' turns back on itself. There is a risk of gaming or misuse of a system that reveals all its secrets, while the end result may turn out to be perverse.[25] Moreover, from a legal perspective, the current data economy, powered by AI, undeniably consists of several elements that point towards invisibility rather than visibility. Data, including that of a personal nature, is essential to new technologies such as AI and ML.[26] Machine learning refers to a subcategory of AI. It means improving the performance of a computer by using data for learning, while it may occur whether supervised or unsupervised.[27] Data protection laws regulate the processing of personal data, while algorithmic tools also imply proprietary software and trade secrets, among others. These areas are thus of utmost importance for utilisation of AI in any field of application, including the media

---

[23]   Ibid., 664–665; see also Hood (n 15) on three different ways to view the relationship between accountability and transparency.

[24]   Dean, 'Publicity's Secret' (n 16) 624–626; Dean, *Publicity's Secret: How Technoculture Capitalizes on Democracy* (n 16) 1–46.

[25]   Byung-Chul (n 15).

[26]   Diakopoulos, 'Enabling Accountability of Algorithmic Media' (n 2) 30; Lindén and Tuulonen (n 7) 35–37, 41, 48; European Broadcasting Union (EBU) (n 1) 33–39. Indeed, more often that not personal data is involved even in industrial applications. See e.g., John Wrigley, Anette Alén-Savikko and Olli Pitkänen, 'Finding the "Personal" in the Industrial Internet: Why Data Protection Law still Matters' in Rosa Ballardini, Olli Pitkänen and Petri Kuoppamäki (eds), *Regulating Industrial Internet Through IPR, Data Protection and Competition Law* (Kluwer Law International 2019).

[27]   Steven W Knox, *Machine Learning: a Concise Introduction* (Wiley 2018) 5; see also European Broadcasting Union (EBU) (n 1) 18–19.

sector in general and journalism in particular.[28] Simultaneously, however, transparency has gained new momentum in the data economy. At the EU level, the Guidelines on Transparency have been updated following the General Data Protection Regulation (EU) 2016/679 (GDPR).[29] They provide practical and interpretative guidance on the 'overarching obligation' related to information provision.[30] According to the guidelines, transparency 'is about engendering trust in the processes which affect the citizen by enabling them to understand, and if necessary, challenge those processes'.[31]

In the context of new technologies and new forms of power, such as AI and algorithms, the overall conceptualisation should arguably enable action and practices based on values that are considered important in society.[32] Utilisation of AI should, according to many, promote equality and reduce bias and harm.[33] All this has implications for policy, law, ethics, and self-regulation. Within the EU, the High-Level Expert Group on Artificial Intelligence set up by the European Commission has issued Ethics Guidelines for Trustworthy AI which tie AI ethics to fundamental rights and the values underlying them. According to these guidelines, the fundamental pillars for trustworthy AI include human dignity and freedom, democracy and rule of law, as well as equality and citizens' rights.[34] There are three dimensions to trustworthiness: these relate

---

[28]   Diakopoulos, 'Enabling Accountability of Algorithmic Media' (n 2) 30; Picard and Pickard (n 14) 11.

[29]   Regulation (EU) 2016/679 of the European Parliament and of the Council of 27 April 2016 on the protection of natural persons with regard to the processing of personal data and on the free movement of such data, and repealing Directive 95/46/EC (General Data Protection Regulation) [2016] OJ L119/1.

[30]   Article 29 Data Protection Working Party, 'Guidelines on Transparency under Regulation 2016/679' (WP260rev.01, adopted on 29 November 2017 and as last revised and adopted on 11 April 2018) 4.

[31]   Ibid., 4.

[32]   Taina Bucher, *If ... Then: Algorithmic Power and Politics* (OUP 2018); Neil M Richards and William D Smart, 'How Should the Law Think about Robots?' in Ryan Calo, A. Michael Froomkin and Ian Kerr (eds), *Robot Law* (Edward Elgar Publishing 2016).

[33]   Larsson (n 19) 307–309. For algorithmic nuisance, see Jack M Balkin, 'The Three Laws of Robotics in the Age of Big Data' (2017) 78 *Ohio State Law Journal* 1217, 1232–1240; Frank Pasquale, 'Toward a Fourth Law of Robotics: Preserving Attribution, Responsibility, and Explainability in an Algorithmic Society' (2017) 78 *Ohio State Law Journal* 1243, 1247–1251. According to Balkin 1238, 'algorithm operators have a duty to the public not to "pollute", that is, unjustifiably externalize the costs of algorithmic decision-making onto others'.

[34]   High-Level Expert Group on Artificial Intelligence set up by the European Commission, 'Ethics Guidelines for Trustworthy AI' (8 April 2019) https://ec .europa.eu/digital-single-market/en/news/ethics-guidelines-trustworthy-ai accessed 4 September 2019.

to lawfulness, ethics, and robustness of AI respectively. The principle of explicability is placed among the foundations, alongside human autonomy, harm prevention, and fairness. Human autonomy ties to the requirements of human agency and human oversight over AI, while transparency and accountability are an essential part of the realisation of trustworthy AI.[35]

According to the Guidelines, explicability is tied to trust in the sense that users' trust must be built and maintained. This is done via transparent processes, by communicating the workings and purposes of the AI systems in question. In particular, automated decisions must be explainable to those affected by them (e.g., to enable contestation). The degree of explanation depends on the context and consequences. However, the Guidelines do admit that reasons for a particular output cannot always be explained (the so-called black box[36]) – but even then, fundamental rights are to be respected, and it is possible to employ other measures, such as transparent communication about system capabilities.[37] Transparency itself is defined as something intertwined with the principle of explicability, covering AI systems themselves and related data and business models. Moreover, transparency is further elaborated in terms of traceability, explainability, and communication. Traceability refers to documentation of relevant data, processes, and algorithms. Traceability enables detection of (reasons behind) mistakes as well as auditing and safeguarding explainability. Explainability, in turn, covers both technical and human processes. There is a balancing between explainability and accuracy, while explanations should also be tailored for the recipients in question. Business model transparency includes clarifying the reasons for employing the AI system in question as well as the degree of influence it has on design choices and decision-making. Lastly, communication involves informing users of the fact that an AI system is being used. AI systems are to be identifiable and a choice should be availanble for users to decline interaction with the system. Moreover, users should be informed of the capabilities and restrictions of AI systems in an intelligible manner.[38]

All this has implications for media as the fourth estate and business when they resort to new technologies, such as AI and algorithms. Traditionally, however, the media is more famous for exposing issues or providing a forum for issues that have been exposed, thereby creating transparency impacts, but not so much a target (something to be exposed) itself.[39] Journalism continues

---

[35]   Ibid., 8, 12–13, 15–16, 18.

[36]   See Frank Pasquale, *The Black Box Society: The Secret Algorithms That Control Money and Information* (Harvard University Press 2015).

[37]   High-Level Expert Group (n 34) 13.

[38]   Ibid., 18.

[39]   Fox (n 15) 666.

to exercise its watchdog role – possibly even with some new dimensions. The data economy needs not only someone to hold those in power accountable for their use of AI but also someone to decipher digits and data. The newsroom arguably needs to develop a 'data-savvy culture', as noted in the EBU Report, and integrate new skills into media practices, including data literacy, mastery of spreadsheets and algorithmic accountability reporting, among others; the legacy media also has an important task in battling and educating on disinformation which employs AI tools (e.g., deep fakes).[40] However, this chapter examines the notion of transparency as a demand targeted at the media itself. Since transparency is linked to the exercise of power, this chapter examines transparency from the perspective of a rights-based approach in the field of media. This refers to a particular view on supplying citizens with 'information and communication rights', whether in terms of normative principles or legal norms, to counter state and corporate power, including algorithmic power.[41]

## 2. TRANSPARENCY AS AN ESSENTIAL MEDIA PRINCIPLE

Transparency is causally linked to accountability also in the media sector,[42] even though the assumption can be challenged as noted. With regard to the media, transparency refers to openness at least in two different ways (although categorizations are many): disclosing how content is produced and allowing the public to participate in the production process.[43] The focus in this chapter is on the former dimension. This dimension might further be divided into disclosure regarding the newsroom, journalists, sources, editorial decision-making and other sides of the production process.[44] Transparency in this regard implies

---

[40] Lindén and Tuulonen (n 7) 33; European Broadcasting Union (EBU) (n 1) 8, 34, 91–93, 101–102, 119, 127.

[41] Marko Ala-Fossi and others, 'Operationalising Communication Rights: The Case of a "Digital Welfare State"' (2019) 8(1) *Internet Policy Review* 2; Hannu Nieminen, 'Communication and Information Rights in European Media Policy' in Leif Kramp and others (eds), *Politics, Civil Society and Participation: Media and Communications in a Transforming Environment* (The Researching and Teaching Communicatins Series, Edition lumière 2016); see also Monica Horten, *The Closing of the Net* (Polity Press 2016) on power online and corporations aiming to shape law and policy.

[42] Larsson (n 19) 301; Michael Karlsson and Christer Clerwall, 'Transparency to the Rescue? Evaluating Citizens' Views on Transparency Tools in Journalism' (2018) 19 *Journalism Studies* 1923. cf Diakopoulos, 'Enabling Accountability of Algorithmic Media' (n 2) 27.

[43] Craft and Heim (n 14) 217; Karlsson and Clerwall (n 40) 1923–1924; Lauri Haapanen, 'Problematising the Restoration of Trust through Transparency: Focusing on Quoting' (2020) *Journalism* 3–4.

[44] See also Haapanen (n 43), ibid.

that the media itself, its practices and institutional structures are being exposed. Transparency is supposed to enable control of journalistic practices by both insiders and outsiders.[45] There are obvious links to the role of the media in society and for democracy whether as a watchdog, an intermediary, or a mediator. Increased transparency accompanied by increased accountability to the public is seen as an instrument in fulfilling the(se) societal role(s).[46] The online environment with bloggers and citizen journalists has arguably contributed to the pressure felt by professional journalists in justifying, opening, and explaining their activity. Moreover, in light of increased suspicion towards the legacy media, especially news production, transparency is supposed to function as a tool to reclaim the public's trust.[47] Craft and Heim talk about 'the modern era of transparency' in the media sector which encompasses self-assessment and reflection over the media's methods of operation.[48]

Indeed, according to the Picard and Pickard model from 2017, accountability and transparency feature among the essential principles for contemporary media and communications policymaking which are tailored to guide decision-making in the field. Other principles include, for example, following umbrella concepts with various subprinciples: catering for fundamental communication and content needs, promoting diversity in ownership of media, protecting users and society, pursuing economic benefits and effective policy outcomes. Much like transparency in general, references to it in the field of the media and journalism often fail to provide any clear definition, target, or way of fullfilling the obligation.[49] According to Picard and Pickard, the principles of accountability and transparency include several dimensions from a consumer perspective, that is, openness and comparability in terms, pricing, and data collection, as well as informing and helping people to understand the technological impacts on content choices. It also includes openness regarding media ownership as well as promotion of media accountability by means of law and self-regulatory measures.[50] For its part, the protection of users and society in Picard and Pickard's model also includes protection of privacy and data security. This relates, for example, to data collection enabling personalisation and targeted services. Transparency should also extend to such data collection and retention, while users should have the choice of opting-in and opting-out, as well as being safeguarded from manipulation and being aware

[45]   Diakopoulos, 'Enabling Accountability of Algorithmic Media' (n 2) 27; Lindén and Tuulonen (n 7) 7, 41.
[46]   Karlsson and Clerwall (n 42) 1924; Craft and Heim (n 14) 217.
[47]   Craft and Heim (n 14) 217; Haapanen (n 43).
[48]   Craft and Heim (n 14) 218.
[49]   Ibid., 217–218.
[50]   Picard and Pickard (n 14) 28–31.

of processes and rights related to data processing.[51] Picard and Pickard also highlight the importance of consumer protection in the field of media and communications, including transparent information on prices, products, and services. This allows for informed choices and comparison between subscriptions and equipment.[52]

As noted, Picard and Pickard speak for accountability backed up by law and self-regulation. Media companies, alongside other content producers and distributers, should be held responsible for harm to individuals and society. On the one hand, accountability is realised via enforcement of laws and regulation, such as provisions on defamation and privacy. On the other hand, accountability may involve a question of violating journalistic ethics and accompanying sanctions.[53] Transparency as such may be referred to as an established ethical principle which comes in many forms, ranging from openness with regard to ownership structures to explaining the framing of topics and selection of sources. It is basically a prerequisite for accountability in that it enables control by the public and is supposed to enable (re)connecting with the public and making its position better or stronger.[54] The background to the principle of transparency lies in openness as a philosophical concept, as pointed out by Picard and Pickard, since it enables the public to spot and evaluate various interests and their effects.[55] Indeed, Diakopoulos notes that traditional manifestations of media transparency include acknowledging sources and relationships with (financial) partners, highlighting expertise, as well as sharing and rectifying mistakes; despite the same ethical basis, transparency might be difficult to specify in practical terms when resorting to algorithmic tools.[56] Moreover, like other essential principles, transparency requires balancing with other dimensions in specific circumstances.[57] The interplay of ethics and law is also of interest since transparency is supposed to surpass the law and draw from benevolence, while also reaching into policy and regulatory debates with its normative effect, sometimes all the way to justifying or competing with legal norms.[58] Indeed, transparency already has practical applications and

---

[51] Ibid., 25–26.
[52] Ibid., 27.
[53] Ibid., 30–31.
[54] Karlsson and Clerwall (n 42); however, the Swedish study reported in the article concentrates on more conventional topics, not including automation and algorithmic tools as such.
[55] Picard and Pickard (n 14) 28–29.
[56] Diakopoulos, 'Enabling Accountability of Algorithmic Media' (n 2) 27; Berns (n 17). See also Lindén and Tuulonen (n 7) 7, 41–43.
[57] Picard and Pickard (n 14) 7.
[58] Berns (n 17) 244–245; Larsson and Heintz (n 15) 6.

manifestations in media related legislation and self-regulation. Legislation is discussed next, while self-regulation is discussed in subsection 4.

## 3.    EXAMPLES OF TRANSPARENCY RULES IN LEGISLATION

Transparency features in law both as a general principle and as specific provisions. Moreover, the links to democratic ideas presented above in subsection 1.2 arguably provide an overall background for the law as well. Two particular examples of transparency in current media-related legislation concern media ownership and data protection. Following the Ethics Guidelines for Trustworthy AI as well as Picard and Pickard's typology presented above, both are relevant where the media and use of AI is concerned.

Guidelines on transparency in the context of the GDPR note that it is a question of "a long established feature" of EU law.[59] More specifically, the Treaty on the Functioning of the European Union (TFEU)[60] includes provisions on open decision-making, close to citizens (Art. 1). For their part, EU institutions must be open and transparent as well as in dialogue with civil society (Art. 11(2) TFEU). Lastly, the Treaty refers to access to information within the EU framework, while stressing the transparent nature of proceedings (Art. 15 TFEU).[61] For its part, media ownership transparency is regulated in the revised Audiovisual Media Services Directive (AVMSD; 2018/1808).[62] Due to the societal position of the media, openness regarding its ownership becomes an important issue. In particular, the media functions as a tool to enable detection of (holders of) powerful interests and informed judgements. It supposedly works against abuses of power. It is not a limitation of ownership as such (cf. competition law), even if it also contributes to assessments of pluralism[63] in the media sector, that is, manifold values and perspectives. It boils down to

---

[59]    Art. 29 WP (n 30) 4.

[60]    Consolidated Version of the Treaty on the Functioning of the European Union [2012] OJ C326/47.

[61]    See also Article 29 WP (n 30) 4 fn 5.

[62]    Directive (EU) 2018/1808 of the European Parliament and of the Council of 14 November 2018 amending Directive 2010/13/EU on the coordination of certain provisions laid down by law, regulation or administrative action in Member States concerning the provision of audiovisual media services (Audiovisual Media Services Directive) in view of changing market realities [2018] OJ L303/69.

[63]    For a detailed account of media pluralism, see Kari Karppinen, *Rethinking Media Pluralism* (Fordham University Press 2012). See also European Broadcasting Union (EBU) (n 1) 50–51 where the Diamond project with a focus on collecting data on diversity is discussed. See https://creativediversitynetwork.com/diamond/ accessed 13 April 2020.

availability of information about ownership.[64] Indeed, at the EU level, the revised Article 5(2) of the AVMS Directive states that national provisions may be adopted that mandate media companies to render information on their ownership structure accessible. However, the article insists that relevant fundamental rights, including the private and family life of beneficial owners, be respected, while pursuing 'an objective of general interest'. The article is accompanied by a mandatory list of other types of information that a media service provider must provide, including its name and contact details as well as notes on competent regulatory authorities or supervisory bodies (Art. 5(1) AVMSD). According to the preamble to the AVMS Directive (Recitals 15–16), media ownership transparency is 'directly linked to the freedom of expression, a cornerstone of democratic systems', while promotion of free speech and media pluralism requires that users have access to information about media companies.

At the EU level, the GDPR includes provisions on transparency and accountability – and the Regulation may function as a signpost with regard to algorithmic tools in general.[65] Transparency is among the building blocks of the Regulation and one of the general principles of processing (Art. 5(1)(a); Recitals 13, 39, 58, 60, 71 GDPR). Similarly, the principle of accountability is integrated throughout the GDPR, alongside a specific provision (Art. 5(2)[66] GDPR). According to the guidelines for transparency, the two are 'intrinsically linked', while transparency has links to fairness and 'empowers data subjects to hold data controllers and processors accountable and to exercise control over their personal data'.[67] However, the GDPR also includes specific obligations for data controllers (i.e., those responsible for data processing) regarding the information to be provided to data subjects (i.e., those whose data is processed). The Regulation includes provisions on information transparency whereby information and communication regarding the processing in question must take place 'in a concise, transparent, intelligible and easily

---

[64]   Picard and Pickard (n 14) 28–29. See also Mark Thompson, 'Media Plurality Series: The Transparency of Media Ownership' (*LSE Blog*, 11 December 2013) https:// blogs.lse.ac.uk/medialse/2013/12/11/the-transparency-of-media-ownership/ accessed 8 April 2020.

[65]   See also Mittelstadt (n 15) 4998; Koulu (n 2) 29.

[66]   Regulation (EU) 2016/679 (n 29) Art. 5(2) GDPR: 'The controller shall be responsible for, and be able to demonstrate compliance with, paragraph 1 ("accountability")'. See also e.g., Arts 7(1); 24 GDPR. For accountability, see e.g., Joseph Alhadeff, Brendan van Alsenoy and Jos Dumortier, 'The Accountability Principle in Data Protection Regulation: Origin, Development and Future Directions' in Daniel Guagnin and others (eds), *Managing Privacy through Accountability* (Palgrave Macmillan 2012) 49–82.

[67]   Article 29 WP (n 30) 5.

accessible form, using clear and plain language' (Art. 12). First, people are to be informed, among others, of the identity of the controller, the purposes and extent of processing, as well as of their rights and the right to lodge a complaint. Secondly, they are to be informed of the logics and function of algorithms, where automated decisions, including profiling, are concerned (Arts 13–14). They also have the right to access data concerning them, along-side information on these issues (Art. 15).[68] The GDPR thus specifies many demands for transparency: transparency involves informing people about the activity and their own position as well as of the manner of providing this information. Indeed, according to the Preamble (Recital 39), people 'should be made aware of risks, rules, safeguards and rights in relation to the processing of personal data and how to exercise their rights in relation to such processing'. With regard to profiling (cf. Art. 22[69] GDPR), people should be made aware of such processing and the consequences thereof (Recital 60). Moreover, to ensure that the information is understandable, visualisation tools and standard-ised icons may also be required, while accessibility could refer to availability on a website (Recitals 58 and 60). Transparency may also be promoted via cer-tification, seals, and marks indicating the level of data protection in products and services (Recital 100). Transparency combined with fairness also requires use of 'appropriate mathematical or statistical procedures for the profiling' as

---

[68]  See also ibid., 6–7.
[69]  Regulation (EU) 2016/679 (n 29) Art. 22 GDPR:
  1.  The data subject shall have the right not to be subject to a decision based solely on automated processing, including profiling, which produces legal effects concerning him or her or similarly significantly affects him or her.
  2.  Paragraph 1 shall not apply if the decision:
    (a)  is necessary for entering into, or performance of, a contract between the data subject and a data controller;
    (b)  is authorised by Union or Member State law to which the controller is subject and which also lays down suitable measures to safeguard the data subject's rights and freedoms and legitimate interests; or (c) is based on the data subject's explicit consent.
  3.  In the cases referred to in points (a) and (c) of paragraph 2, the data controller shall implement suitable measures to safeguard the data subject's rights and freedoms and legitimate interests, at least the right to obtain human interven-tion on the part of the controller, to express his or her point of view and to contest the decision.
  4.  Decisions referred to in paragraph 2 shall not be based on special categories of personal data referred to in Article 9(1), unless point (a) or (g) of Article 9(2) applies and suitable measures to safeguard the data subject's rights and freedoms and legitimate interests are in place.

well as measures to ensure that risks are minimized in terms of errors, interests and rights of the data subject, as well as discriminatory effects (Recital 71).[70]

According to the guidelines for transparency, visualisation tools enable effective communication without and alongside extensive written documents and reports, while information provision may also happen by resorting to the so-called layered approach. All in all, the demand for transparency may be met with a combination of tools. For its part, layering means that key points are delivered in a short notice on the first layer with links to more detailed information on each point on the second layer. Then, some specific issues may be expanded by providing more links and material on subsequent layers. However, the first layer should already enable a clear overview and the aim is not to offer a complicated web of links.[71]

With regard to transparency, data protection law includes one more interesting aspect. According to some views, the GDPR actually includes a 'right to explanation' promoting accountability and transparency that is applicable to automated decisions and AI-driven systems. This entitlement, however, is not as a dedicated right but rather a constructed right based on Articles 13–15 GDPR.[72] Some rather talk about the 'right to be informed'.[73] This would indeed be very similar to the 'right to be forgotten' in the Data Protection Directive (95/46/EC)[74] as interpreted by the CJEU.[75] In interpreting this right, functionality and flexibility should be promoted according to Selbst and Powles, while the right should enable exercise of data subjects' rights (even under a human rights lense).[76] However, the GDPR also includes explicit provisions on balancing personal data protection and freedom of expression and information – both safeguarded as fundamental rights in the EU Charter (Arts 8 and 11). Thereby, within the framework of Article 85, Member States should provide exemptions and derogations, for example, for processing conducted for *journalistic purposes* (as to which see Chapter 3 in this volume). According to the Regulation

---

[70]  Article 29 WP (n 30) 6–12, 22.

[71]  Ibid., 19–20, 25–26.

[72]  Andrew Selbst and Julia Powles, 'Meaningful Information and the Right to Explanation' (2017) 7 *International Data Privacy Law* 233. cf critique e.g., Sandra Wachter, Brent Mittelstadt and Luciano Floridi, 'Why a Right to Explanation of Automated Decision-Making Does Not Exist in the General Data Protection Regulation' (2017) 7 *International Data Privacy Law* 76.

[73]  Wachter, Mittelstadt and Floridi (n 72).

[74]  Directive 95/46/EC of the European Parliament and of the Council of 24 October 1995 on the protection of individuals with regard to the processing of personal data and on the free movement of such data [1995] OJ L281/31.

[75]  Case C-131/12 *Google Spain SL and Google Inc. v Agencia Española de Protección de Datos (AEPD) and Mario Costeja González* ECLI:EU:C:2014:317.

[76]  Selbst and Powles (n 72).

(Preamble, Recital 153), reconciling data protection with free speech may require exemptions and derogations, in particular where audiovisual media and news archives are concerned. These may target many parts of the Regulation, including general principles, data subject's rights, and supervisory authorities (Art. 85(2); Recital 153). Moreover, Article 85(2) states that the importance of free speech in democratic society makes it 'necessary to interpret notions relating to that freedom, such as journalism, broadly'. Member States must notify the EU Commission of the solutions they adopt to this end (Art. 85(3)). With regard to Finland, the national Data Protection Act (1050/2018; DPA[77]) includes provisions specifying the need to safeguard freedom of expression as well as the reach of the journalistic exemption. According to Section 27 DPA, the applicability of several articles of the GDPR is excluded where journalistic purposes are concerned (e.g., Arts 5(1)(c)–(e); 6–7, 9–10, 11(2); 12–22), while some other articles are applicable "only where appropriate" (e.g., Arts 5(1)(a); 5(2); 24–26). It seems that the general principle of transparency in Article 5(1) similar to the principle of accountability in Article 5(2) applies to some extent, but not the articles providing a basis for the disputed 'right to explanation'.

These legal norms cover some parts of media practices. The utilisation of AI in the media is discussed next in order to examine the scope of transparency demands in algorithmic journalism. The purpose is to investigate the feasibility of a dedicated legal right, taking into account the current regulatory and self-regulatory framework for transparency in the media.

## 4.    THE EMPEROR IN NEW CLOTHES

### 4.1    Transparency in Algorithmic Journalism

AI and automation may be involved in various stages of the content production process and with or without direct human intervention (i.e., from semi-automated to fully automated or autonomous). Indeed, templates have been the governing basis for robotic journalism in text format – thereby not really amounting to AI. Developing technologies around natural language processing (NLP) and especially natural language generation (NLG) as subcategories of AI are, however, slowly freeing the (robot) journalist from the template. Here, it is a question of generating text in natural language from computational input. Then again, some tools may rather be limited to the newsroom (e.g., automated proofreading and translation) or producing graph-

---

[77]    Data Protection Act (1050/2018) (FI), unofficial translation by the Ministry of Justice available at www.finlex.fi/en/laki/kaannokset/2018/en20181050.pdf accessed 22 March 2020.

ics, while others produce content automatically for the eyes of the public.[78] Transparency as a guiding principle in the media sector is certainly not limited to questions of content production with the help of algorithmic tools. However, transparency becomes a particularly interesting phenomenon in the context of computational or algorithmic journalism. This is because the use of AI, like computational journalism in general, might imply the opposite trend of opacity in the form of blind spots for biases and unexplainable black boxes or logics of operation, especially with (unsupervised) machine learning.[79] In addition, 'tacit power' is involved in algorithmic tools.[80]

Diakopoulos elaborates on a transparency model where disclosable information is specified as follows: Where data is concerned, questions of accuracy, validation, and cleanliness should be addressed, while disclosure on modelling should include methods, software, and rules. Moreover, inference should be opened with regard to error analysis and confidence values. Finally, transparency should be integrated into the user experience (UX) in terms of an interactive interface with, for example, notifications on algorithms.[81] As for data, questions of volume and frequency as well as variety become important alongside accuracy.[82] In terms of content production, Montal and Reich have identified different types of demands related to transparency, including *disclosure transparency* and *algorithmic transparency*. These refer to openness with regard to how news and other types of content are framed and produced, what sources and data are used, and how the algorithms employed work, as well as their methodology.[83] Indeed, transparency may be exercised in practice by

---

[78] Lindén and Tuulonen (n 7) 24, 27, 45; Dörr (n 1) 702–705; European Broadcasting Union (EBU) (n 1) 21–27, 30–32, 57, 64, 93, 109. See, on the one hand, Reuters' human–machine collaboration described in the EBU Report where robots suggest stories for human reporters to evaluate and on the other hand Dutch sport broadcasting coverage without human involvement, European Broadcasting Union (EBU) (n 1) 24–27.

[79] McKelvey (n 15) 599; Coddington, 'Clarifying Journalism's Quantitative Turn' (n 2); Nicholas Diakopoulos and Michael Koliska, 'Algorithmic Transparency in the News Media' (2016) 5 *Digital Journalism* 809; Mittelstadt (n 15) 4996–4997; Diakopoulos, 'Enabling Accountability of Algorithmic Media' (n 2) 26–27; European Broadcasting Union (EBU) (n 1) 99.

[80] Lindén and Tuulonen (n 7) 28–30.

[81] Diakopoulos, 'Enabling Accountability of Algorithmic Media' (n 2) 28–30.

[82] Lindén and Tuulonen (n 7) 35–37.

[83] Montal and Reich, 'The Death of the Author, the Rise of the Robo-Journalist Authorship' (n 15) 54. See also Craft and Heim (n 14); Dalen (n 11); Diakopoulos and Koliska (n 79); Graefe (n 12); Coddington, 'Clarifying Journalism's Quantitative Turn' (n 2); Picard and Pickard (n 14). For a practical execution, see e.g., Alexander Spangher 'Building the Next New York Times Recommendation Engine' (*NYT Open*, 11 August 2015) https://open.nytimes.com/building-the-next-new-york-times-recommendation

accompanying news reports with editorials, links to original sources and ethical guidelines, as well as by adding notes on (up)dates and corrections. Moreover, disclosure also takes the form of bylines, that is, credits or attribution of news stories to their writers, as well as 'mug shots' and information on journalists' backgound and interests. Byline policies in the field of journalism have thus far been rather human-centric since news is regularly accompanied by names of human journalists or news agencies.[84] Indeed, crediting a machine instead of a person might have surprising effects depending on the level of credibility and corruption linked to the media sector.[85] As a comparison, Larsson looks at transparency from the point of view of platforms. He identifies seven dimensions which have to do with ownership of software and data, prevention of gaming the system, data literacy, explainable algorithms, tracking and personalisation, as well as the complexity of data-driven ecosystems and autonomous systems.[86] All these appear to be relevant for the legacy media as well.

Following Coddington's typology, it is especially the question of openness that separates computational journalism from data journalism. Whereas data journalism follows an open source ideology with regard to product and process, computational journalism cannot meet those demands due to algorithmic transparency being more difficult than data transparency.[87] Then again, computation and algorithms might also imply the opposite, that is, the ability to trace and explain functions that otherwise would be obscure – such as those (unconsciously) taking place inside the human mind. Indeed, as noted in the EBU Report, humans in the newsroom need to be increasingly aware of their own routines, assumptions, and choices in order to be able to give instructions to AI tools.[88]

---

-engine-19ac4715b9fa accessed 4 September 2019. See however Larsson and Heintz (n 15) 2–3 on the conceptual distinction between 'AI transparency' and 'algorithmic transparency' whereby the former concept is wider than the latter.

[84]    Montal and Reich, 'The Death of the Author, the Rise of the Robo-Journalist Authorship' (n 15) 55; Haapanen (n 43) 3–4.

[85]    Lindén and Tuulonen (n 7) 30–31. See also Jaemin Jung and others, 'Intrusion of Software Robots into Journalism: The Public's and Journalists' Perceptions of News Written by Algorithms and Human Journalists' (2017) 71 *Computers in Human Behavior* 291.

[86]    Larsson (n 19) 300–303.

[87]    Nicholas Diakopoulos, 'Algorithmic Accountability Reporting: On the Investigation of Black Boxes' (2014) Tow Center for Digital Journalism, Columbia University www.nickdiakopoulos.com/wp-content/uploads/2011/07/Algorithmic-Accountability-Reporting_final.pdf accessed 9 April 2020; Coddington, 'Clarifying Journalism's Quantitative Turn' (n 2) 337, 341.

[88]    European Broadcasting Union (EBU) (n 1) 45–46. The Report discusses reflective practice groups in the Austrian public service media company, ORF (ibid). See also Diakopoulos, 'Enabling Accountability of Algorithmic Media' (n 2) 27.

As noted in subsection 1.2 above, the EU AI Ethics Guidelines require identification as well as both explicability and explanation. For its part, the EBU Report refers to the Guidelines, noting that AI ethics really does not differ from ethics in general but AI does bring about some particular challenges, such as a lack of transparency due to the black box problem. In the report, transparency means communicating the use of AI.[89] In the context of Picard and Pickard's model regarding the media in particular, the principles of accountability and transparency include informing the public of automation and algorithms. The focus is on openness regarding technological influences, among others, on content choices, automatic selection and related biases.[90] Picard and Pickard refer to these principles as something that work against or to reveal otherwise concealed choices, effects, and informational biases regarding marketing, news, automated content production (by 'robots') and algorithmic functions, such as personalisation and filtering (one might called it consumer protection of sorts in a data economy). The principles also aim to safeguard transparency and the public's understanding of these invisible structures and functions, often involving trade secrets and proprietary software that actually work towards secrecy rather than publicity. Indeed, the idea of full disclosure is not applicable here – also due to its downside of enabling (undesired) third party manipulation. The public should nevertheless be able to make informed judgments on the reliability and importance of media content. This could also be promoted via requirements related to labelling, including those related to notifications of algorithmic preferences in cases of ownership or financial interests.[91] Mittelstadt talks about a need for algorithmic auditing and a possible need for a regulatory agency or a trusted third party to which meaningful notices would be submitted.[92]

These elements are essentially part of disclosure transparency and algorithmic transparency in the media sector. The essence, following Picard and Pickard's ideas, is to enable informed judgements, whether in terms of reliability or importance of media content. This in turn might be linked to enabling the public to oversee the media in its use of algorithmic tools and safeguarding that the media continues to act according to established journalistic standards in the fields of both ethics and law. What is opened to the public are methods of journalism and other forms of content production or curation. This is currently accompanied by legal protection afforded to data subjects and consumers in terms of processing personal data. The media must thus open up its practices

---

[89]   European Broadcasting Union (EBU) (n 1) 90, 111–112.
[90]   Picard and Pickard (n 14) 29–30.
[91]   Ibid. See also Carlson (n 12); Mittelstadt (n 15) 4996.
[92]   Mittelstadt (n 15) 4994–4998 with references.

and methods of information processing. Here, one might draw analogies with scientific practices which gain their reliablity via methods and their openness. Algorithmic tools may also provide new opportunities to watch the watchdog: content may be tested and scanned for biases and polarisation, for example. These ideas of democratic participation and informed judgments are linked to the human oversight requirement put forward in the AI Ethics Guidelines. The downside is that such a requirement often rests on problematic assumptions of a human being in control and may end up meaning an unrealistic burden for the person supposedly in control of the machine – as pointed out by Koulu.[93]

Diakopoulos provides one example of transparency in the context of an automated social media newsbot based on his model discussed above: information was made available on a webpage, such as opening the code and describing the data, as well as providing links to research around the design of the automated agent in question. This information then enabled both media companies to draw from the code and the public to find out who designed the robot and how its decision-making works.[94] As for the legacy media, for example in Finland, the national public service broadcaster Yleisradio (Yle) has opened the code of its newsbot, called Voitto, to encourage collaboration among developers.[95] For its part, *The New York Times* also offers some interesting examples of transparency in action via its NYT Open service: it offers the public insights into the processes underlying its digital products.[96] For example, one article reports on the necessary engineering for traffic peaks related to election coverage.[97] However, many options are available for making transparency happen – alongside text-based information, open source codes, and written coverage. Various types of visualisation tools and layered approaches to delivering information could also be employed. Moreover, information could be offered both in accessible format and by means of gradual extension of available information according to the needs and desires of each individual member of the public. Similar solutions are already utilised to fulfill information duties in the field of data protection and consenting, as explained in subsection 3 above. The embedding of wider democratic values as well as journalistic values into

---

[93]   Koulu (n 2) 22–23, 31–32, 45–46. See also High-Level Expert Group (n 34) 12, 14–16. For a tool developed for testing content by Stanford University see European Broadcasting Union (EBU) (n 1) 77–78.
[94]   Diakopoulos, 'Enabling Accountability of Algorithmic Media' (n 2) 31–33.
[95]   See https://github.com/Yleisradio/avoin-voitto accessed 4 May 2020.
[96]   See https://open.nytimes.com/ accessed 3 May 2020.
[97]   See Kriton Dolias and Vinessa Wan, 'How We Prepared New York Times Engineering for the Midterm Elections' (*NYT Open*, 15 Febuary 2019) https:// open.nytimes.com/how-we-prepared-new-york-times-engineering-for-the-midterm -elections-2a615fe4196e accessed 27 March 2020.

algorithms is also necessary.[98] Needless to say, this type of content production requires an multitalented interdisciplinary team in the newsroom, consisting not only of traditional journalists, but tech-savvy journalists (including data journalists), data scientists and statisticians, programmers, and designers, among others.[99]

## 4.2    Pioneering Self-regulatory Tools: Case Studies from Finland

In the field of mass media, the Finnish self-regulatory body, the Council for Mass Media (CMM), has been at the forefront in responding both to the increased use of algorithms in newsrooms and to related developments in legislation. In 2018, the CMM issued its first decision around the use of automation in the media, followed in late 2019 by publication of a dictum concerning algorithmic journalism. The CMM has thereby been the first in Europe, if not internationally, to tackle the issue with general guidelines.[100] The CMM interprets the Guidelines for journalists[101] and may issue non-binding decisions in response to complaints. The guidelines as such are technology-neutral and apply across the media sector. However, despite all major Finnish media companies being part of the voluntary self-regulatory system, not all media companies have bound themselves to the Guidelines or to the CMM.

In early 2018, the CMM started a campaign around a label for 'accountable journalism'[102] (see Figure 2.1 below), aiming for permanent use thereof. The label enables the public to identify media content produced according to the Guidelines and to separate it from disinformation and new forms of marketing, among others. Its use is free for members of the CMM bound by the Guidelines.[103]

---

[98]   See e.g., European Broadcasting Union (EBU) (n 1) 12–14, 88–94. The Report discusses a Swedish newspaper publisher called Mittmedia (ibid., 12–14), while also pointing to the wider question of value-based journalism (ibid., 88–94). Moreover, the common good could also be integrated into AI (ibid., 49).

[99]   European Broadcasting Union (EBU) (n 1) 8, 113.

[100]   Elina Grundström, Lauri Haapanen and Sakari Ilkka, 'JSN määritteli algoritmit osaksi journalistista työtä' (2019) 42(4) Media & Viestintä 253 https://journal.fi/mediaviestinta/article/view/88457 accessed 18 March 2020.

[101]   Council for Mass Media (CMM), 'Guidelines for Journalists and an Annex. Guidelines operative from 1 January 2014' www.jsn.fi/en/guidelines_for_journalists/ accessed 18 March 2020.

[102]   See 'Mistä tiedät, että uutinen on totta?' https://vastuullistajournalismia.fi/merkki/ accessed 18 March 2020.

[103]   See Manu Marttinen, 'JSN lanseerasi vastuullisen journalismin merkin' (*Journalisti*, 2 March 2018) www.journalisti.fi/artikkelit/2018/3/0.28938000-151971 365465/ accessed 20 March 2020.

*Figure 2.1*     *Finnish and Swedish versions of the label for accountable journalism*

From the point of view of transparency, a few provisions of the Guidelines are particularly noteworthy. According to Section 2, decisions around media content must be taken in accordance with journalistic principles, while that power must never be outsourced from the editorial office. Section 4 states that journalists must not misuse their position or compromise their independence and professional ethics. Sections 7 and 9 of the Guidelines respectively include duties to indicate sources and obtain information openly. Moreover, advertising and editorial content must be separated (Section 16).[104]

In 2018, the CMM was faced with the first case around algorithmic tools in journalism. A newspaper offered information related to companies on its website. The content was automatically updated from an official database. Following a request for correction, the newspaper advised the complainant to turn to the authority providing the database. The CMM concluded that the newspaper did not transfer editorial decision-making power outside the editorial office when asking the complainant to request correction from the data source as well. Moreover, the information service of the newspaper in question clearly stated where and on what basis the data was collected and how correction could be requested.[105] These findings are essential from the point of view of using algorithmic tools as well as safeguarding transparency in the media. The CMM also conducted a study among its members and found that algorithmic tools were widely used in journalistic practices, especially with regard to personalisation. In late 2019, the CMM published a dictum concerning news automation and personalisation which was drafted by a working group including not only key members of the Council but also a couple of

---

[104] Guidelines for Journalists 2014 (n 101).
[105] Council for Mass Media (CMM) Decision 6887/SL/18 of 21 November 2018 www.jsn.fi/paatokset/6887-sl-18/?year=2018 accessed 30 April 2020.

key stakeholders (i.e., editors-in-chief of major Finnish newspapers and the director of Yle News Lab).[106] The arguments behind the dictum rely on press freedom whereby the CMM wanted to take precautionary measures instead of letting journalism be regulated by authorities or platforms. However, at the same time, it wanted to avoid over-detailed or too far-reaching regulation which would soon become outdated. On the one hand, algorithmic tools are seen as indispensable for the media sector facing pressures of efficiency and quality. On the other hand, a need for transparency and accountability has been identified, and transparency in the eyes of the public is especially important for the credibility of journalism.[107]

The dictum tackles only specific areas of automation in the media, that is, news automation and personalisation. These cover newsbots, voting aid applications, and targeted recommendations, among others. The dictum clarifies the applicability of Sections 2, 7, and 9 of the Guidelines for Journalists. Along these lines, news automation always involves journalistic decision-making (e.g., what is published and to whom). Editorial decisions cannot be outsourced to programmers outside the newsroom. This, however, does not imply in-house development only. Indeed, editors-in-chief have to make sure that developers of digital media services respect the Guidelines for journalists. Editors-in-chief must also understand the basic logics behind the algorithms they employ, while bearing responsibility for their algorithmic tools. The dictum includes two recommendations. First, the public must be informed of the use of automation as well as data sources when machine-generated content is published. Secondly, personalisation and data collection are subject to similar information duties. Relevant information must be provided transparently and intelligibly.[108] These are, however, not further elaborated. Interestingly, Diakopoulos also refers to the 'numerous editorial decisions' embedded in the social media newsbot he uses as an example of his transparency model. These concern, among others,

---

[106] Grundström, Haapanen and Ilkka (n 100) 254–258.

[107] Ibid., 253–257; Anette Alén-Savikko, 'The Council for Mass Media Publishes Dictum on the Use of Algorithms in Journalism' (2020) 2020-1 IRIS – Legal Observations of the European Audiovisual Observatory 38; European Broadcasting Union (EBU) (n 1). Then again, algorithmic tools in content production also require substantial investments, European Broadcasting Union (EBU) (n 1) 63.

[108] Council for Mass Media (CMM), 'Dictum on designating news automation and personalisation 2019. *Lausuma uutisautomatiikan ja personoinnin merkitsemisestä 2019*' (30 October 2019) http://www.jsn.fi/lausumat/lausuma-uutisautomatiikan-ja -personoinnin-merkitsemisesta-2019/ accessed 18 March 2020; Grundström, Haapanen and Ilkka (n 100) 257–258; Alén-Savikko (n 107) 38. See also Lindén and Tuulonen (n 7) 39.

the origin and sampling of the data as well as managing, filtering, and ranking of various end-user activities.[109]

In the media field, like many others, self-regulation is employed to counter abuses of power, and utilisation of algorithmic tools is not to provide an avenue for escaping this regulation,[110] as is evident from the CMM's approach. However, as shown by the CMM's decision and dictum, this 'technology-neutral' approach and application of traditional ethical guidelines to AI and automation still needs to translate general principles into practice, that is, to some sort of technology-specific considerations. This means interpreting the ethical concerns involved and solutions to them. Much like AI ethics in general, media self-regulation also appears as a rather deterministic collection of concerns to which reaction is called for.[111] With this in mind, calls have been voiced for a more open media ethics and ethics of difference, bringing together legacy and algorithmic media, journalists and citizens all over the globe to discuss ethical practices.[112] With regard to the interaction between law and ethics, self-regulatory solutions may affect or pave the way for legal regulation in the long run – even if the aim is, rather, to self-regulate before somebody else does it.[113] The strict view on editorial control over AI may also be seen as yet another manifestation of the human oversight requirement in the AI Ethics Guidelines, albeit in the specific context of the media and with downsides pointed out by Koulu.[114] However, the CMM dictum does acknowledge the role of developers as well, while stressing the need for human collaboration instead of allocating full agency to machines.[115]

## 5.    CONCLUSIONS: TOWARDS A RIGHTS-BASED APPROACH?

Transparency is linked to accountability, while both are linked to democratic ideals and processes. Therefore, they stand at the heart of media practices – also when relying on automation and AI. However, relations between these elements are far from causal and self-evident. Despite its frequent use, transparency is often itself (quite paradoxically!) left without explanation and

---

[109]   Diakopoulos, 'Enabling Accountability of Algorithmic Media' (n 2) 32.
[110]   See e.g., Pasquale, 'Toward a Fourth Law of Robotics' (n 33).
[111]   Koulu (n 2) 22, 41; see ibid., 39, 44 on the tension between technology neutrality and a technology-oriented approach.
[112]   See e.g., Stephen J A Ward, *Ethics and the Media: An Introduction* (CUP 2011) 207–271.
[113]   See also Larsson and Heintz (n 15).
[114]   Koulu (n 2) 22–23, 31–32, 45–46; High-Level Expert Group (n 34) 12, 14–16.
[115]   cf Koulu (n 2) on the AI Ethics Guidelines; see High-Level Expert Group (n 34).

elaboration of its practical implications. This is also true in the media sector. The law includes transparency as an overarching principle and as specific provisions in the field of media ownership and data protection. However, transparency in algorithmic journalism cannot rely on this legal basis alone due to their scope of application and the so-called journalistic exemption in the GDPR. However, impressive self-regulatory instruments are being developed to safeguard transparency in content production. The Finnish self-regulatory model is at the forefront of development. This is partly due to the pressure of possible other types of regulation (legislation) or the fear of various platforms, whether specialised in content provision or social media, getting to regulate practices. Moreover, development of this sort can be seen in line with the AI Ethics Guidelines requiring human oversight, AI identification, as well as explicability and explanation.

In the light of this chapter, AI in the media seems to refer to various degrees of automation boosted by algorithmic tools as well as data utilisation: it refers, for example, to the move towards (semi)autonomous functions in content production. Some algorithmic tools still mostly serve the newsroom instead of targeting the public sphere directly. Nonetheless, the absence of human editing is pursued. All in all, the move fits under the labels of computational journalism, algorithmic journalism, and even robot journalism. However, not all forms or degrees of automation in content production can be classified as AI. Moreover, not all areas of content production are apt for automation – there is a need to find optimal collaboration between humans, that is, a multitalented team, and machines. This calls for a dissection of the principles and practices of journalism and a model based on interaction between humans and machines (Figure 2.2).[116]

If transparency is to play a crucial role in opening up the technological workings behind (algorithmic) media practices, it must acknowledge its remits and limits. Transparency is, as outlined in this chapter, about access, availability, and comprehensibility of information related to the production process. This type of information transparency in algorithmic journalism covers several areas. It refers to disclosure and explicability in terms of the sources and methods of journalism, including media ethics. The main areas here are the following: First, the media should disclose how their news and other content is produced, including information on their use of algorithmic tools. Second, they should specify what kind of data or data sources are used as well as offer necessary references. Thirdly, the media should explain the way(s) in which

---

[116] Lindén and Tuulonen (n 7) 5, 7, 10, 45; see also Koulu (n 2) 45; for more on the critique of the humans-are-better-at/computers-are-better-at (HABA-MABA) model, see Koulu (n 2) 19–20.

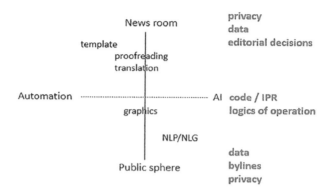

*Figure 2.2*     *Examples of automation and AI in content production with*
                 *relevant transparency issues*

the data is processed and interpreted, including how their algorithmic tools
work. However, according to Fox, disclosure that relies on a voluntary basis
(entirely) is by nature limited since there is a push towards concealing unflat-
tering details. Obligatory disclosure in turn suffers from problems related to
quality control and under-reporting. Moreover, mere access to information
does not imply accountability. Transparency and accountability overlap where
there is a 'capacity to demand explanations' and a corresponding 'capacity
to produce answers'.[117] The question thus remains whether the public should
eventually have a legal right to identify computer-generated content and access
information about the background data and logics of operation? This would
reach beyond self-regulated media companies and beyond benevolence. How
would such a right be guaranteed and realised? Transparency as a right would
most probably be difficult to achieve in practice – going beyond the framework
and scope of application of the GDPR.[118] Then again, some data protection
laws might exclude journalism from the provisions behind the 'right to explanation' even if journalism remains within the scope of the general principle of
transparency. For its part, algorithmic auditing, coupled with the establishment
of a regulatory authority, could provide an instrument to achieve transparency
– however, many open questions remain in these regards.[119] Then again, the

---

[117] Fox (n 15) 666–667; see also Hood (n 15) 991. Indeed, Haapanen (n 43) 3, 13
notes that the end result of impression management among journalists and seeing transparency as a 'promotional tool' may be the disclosure of socially acceptable practices
only – leaving actual practices largely unreaveled.

[118] Mittelstadt (n 15) 4998.

[119] Ibid.

critique of transparency points out that disclosure rests on the assumption that people can understand sophisticated technology, as noted by Koulu, and that this understanding in turn provides adequate safeguards for the underlying values; along these lines, establishing a legal right seems like an easy way out of the pressing societal debates around power imbalances, while also potentially fading out the value basis of ethics.[120] More importantly, as pointed out by Byung-Chul, the ultimate goal of securing trust may not even be achieved since transparency taken to the extreme may rather imply control and uniformity, the erasure of Otherness.[121] There might thus be a call for a new type of media ethics, as pointed out – one that bridges the gap between disclosure and participation, since transparency becomes an issue including both dimensions. This could even tackle some power imbalances, instead of boosting them.

For its part, technology itself offers some opportunities for meaningful transparency in algorithmic journalism as well: content production could rely on codes that label or 'self-certify' responsible journalism. Alongside informing on automation itself, content produced in line with self-regulation could be labelled as 'accountable'. Indeed, the GDPR (Recital 100) also refers to certification, seals, and marks 'in order to enhance transparency and compliance' which enable informed assessments by individuals. For his part, Pasquale talks about 'responsibility-by design' as a way of regulating AI.[122] This, however, requires close cooperation among people, that is, journalists and programmers, much like ethical AI in general. The challenge is also to acknowledge human agency but not to resort to false assumptions, such as those concerning human capabilities to exercise oversight or those linking objectivity and independence to algorithms.[123]

Transparency in algorithmic journalism currently functions as a Janus-faced[124] principle, seemingly combining the legitimate interests of the public and (traditional) responsibilities of the editorial media vis-à-vis their use of new tools. In the background, transparency also amounts to a more general principle in the platform economy, powered by AI. For the time being it operates principally in the area of ethics and self-regulation, sometimes coupled with either

---

[120]  Koulu (n 2) 35, 45–46.

[121]  Byung-Chul (n 15) vii–viii; see also Haapanen (n 43) 14 on the need to examine how and under which conditions transparency could actually promote trust.

[122]  Pasquale, 'Toward a Fourth Law of Robotics' (n 33) 1252–1254; see also Balkin (n 33) 1240: '(T)he state must decide how best to make businesses internalize their costs.'

[123]  See also Koulu (n 2). For his part, Ward (n 112) 118–160 talks about a new kind of multi-dimensional objectivity in journalism.

[124]  See also Fox (n 15) 667–668 on the 'two faces of transparency' albeit in a different meaning.

a loose or a specific connection to legal rights and responsibilities. Caution is adviced in terms of any efforts to turn transparency into a dedicated legal right in algorithmic journalism. Similar to other research in the area, this chapter calls for insights across disciplines to shed light on transparency in this field.[125]

---

[125]   Larsson and Heintz (n 15); Haapanen (n 43).

# 3. The journalistic exemption in personal data processing

## Päivi Korpisaari[1]

## 1. INTRODUCTION: HOW TECHNOLOGY HAS AFFECTED PERSONAL DATA PROTECTION AND NEWS PRODUCTION

The General Data Protection Regulation (GDPR)[2] entered into force on 25 May 2016 and has been applicable since 25 May 2018, after a transitional period of two years. The purpose of the GDPR is to protect the fundamental rights and freedoms of natural persons – especially the right to personal data protection – and to harmonize European personal data regulation, thus promoting the European single market by ensuring the free flow of data between EU Member States.[3]

Reform was necessary because technological development and globalization present new threats and challenges to protection of personal data. For example, ways to collect, use and share personal data have increased significantly, giving rise to new business ideas but also endangering the right to private lives and protection of personal data. Current technology and increased capacity to store and process information enable both private companies and public authorities to exploit personal data on an unprecedented scale. In turn, natural persons share ever more of their private information publicly and

---

[1]  This chapter is written as part of the 'Viha ja julkisuus' (Hate and publicity) research project, funded by Helsingin Sanomain Säätiö and where legal research is led by the author. The author expresses her thanks to LL.D Jan Oster and LL.M. doctoral candidate Sam Wrigley for their valuable comments. Of course, any mistakes are the author's. The author thanks Kenneth Quek for language revision of the first draft of this text and Christopher Goddard for checking the second version.
[2]  Regulation (EU) 2016/679 of the European Parliament and of the Council of 27 April 2016 on the protection of natural persons with regard to the processing of personal data and on the free movement of such data, and repealing Directive 95/46/EC (General Data Protection Regulation, GDPR) [2016] OJ L119/1.
[3]  See GDPR (n 2) Recitals 2–4 and Art 1.

globally – sometimes knowingly but often also without a full understanding of their actions.[4]

Technological developments have also affected journalistic activities. Technological tools can collect, organize, classify, and sort information for journalistic purposes,[5] and even write magazine articles.[6] They can also be used to visualize narration. AI can find connections in mass data much more quickly than a human being and thus be of great help to journalists in their work.[7] AI or automation can cut down journalists' time and effort, thus reducing costs and releasing journalists to pursue more challenging tasks.[8]

Machine-learning techniques can also be used to scan through social media feeds and present trending issues as news topics and predict the popularity or 'virality' of stories. AI helps to decide what content to promote and for whom. That way AI also influences the issues and events that journalists regard as worth further investigation.[9] Newsbots in turn may disseminate news in private

---

[4]    See GDPR (n 2) Recital 6. According to Special Eurobarometer 487a (March 2019) 'The General Data Protection Regulation', a survey requested by the European Commission, Directorate-General for Justice and Consumers, 56 per cent of social network users had tried to change the privacy settings of their personal profile from the default settings, while 43 per cent had not tried to do that. In 2015 60 per cent had tried to change settings. Trust in social network sites (29 per cent) and lack of knowledge how to change them (27 per cent) were the main reasons why respondents had not tried to change default privacy settings. No less than 20 per cent of respondents were not worried about sharing their personal data (Summary of Special Eurobarometer 487a pp. 18 and 20 and Special Eurobarometer 487a, Report, The General Data Protection Regulation p. 4). Those who had changed their privacy settings were more likely to have heard of the GDPR than those who had not (80 vs 65 per cent, p 21 of the report; see also pp. 56–68).

[5]    See the examples in Jonathn Stray, 'What Do Journalists Do with Documents? Field Notes for Natural Language Processing Researchers' (Computation + Journalism Symposium, Palo Alto, CA, September/October 2016) https://journalism.stanford .edu/cj2016/files/What do journalists do with documents.pdf accessed 23 April 2021; Jonathan Stray, 'Making Artificial Intelligence Work for Investigative Journalism' (2019) 7(8) *Digital Journalism* 1076, 1083–84; Shangyuan Wu, Edson C Tandoc Jr and Charles T Salmon, 'Journalism Reconfigured: Assessing Human–Machine Relations and the Autonomous Power of Automation in News Production' (2019) 20(10) *Journalism Studies* 1440.

[6]    Wu and others (n 5) 1440–44.

[7]    Stray, 'Making Artificial Intelligence Work for Investigative Journalism' (n 5) 1080.

[8]    Wu and others (n 5) 1453.

[9]    Wu and others (n 5) 1447, 1453.

messaging channels such as Facebook Messenger.[10] Currently, AI is more often used in story distribution and promotion than story production.[11]

Even though AI can help journalists in many ways, many tasks remain that it cannot do. Developing AI to produce articles other than fairly simple ones is still so expensive today that it is not yet economically viable. Public data is not always publicly available on the Internet, but must be found, requested or purchased. Once data is gathered, AI can help to process it.[12] AI cannot interview persons either[13] – or perhaps it could, but surely the results would not be as good as when a human being is talking and interviewing another human being and deciding how to lead the discussion. Additionally, the need for accuracy might be difficult to fulfil in directly AI-generated storytelling, because AI systems may contain errors, or data can be ambiguous. This means that AI-generated results should be checked and often modified by a human being to avoid incorrect results, libel suits and false journalism.[14] Human journalists are also needed to set the parameters and goals for machines.[15] It can thus be said that AI-generated transformation of journalism will rather enhance than replace journalistic work.[16]

## 2.    THE CONCEPT OF PERSONAL DATA AND SCOPE OF APPLICATION OF THE GDPR

According to Article 2(1), the GDPR 'applies to the processing of personal data wholly or partly by automated means and to the processing other than by automated means of personal data which form part of a filing system or are intended to form part of a filing system'. Some exceptions to this exist, for

---

[10]    Heather Ford and Jonathon Hutchinson, 'Newsbots That Mediate Journalist and Audience Relationships' (2019) 7(8) *Digital Journalism* 1013, 1014–15.

[11]    Stray, 'Making Artificial Intelligence Work for Investigative Journalism' (n 5) 1076–79. Automation is more used in investigative work than news production. Not all automated data processing is considered as AI. It is also important to understand that computational journalism is not the same as using AI when producing journalistic products.

[12]    Stray, 'Making Artificial Intelligence Work for Investigative Journalism' (n 5) 1083–84, 1093.

[13]    Ibid., 1084.

[14]    Ibid., 1094; Wu and others (n 5) 1451. There might be a risk of a libel suit. Also the ethics of journalism requires that information that is published be verified.

[15]    Wu and others, ibid., 1454.

[16]    Mark Hansen, Meritxell Roca-Sales, Jonathan M Keegan and George King, 'Artificial Intelligence: Practice and Implications for Journalism', Platforms and Publishers: Policy Exchange Forum, 13 June 2017, Columbia Journalism School Organized by the Tow Center for Digital Journalism and the Brown Institute for Media Innovation, September 2017, 2.

example the so-called 'household exemption'.[17] The Court of Justice of the EU (CJEU) has outlined that publishing personal data on the Internet is not private use and thus does not fall under the household exemption.[18] Nor is collecting data from public places for private purposes considered private use.[19]

Because any kind of information relating to an identified or identifiable natural person counts as personal data,[20] journalists process a great deal of personal data with their journalistic activities. They collect and store personal data that they use or that they think they might be able to use as background information, and they also publish a lot of personal data both as individual data and as a register. Because of the wide applicability of the GDPR, some exemptions had to be made to guarantee freedom of expression. Without exemptions, for example, the principles of transparency, data minimization and storage limitation that are set in Article 5 GDPR, would hinder journalistic activities. Moreover, exercise of the rights of data subjects could prevent full exercise of journalistic activity. For instance, if investigative journalists were required to inform those whom they investigate, and give them access to their data, this could in some cases compromise the entire project.[21] In turn, the requirement of lawful grounds for processing in GDPR Articles 6 and 9 would in many cases prohibit the publication of data, because not always are any of the lawful grounds for processing data involved when a publication is disseminated for the audience. That is why Article 85 GDPR regulates exemption of the applicability of the GDPR relating to 'journalistic purposes'. This Article reads as follows:

85. Processing and freedom of expression and information
1. Member States shall by law reconcile the right to the protection of personal data pursuant to this Regulation with the right to freedom of expression and information, including processing for journalistic purposes and the purposes of academic, artistic or literary expression.

---

[17] GDPR (n 2) Art 2(2)c.
[18] See Case C–101/01 *Bodil Lindqvist (Lindqvist)* EU:C:2003:596 [2003] ECR I–12971. Even though the case was decided by applying the DPD, there is no indication that the GDPR would depart from this standpoint. However, see Recital 18 GDPR (n 2), according to which 'household activities could include correspondence and the holding of addresses, or social networking and online activity undertaken within the context of such activities'.
[19] See Case C–212/13 *František Ryneš v Úřad pro ochranu osobních údajů* EU:C: 2014:2428 (11 December 2014).
[20] See text relating to the GDPR Art 4(1) below.
[21] Natalija Bitiukova, 'Journalistic Exemption Under the European Data Protection Law' (2020) Vilnius Institute for Policy Analysis, Policy Paper Series 2020, 18. https://ssrn.com/abstract=3531977 accessed 15 November 2020.

2. For processing carried out for journalistic purposes or the purpose of academic artistic or literary expression, Member States shall provide for exemptions or derogations from Chapter II (principles), Chapter III (rights of the data subject), Chapter IV (controller and processor), Chapter V (transfer of personal data to third countries or international organisations), Chapter VI (independent supervisory authorities), Chapter VII (cooperation and consistency) and Chapter IX (specific data processing situations) if they are necessary to reconcile the right to the protection of personal data with the freedom of expression and information.
3. Each Member State shall notify to the Commission the provisions of its law which it has adopted pursuant to paragraph 2 and, without delay, any subsequent amendment law or amendment affecting them.

Journalistic exemption is limited to journalistic processing, so it does not apply to other activities by media outlets. For instance, when processing personal data for subscriber registration and billing, employees' employment and salary issues, or direct marketing purposes, media companies are regarded as 'normal' data controllers that must comply with the entire GDPR.[22]

Regarding the wording of the regulation, it is worth noting that 'freedom of expression and information' is mentioned as a factor that must be balanced with protection of personal data. Journalistic purposes and purposes of academic, artistic or literary expression are subcategories that are mentioned thereafter. Therefore, one may presume that some guidance could be gained from the nature of these activities. This all raises the question: When such a 'journalistic purpose' is involved, is this exemption applicable? And how does the use of AI and automated tools affect the concept of 'journalism'?

## 3. RESEARCH QUESTION: THE CONCEPT OF JOURNALISM IN A CHANGING MEDIA ENVIRONMENT

Some decades ago, it was easier to define what journalism was, and what was meant by journalistic purpose. Journalism was regarded as a profession,[23] and the concept of journalism was linked to publishing information and other

---

[22] Council of Europe Committee on Media and Information Society and the Consultative Committee of Convention, 'Guidelines on safeguarding privacy in the media' [June 2018] 34, Available at https://rm.coe.int/ guidelines-on-safeguardin g-privacy-in-the-media-additions-after-adopti/16808d05a0, accessed 6 November 2020.

[23] Scott Gant, *We're All Journalists Now: The Transformation of the Press and Reshaping of the Law in the Internet Age* (Free Press 2007) and Deborah Gabriel, 'Book Review: We're All Journalists Now: Scott Gant' (*People with Voices*, 7 February 2011) http://peoplewithvoices.com/2011/02/07/were-all-journalists-now-scott-gant/ accessed 6 November 2020.

content within the activities of established media companies. Additionally, the same kind of values, strategies and formal codes were widely shared by journalists.[24] Journalistic work was also related to the public service (journalists as 'watchdogs' and disseminators of information), objectivity, autonomy, immediacy (instantaneous working practices) and journalistic ethics.[25]

The advent of the Internet has made publishing faster and cheaper than before, and people other than journalists can also publish content to a large audience.[26] Boundaries have blurred between journalism and other forms of public communication, and in addition to journalists, media audiences can contribute to content production.[27] Anyone can set up a website or an online magazine to publish texts, images and videos. AI-generated bots can create, disseminate and target content without human interaction.[28] This raises the question whether – and how – we can defend the privileges that are granted for the purposes of journalism, if a large group of people – and businesses and other entities that disseminate AI-generated information – are entitled to them. And it is also worth pondering whether there are any qualitative criteria for the concept of journalism or can any information extracted by artificial intelligence be published as journalism?

Judge Wojtyczek's dissenting opinion in *Guseva v Bulgaria*[29] illustrates this very well: he points out that the case-law of the European Court of Human Rights (ECtHR) concerning the rights of journalists and the press was developed in the 1970s and 1980s. The situation is completely different now, when information circulates with the help of new technologies on the Internet and the 'press has lost its quasi-monopoly on imparting information and access to public debate has been democratised'. Therefore Judge Wojtyczek opines that the fundamental right of access to information should be guaranteed equally

---

[24] Mark Deuze, 'What Is Journalism? Professional Identity and Ideology of Journalists Reconsidered', (2005) 6(4) *Journalism* 442, 444–47. See also Mark Deuze, 'What Journalism Is (Not)' (2019) 5(3) *Social Media + Society* 1, where the writer emphasizes that the media industry does not define what journalism is, but 'the idea(l)s, debates, and practices of journalists inhabiting these institutions do'. The writer sees that journalism is produced by persons that are quite passionate towards their work.
[25] Deuze 'What Is Journalism' (n 24) 446–50 provides an overview to this opinion, referring to many sources.
[26] Tim Gleason, 'If We Are All Journalists, Can Journalistic Privilege Survive?' (2015) 22(4) *Javnost – The Public* 375, 375–76; Deuze, 'What Journalism Is (Not)' (n 24) 3.
[27] Gleason, 'If We Are All Journalists' (n 26) 375–76.
[28] Stray, 'Making Artificial Intelligence Work for Investigative Journalism' (n 4) 1076–79.
[29] *Guseva v Bulgaria* App no 6987/07 (ECtHR, 17 February 2015), Opinion of Judge Wojtyczek.

to every citizen. No better rights should be given to journalists or persons representing NGOs,[30] because 'Access to information should not depend on the status of the person requesting information'. He writes in his opinion:

> It is no exaggeration to say that today we, the citizens of European States, are all journalists. We (at least many of us) directly access different sources of information, collect or request information from public authorities, impart information to other persons and publicly comment on matters of public interest. We directly participate in public debate through various channels, mainly through the Internet. We are all social watchdogs who oversee the action of the public authorities. Democratic society is – inter alia – a community of social watchdogs. The old distinction between journalists and other citizens is now obsolete. In this context, the case-law hitherto on the functions of the press seems out of date in 2015 and should be adapted to the latest social developments.

Journalism has been seen as involving an even wider range of people participating in public debates. In addition, technology has enabled bot journalism, and in the future artificial intelligence will increasingly produce and target news content. In this case, it will also be considered whether application of the journalistic exemption is affected by whether content was produced by a human or a bot. Hence, the aim of this study is to find out how the concept of 'journalistic purpose' should be interpreted in the context of the GDPR, in the present media environment where disseminating information is easier than ever before and may also be done without human interaction.[31]

There is as yet no case law on automation, so the purpose of this chapter is to present the kind of environment in which 'artificial intelligence' enters. The subjects of review are the significance of the author's role, the communication channel and the content of the publication. The scope of exception is also briefly examined. In order to study this, the chapter proceeds as follows. Section 4 introduces freedom of expression and media freedom and explains their importance in democratic societies. In Section 5, the right to private life and protection of personal data are discussed. Section 6 introduces regulation and court practice relating to the 'journalistic exemption' in the field of personal data protection. Lastly, an analysis and conclusions are drawn in section 7.

---

[30]   He refers to a judgment where the majority (five out of seven) mentions five times (in paras 36, 37, 52, 53 and 54) that the applicant 'was an activist in a non-governmental organisation which was active in the area of animal protection and that her purpose was to inform the public'.

[31]   See Chapter 9 in this book where Pihlajarinne and others write that 'Some estimate that by 2030, a large majority of news items will already be written by machines.'

# 4.  FREEDOM OF EXPRESSION AND MEDIA FREEDOM AS FUNDAMENTAL AND HUMAN RIGHTS

The aims of freedom of expression and personal data protection can sometimes be difficult to reconcile, because freedom of expression is intended to facilitate dissemination of information and personal data protection imposes restrictions on the dissemination and other processing of personal data. Freedom of expression – an essential value in every democratic society and a fundamental right in European law – is guaranteed by Article 11 Charter of Fundamental Rights of the European Union (CFEU).[32] According to Article 11(1), the right to freedom of expression belongs to everyone, and includes 'freedom to hold opinions and to receive and impart information and ideas without interference by public authority and regardless of frontiers'. CFEU Article 11(2) states that the 'freedom and pluralism of the media shall be respected'.

The right to freedom of expression is also guaranteed by the European Convention on Human Rights (ECHR). According to CFEU Article 52(3) the rights that it guarantee bear the same meaning and scope as respective rights in the ECHR, except when EU law provides more extensive protection. This means that the practice of the ECtHR can give guidance on the interpretation of rights guaranteed in the CFEU and EU regulation.

The ECtHR has interpreted the scope of freedom of expression hundreds of times and freedom of expression has enjoyed wide protection. It includes the freedom to hold opinions as well as to receive and impart information and ideas. It constitutes 'one of the essential foundations of a democratic society and one of the basic conditions for its progress'.[33] Freedom of expression is also a social good, promoting truth, democracy and participation. It can also be regarded as an end in-and-of itself, promoting individual self-fulfilment, and as an individual good.[34] As well as protecting positive and insignificant (or oth-

---

[32] CFEU [2000] OJ C364/01.

[33] European Court of Human Rights (ECtHR), e.g., *Handyside v The United Kingdom* App no 5493/72 (ECtHR, 7 December 1976) Series A no 24; *Barthold v Germany* App no 8734/79 (ECtHR, 25 March 1985) Series A no 90; *Zana v Turkey* [GC] App no 18954/91 (ECtHR, 25 November 1997) Reports of Judgments and Decisions 1997–VII; *Axel Springer AG v Germany* [GC] App no 39954/08 (ECtHR, 7 February 2012); *von Hannover v Germany No. 2* [GC] App nos 40660/08 and 60641/08 (ECtHR, 7 February 2012) ECHR 2012; *Gillberg v Sweden* [GC] App no 41723/06 (ECtHR, 3 April 2012).

[34] See *Satakunnan Markkinapörssi Oy and Satamedia Oy v Finland* [GC] (*Satakunnan Markkinapörssi* [ECtHR GC]) App no 931/13 (ECtHR, 27 June 2017); Thomas I Emerson, 'Toward a General Theory of the First Amendment' (1963) 72 *Yale LJ* 877, 878–79; Jan Oster, *Media Freedom as a Fundamental Right* (CUP 2015)

erwise neutral) expressions, freedom of expression also applies to expressions that offend, shock or disturb.[35]

It is important to note that the right to freedom of expression protects not only the right to disseminate information, but also the right to receive information. Every time we limit the right to disseminate information, we also limit the right to receive it.

Media freedom is an essential right partly overlapping with the notion of freedom of expression.[36] Media freedom creates the conditions for more diverse public debate. It is important that personal data protection does not unduly restrict public debate and access to information. The ECtHR has emphasized the essential role in a democratic society played by the press, whose task it is to impart information and ideas and act as a 'public watchdog', disseminating information to the public. The media play a vital role in facilitating and fostering the public's right to receive and impart information and ideas. The ECtHR has also held that 'the gathering of information is an essential preparatory step in journalism and is an inherent, protected part of press freedom'.[37] Journalistic activities are subject to special rights in the practice of the ECtHR and in many countries' legal orders, such as the right to protect the confidentiality of their information sources and the exception to the application of personal data legislation. In return, journalists are often committed to following their own ethical guidelines.[38]

---

13–20; and Päivi Korpisaari, 'Balancing Freedom of Expression and the Right to Private Life in the European Court of Human Rights – Application and Interpretation of the Key Criteria' (2017) 22 *Communications LJ* 39, 39.

[35] For example, *Hertel v Switzerland* App no 25181/94 (ECtHR, 25 August 1998) Reports of Judgments and Decisions 1998–VI; *Steel and Morris v The United Kingdom* App no 68416/01 (ECtHR, 15 December 2005) ECHR 2005–II; *Stoll v Switzerland* [GC] App no 69698/01 (ECtHR, 10 December 2007) ECHR 2007–V; *Mouvement raëlien suisse v Switzerland* [GC] App no 16354/06 (ECtHR, 13 July 2012) ECHR 2012 (extracts).

[36] For a closer analysis see Oster, 'Media Freedom as a Fundamental Right' (n 34) and for a conclusion see pp. 268–70.

[37] *Dammann v Switzerland* App no 77551/01 (ECtHR, 25 April 2006) para 52; *Shapovalov v Ukraine* App no 45835/05 (ECtHR, 31 July 2012) para 68; *Magyar Helsinki Bizottság v Hungary* [GC] App no 18030/11 (ECtHR, 8 November 2016) para 130; and *Satakunnan Markkinapörssi* [ECtHR GC] (n 34) para 128. See also *Nordisk Film & TV A/S v Denmark* [DEC] App no 40485/02 (ECtHR, 8 December 2005) ECHR 2005–XIII; and *Haldimann and Others v Switzerland* App no 21830/09 (ECtHR, 24 February 2015) ECHR 2015.

[38] See, e.g., *Satakunnan Markkinapörssi* [ECtHR GC] (n 34) para 183, where the Court states that;

in the area of press freedom the Court has held that, by reason of the duties and responsibilities inherent in the exercise of the freedom of expression, the safeguard afforded by Article 10 to journalists in relation to reporting on issues

In recent court practice, NGOs have also enjoyed wide protection of freedom of expression and access to information, and their role as an important disseminator of information and opinions has been recognized.[39] The ECtHR has stated that 'when an NGO draws attention to matters of public interest, it is exercising a public watchdog role of similar importance to that of the press'.[40] In view of the functions and purpose of freedom of expression, it is not justified to limit the application of freedom of expression on the basis of the formal status of the person or entity expressing it. This also raises the question: should NGOs also belong under the 'journalistic exemption' and if so, under what conditions? And why only NGOs, or should everyone enjoy the same protection regardless of whether they act as a representative of the media or some association?

However, freedom of expression is not unlimited. It can be limited following the conditions set out in Article 10(2) of the ECHR.[41] Restrictions have to be prescribed by law, necessary in a democratic society, and protect the interests that are mentioned in Article 10(2). All limitations to freedom of expression have to be construed strictly, and the need for any restriction must be established convincingly. For example, the right to private life or protection of personal data can be reasons for restricting freedom of expression.

## 5.     THE RIGHT TO FAMILY AND PRIVATE LIFE AND PROTECTION OF PERSONAL DATA

The right to private and family life, home and communications is guaranteed by Article 7 of the CFEU.[42] In turn, Article 8(1) of the CFEU guarantees the right to protection of personal data. According to Article 8(2) CFEU:

> Such data must be processed fairly for specified purposes and on the basis of the consent of the person concerned or some other legitimate basis laid down by law. Everyone has the right of access to data which has been collected concerning him or her, and the right to have it rectified.

---

of public interest is subject to the proviso that they are acting in good faith in order to provide accurate and reliable information in accordance with the ethics of journalism.
See also *Magyar* [GC] (n 37) para 159 with further references.

[39] See, e.g., *Youth Initiative for Human Rights v Serbia* App no 48135/06 (ECtHR, 25 June 2013).

[40] *Animal Defenders International v The United Kingdom* [GC] App no 48876/08 (ECtHR, 22 April 2013) ECHR 2013 (extracts) para 103.

[41] See also CFEU (n 32) 52(1).

[42] CFEU (n 32).

Compliance with rules concerning personal data protection are subject to control by an independent authority (Art 8(3) CFEU). The right to respect for private and family life is also guaranteed by Article 8 of the ECHR. This Article also grants protection for personal data, at least to some extent.[43] It is important to note that not all personal data belongs to the sphere of private life: some personal data can be part of a person's public sphere and not protected as private information, but still fall under the protection of personal data.

According to the GDPR Article 4(1):

> '[P]ersonal data' means any information relating to an identified or identifiable natural person ('data subject'); an identifiable natural person is one who can be identified, directly or indirectly, in particular by reference to an identifier such as a name, an identification number, location data, an online identifier or to one or more factors specific to the physical, physiological, genetic, mental, economic, cultural or social identity of that natural person.

Recital 26 GDPR states that 'account should be taken of all the means reasonably likely to be used' to identify a natural person directly or indirectly. Attention should also be paid to 'all objective factors, such as the costs of and the amount of time required for identification, taking into consideration the available technology at the time of the processing and technological developments'. The concept of personal data is thus wide, and the CJEU has also interpreted it broadly.[44]

The right to private life covers the physical, psychological and moral integrity of a person,[45] as well as the right to establish and develop relationships

---

[43]  For example, *S and Marper v The United Kingdom* [GC] App nos 30562/04 and 30566/04 (ECtHR, 4 December 2008) ECHR 2008; *LH v Latvia* App no 52019/07 (ECtHR, 29 April 2014); *Ben Faiza v France* App no 31446/12 (ECtHR, 8 February 2018).

[44]  See, e.g., Case C–582/14 *Patrick Breyer v Bundesrepublik Deutschland* EU: C:2016:779 (19 October 2016) [2017] 2 CMLR 3, where the dynamic internet protocol address of a visitor constituted personal data when the administrator of a website had the legal means of allowing it to identify the visitor with additional information, which was held by the internet access provider. See also Case C–70/10 *Scarlet Extended SA v Société belge des auteurs, compositeurs et éditeurs SCRL (SABAM)* EU: C:2011:771 (24 November 2011) [2012] ECDR 4, where the Court held that static IP addresses were personal data 'because they allow users to be precisely identified' by the Internet service provider. See also Case C–434/16 *Peter Nowak v Data Protection Commissioner* EU:C:2017:994 [2017] and Commission, Article 29 WP, 'Opinion 4/2007 on the Concept of Personal Data' (WP 136, 01248/07/EN) and 'Opinion 05/2014 on Anonymisation Techniques' (WP 216, 0829/14/EN).

[45]  See, e.g., Jill Marshall, *Personal Freedom through Human Rights Law?: Autonomy, Identity and Integrity Under the European Convention on Human Rights* (Martinus Nijhoff Publishers 2009); Daniel Solove, *Understanding Privacy* (Harvard

with other human beings.[46] Notably, activities of a professional or business nature may also belong to the concept of private life.[47] The right to a private life guarantees dignity and autonomy, since revealing private matters without consent takes away an individual's control and can deprive them of their dignity or reputation in the eyes of others.[48] The right to a private life may also cover protecting reputation[49] and honour.[50]

States also have the duty to guarantee fulfilment of human rights between individuals.[51] When the right of freedom of expression and information collides with the right to private life, the right solution can be found by balancing them and guaranteeing their essential core. Some balancing has been done by the legislator, but as legislation cannot be exhaustive, some balancing activity must be done by interpretation when applying legislation. For example, the ECtHR has developed and applied a balancing test with several criteria, such as contributing to a debate of general interest, how well known the person concerned is, the method of obtaining information and its veracity, the content, form and consequences of the publication, and the severity of sanction.[52]

## 6.    RECONCILING FREEDOM OF EXPRESSION AND INFORMATION AND THE RIGHT TO PROTECTION OF PERSONAL DATA

### 6.1    Introduction to Regulation

In the first proposals regarding Article 85 (Art 80 at that time) the proposed name of the Article was 'Processing of personal data and freedom of expression', but in the last proposal the title was 'Processing of personal data and

---

UP 2008); Gloria González Fuster, *The Emergence of Personal Data Protection as a Fundamental Right of the EU* (Springer 2014).

[46]    See especially Beate Roessler and Dorota Mokrosinska (eds), *Social Dimensions of Privacy: Interdisciplinary Perspectives* (CUP 2015).

[47]    *Niemietz v Germany* (ECtHR, 16 December 1992) Series A no 251–B; *Von Hannover v Germany No. 2* [GC] (n 33). More closely, see Korpisaari (n 34).

[48]    Korpisaari (n 34) 39.

[49]    *Chauvy and Others v France* App no 64915/01 (ECtHR, 29 June 2004) ECHR 2004–VI; *White v Sweden* App no 42435/02 (ECtHR, 19 September 2006); *Fürst-Pfeifer v Austria* App nos 33677/10 and 52340/10 (ECtHR, 17 May 2016).

[50]    *Radio France and Others v France* App no 53984/00 (ECtHR, 30 March 2004) ECHR 2004–II; *A v Norway* App no 28070/06 (ECtHR, 9 April 2009).

[51]    This may require active measures by States, such as legislation. See, e.g., *KU v Finland* App no 2872/02 (ECtHR, 2 December 2008) ECHR 2008; and *Khurshid Mustafa and Tarzibachi v Sweden* App no 23883/06 (ECtHR, 16 December 2008).

[52]    These were laid down on 7 February 2012 in Grand Chamber cases *Axel Springer AG v Germany* [GC] (n 33) and *Von Hannover v Germany No. 2* [GC] (n 33).

freedom of expression and information'. Finally, in the GDPR the title is 'Processing and freedom of expression and information'. Mentioning the right to information as well better describes the purpose of exemption.

Article 85 GDPR obliges Member States to adopt national regulation to guarantee the right of freedom of expression and information. It replaces Article 9 of the repealed Personal Data Protection Directive (DPD).[53] Recital 153 of the GDPR refers to Article 11 of the Charter and 'in particular to the processing of personal data in the audiovisual field and in news archives and press libraries'. According to the recital, in 'order to take account of the importance of the right to freedom of expression, it is necessary to interpret notions relating to that freedom, such as journalism, broadly'. This raises the crucial question how we balance the two different rights – the right to protection of personal data on the one hand and the right to freedom of expression and information on the other. How is and should the concept of journalism be defined, and what activities belong under the special protection guaranteed for journalism in Article 85?

To answer this, I first seek guidance from the wording of the GDPR and former DPD, and then analyse the purpose and interpretation of the exception with the help of legal literature and the case law of the CJEU and ECtHR. Finally, I will do some analysis and draw conclusions.

The DPD referred to 'processing of personal data carried out solely for journalistic purposes' while Article 85 of the GDPR only talks about 'processing carried out for journalistic purposes'. The word 'solely' no longer appears, possibly indicating a wider interpretation of 'journalistic purposes' than under the DPD, the former governing legislation. On the other hand, conclusions drawn from erasure of the word 'solely' should not be too far-reaching because the former definition with 'solely for journalistic purposes' was very strict in literally excluding all processing that included processing for other than journalistic purposes, even to a small extent. Nevertheless, commercial intent to make a profit has not been considered as precluding certain activities from being considered journalistic.[54]

For example, the old criterion 'solely for journalistic purposes' excluded marketing and advertising, because these also involved purposes other than a journalistic purpose – selling or branding products or services. Given the purposes of freedom of expression and personal data protection, there are good

---

[53]   Council Directive 95/46/EC of the European Parliament and of the Council of 24 October 1995 on the Protection of Individuals with regard to the Processing of Personal Data and on the Free Movement of such Data (DPD) [1995] OJ L281/31.

[54]   See para 59 in CJEU Case C–73/07 *Tietosuojavaltuutettu v Satakunnan Markkinapörssi Oy and Satamedia Oy* (*Satakunnan Markkinapörssi* [CJEU]) EU:C: 2008:727 (16 December 2008).

reasons to argue that it is still true that those activities do not fall within the scope of the exemption, even though the word 'solely' no longer exists in the GDPR. The purposes of marketing and advertising differ from the purposes of journalism. Lobbying is a more difficult activity to evaluate, because – just like part of journalism – lobbying also aims to influence decision-making. But because lobbying mostly promotes the interests of the client according to an agreement with the client, one would not consider it as 'journalism' in the meaning of the GDPR, even though lobbying has many virtues and enjoys general protection of freedom of expression.[55] So far the question remains unresolved whether collecting information by automated tools about the habits and preferences of readers of online papers and magazines, and then using artificial intelligence to influence the topics of content and targeting of news, amounts to processing for journalistic purposes. Opinions can be expressed for and against: such activities can be equated in part with consumer research and marketing, but on the other hand they also have a real impact on journalistic content as well as news headlines and topics.

It is even more difficult to draw the line between journalism and opinion-building that is not marketing or lobbying as such, but which aims to discuss matters of general interest and affect general opinion-building. For example in *Animal Defenders International v The United Kingdom*[56] the NGO in question resisted abuse of chimps in entertainment. The ECtHR stated that 'when an NGO draws attention to matters of public interest, it is exercising a public watchdog role of similar importance to that of the press' and therefore the margin of appreciation was narrower than normally (paras 103–104). Here the Court gave weight to an NGO's overall aims and activities in drawing attention to matters of public interest, not only to the circumstances in a particular case. However, the matter related to advertising in certain media, not to the journalistic exemption regarding personal data protection, so no direct conclusions can be drawn from this case relating to the concept of journalism in the context of the GDPR.[57]

---

[55]   In Point 7 of the Interinstitutional Agreement between the European Parliament and the European Commission on the transparency register for organisations and self-employed individuals engaged in EU policy-making and policy implementation [2014] OJ lobbying is defined as:

> all activities … carried out with the objective of directly or indirectly influencing the formulation or implementation of policy and the decision-making processes of the EU institutions, irrespective of where they are undertaken and of the channel or medium of communication used.

[56]   *Animal Defenders International v The United Kingdom* (n 40) paras 103–104.

[57]   The Court ruled that the UK did not violate freedom of speech when it banned political advertising on television and radio because this did not ban all political speech

## 6.2    Short History of Article 85 GDPR

The wording of the article and recital concerning journalistic exemption varied during the preparatory process. Unfortunately, it has been difficult to find any information on why it varied, and how and why the existing wording was formed. However, the regulatory options presented earlier shed light on the types of regulatory models that were rejected, so they may give guidance with interpreting the current provision.

At the Commission's proposal on January 2012, the proposed Article 80 and Recital 121 included the word 'solely'.[58] Draft Recital 121 also explained that it was a question of journalism if the object of the activity was 'the disclosure to the public of information, opinions or ideas, irrespective of the medium which is used to transmit them'. Such activities 'should not be limited to media undertakings and may be undertaken for profit-making or for non-profit making purposes'.[59] Even though this text does not exist in the final version of the GDPR, the same conclusion can be drawn from the recent wording of the GDPR where the word 'solely' no longer appears. Additionally the case-law of the CJEU interpreting the DPD, and the case-law of the ECtHR – which will be explained shortly hereafter – refer to this interpretation.

At the parliamentary legislative resolution on 12 March 2014 the journalistic exemption was not mentioned at all. A proposal suggested that exemptions or derogations should be provided on specific data processing situations mentioned in Chapter IX 'whenever it is necessary in order to reconcile the right to the protection of personal data with the rules governing freedom of expression in accordance with the Charter'. The journalistic exemption was not mentioned in recitals either but had been erased.[60] Specific processing situations in a suggested chapter were access to documents, health data, the employment and security context, processing for historical, statistical and scientific research

---

(only advertisements), and there were other avenues available through which political advertising could still be expressed.

[58]    Commission, 'Proposal for a Regulation of the European Parliament and of the Council on the protection of individuals with regard to the processing of personal data and on the free movement of such data (General Data Protection Regulation)' (GDPR Proposal) COM (2012) 11 final – 2012/0011 (COD), document 52012PC0011, p. 35. https://eur-lex.europa.eu/legal-content/EN/TXT/PDF/?uri=CELEX:52012PC0011& from=EN, accessed 28 June 2021.

[59]    Ibid.

[60]    European Parliament, 'Legislative Resolution of 12 March 2014 on the Proposal for a Regulation of the European Parliament and of the Council on the Protection of Individuals with regard to the Processing of Personal Data and on the Free Movement of such Data' (General Data Protection Regulation) COM(2012)0011 – C7–0025/2012 – 2012/0011(COD).

purposes, archive services, the religious context and obligations of secrecy. Further, an article was suggested in Chapter IX such that 'This Regulation shall not have the effect of modifying the obligation to respect fundamental rights and fundamental legal principles as enshrined in Article 6 of the TEU [Am. 198].'[61]

Then again, at the General Approach of the Council adopted on 15 June 2015, the journalistic exemption had come back.[62] Proposed Article 80(1) suggested that:

> The national law of the Member State shall (…) reconcile the right to the protection of personal data pursuant to this Regulation with the right to freedom of expression

---

[61]   See suggestion for Recital 121:
(121) ~~The processing of personal data solely for journalistic purposes, or for the purposes of artistic or literary expression should qualify for exemption~~ *Whenever necessary, exemptions or derogations* from the requirements of certain provisions of this Regulation *for the processing of personal data should be provided for* in order to reconcile the right to the protection of personal data with the right to freedom of expression, and notably the right to receive and impart information, as guaranteed in particular by Article 11 of the Charter. ~~This should apply in particular to processing of personal data in the audiovisual field and in news archives and press libraries.~~ Therefore, Member States should adopt legislative measures, which should lay down exemptions and derogations which are necessary for the purpose of balancing these fundamental rights. Such exemptions and derogations should be adopted by the Member States on general principles, on the rights of the data subject, on controller and processor, on the transfer of data to third countries or international organisations, on the independent supervisory authorities, ~~and~~ on co-operation and consistency *and on specific data processing situations*. This should not, however, lead Member States to lay down exemptions from the other provisions of this Regulation. In order to take account of the importance of the right to freedom of expression in every democratic society, it is necessary to interpret notions relating to that freedom~~, such as journalism,~~ broadly~~. Therefore, Member States should classify activities as "journalistic" for the purpose of the exemptions and derogations to be laid down under this Regulation if the object of these~~ *to cover all* activities ~~is~~ *which aim at* the disclosure to the public of information, opinions or ideas, irrespective of the medium which is used to transmit them*, also taking into account technological development*. They should not be limited to media undertakings and may be undertaken for profit-making or for non-profit making purposes.
[62]   Proposal for a Regulation of the European Parliament and of the Council on the protection of individuals with regard to the processing of personal data and on the free movement of such data (General Data Protection Regulation) – Preparation of a general approach. Brussels, 11 June 2015, 9565/15, Interinstitutional File: 2012/0011 (COD). The same wording also appears in an earlier Proposal for a Regulation of the European Parliament and of the Council on the protection of individuals with regard to the processing of personal data and on the free movement of such data (General Data

and information, including the processing of personal data for journalistic purposes and the purposes of academic, artistic or literary expression.

The proposed Article did not contain the word 'solely', but it appeared in the proposed recital.

The exemption in Article 85 of the GDPR and the concept of journalism within are quite broad and leave wide leeway for Member States to strike a balance between protection of personal data and freedom of expression and information. As Bitiukova points out, this runs counter to the aim of building a 'more coherent data protection framework in the Union'[63] and might also cause problems when individual journalists operate across several Member States.[64] However, Article 85(3) contains an obligation to notify the Commission of the provisions that have been adopted pursuant to Article 85(2).

There are many different national implementations of Article 85 GDPR.[65] Bitiukova has summarised that national implementation of Article 85 varies for example regarding the personal scope of exemption, what activities are exempted and which rules do not apply as a result of the exemption.[66] To illus-

---

Protection Regulation) = Partial general approach = Orientation debate, Brussels, 1 December 2014, 16140/14, Interinstitutional File: 2012/0011 (COD).

[63]  See Bitiukova (n 21) 17–18. Quotation Recital 7 of the GDPR. Relating to the national margin of appreciation, see also judgment of 24 September 2019, Case C–507/17 *Google Inc v Commision nationale de l'informatique et des libertés (CNIL)* EU:C:2019:772 (24 September 2019), where the CJEU found (in para 72) that national authorities are:

> competent to weigh up, in the light of national standards of protection of fundamental rights (...) a data subject's right to privacy and the protection of personal data concerning him or her, on the one hand, and the right to freedom of information, on the other, and, after weighing those rights against each other, to order, where appropriate, the operator of that search engine to carry out a de-referencing concerning all versions of that search engine.

See also para 69.

[64]  Bitiukova, ibid., 18.

[65]  Ibid., 20–27. Annex 1 contains a list of some national implementations of exemption, see p. 31–34. David Erdos has made comprehensive inquiries with data protection authorities about application of the exception, and analysed the national implementation in his articles 'Statutory Regulation of Professional Journalism Under European Data Protection: Down But Not Out?' (2016) 8 *JML* 229 and 'European Data Protection Regulation and Online New Media: Mind the Enforcement Gap' (2016) 43 *Journal of Law and Society* 534, 55. For Member States' notifications relating to national implementations, see European Commission, 'EU Member States notifications to the European Commission under the GDPR' https://ec.europa.eu/info/law/law-topic/data-protection/data-protection-eu/eu-countries-gdpr-specific-notifications_en accessed 29 November 2020.

[66]  Bitiukova, ibid., 19–27.

trate, Austria provides the exemption only for 'media undertakings, media services and their employees',[67] which seems to be contrary to CJEU case-law.[68]
In return, exemption for those who fall under its protection is complete: not
even data secrecy applies to employees of media undertakings and media services.[69] In Romanian law the scope of exemption is very narrow: application
requires that the question is of personal data which was clearly made public by
the data subject or data that relates to a public person or to the public character
of the acts in which the data subject is involved. If these narrow conditions
are met, processing is entirely excluded from the obligations of Chapters
II–IX.[70] The Association for Technology and Internet has lodged a complaint
with the European Commission of infringement of EU law in this respect.[71]
The Bulgarian Constitutional Court in turn declared the Bulgarian provision
relating to the journalistic exemption unconstitutional on 15 November 2019,
because it established ten criteria that were too vague and unclear for exemption.[72] The British form of national regulation, for its part, requires public
interest in publication and demands consideration of self-regulation within the
respective field.[73] This view does not provide any relief to journalism whose

---

[67]   Günther Leissler, Patrizia Reisinger and Janos Böszörmenyi, 'National
Adaptations of the GDPR in Austria' in Karen Mc Cullagh, Olivia Tambou and Sam
Bourton (eds), *National Adaptations of the GDPR* (Collection Open Access Book,
Blogdroiteuropeen, Luxembourg February 2019), 35, 39 https://wp.me/p6OBGR-3dP
accessed 13 December 2020.
[68]   See later on Case C–345/17 *Sergejs Buivids v Datu valsts inspekcija (Buivids)*
EU:C:2019:122 (14 February 2019).
[69]   Leissler and others (n 67) 39.
[70]   Unofficial translation from Romanian prepared by PrivacyOne https://privacyon
.ro/wp-content/uploads/2018/12/Romanian-GDPR-implementation-law-English
-translation.pdf accessed 13 December 2020.
[71]   Valentina Pavel, European Commission, Complaint – Infringement of EU law,
2018, Romania, https://www.apti.ro/sites/default/files/Complaint%20on%20Romanian
%20implementation%20of%20the%20GDPR%20-%20ApTI.pdf accessed 13 December 2020.
[72]   Bitiukova (n 21) 22–24; and Commission Staff Working Document, 2020 Rule
of Law Report, Country Chapter on the rule of law situation in Bulgaria, Brussels,
30.9.2020 SWD(2020) 301 final, p. 17.
[73]   See Data Protection Act 2018, Sched 2, part 5 'Exemptions etc. based on Article
8582) for reasons of freedom of Expression and information', para 26, https://www
.legislation.gov.uk/ukpga/2018/12/schedule/2/enacted accessed 7 December 2020.
See also Information Commissioner's Office (ICO), 'Guide to the General Data
Protection Regulation (GDPR): Exemptions' https://ico.org.uk/for-organisations/guide
-to-data-protection/guide-to-the-general-data-protection-regulation-gdpr/exemptions/
#ex16 accessed 7 December 2020; Karen Mc Cullagh, 'UK: GDPR Adaptations and
Preparations for Withdrawal From the EU' in Mc Cullagh, Tambou and Bourton (eds)
(n 67) 112–19.

content is not in the public interest, nor does it define what is meant by the public interest. In a way, entertainment and the arts can also be seen as serving the public interest, as they provide important entertainment for people. Thus, to guarantee journalistic freedom and the audience's right to receive information and ideas – which is an essential part of freedom of expression – it seems that the concept of general interest should not be interpreted too narrowly in this context. Reference by the British Data Protection Acts to codes of practice and the BBC Editorial Guidelines, the Ofcom Broadcasting Code and the Editors' Code of Practice is a quite questionable requirement for the exemption, because those guidelines are not established via the democratic legislative process, and they affect the use of fundamental and constitutional rights.

To wrap up this section, the examples above demonstrate the fact of much national variation relating to implementation of the journalistic exemption. Some guidance from the European Data Protection Board would be necessary in this respect, even though the guidelines would have had a greater impact if they had already been given shortly after the entry into force of the GDPR when national legislation was being prepared.

## 6.3    Interpretation of the Journalistic Exemption in Court Practice

The purpose of the exemption is to reconcile the right to protection of personal data with the right to freedom of expression and information. This means that the concept of journalism must be interpreted with those aims in mind.[74] This also sets limits to interpretation: personal data protection should not hinder journalistic information-gathering, maintaining a journalistic background database, combining, sorting and categorizing information with the help of AI for publication purposes and publishing personal data when that happens for journalistic purposes and as part of journalistic activity. On the other hand, the concept of journalism should not be interpreted so broadly that it nullifies the purpose of the data protection regulation or allows data protection legislation to be circumvented under the pretext of journalism.[75]

---

[74] See, e.g., *Satakunnan Markkinapörssi* [CJEU] (n 54) para 51:
It must be observed, as a preliminary point, that, according to settled case-law, the provisions of a directive must be interpreted in the light of the aims pursued by the directive and the system it establishes (see, to that effect, Case C–265/07 *Caffaro* [2008] ECR I–7085, para 14).

[75] See ibid., point 52:
In that regard, it is not in dispute that, as is apparent from Article 1 of the directive, its objective is that the Member States should, while permitting the free flow of personal data, protect the fundamental rights and freedoms of natural persons and, in particular, their right to privacy, with respect to the processing of personal data' and 53: 'That objective cannot, however, be pursued without having regard

The court practice of the CJEU and ECtHR provides some guidance and boundary conditions, but it still leaves a considerable margin of appreciation for the Member States. Even though the judgments concerned applying the DPD, the principles of interpretation remain relevant. It can be seen from the wording of the GDPR that the concept of journalistic purpose is at least not narrower than before, because the word 'solely' has been deleted. On the other hand, I have not found any documentation in the preparatory documents for the GDPR to indicate that the scope of the derogation had been intended to change at all.

In the well-known *Google Spain*[76] case, the CJEU ruled that Google, as a commercial search engine that gathered personal information for profit, had to remove links to private information when asked, provided that the information was no longer relevant. The Court stated at point 85 that:

> Furthermore, the processing by the publisher of a web page consisting in the publication of information relating to an individual may, in some circumstances, be carried out 'solely for journalistic purposes' and thus benefit, by virtue of Article 9 of Directive 95/46, from derogations from the requirements laid down by the directive, *whereas that does not appear to be so in the case of the processing carried out by the operator of a search engine*. It cannot therefore be ruled out that in certain circumstances the data subject is capable of exercising the rights referred to in Article 12(b) and subparagraph (a) of the first paragraph of Article 14 of Directive 95/46 against that operator but not against the publisher of the web page.[77]

Thus, the Court concluded that publishing on the Internet may 'in some circumstances' fall under the journalistic exemption, but processing in a search engine was not journalism.

The applicability of the journalistic exemption and its national application was also involved in a case that was first decided by the Grand Chamber of the CJEU and thereafter by the Grand Chamber of the ECtHR. Both judgments concerned the same course of events. These began in 2002, when the Finnish limited liability company, Satakunnan Markkinapörssi Oy, started publishing the newspaper *Veropörssi*. This contained articles, summaries and advertisements, but its main purpose was to publish personal tax information that related to private individuals. In 2003, Satakunnan Markkinapörssi Oy began to transfer personal data published in *Veropörssi*, in the form of CD-ROM discs, to

---

to the fact that those fundamental rights must, to some degree, be reconciled with the fundamental right to freedom of expression.

[76]  Case C–131/12 *Google Spain SL and Google Inc. v Agencia Española de Protección de Datos (AEPD) and Mario Costeja González (Google Spain)* [GC] EU:C: 2014:317 (13 May 2014) EUECJ.

[77]  Emphasis added.

the limited liability company Satamedia Oy, which was owned by the same shareholders. The purpose of the data transfer was to run a text-messaging service allowing mobile telephone users to request tax information relating to other individuals (= how much their earned income and capital income were and how much taxes they had paid) and receive information published in *Veropörssi* on their telephone, for a charge of approximately EUR 2. Personal data were removed from that service on request.

The database had been created using information that had already been published in 2002 in *Veropörssi* on the income and assets of 1.2 million individuals. This amounted to a third of all taxable persons in Finland, among whom were well-known personalities, high-earning individuals, ordinary citizens and also low-income individuals. The taxation information that was published was publicly available information as such, but it was only available at tax offices. Only for journalistic purposes could it be provided in electronic format. Following complaints from individuals allegeing infringement of their right to privacy, the Data Protection Ombudsman brought administrative proceedings concerning the manner and extent of the applicants' processing of taxation data. The companies invoked the journalistic exemption. After the request had been dismissed by the Data Protection Board and the Helsinki Administrative Court, the Data Ombudsman brought the case to the Supreme Administrative Court, which asked the CJEU for a preliminary ruling relating to the journalistic exemption.

The CJEU[78] declared in its Grand Chamber judgment of 16 December 2008 that the case concerned an activity in which personal data was:

- collected from documents in the public domain held by the tax authorities and processed for publication,
- published alphabetically in printed form by income bracket and municipality in the form of comprehensive lists,
- transferred onward on CD-ROM to be used for commercial purposes, and
- processed for the purposes of a text-messaging service whereby mobile telephone users can, by sending a text message containing details of an individual's name and municipality of residence to a given number, receive in reply information concerning the earned and unearned income and assets of that person.

Then the Court pointed out in paragraph 56 that 'in order to take account of the importance of the right to freedom of expression in every democratic society', it was necessary 'to interpret notions relating to that freedom, such as journalism, broadly'. The journalistic exemption did not apply 'only to

---

[78]    *Satakunnan Markkinapörssi* [CJEU] (n 54).

media undertakings but also every person engaged in journalism' (para 58). The purpose of making a profit did not, as such, preclude such activities from being undertaken 'solely for journalistic purposes' (para 59). The Court found that an activity could be 'classified as "journalistic activities" if their object is the disclosure to the public of information, opinions or ideas, irrespective of the medium which is used to transmit them. They are not limited to media undertakings and may be undertaken for profit-making purposes' (para 61). Finally, the Court concluded that processing 'solely for journalistic purposes' is involved when 'the sole object of those activities is the disclosure to the public of information, opinions or ideas' (para 62). According to the Court, it was a matter for the national court to determine whether that was the case.

In September 2009, the Finnish Supreme Court found[79] that publication of the entire database as such could not be considered journalistic activity but as processing of personal data, which they had no right to perform. The court referred the case back to the Data Protection Board, which forbade the applicant companies from processing taxation information to the extent that they had done in 2002 and from passing such data to the SMS service. This decision was ultimately upheld by the Supreme Administrative Court in June 2012. After that, the applicant companies filed a claim against Finland in the ECtHR, claiming that the ban on processing and publishing taxation data violated their rights to freedom of expression, alleging that the ban had amounted to censorship as well as discrimination vis-à-vis other newspapers, which were able to continue publishing such information.

Finally, in June 2017 the Grand Chamber of the ECtHR adjudged that the Finnish authorities had acted within their margin of appreciation and found no violation of Article 10.[80] The Court emphasized that the rights under Articles 10 and 8 of the Convention deserved equal respect (paras 123, 163), and that the heart of the case lay in striking the right balance between those two competing rights (para 122).

The Court agreed with the conclusion of the Supreme Administrative Court, namely that publication of taxation data in the manner and to the extent described did not contribute to a debate of public interest, and the publication could not be considered to have been carried out for a solely journalistic purpose. Furthermore, the Court noted that collection, processing and dissemination of data had been conducted on a bulk basis, in a way that impacted

---

[79]   Case KHO:2009:82 *Tietosuojavaltuutettu v Satakunnan Markkinapörssi Oy and Satamedia Oy* (*Satakunnan Markkinapörssi* [KHO]) [2009] 23 September 2009/2303 Supreme Administrative Court of Finland (Korkein hallinto-oikeus, KHO).
[80]   Also the Chamber judgment 21 July 2015 found by six votes to one in favour of Finland.

the entire adult population. As media companies, the applicants should have understood that:

> the mass collection of data and its wholesale dissemination – pertaining to about one third of Finnish taxpayers or 1.2 million people, a number 10 to 20 times greater than that covered by any other media organization at the time – might not be considered as processing 'solely' for journalistic purposes (para 151).

The data was also obtained in an unusual way, circumventing the normal channels used by journalists to obtain such information.[81] Such dissemination of personal data had made it accessible in a manner and to an extent that had not been intended by the legislator. It also differed from the manner and extent to which other media outlets published tax data. Finally, the Court noted that tax information was not publicly accessible in most countries in Europe, so there was no unified European view of this, and that the authorities had not placed a total ban on publication.

The outcome of the judgment appears fair and correct. It seems that the companies tried to circumvent personal data legislation regarding their SMS business by publishing raw (tax) data as such. The cooperation and ownership of the companies pointed in that direction. At that time, there was an unsuccessfully worded provision in the Finnish Personal Data Act (523/1999) which stated that 'This Act does not apply to personal data files containing, solely and in unaltered form, data that have been published by the media.' As Hins has noted, Finnish law on personal data generally excluded processing of personal data for purposes of journalism from almost all provisions in the law, and thus ignored the requirement of Article 9 of the DPD, namely that such an exception is only allowed insofar as it is 'necessary' for the protection of freedom of speech. Thus, Finland had implemented the DPD incorrectly. This may be the reason why the CJEU emphasized that 'derogations and limitations in relation to the protection of data' 'must apply only in so far as is strictly necessary', even though the DPD did not use the word 'strictly'.[82]

The purpose of this subsection was to enable internal background information registers for media outlets, meaning that media companies could store information that had already been published in the media. Now the appellants invoked this provision to circumvent personal data legislation. The legislator

---

[81]   The data had been collected in tax offices instead of electronic channels provided for journalistic purposes after the data protection authority had asked for more information on the company's activities.

[82]   Wouter Hins, 'Case C–73/07, *Tietosuojavaltuutettu v Satakunnan Markkinapörssi Oy and Satamedia Oy* with annotation by W Hins', Judgment of the Grand Chamber of 16 December 2008, (2010) 47(1) CML Rev 215, 232.

had not intended that media companies could publish any personal register files whatsoever under the claim of journalistic exemption. Nor had the legislator meant that anyone could process this bulk data for any purposes in any possible way once it had been published. If this kind of publishing were possible without any restrictions regarding protection of personal data, under the guise of the journalistic exemption, then personal data legislation could have been circumvented, resulting in significant harm, inconvenience and suffering for data subjects from publication of the data.[83] As Advocate General Kokott puts it: exceptions to a general principle of personal data protection 'must be interpreted strictly in order not to undermine the general principle unduly'. If Article 9 were interpreted too broadly there would be a risk of encroaching on the fundamental right to privacy.[84]

There is one more judgment relating to the journalistic exemption. In *Buivids*[85] the CJEU repeated the principles that it and the ECtHR had expressed in the *Satakunnan Markkinapörssi* cases. Mr Buivids had made a video recording in a police station while he was making a statement in the context of an administrative proceeding that had been brought against him. He had then published the video, which showed police officers going about their duties in the police station, on the Internet site www.youtube.com. The National Data Protection Agency then charged that he had violated personal data protection legislation. The CJEU wrote (para 55) regarding the journalistic exemption that:

> the fact that Mr Buivids is not a professional journalist does not appear to be capable of excluding the possibility that the recording of the video in question and its publication on a video website, on which users can send, watch and share videos, may come within the scope of that provision.

Thus, the Court confirmed that application of the journalistic exemption did not require that the party relying on the exception had been hired as a journalist for some media (newspaper, magazine, radio, television, web publication). Again, this outcome appears equitable for many reasons. First, freedom of expression belongs to everyone, and it would be haphazard use of the law to grant special protection only on the basis of formal criteria or an employment relationship

---

[83]   Actually, there were already indications of the misuse of this exception: a magazine had published a list of members of Suomen Mensa ry (Mensa Finland), referring to this exception. The prosecutor did not raise charges, because he/she considered the publication to be under the journalistic exemption.

[84]   *Satakunnan Markkinapörssi* [CJEU] (n 54), Opinion of Advocate General Kokott, delivered on 8 May 2008, para 58. Reference for a preliminary ruling of Supreme Administrative Court of Finland: *Satakunnan Markkinapörssi* [KHO] (n 79).

[85]   *Buivids* (n 68); *Satakunnan markkinapörssi* [ECtHR GC] (n 34).

or equivalent. Private bloggers, vloggers and NGOs may play a significant role in disseminating information of general interest and it would go against the principle of equality to exclude them totally from the scope of protection of freedom of expression just because of their status as non-journalists.[86] Second, there is no authoritative definition of 'journalist'.[87] Therefore, it would be difficult to draw a distinction between a journalist and a non-journalist.

In *Buivids,* the Court referred to teleological interpretation, where 'the provisions of a directive must be interpreted in the light of the aims pursued by the directive and the system which it establishes'. Therefore, it was important to interpret the concept of journalism broadly. It was the national courts' task to evaluate whether it appeared from the video posting 'that the sole purpose of the recording and publication of the video was the disclosure to the public of information, opinions or ideas' (para 59), taking into consideration that the purpose of the video was to draw attention to alleged police malpractice (para 60). However, establishing such malpractice was not a condition for the journalistic exemption (para 61). The Court also noted that the journalistic exemption had to be applied only when it was necessary to achieve a balance between the fundamental rights to privacy and to freedom of expression (paras 63–64).

The CJEU also referred to the ECHR and the practice of the ECtHR in interpreting it (para 65).[88] Relevant criteria included whether the expression contributes to a debate of general interest; how well-known the person concerned is, and what is the subject of the report; the prior conduct of the person concerned; the content, form and consequences of the publication; and the circumstances under which the information was obtained, and its veracity. Also relevant were what opportunities the controller had to mitigate the extent of interference with the right to privacy.[89]

In the Court's opinion, recording and publishing a video without the persons concerned being informed is interference in private life (para 67). Finally, the

---

[86] Of course, it is possible that the amount of protection may vary depending on circumstances – e.g., the responsibility of the editor-in-chief of a magazine can serve as a counterweight when the magazine relies on protection of information sources or the right to anonymous expression. But it would seem unfair to categorically exclude certain groups of persons from protection just because of their status, without any possibility for discretion *in casu.*

[87] Relating to concepts of journalism see Tim P Vos, 'Journalism' in Tim P Vos (ed), *Journalism* (De Gruyter 2018); Deuze, 'What Is Journalism' (n 24); Deuze, 'What Journalism Is (Not)' (n 24) 1–4.

[88] Also Recital 37 of the DPD (n 53) refers to Art 10 of the ECHR.

[89] Here the Court refers to Grand Chamber judgment of the ECtHR of 27 June 2017, *Satakunnan Markkinapörssi* [ECtHR GC] (n 34) para 165. More closely about those criteria, see Korpisaari (n 34) and GC cases *Von Hannover No. 2* [GC] (n 33) and *Axel Springer* [GC] (n 33), both on 7 February 2012.

Court emphasized that recording and publishing the video could be considered 'processing of personal data solely for journalistic purposes' if it was 'apparent from that video that the sole object of that recording and publication thereof [was] the disclosure of information, opinions or ideas to the public'. In this case, the Court left it to the national courts to determine whether this was the case. What is interesting is that, according to the Court, evaluating journalistic purpose had to be based on the content of the video (paras 59, 67). Therefore AI-created content could belong in the sphere of exemption. It is also important to acknowledge that in the practice of the ECtHR information concerning a person's private life in the form of a photo has enjoyed greater protection than information in the form of written text. A video recording infringes a person's private life even more than a photo.[90] Therefore, the nature of a publication may also bear some significance – at least at that stage when the court is considering whether infringement on a person's private life and personal data protection is strictly necessary, as the GDPR (and CJEU) requires. It also bears significance when the court is considering the proportionality of the infringement or whether imposing a sanction on the use of freedom of expression might bear a chilling effect on using freedom of expression in the future.[91]

## 7.   ANALYSIS AND CONCLUSIONS

The practice of the CJEU and ECtHR does not provide precise guidance on the criteria of 'journalistic purpose' or the concept of journalism in the present media environment. However, some analysis and conclusions can be drawn.

First, the concept of journalism must be assessed in the light of the purpose and context of the provision. Its purpose is to guarantee dissemination and reception of information as part of freedom of expression. However, the journalistic exemption must not nullify protection of privacy and the purpose of the data protection regulation. As the CJEU pointed out in the case of *Satakunnan Markkinapörssi* (para 46):

> it must be held that a general derogation from the application of the [Data Protection] directive in respect of published information would largely deprive the directive of

---

[90]   See, e.g., *Peck v The United Kingdom* App no 44647/98 (ECtHR, 28 January 2003) ECHR 2003–I, para 80; *Sciacca v Italy* App no 50774/99 (ECtHR, 11 Jan 2005) ECHR 2005–I, para 29; and *Reklos and Davourlis v Greece* App no 1234/05 (ECtHR, 15 January 2009) para 40; *Von Hannover v Germany No. 2* [GC] (n 33) para 103; *Kahn v Germany* App no 16313/10 (ECtHR, 17 March 2016) para 74; *López Ribalda and Others v. Spain* [GC] App nos 1874/13 and 8567/13 (ECtHR, 17 October 2019) paras 87–91.
[91]   See, e.g., *Heinisch v Germany* App no 28274/08 (ECtHR, 21 July 2011) ECHR 2011 (extracts) para 91.

its effect. It would be sufficient for the Member States to publish data in order for those data to cease to enjoy the protection afforded by the directive.

For example, in *Satakunnan Markkinapörssi*, the magazine was apparently set up solely for the purpose of publishing tax information (and to forward it to an SMS service), and a similar logic could be used to set up a media project around any subject to publish related personal registers and claim that it is journalism, thus falling under the journalistic exemption. If such activity were to be covered by the journalistic exemption, it would undermine the basis of personal data protection. Vice versa, the concept of journalistic purpose must not be interpreted so strictly that it would prevent the production of journalistic content. An overly strict interpretation might also have a chilling effect on the future activities of media companies, NGOs and other persons that wish to disseminate ideas and information or create new technologies for the creation of journalistic content.

In *Satakunnan Markkinapörssi* and *Buivids,* the CJEU left it to the national courts to determine whether the activity in question was journalistic. In *Google Spain* the CJEU held that search engine activities did not fall under the journalistic exemption. The reasoning behind this was not the fact that the outcome of search engine activity was generated automatically but the nature of the activity as such, which was not producing content but merely classifying and presenting content that had already been created.

In journalistic literature a certain kind of professionalism has traditionally been associated with the concept of journalism, but with the transformation of journalism (online media, user-centred communication, user-generated content, and changes in journalistic work, workspaces and the economics of journalism) the definition of journalism has also changed.[92] The boundaries between 'journalistic, institutional media' and other types of mass communication have become fluid and unclear[93] when the privilege of reaching large audiences has expanded from journalists representing traditional media to bloggers, vloggers, Instagram-celebrities and amateur journalists who can disseminate their ideas, opinions and photos worldwide in seconds.[94] The courts in turn have adopted a more functional approach where the purpose of

---

[92]   See e.g., Mark Deuze and Tamara Witschge, 'Beyond Journalism: Theorizing the Transformation of Journalism' (2018) 19 *Journalism* 165, 169–74; Vos (n 87) 3–5.

[93]   See Ellen Hovlid, 'Finding a Judicial Definition of Journalism. A Challenging Exercise in the Digital Age' in Mart Susi (ed), *Human Rights, Digital Society and the Law – A Research Companion* (Routledge 2019) 209, 209–10.

[94]   See Jan Oster, *European and International Media Law* (CUP 2016) 9.

the publication is a decisive factor.[95] This emphasizes the nature and purpose of journalistic activities instead of giving weight to the connection between a journalist and media institutions, membership in a professional association, or commitment to the guidelines or ethics followed by journalists.[96] This functionalistic approach does not as such preclude content created by artificial intelligence from being considered journalistic.

AI and automated tools can be of great help when gathering background information for journalistic purposes. The ECtHR has stated that gathering information is an important part of the journalistic process and as such protected as part of press freedom.[97] Therefore, it is justified to extend the journalistic exemption to collection and storage of data for journalistic purposes. Of course, adequate data security measures are required.

In *Buivids* the CJEU referred to the case-law of the ECtHR, where it had laid down the criteria for balancing the rights to private life and freedom of expression. As already mentioned, those were: contribution to a debate of public interest; how well-known is the person affected and the prior conduct of the person concerned; the subject of the news report; the content, form and consequences of the publication; and the manner and circumstances in which the information was obtained, as well as its veracity. While it is understandable that these criteria are relevant when the Court is deciding whether the national courts (and legislators) have acted within their margin of appreciation or whether a violation has occurred of such human rights as private life (including protection of personal data) or freedom of expression, these criteria are not suitable for assessing whether a certain action is journalism or not. There can be good journalism or poor-quality journalism, major news topics, investigative journalism, or idle gossip and sensational journalism, professional journal-

---

[95] For example ECtHR *Társaság a Szabadágjandokért v Hungary* App no 37374/05 (ECtHR, 14 April 2009) para 27: 'The function of the press includes the creation of forums for public debate. However, the realisation of this function is not limited to the media or professional journalists.' In this case – which related to access to information – the Court emphasized 'civil society's important contribution to the discussion of public affairs' and pointed out that because the applicant was 'an association involved in human rights litigation with various objectives' it could 'therefore be characterised, like the press, as a social "watchdog".' Therefore its activities deserved similar protection to that afforded to the press. See also *Österreichische Vereinigung zur Erhaltung, Stärkung und Schaffung v Austria* App no 39534/07 (ECtHR, 28 November 2013).

[96] Hovlid (n 93) 210–11; Oster, (n 94) 9.

[97] *Shapovalov v Ukraine* (n 37) para 68; *Dammann v Switzerland* (n 37) para 52; *Magyar* [GC] (n 37) para 130; and *Satakunnan Markkinapörssi* [ECtHR GC] (n 34) para 128. See also *Nordisk Film & TV A/S v Denmark* (n 37) and *Haldimann and Others v Switzerland* (n 37).

ism or modest journalistic output produced by a beginner or an association. But it would still be wrong to say that bad journalism is not journalism.

On the other hand, for the sake of personal data protection, exemptions should not be applied to every blogger or vlogger who writes about their everyday life. For example, in the *Lindqvist* case[98] Mrs Lindqvist had used her freedom of expression by setting up an Internet page where she referred to various persons who were identified by name or by other means. She mentioned their telephone numbers, working conditions, hobbies and state of health. This blog was a non-profit-making leisure activity for her. The CJEU held (para 47) that the household exemption could only relate to activities which were carried out in the course of private or family life of individuals, and that this was 'clearly not the case with the processing of personal data such a way that it was accessible on the internet for an indefinite number of people'. Mrs Lindqvist had not even invoked the journalistic exemption. Relating to her freedom of expression the Court found (paras 85–86) that a balance between the rights and interests involved had to be found primarily at national level. Fundamental rights were of particular importance, and Mrs Lindqvist's freedom of expression had 'to be weighed against the protection of the private life of the individuals whom she had been writing about'. This example illustrates that the journalistic exemption cannot be available to every person who runs a blog, but on the other hand, the fact that the journalistic exemption is not applicable does not mean that there would be no protection for a person's freedom of expression.

It is true that, if the concept of journalism is too broad and if the privileges offered for journalists are available in too many situations, they might become difficult to defend[99] and might seem unfair. However, rather than trying to narrow the concept of journalism as much as possible so that sensational voyeurism does not infringe on anyone's privacy or personal data, there should be scope for more flexible consideration instead of an either–or type of solution. The dangers of a broad definition of journalism can be avoided if additional criteria are set as conditions for privileges or if privileges (exemptions of personal data protection) only go as far as is strictly necessary for the purpose of freedom of expression. As the CJEU emphasized in *Satakunnan Markkinapörssi* (para 56), the concept of journalism must be interpreted broadly, but derogations and limitations to protection of privacy must apply only so far as is strictly necessary.

If the criterion of 'general interest' is to be maintained, that should be stated as a requirement in national laws and be a separate criterion from the concept

---

98   *Lindqvist* (n 18).
99   See Oster (n 94) 9 and Hovlid (n 93) 211.

of journalism, because expressions that are not of general interest can also be journalism. A balance must be struck in national implementation so that the special rights guaranteed to journalism are reasonable and justified. It can be read from the practice of the ECtHR that there is a sliding scale: deeper limitations to private life are justified if there is general interest in publication, while a narrower scope for limitations to private life applies if general interest in publication does not exist. From the point of view of the individual, publishing information may be much more harmful than collection and processing of personal data prior to publication.

Exhaustive lists of criteria are questionable, as they may not apply to all cases deserving of an exception or, on the other hand, they might provide exceptions in cases that might not deserve it, or which might not be provided by an open weighing and balancing test that considers the right value of different fundamental rights. Flexible balancing criteria would probably best fulfil the purpose of the exemption, because the media environment changes so quickly, and flexible criteria would make it possible to take into consideration all the relevant circumstances. The downside of open clauses that require weighing and balancing is that sometimes a publisher may be uncertain whether the exemption applies. But in terms of the professional media this probably would not cause problems – unless they extend their activities to an area that is no longer traditional journalism. An example is the 'tax machines' that operate on the Internet, and are made by the Finnish 'traditional' media. These are digital personal registers, where information may be obtained for free without registration. 'Tax machines' contain information on every person that has earned at least 100 000 (the limit may vary depending on the media) euros a year, which means 1–2 per cent of persons that have taxable income. One person's income can be seen for many years back. Otherwise the information is only obtainable at the tax office or by making a phone call to the tax authorities. The Finnish Data Ombudsman found in its decision 27.10.2021 (9970/163/2019) that the information was processed for journalistic purposes. It also emphasised that assessing the content of journalistic decisions made by editorial staff was not within the Ombudsman's authority. The decision is not yet final.

The definition of journalism and the scope of the journalistic exemption are already difficult to interpret in current circumstances. It has been predicted that in the future AI will produce articles on a large scale and that it will resemble human work more than before. Using AI will also be considered normal.[100] This makes it even more difficult to assess what is journalism and

---

[100] Aljosha Karim Schapals and Colin Porlezza, 'Assistance or Resistance? Evaluating the Intersection of Automated Journalism and Journalistic Role Conceptions' (2020) 8(3) *Media and Communication* 16, 19.

what is accepted within the journalistic exemption. The further the journalistic exemption is expanded from the context of its original circumstances, the more questionable its utilisation might become. Especially in the case of automated journalism and the speed of technological progress taking place, applying the journalistic exemption should be considered carefully. However, a certain level of flexibility is needed and the technology used should not be in a dominant or even prominent position when assessing the case.

It is also important to note that personal data protection regulation is not the only way to protect private life and personal data. Additionally, criminal or compensation liability may be applicable – for example if private or false information has been disseminated.[101] Finally, even though the journalistic exemption would not be applicable, publication may be justified because one of the legal grounds for processing is involved. Publication may be in the public interest or there might be a legitimate interest for publication as GDPR 6(1) (e) and (f) state. The fact that the journalistic exemption does not apply does not imply no protection for freedom of expression and information.

---

[101]  I refer for example to national regulations relating to defamation and disseminating private information.

PART II

Trust, disinformation and platforms

# 4. Social media platforms as public trustees: an approach to the disinformation problem

**Philip M. Napoli and Fabienne Graf**

Within the context of this volume's focus on responsibilities associated with the implementation of artificial intelligence in the media sector, one pressing question involves whether social media companies (who have now largely given up the idea that they are technology companies and not media companies) bear specific responsibilities related to the algorithmic dissemination of disinformation on their platforms. Certainly, the evolving legal obligations in this regard vary significantly from country to country. This chapter focuses specifically on the United States, and a possible mechanism for imposing disinformation-related responsibilities upon these platforms, despite a legal environment that, due to the First Amendment, has long offered media organizations substantial protections from any form of content regulation. Recent developments in the USA, such as the January 6th insurrection, and the ongoing resistance to basic coronavirus-related safety precautions (such as mask-wearing), have highlighted the negative social and political consequences of widespread disinformation.

The disinformation problem affecting the USA (and many other countries around the world) is certainly not isolated to the social media realm. Indeed, recent research has highlighted the role that the broad spectrum of news media and government officials play in facilitating the production and flow of disinformation.[1] However, social media platforms play a significant role in the contemporary disinformation ecosystem, often serving as a point of

---

[1] Yochai Benkler and others, 'Mail-In Voter Fraud: Anatomy of a Disinformation Campaign' (2020) The Berkman Klein Center for Internet & Society Research Publication Series https://cyber.harvard.edu/publication/2020/Mail-in-Voter-Fraud -Disinformation-2020 accessed December 12, 2020; S Evanega, M Lynas, J Adams and K Smolenyak, 'Coronavirus Misinformation: Quantifying Sources and Themes in the COVID-19 "Infodemic"' (2020) https://allianceforscience.cornell.edu/wp-content/ uploads/2020/09/Evanega-et-al-Coronavirus-misinformationFINAL.pdf accessed December 12, 2020.

origin for disinformation that then finds its way into mainstream news media; facilitating the rapid rate of distribution (virality); and enabling a degree of microtargeting of disinformation at target audiences that cannot be achieved with other media.[2]

Yet, from a regulation and policy standpoint, the federal government in the USA has done virtually nothing to confront the social media disinformation problem. None of the many pieces of social media-related legislation that are at various stages of consideration within Congress address the disinformation problem in any direct way.[3] Nor have any of the regulatory agencies with potential jurisdiction in this space (such as the Federal Trade Commission (FTC), the Federal Communications Commission (FCC), and the Federal Election Commission (FEC)) introduced substantive regulatory interventions.

Needless to say, it is fair to ask whether any government oversight of platforms' policing of disinformation is advisable, particularly in the current political environment, and whether it would even be feasible within the contemporary parameters of the First Amendment. However, as American democracy and public health strain under the weight of the country's commitment to absolutist First Amendment principles,[4] it seems reasonable to consider whether some kind of regulatory interventions related to platforms' policing of disinformation – or at least the algorithmic systems that are central to its dissemination – are possible.

That question is the focal point of this chapter, which explores relevant precedent for disinformation-related regulation in the US media sector; and then considers whether the underlying rationale that justified such regulation is relevant to the social media context. Specifically, this chapter considers whether the public trustee governance model that applies to broadcasting in the USA might be applicable in the social media context; and whether the type

---

[2]    See e.g., Y Benkler, R Faris and H Roberts, *Network Propaganda: Disinformation, Manipulation, and Radicalization in American Politics* (OUP 2018); P Howard, *Lie Machines: How to Save Democracy from Troll Armies, Deceitful Robots, Junk News Operations, and Political Operatives* (Yale UP 2020); P M Napoli, *Social Media and the Public Interest: Media Regulation in the Disinformation Age* (Columbia UP 2019a).

[3]    It is important to note here that legislative efforts to curb 'anti-conservative bias' (see e.g., Online Freedom and Viewpoint Diversity Act, 2020) do not equate with efforts to combat disinformation. Online Freedom and Viewpoint Diversity Act (2020), 116th Congress, 2nd Session https://www.commerce.senate.gov/services/files/ 94D0F3C6-B927-46D2-A75C-17C78D0D92AA accessed December 12, 2020.

[4]    See, e.g., Emily Bazelon, 'Free Speech Will Save Our Democracy: The First Amendment in the Disinformation Age' *New York Times Magazine* (13 October 2020) https://www.nytimes.com/2020/10/13/magazine/free-speech.html accessed December 12, 2020.

of disinformation-related regulations that have accompanied this public trustee model might therefore be feasible within the social media context as well.

## 1. THE FIRST AMENDMENT, FALSITY, AND SOCIAL MEDIA REGULATION

The most obvious reason for federal inaction on the disinformation front is the broad First Amendment protections that are granted to false speech – even intentional false speech. The relationship between the First Amendment and false speech (particularly political false speech) is not entirely clear cut.[5] As legal scholar Frederick Schauer[6] has pointed out, First Amendment theory has seldom grappled with the issue of truth versus falsity – or, in today's vernacular, facts versus 'alternative facts'. Rather, traditional thinking about the First Amendment assumes that, in a robust speech environment, individuals will have access to – and will consider – all of the relevant information necessary to distinguish truth from falsity. Falsity ultimately receives a substantial amount of protection in order to assure that no government suppression of truthful speech takes place.

From this standpoint, it is worth considering the most recent Supreme Court decision that has addressed the First Amendment status of political disinformation. *United States v Alvarez*[7] elevated what was already a very high bar for any possible government interventions related to false speech to 'a virtually impossible bar for the government to overcome'.[8] In this decision, a California elected official gave a speech in which he lied about having won the Congressional Medal of Honor. This particular falsity violated the Stolen Valor Act,[9] which made it a crime to misrepresent one's military service record.

In its decision declaring the Stolen Valor Act unconstitutional, the Court catalogued the various categories of speech that have historically merited lower levels of First Amendment protection (obscenity, advocacy likely to provoke lawless action, defamation, and the like). However, the Court refused to place intentional false speech designed to misinform and manipulate voters

---

[5]    R N Spicer, *Free Speech and False Speech: Political Deception and Its Legal Limits (or Lack Thereof)* (Palgrave Macmillan 2018); G E White, 'Falsity and the First Amendment' (2019) *72*(3) *SMU L Rev* 513.

[6]    F Schauer, 'Facts and the First Amendment' (2009/2010) *57*(4) *UCLA L Rev* 897.

[7]    *United States v Alvarez* [2012] 567 US 709.

[8]    R K L Collins, 'Exceptional Freedom – the Roberts Court, the First Amendment and the New Absolutism' (2013) *76 Albany L Rev* 409, 428.

[9]    Stolen Valor Act (2005). Pub.L. 109–437.

(a fair characterization of Alvarez's falsity[10]) within this collection of speech categories eligible for content-based restrictions. Limiting such expressions violated what the Court viewed as the 'common understanding that some false statements are inevitable if there is to be an open and vigorous expression of views'.[11]

In addition, the Court noted that its previous statements, such as '[f]alse statements of fact are particularly valueless [because] they interfere with the truth-seeking function of the marketplace of ideas'[12] and that false statements 'are not protected by the First Amendment in the same manner as truthful statements',[13] were contextually irrelevant because they involved a 'legally cognizable harm associated with a false statement'.[14] The Court did not see the lying engaged in by Alvarez as producing such harm. As the health of our democracy, and the physical health of the American public, strain under the weight of widespread political disinformation, this question of the presence of cognizable harms associated with political disinformation seems more difficult to dismiss today than it was just eight years ago, when the Supreme Court reached its decision.

Perhaps the most ironic aspect of the current moment, in which the dis-information ecosystem is operating so vigorously in areas as wide-ranging as elections, public health, and race relations, is the fact that the focus of many policymakers has been on altering policies pertaining to social media platforms in ways that would actually facilitate the dissemination of more, rather than less, disinformation.[15] These efforts are directed at Section 230 of the Communications Decency Act, which grants digital platforms broad immunities from civil liability for the third-party content that they host. A key

---

[10]   Spicer (n 5).
[11]   *United States v Alvarez* [2012] (n 7) p. 718.
[12]   *Hustler Magazine, Inc. v Falwell* [1988] 485 US 46, p. 52.
[13]   *Brown v Hartlage* [1982] 456 US 45–61, p. 52.
[14]   *United States v Alvarez* [2012] (n 7) 2545.
[15]   Executive Order on Preventing Online Censorship (28 May 2020). https://www .whitehouse.gov/presidential-actions/executive-order-preventing-online-censorship/ accessed December 12, 2020; Limiting Section 230 Immunity to Good Samaritans Act (2020). 116th Congress, 2nd Session, https://www.hawley.senate.gov/sites/default/ files/2020-06/Limiting-Section-230-Immunity-to-Good-Samaritans-Act.pdf accessed December 12, 2020; U.S. Department of Justice (2020). Department of Justice's Review of Section 230 of the Communications Decency Act, https://www.justice.gov/ file/1319326/download accessed December 12, 2020.

provision of Section 230 is that no interactive computer service provider shall be subject to civil liability for:

> any action voluntarily taken in good faith to restrict access to or availability of material that the provider or user considers to be obscene, lewd, lascivious, filthy, excessively violent, harassing, or otherwise objectionable, whether or not such material is constitutionally protected.[16]

Efforts to revise, or limit the scope of, Section 230 liability immunity have been primarily directed at narrowing these reasons that platforms can filter content without incurring civil liability. So, for example, the National Telecommunications and Information Administration, acting in response to a White House executive order, petitioned the FCC to issue a regulation interpreting the 'otherwise objectionable' language in Section 230 as 'any material that is similar in type to obscene, lewd, lascivious, filthy, excessively violent, or harassing materials'.[17] Similarly, the US Department of Justice[18] proposed revising Section 230 by replacing the phrase 'otherwise objectionable' with 'unlawful'.[19] And, in the recently introduced Online Freedom and Viewpoint Diversity Act,[20] conservative members of Congress proposed replacing 'otherwise objectionable' language with the phrase 'promoting self-harm, promoting terrorism, or unlawful'.[21]

All of these proposed revisions seek to limit the extent to which social media companies will take action against false information posted to their platforms, by exposing them to civil liability for efforts to police the content on their platforms that extends beyond the narrower range of content categories that these proposals lay out. These proposed revisions thus compound the lack of government authority to intervene on the disinformation front with a potential reduction in social media platforms' incentives to intervene on the disinformation front.

These proposed revisions have been widely recognized as politically motivated efforts to compel large digital platforms to scale back the enforcement

---

[16]   47 USC § 230 (c) (2) (A).

[17]   National Telecommunications and Information Administration. *Petition for Rulemaking to Clarify Section 230 of the Communications Decency Act* (27 July 2020), 38 https://www.ntia.gov/fcc-filing/2020/ntia-petition-rulemaking-clarify-provisions -section-230-communications-act accessed December 12, 2020.

[18]   US Department of Justice (2020) (n 15).

[19]   (n 12) 1.

[20]   (n 3).

[21]   (n 3) 3.

of their disinformation-related content moderation policies.[22] The contention that these platforms actively seek to 'suppress conservative voices' has long been a rallying cry for these efforts.[23] However, the empirical evidence of such suppression efforts is lacking.[24] And, of course, any efforts to ascertain bias in social media platforms' content moderation policies need to take into consideration the very real possibility that, for whatever reason, conservative voices may in fact objectively violate platforms' policies regarding falsity more frequently and more aggressively than their liberal counterparts.[25]

But even more legitimately well-intentioned efforts to modify Section 230 would likely not do much to address the disinformation problem. As public interest advocate Harold Feld has noted, any targeted or complete elimination of Section 230 'would do little to get at the kinds of harmful content increasingly targeted by advocates'.[26] So, for instance, even absent Section 230, large swathes of disinformation that do not injure individual or organizational reputations through the violation of libel and defamation laws would remain unaffected.[27] As the Stigler Committee for the Study of Digital Platforms has

[22]   S Overton, 'Testimony before the Subcommittee on Elections, House Administration Committee, U.S. House of Representatives, Hearing on "Voting Rights and Election Administration: Combating Misinformation in the 2020 Election"' (6 October 2020) https://jointcenter.org/wp-content/uploads/2020/10/HHRG-116-HA08-Wstate-OvertonS-20201006.pdf accessed December 12, 2020; A Robertson, 'Let's Go through Trump's Terrible Internet Censorship Order, Line by Line' (29 May 2020) *The Verge* https://www.theverge.com/2020/5/29/21273191/trump-twitter-social-media-censorship-executive-order-analysis-bias accessed December 12, 2020.

[23]   See, e.g., S Bond, 'Trump Accuses Social Media of Anti-Conservative Bias after Twitter Marks His Tweets' (*NPR*, 27 May 2020) https://www.npr.org/2020/05/27/863422722/trump-accuses-social-media-of-anti-conservative-bias-after-twitter-marks-his-twe accessed December 12, 2020; C Young, 'How Facebook, Twitter, Silence Conservative Voices Online' (*The Hill*, 28 October 2016) https://thehill.com/blogs/pundits-blog/media/303295-how-facebook-twitter-are-systematically-silencing-conservative. accessed December 12, 2020.

[24]   See, e.g., O Darcy, 'Trump says Right Wing Voices are Being Censored. The Data says Something Else' *CNN* (New York, 28 May 2020) https://www.cnn.com/2020/05/28/media/trump-social-media-conservative-censorship/ accessed December 12, 2020; R Kraus, 'Once Again, There is no Anti-conservative Bias on Social Media' (*Mashable*, 28 July 2020) https://mashable.com/article/anti-conservative-bias-facebook/ accessed December 12, 2020.

[25]   A Guess, J Nagler and J Tucker, 'Less Than You Think: Prevalence and Predictors of Fake News Dissemination on Facebook' (2019) 5(1) *Science Advances*, eeau4586.

[26]   H Feld, *The Case for the Digital Platform Act: Breakups, Starfish Problems, and Tech Regulation.* (Public Knowledge and the Roosevelt Institute 2019) 141.

[27]   T Hwang, 'Dealing With Disinformation: Evaluating the Case for CDA 230 Amendment' (2017) http://dx.doi.org/10.2139/ssrn.3089442 accessed December 12, 2020.

noted, 'Section 230 is not directly related to some of the most problematic discourse harms, such as disinformation ...'.[28]

Other policy interventions that appear to be gaining traction, such as antitrust enforcement against the dominant digital platforms,[29] have no clear relationship to addressing the disinformation problem.[30] How does breaking up Facebook or Google, or forcing them to share data with competitors, counteract the disinformation problem? Perhaps the fragmentation of the social media audience would contribute to a reduction in the spread of disinformation. Or perhaps a more competitive social media marketplace would incentivize individual platforms to police disinformation more aggressively, as a means of attracting and retaining users. Such indirect effects may be a possibility, but these relationships are purely speculative.

Historically, US media policymakers have opted to use structural regulation as a means of indirectly affecting content, as a strategy for avoiding First Amendment challenges. So, for example, the FCC has employed broadcast licence allocation criteria that favour locally-based applicants in an effort to assure that communities receive more content that meets their particular needs and interests. Similarly, the FCC has adopted regulations designed to increase ownership of media outlets by under-represented groups in an effort to diversify the content available to audiences.[31] Such diversity goals could, in theory, be addressed by breaking up large platforms such as Facebook and Google; however, any logical grounds for a connection between breaking up these large platforms and diminishing the prominence of disinformation (or even increasing the prominence of news/information that effectively combats disinformation) are not at all clear.

The bottom line is that even indirectly addressing the disinformation problem is not a core goal of the antitrust efforts directed at digital platforms.

---

[28]  Stigler Committee for the Study of Digital Platforms (2019) Report of the Media Subcommittee, http://www.columbia.edu/~ap3116/papers/MediaReportFinal .pdf accessed December 12, 2020 p. 50.

[29]  See, e.g., House Judiciary Committee's Subcommittee on Antitrust, Commercial, and Administrative Law (2020). Investigation of Competition in Digital Markets, https://judiciary.house.gov/uploadedfiles/competition_in_digital_markets.pdf accessed December 12, 2020; *US v Google* (2020, October 20). Complaint filed in the United States District Court, District of Columbia Circuit, https://www.justice.gov/opa/press -release/file/1328941/download accessed December 12, 2020.

[30]  For an overview of this argument, see R H Frank, 'The Economic Case for Regulating Social Media' *New York Times* (New York, 11 February 2021) https://www .nytimes.com/2021/02/11/business/social-media-facebook-regulation.html accessed December 12, 2020.

[31]  P M Napoli, *Foundations of Communications Policy: Principles and Process in the Regulation of Electronic Media* (Hampton Press 2001).

In the 450-page report on competition in digital markets released by the House Judiciary Committee's Subcommittee on Antitrust, Commercial, and Administrative Law (2020),[32] the term 'disinformation' appears exactly once. One could even make the argument that a more fragmented social media landscape could make the policing of disinformation more erratic and piecemeal,[33] given the substantial resources that are needed to police disinformation effectively (something that even the largest and most well-resourced platforms have yet to achieve).

And so, tackling the disinformation problem on social media remains purely within the completely voluntary efforts undertaken by the platforms themselves.[34] Given their disappointing track record thus far, many have questioned whether the platforms are sufficiently incentivized to perform as well as they could;[35] which raises the question of whether some sort of government oversight could provide further incentive. Despite the broad First Amendment protections provided to false speech described in the previous section, there is in fact a precedent for such an approach.

## 2.   FEDERAL REGULATION OF DISINFORMATION: THE FCC'S BROADCAST HOAX AND NEWS DISTORTION RULES

Exploring this precedent involves revisiting a medium that is of steadily diminishing importance within the contemporary media ecosystem – terrestrial

---

[32]   House Judiciary Committee's Subcommittee on Antitrust, Commercial, and Administrative Law (n 30).

[33]   S Aral, 'Breaking Up Facebook Won't Fix Social Media' (3 September 2020) *Harvard Business Review*, https://hbr.org/2020/09/breaking-up-facebook-wont-fix -social-media accessed December 12, 2020.

[34]   F Nuñez, 'Disinformation Legislation and Freedom of Expression' (2020) *10*(2) *U.C. Irvine L Rev* 783.

[35]   P M Barrett, 'Social Media Can Be an "Arbiter of the Truth" After All' (*Politico*, 14 April 2020b) https://www.politico.com/news/agenda/2020/04/14/social -media-coronavirus-184438 accessed December 12, 2020; B Chakravorti, 'Social Media Companies Are Taking Steps to Tamp Down Coronavirus Misinformation – But They Can Do More (*The Conversation,* 30 March 2020) https://theconversation .com/social-media-companies-are-taking-steps-to-tamp-down-coronavirus -misinformation-but-they-can-do-more-133335 accessed December 12, 2020; E P Goodman, and K Kornbluh, 'Social Media Platforms Need to Flatten the Curve of Dangerous Misinformation' (*Slate*, 21 August 2020) https://slate.com/technology/ 2020/08/facebook-twitter-youtube-misinformation-virality-speed-bump.amp accessed December 12, 2020?; A Marantz, 'Why Facebook Can't Fix Itself' (*New Yorker*, 12 October 2020) https://www.newyorker.com/magazine/2020/10/19/why-facebook-cant -fix-itself accessed December 12, 2020.

broadcasting. In an era of more than 500 cable networks, online streaming of music and video, and countless mobile device applications, terrestrial broadcasting represents a shrinking slice of the overall media pie. Broadcasting as a means of accessing media content is practically alien to young people in the USA today. Viewers of broadcast television in the USA are, for the most part, approaching or past retirement age.[36] Even these viewers are, in most cases, not accessing broadcast signals directly, but rather through an intermediary such as a cable service provider or online streaming service, making broadcast transmission largely superfluous. So it is, admittedly, a bit odd to be looking to broadcasting for guidance as to how to regulate social media, a medium that would seem to have little in common with broadcasting.

But within the vast array of differences between broadcasting and social media are also some important similarities. Each, at their peak, has represented the most far-reaching and immediate distribution platform available. From a structural standpoint, each represents a model in which substantial gatekeeping authority is invested with a fairly limited number of gatekeepers. And the early history of each is inextricably intertwined with some of modern history's most significant advances in technologically-driven propaganda campaigning.[37] As technology journalist Julia Angwin recently stated, 'social media platforms are the broadcasting networks of the 21st century'.[38]

In sum, drawing upon models of broadcast regulation to inform current thinking about social media regulation may seem anachronistic at first blush; but the reality is that many analysts have come to recognize the ways in which social media have 'transformed the internet into something more like television'.[39] Therefore, looking to the broadcast medium for guidance may not be as outlandish as it initially seems,[40] particularly in light of the fact that broad-

---

[36] Marketing Charts, 'How the median age of TV viewers differs across platforms' (11 December 2018), https://www.marketingcharts.com/television/tv-audiences-and-consumption-106649 accessed December 12, 2020.

[37] Broadcasting in the case of the rise of Nazi Germany, see R L Bytwerk, *Bending Spines: The Propagandas of Nazi Germany and the German Democratic Republic* (Michigan State UP 2004), and social media in the case of 21st century election interference in the US, the UK, and many other national contexts, see Napoli, 2019a (n 2).

[38] J Angwin, 'Auditing the Algorithms of Disinformation'. (*The Markup*, 17 October 2020), 1. https://www.getrevue.co/profile/themarkup/issues/auditing-the-algorithms-of-disinformation-284735 accessed December 12, 2020.

[39] D Kay, *Speech Police: The Global Struggle to Govern the Internet* (Columbia Global Reports 2019), 12.

[40] See J Samples and P Matzko, 'Social Media Regulation in the Public Interest: Some Lessons From History' (Essay Series: The Tech Giants, Monopoly Power, and Public Discourse, Knight First Amendment Institute at Columbia University, 4 May 2020) https://knightcolumbia.org/content/social-media-regulation-in-the-public-interest-some-lessons-from-history accessed December 12, 2020.

casting represents the only medium in which regulations that directly address the dissemination of disinformation are in place.

The first of these regulations – the broadcast hoax rule – prohibits broadcast licensees from knowingly broadcasting false information concerning a crime or catastrophe, if the licensee knows beforehand that 'broadcasting the information will cause substantial "public harm"'.[41] This public harm must be immediate and cause direct and actual damage to the property, health, or safety of the general public, or divert law enforcement or public health and safety authorities from their duties.

From the standpoint of contemporary debates about disinformation, these restrictions reflect a fairly narrow range of what might be considered identifiable fake news. However, the references in this regulation to the health and safety of the American public naturally call to mind the ongoing (as of this writing) coronavirus pandemic. Indeed, the public interest advocacy organization, Free Press,[42] petitioned the FCC to investigate the possibility that broadcasters who disseminated false coronavirus information, through the broadcast of false statements uttered by President Trump during his coronavirus task force appearances, or through the distribution of programming containing similar falsities, such as the Rush Limbaugh Show, were in violation of this regulation. The FCC immediately denied Free Press's petition, contending that it is not the Commission's role to act as a 'self-appointed, free-roving arbiter of truth in journalism'[43] and that the concerns raised by Free Press extended beyond the narrow parameters of the broadcast hoax rule.

Since the late 1960s, the FCC has also maintained a more general policy that it will 'investigate a station for news distortion if it receives documented evidence of such rigging or slanting, such as testimony or other documentation, from individuals with direct personal knowledge that a licensee or its management engaged in the intentional falsification of the news'.[44] According to

---

[41]   Federal Communications Commission (n.d.). Consumer Guide: Broadcasting false information, http://transition.fcc.gov/cgb/consumerfacts/falsebroadcast.pdf accessed December 12, 2020.

[42]   Free Press, 'Emergency Petition for Inquiry Into Broadcast of False Information on COVID-19' (26 March 2020) https://www.freepress.net/sites/default/files/2020-03/free_press_petition_for_inquiry_to_fcc_re_broadcast_misinformation.pdf accessed December 12, 2020.

[43]   Federal Communications Commission, 'Letter Re: Free Press Emergency Petition for Inquiry Into Broadcast of False Information on COVID-19' (6 April 2020), 2 https://docs.fcc.gov/public/attachments/DA-20-385A1.pdf accessed December 12, 2020.

[44]   Federal Communications Commission, 'The Public and Broadcasting' (2008), 11 https://www.fcc.gov/media/radio/public-and-broadcasting#DISTORT accessed December 12, 2020.

the Commission, 'of particular concern would be evidence of the direction to employees from station management to falsify the news. However, absent such a compelling showing, the Commission will not intervene'.[45] Indeed, news distortion investigations have been rare (especially since the deregulatory trend that began in the 1980s), and have seldom led to any significant repercussions for broadcast licensees.[46]

That being said, the FCC's news distortion policy re-emerged recently. Specifically, in 2018, a dozen Democratic members of Congress wrote a letter to the FCC seeking a news distortion investigation of the Sinclair Broadcast Group.[47] Sinclair, which owns nearly 200 television stations across the USA, received a substantial amount of attention at the time for requiring anchors for the local newscasts that it produces across the country to read from the same centrally-produced scripts and for distributing to its stations highly polarizing, and often factually questionable 'must run' news/editorial segments.[48] As the members of Congress noted in their letter, 'Sinclair may have violated the FCC's long-standing policy against broadcasters deliberately distorting news by staging, slanting, or falsifying information.'[49] This request was also promptly declined, the very next day, with FCC Chairman Ajit Pai[50] (2018) citing his commitment to the First Amendment and freedom of the press.[51]

---

[45]   Federal Communications Commission, 2008, (n 44) 11.

[46]   C Raphael, 'The FCC's News Distortion Rule: Regulation by Drooping Eyelid' (2001) 6(3) *Communication Law & Policy* 485; for a detailed critique of the FCC's news distortion policy, see L Levi, 'Reporting the Official Truth: The Revival of the FCC's News Distortion Policy' (2000) *78(4) Washington University Law Quarterly* 1005.

[47]   M Cantwell and others, 'Letter to Ajit Pai, Chairman, Federal Communications Commission' (11 April 2018) https://www.cantwell.senate.gov/imo/media/doc/ 04112018%20Sinclair%20News%20Distortion%20Letter%20w%20Signatures.pdf accessed December 12, 2020.

[48]   J Fortin and J E Bromwich, 'Sinclair Made Dozens of Local News Anchors Recite the Same Script' (*New York Times*, 2 April 2018) https://www.nytimes.com/ 2018/04/02/business/media/sinclair-news-anchors-script.html accessed December 12, 2020.

[49]   Cantwell and others 2018 (n 47).

[50]   A Pai, 'Letter to the Honorable Maria Cantwell, U.S. Senate' (12 April 2018). https://cdn.arstechnica.net/wp-content/uploads/2018/04/ajit-pai-to-democrats-april -2018.pdf accessed December 12, 2020.

[51]   It is worth noting that Sinclair has subsequently received a fair amount of attention for disseminating coronavirus conspiracy theories and misinformation both through its news broadcasts and its websites (Farhi, 2020; Pleat, 2020), though these actions have yet to generate any similar push for the FCC to investigate. P Farhi, 'Sinclair Yanked a Pandemic Conspiracy Theory Program. But It Has Stayed in Line With Trump on Coronavirus' (*Washington Post,* 31 July 2020) https://www.washingtonpost .com/lifestyle/media/sinclair-yanked-a-pandemic-conspiracy-theory-program-but-it

As obscure as these regulations have been through much of their history,[52] their existence still runs counter to the expansive First Amendment protections for falsity outlined in the previous section. How can this contradiction be reconciled? The answer lies in a statement made by the FCC when the concept of the news distortion policy was first introduced in 1949: a broadcaster 'would be abusing his position as a *public trustee* of these important means of mass communications were he to withhold from expression over his facilities relevant news of facts concerning a controversy or to slant or distort the news'.[53] It is this notion of broadcaster as public trustee that is key to understanding why, in certain contexts, federal regulation of the dissemination of disinformation through electronic media is actually permissible within the highly protected standards for intentional falsity that have been established under the First Amendment.

## 3.    PUBLIC RESOURCES AND PUBLIC TRUSTEES IN ELECTRONIC MEDIA REGULATION

When we think about why we regulate media, it is important to recognize that there are two components to how we answer that question. The first component has to do with the underlying *motivations*. By motivations we mean the underlying problems being addressed and/or principles being pursued. Media regulations have, of course, been implemented on behalf of a wide range of motivations, ranging from protecting children from adult content, to preserving and promoting competition, to protecting domestic cultural expression, to enhancing the diversity of sources and content available to media users.[54]

In the US, with its strong First Amendment tradition, motivations alone are seldom adequate for facilitating regulatory interventions. These motivations must be accompanied by compelling *rationales*. Rationales, in this case, refers to technologically derived justifications for imposing regulations that, to

---

-has-stayed-in-line-with-trump-on-coronavirus/2020/07/31/5d90a296-d021-11ea-8c55 -61e7fa5e82ab_story.html accessed December 12, 2020; Z Pleat, 'Sinclair Stations Set to Air Eric Bolling Monologue Claiming Masks and Lockdown Precautions Do Not Help Slow the Spread of Covid-19' (*Media Matters for America,* 15 October 2020) https://www.mediamatters.org/sinclair-broadcast-group/sinclair-stations-set-air-eric -bolling-monologue-claiming-masks-and accessed December 12, 2020.

[52]    For a detailed historical analysis of the application of these policies, see J Timmer, 'Potential FCC Actions Against "Fake News": The News Distortion Policy and the Broadcast Hoax Rule' (2019) 24(1) *Communication Law & Policy* 1.

[53]    Federal Communications Commission, 'Editorializing by Broadcast Licensees' (1949) 13 FCC Rcd 1246, 1246. Emphasis added.

[54]    See Napoli 2019a, *Social Media and the Public Interest: Media Regulation in the Disinformation Age* (n 2).

a certain extent, infringe on media outlets' speech rights. The logic here is that certain characteristics of a medium may justify a degree of regulatory intervention. The underlying premise of this approach is that particular characteristics of a medium may warrant a greater emphasis on collective speech rights over individual speech rights; or that the medium may have a capacity for influence or harms that make some intrusion on speech rights permissible on behalf of the broader public interest. These rationales serve as a mechanism for pursuing regulatory objectives within the context of a free speech tradition that is intrinsically hostile to government intervention, regardless of the broader public interest values that these interventions might serve.

So, for instance, electronic media regulation in the USA has been justified by a wide range of medium characteristics. Broadcasting (and, to a lesser extent, cable television) have been regulated in part on the basis of these media being *uniquely pervasive*.[55] Failed efforts were even made to apply this uniquely pervasive characterization to the Internet back in the 1990s, when Congress was attempting to impose strict indecency regulations on online content providers.[56] Within these contexts, the notion of pervasiveness appears to relate to the distinctive reach, ease of access, and/or impact that certain media may have – particularly in relation to allowing children to be exposed to adult content.

Media such as cable and satellite television have been regulated on the basis that their functionality is *reasonably ancillary* to the functionality of other, more heavily regulated media (namely, broadcasting).[57] The logic here is that, to the extent that one medium serves an important role in the distribution of – and audience access to – another, more heavily regulated medium, then that more heavily regulated medium's regulatory framework may, to some extent, be imposed on the other medium.

Looking specifically at broadcasting, the most frequently utilized (as well as most frequently criticized) rationale for regulation is the notion that broadcasters utilize a *scarce public resource*.[58] Here, the key contention is that broadcasters' use of the broadcast spectrum represents the use of a publicly held resource for which more parties are seeking access than the spectrum can accommodate – thus justifying a governmental role in allocating the spectrum

---

[55]  J D Wallace, 1998, 'The Specter of Pervasiveness Pacifica, New Media, and Freedom of Speech' *CATO Institute* https://object.cato.org/sites/cato.org/files/pubs/pdf/bp-035.pdf accessed December 12, 2020.

[56]  P M Napoli, 'User Data as Public Resource: Implications for Social Media Regulation' (2019b) *11*(4) *Policy & Internet* 439.

[57]  For an overview of this rationale, see Napoli (n 2).

[58]  See C W Logan Jr, 'Getting Beyond Scarcity: A New Paradigm for Assessing the Constitutionality of Broadcast Regulation' (1997) *85*(6) *California L Rev* 1687.

and, to some extent, dictating behavioural guidelines for those privileged few granted access.

These rationales that have justified the regulation of previous generations of media have, over the years, been analysed and critiqued in depth.[59] Most of them do not hold up particularly well under scrutiny – a pattern that would suggest that the typical approach to media regulation is for policymakers to move forward on regulatory interventions on behalf of specific motivations, with the consideration and articulation of rationales being something of an afterthought to buttress these regulatory interventions against critiques of government overreach and any accompanying legal challenges.[60]

In the USA, what may be the most sound and resilient rationale that has been put forth for the regulation of broadcasting is the notion that broadcasters utilize a *public resource,* and as privileged users of this publicly held resource, must abide by certain fiduciary responsibilities that take the form of government-crafted and enforced public interest obligations. These public interest obligations can take the form of impositions on broadcasters' speech rights, but such impositions are, to some extent, permissible as conditions of access to the resource to which the broadcasters have been granted. As articulated by Logan, 'in return for receiving substantial benefits allocated by the government, broadcasters must abide by a number of public interest conditions that, in the absence of government allocation, would be found unconstitutional'.[61] This model is built upon the well-established notion that the broadcast spectrum is 'owned by the people'.[62] Consequently, 'the people' are entitled to specific types of public service above and beyond what broadcasters would provide free to audiences as part of their normal business practices.

This public resource, or *quid pro quo* rationale, as it is sometimes called[63] has been described as being 'overshadowed'[64] in legal discussions evaluating the constitutionality of broadcast regulation by scholars' and critics' emphasis on dissecting the logic of the associated scarcity rationale. It is important to distinguish between this scarcity rationale and the related public resource/*quid*

---

[59]   See e.g., T G Krattenmaker and L A Powe Jr, *Regulating Broadcast Programming* (Cambridge MA, MIT Press 1994); M L Spitzer, 'The Constitutionality of Licensing Broadcasters' (1989) *64*(5) *New York University L Rev* 990.

[60]   For further discussion of this issue, see Napoli (n 2).

[61]   Logan (n 58) 1732.

[62]   J W Berresford, 'The Scarcity Rationale for Regulating Broadcasting: An Idea Whose Time Has Passed' (2005) *Federal Communications Commission Media Bureau Staff Research Paper* https://transition.fcc.gov/ownership/materials/already-released/scarcity030005.pdf accessed December 12, 2020.

[63]   See e.g., Daniel P Graham, 'Public Interest Regulation in the Digital Age' (2003) *11*(1) *CommLaw Conspectus* 97; Spitzer, 1989 (n 59).

[64]   Logan (n 58) 1691.

*pro quo* rationale. As much as the two rationales are interconnected through the notion of the broadcast spectrum as a 'scarce *public* resource', it is important to emphasize that the public resource rationale can operate independently of the notion of scarcity. That is, as much as the logic of regulating a medium on the basis of its use of a resource that is 'scarce' is subject to a wide range of critiques,[65] the logic of regulating the medium on the basis of its use of a resource that is publicly-owned is inherently much more sound.[66] Even staunch opponents of media regulation have acknowledged that the public resource rationale is fundamentally stronger than the range of other, more fragile, rationales that have been articulated over the years.[67]

And so, obligations such as those described above that require broadcasters to abstain from the dissemination of disinformation, are permissible under the lower standards of First Amendment protection that are afforded to public trustees of a public resource – broadcast licensees. And, as much as broadcasting and social media are dramatically different communications technologies, as the next section illustrates, nevertheless social media platforms may in fact merit classification as public trustees of a very different public resource. And as public trustees, they then may be similarly prohibited from knowingly disseminating disinformation.

## 4.   SOCIAL MEDIA PLATFORMS AS PUBLIC TRUSTEES

Treating social media platforms as public trustees is not a new idea. The idea has been suggested elsewhere, though it has not been explored in much detail.[68]

---

[65]   Exploring these critiques is beyond the scope of this chapter; but see e.g., Krattenmaker and Powe, 1994 (n 59); Spitzer, 1989 (n 59).

[66]   And, importantly, the Supreme Court has acknowledged that the public resource/ *quid pro quo* rationale operates independently of the scarcity rationale. As the Court noted in the landmark *Red Lion Broadcasting v Federal Communications Commission*, 395 U.S. 367 (1969) decision, 'Even where there are gaps in spectrum utilization, the fact remains that existing broadcasters have often attained their present position because of their initial government selection' (at 400). The key point in this statement is the phrase 'even where there are gaps in spectrum utilization'. This phrase emphasizes that even in those contexts where the scarcity rationale does not hold up (because there is apparently more spectrum available than there is demand), the public interest regulatory framework imposed by the FCC still applies, on the basis of broadcasters' utilization of a government-allocated resource.

[67]   See e.g., Krattenmaker and Powe, 1994 (n 59).

[68]   See e.g., P M Regan, 'Reviving the Public Trustee Concept and Applying It to Information Privacy Policy' (2017) *76 Maryland L Rev* 1025; H Whitney, 'Search Engines, Social Media, and the Editorial Analogy' in D E Pozen (ed), *The Perilous Public Square: Structural Threats to Free Expression Today* (Columbia UP, in press)

In the U.K., a somewhat related concept has been developed – for a statutory 'duty of care' that encompasses policing for disinformation.[69] What has been missing, however, from these earlier discussions of social media platforms as public trustees is a detailed exploration of the established characteristics and criteria of the public trust model, and how those might apply in developing a regulatory framework for social media platforms. In the approach outlined here, we propose treating the massive aggregations of user data that serve as the economic foundation of these platforms as a *public resource.* Within the context of the public trust framework, this means treating aggregate user data as the *trust property* which effectively triggers the classification of the digital platforms as public trustees.

As a starting point for this analysis, it is important to flesh out the public trustee concept and the broader public trust doctrine in which it is embedded,[70] since the public trustee terminology has a tendency to be used somewhat loosely. The public trust doctrine has its origins in English common law, but with roots dating back to ancient Rome, where concepts such as *res publica* (a common asset) and *res communis* (property that is open to all) were first developed.[71]

The doctrine has become largely dormant in its country of origin,[72] but has become well-established in the USA and many other countries, typically in relation to environmental resources.[73] The public trust doctrine has its origins in the governance of natural resources such as waterways (and the preservation of public access to these waterways as transportation channels), but

---

115–149; T Wu, 'Is the First Amendment Obsolete?' in D E Pozen (ed), ibid., *The Perilous Public Square: Structural Threats to Free Expression Today* (Columbia UP, in press) 15–43.

[69]   Online Harm Reduction – a Statutory Duty of Care and Regulator https://d1ssu070pg2v9i.cloudfront.net/pex/carnegie_uk_trust/2019/04/08091652/Online-harm-reduction-a-statutory-duty-of-care-and-regulator.pdf accessed December 12, 2020.

[70]   See J L Sax, 'The Public Trust Doctrine in Natural Resources Law: Effective Judicial Intervention' (1970) 68(3) *Michigan L Rev* 471.

[71]   RA Epstein, 'Property Rights and Governance Strategies: How Best to Deal with Land, Water, Intellectual Property, and Spectrum' (2016) *14*(2) *Colorado Technology L J* 181.

[72]   M Willers and E Shirley, 'The Public Trust Doctrine's Role in Post-Brexit Britain' (*Garden Court Chambers,* 31 March 2017) https://www.gardencourtchambers.co.uk/news/the-public-trust-doctrines-role-in-post-brexit-britain accessed December 12, 2020.

[73]   M C Blumm and R D Guthrie, 'Internationalizing the Public Trust Doctrine: Natural Law and Constitutional Statutory Approaches to Fulfilling the Saxion Vision' (2012) *45 U.C. Davis L Rev* 741.

has expanded over time to include wildlife, parklands, and the atmosphere – including the electromagnetic spectrum.[74]

The public trust doctrine 'requires that certain property be used for public benefit, because of either its unique characteristics or its essentially public nature'.[75] A public trust involves three elements: (1) a *trustee*, who holds the trust property and is subject to *fiduciary duties* to deal with it for the benefit of another; (2) a *beneficiary*, to whom the trustee owes *fiduciary duties* to deal with the trust property for their benefit; and (3) a *trust property*, which is held by the trustee for the beneficiary.[76]

Typically, the government is the trustee of these natural resources and must manage them subject to fiduciary duties.[77] However, in some instances, the government essentially delegates trustee responsibilities to private actors. This is the case with the system of broadcast regulation in the USA, in which broadcast licensees receive access to the broadcast spectrum (but do not own it); and in exchange for such access are designated as public trustees of the airwaves.[78] As public trustees, these broadcasters have historically been subject to a wide range of fiduciary duties in the form of an ever-evolving set of public interest obligations, some of which represent intrusions upon their speech rights.[79] In addition, it is also important to note that government ownership of the resource has never been an inherent component of the public trust doctrine.[80, 81]

In the framework being proposed here, user data aggregators such as Facebook and Twitter are the trustees. The public whose personal data are being aggregated and monetized are the beneficiaries. The trust property, in this case, is the aggregate user data.

Obviously aggregate user data and the broadcast spectrum appear to have very little in common in terms of their resource characteristics. It is important to note, however, that the nature of the resources that fall within the public trust framework 'will necessarily change over time, as scientific knowledge

---

[74] D Quirke, 'The Public Trustee Doctrine: A Primer' (2016) White Paper, University of Oregon School of Law Environmental and Natural Resources Law Center.

[75] K Corbett, 'The Rise of Private Property Rights in the Broadcast Spectrum' (1996) 46 *Duke L J* 611, 615.

[76] Quirke (n 74) 2.

[77] Ibid.; Sax, 'The Public Trust Doctrine in Natural Resources Law' 1970 (n 70).

[78] *Red Lion Broadcasting v. FCC*, 1969 (n 66).

[79] See Napoli 2019b (n 56).

[80] D J Patalano, 'Police Power and the Public Trust: Prescriptive Zoning Through the Conflation of Two Ancient Doctrines' (2001) 28 *Boston College Environmental Affairs L Rev* 683.

[81] As Patalano, ibid. notes, in early public trust cases, 'legal title to common property vested ... in *the people*', (n 80) p. 709, emphasis in original.

and societal awareness advance'.[82] It has also been noted that application of the public trust doctrine has steadily expanded over time,[83] and that 'there is no theoretical reason why the public trust doctrine should be limited to disputes over the disposition of the public waterways or lands to which it has been applied traditionally'.[84] These observations from public trust scholars are particularly important as we consider the expansion of the public trust doctrine here to a new context – aggregate user data – as these observations help to justify expansion of the public trustee model to social media platforms.

## 5.    APPLYING THE PUBLIC TRUSTEE MODEL TO DOMINANT DIGITAL PLATFORMS: AGGREGATE USER DATA AS PUBLIC RESOURCE

As was noted above, the notion of treating large digital platforms as public trustees is not new. Regan, for instance, argues for a number of specific reasons why treating these platforms as public trustees would make sense. As she notes:

> First, the large online players are operating at the scope and scale where 'public interest, convenience, and necessity' demand that they be more regulated. Second, a public trustee approach avoids the somewhat messy issues of proving 'concentration' and anti-competitive behavior entailed in antitrust regulation. Third, the public trustee approach draws upon the link between privacy and trust that has emerged from public opinion surveys and the academic literature on privacy.[85]

A key point in this passage is that categorizing these platforms as public trustees could represent the most logical and effective point of entry for any regulatory interventions. Another key point is that the public trustee framework would only apply to those platforms operating at a scope and scale that trigger broader concerns about the public interest implications of how they operate and are being used. Reflecting this perspective, the proposal being put forth

---

[82]   Quirke (n 74) 8; see also J L Sax, 'Liberating the Public Trust Doctrine from Its Shackles' (1980) *14 UC Davis L Rev* 185.

[83]   H M Babcock, 'What Can Be Done, if Anything, About the Dangerous Penchant of Public Trust Scholars to Overextend Joseph Sax's Original Conception: Have We Produced a Bridge Too Far?' (2015) *23*(3) *New York University Environmental L J* 390.

[84]   P A Barresi, 'Mobilizing the Public Trust Doctrine in Support of Publicly Owned Forests as Carbon Dioxide Sinks in India and the United States' (2012) *23*(1) *Colorado Journal of International Environmental Law and Policy* 39, 51.

[85]   Regan 2017 (n 68), p. 1037.

here is similarly oriented, applying only to the most dominant platforms, while leaving smaller, upstart platforms free from public trustee burdens.

What is missing from Regan's[86] analysis, and from the other inquiries into the possibility of applying the public trustee doctrine to large digital platforms, is a clear articulation of the nature of the trust property at issue, and how it meets the public resource criteria that are traditionally associated with the type of resources that are treated as under public trust.

Accomplishing this task requires that we delve into the nature of user data, and the ambiguous and contested realm of the appropriate property status of such data. As a starting point, it is important to note that wide-ranging debate persists over whether individuals should have property rights over their user data.[87] Arguments for granting individuals property rights in their user data and arguments for denying individuals property rights in their user data both make compelling cases.[88]

The persistence of these debates can be attributed to the distinctive, ambiguous, and complex characteristics of user data as a resource. While there seems to be general agreement that user data represent a valuable resource, exactly what kind of resource they are remains difficult to pin down. The well-known 'data is the new oil' metaphor has been widely debated,[89] raising questions over if, or how, policymakers should treat user data as a natural, depletable resource like oil. The lack of a fully satisfactory analogy is highlighted by the fact that the World Economic Forum described personal data as a 'new asset class'.[90]

Given the novel, ambiguous character of user data, perhaps it is not surprising that 'no jurisdiction either in the US or Europe has adopted or comprehensively considered the option to legally introduce property rights in personal

---

[86]  Ibid.
[87]  For an overview, see Napoli 2019b (n 56).
[88]  P M Napoli, 'Defining Data' (2020b) *47*(4) *InterMedia* 36–40.
[89]  See e.g., A Hasty, 'Treating Consumer Data Like Oil: How Re-Framing Digital Interactions Might Bolster the Federal Trade Commission's Privacy Framework' (2015) *67*(2) *Federal Communications L J* 293–323; D Hirsch, 'The Glass House Effect: Big Data, the New Oil, and the Power of Analogy' (2014) *66*(2) *Maine L Rev* 374; B Marr, 'Here's Why Data Is Not the New Oil' *Forbes* (5 March 2018) Retrieved from https://www.forbes.com/sites/bernardmarr/2018/03/05/heres-why-data-is-not-the-new-oil/#6ab9b0623aa9 accessed December 12, 2020; 'The World's Most Valuable Resource Is No Longer Oil, but Data' *The Economist* (6 May 2017) Retrieved from https://www.economist.com/leaders/2017/05/06/the-worlds-most-valuable-resource-is-no-longer-oil-but-data accessed December 12, 2020.
[90]  World Economic Forum, 'Personal Data: The Emergence of a New Asset Class' (An Initiative of the World Economic Forum, January 2011) 5.

data'.[91] In the USA, while some lawmakers have embraced the notion that 'you own your data', no legislation formalizing this perspective has yet to make it through Congress.[92]

In Europe, the General Data Protection Regulation (GDPR) is perhaps the most comprehensive effort to date to impose a concrete regulatory framework on the aggregation and usage of user data; yet it falls short of establishing users' explicit property rights in their data. As Daniel Chase (2018) describes the GDPR, 'While the EU's dignity-approach might cringe at the idea of personal data as property, their regulatory approach practically embodies property rights law. Though property is not mentioned once in the EU's GDPR, its protections ... are all crucial elements of American property law.'[93] Yet the GDPR's provisions 'stop short of confirming that personal data can definitively be considered property'.[94] In fact, the term 'property' is almost completely absent from the text of the GDPR, appearing only twice in relation to tangential issues.[95] Thus, some form of 'quasi-property rights' may be inherent in personal data, which suggests that 'there are perhaps additional dimensions to the ongoing ... debate that are yet to be fully explored'.[96]

The debates and policy initiatives centred on the question of property rights in user data would seem to indicate that, while some form of property rights is appropriate, traditional notions of individual property rights do not quite fit. In sum, the situation described thus far seems to indicate that we need 'A new paradigm for understanding what data is – and what rights pertain to it'.[97]

---

[91]    N Purtova, 'The Illusion of Personal Data as No One's Property (2015) 7(1) *Law, Innovation and Technology* 83, 85.

[92]    R McNamee, *Zucked: Waking up to the Facebook Catastrophe* (Penguin Press 2019).

[93]    D Chase, 'Who Owns the Data? An Argument for a Property Rights Approach to Transatlantic Data Protection' *Medium* (22 May 2018), 5 https://medium.com/ @Daniel_Chase_/who-owns-the-data-an-argument-for-a-property-rights-approach-to -transatlantic-data-protection-ddc5cc8fc212 accessed December 12, 2020; see also H Pearce, 'Personality, Property and Other Provocations: Exploring the Conceptual Muddle of Data Protection Rights Under EU Law' (2018) *4*(2) *European Data Protection L Rev* 190.

[94]    Pearce, ibid., 201.

[95]    Specifically, in relation to the use of user data in the workplace to protect employee or customer property; and in relation to the provision requiring data aggregators to provide users with remote access to their personal data, but not in a way that would facilitate access to the aggregators' intellectual property (which is being treated as something separate from the aggregate user data).

[96]    For a more detailed discussion, see Pearce 2018 (n 93) 208.

[97]    M Tisne, 'It's Time for a Bill of Data Rights' *MIT Technology Review* (14 December 2018) https://www.technologyreview.com/s/612588/its-time-for-a-bill-of -data-rights/ accessed December 12, 2020.

The proposal being put forth here is an effort to flesh out such a new paradigm. The recommendation here is that we approach property rights in user data not from an individual property rights perspective, but rather from a collective property rights perspective. That is, we think about aggregate user data as a collectively-owned resource – 'owned by the people' in a manner similar to how policymakers in the US approach the broadcast spectrum.[98] Such an approach would not only capture some of the distinguishing characteristics of user data described above; it would also reflect where the value in user data resides.

Whatever the exact nature of someone's individual property rights in their own user data, when these data are aggregated across millions of users, their fundamental character changes in such a way that they are best conceptualized as a public resource. Certainly, it is in this massive aggregation that the economic value of user data emerges. As Tisne notes, 'contemporary technology markets extract value from collective data'; however, '[o]ur laws respond to individual harms and have not changed to reflect changes in technology'.[99] Similarly, Zuboff notes that:

> Individual users' meanings are of no interest to Google or other firms ... In this way, the methods of production of 'big data' from small data and the ways in which 'big data' are valued reflect the formal indifference that characterizes the firms relationship to its population of 'users.' Populations are the sources from which data extraction proceeds.[100]

Also, collective benefits arise when individual-level data are aggregated, as this allows for the observation of broader patterns that might otherwise go unnoticed, or the formulation of generalizable insights.[101] This is why Tisne[102] notes that 'cumulatively, [data] is a *collective good*'. Thus, in this collective formulation of a valuable resource, we should consider a form of collective ownership.

Reflecting this position, some privacy advocates have suggested that recent legislative proposals to require platforms to determine and disclose to individ-

---

[98]  See Berresford, 2005 (n 62).

[99]  M Tisne, 'The Data Delusion: Protecting Individual Data Isn't Enough When the Harm Is Collective' (2020) Stanford Cyber Policy Center White Paper https://cyber.fsi .stanford.edu/publication/data-delusion accessed December 12, 2020, p. 4.

[100]  S Zuboff, 'Big Other: Surveillance Capitalism and the Prospects of an Information Civilization' (2015) *30*(1) *Journal of Information Technology* 75, 79.

[101]  Tisne, 2018 (n 97).

[102]  Ibid., emphasis added.

ual users the value of their data[103] are fundamentally problematic. Instead, they propose a collective negotiation model, in which individuals band together to form a 'privacy union' to collectively negotiate the value of their aggregate data and the terms and conditions for its use.[104] As Zuboff[105] has argued, 'Data ownership is an individual solution when collective solutions are required.'

The presence of this value in the aggregation of user data can be seen as a form of value transfer for which the public should be compensated above and beyond the free service that the individual user receives from the platform. This proposal to treat aggregate user data as a public resource obviously involves a substantial reorientation in terms of how policymakers and platforms approach user data, which has generally involved a continuum ranging from individual ownership to platform ownership. Collective ownership clearly represents something very different, particularly in terms of the regulatory interventions it potentially facilitates.

To illustrate this point, it is worth delving a bit more deeply into the analogy with the broadcast spectrum. From a property standpoint, spectrum has been characterized as a common asset, or what the Romans termed *res publica*.[106] This concept serves as the foundation for the public trust doctrine, a characterization that seems particularly well-suited to aggregate user data as well, given the unique resource characteristics of user data described above.

In both the spectrum and user data cases, there is a public character to the resource. Also in both cases, there is no expectation that this resource is legitimately accessible by the entirety of the public.[107] Rather, the access limitations inherent in the resource compel the imposition of public service obligations upon those who do obtain access, in order to assure that the public accrue benefits from their collectively held resource.

---

[103] For example, the Designing Accounting Safeguards to Help Broaden Oversight and Regulations on Data Act. 2019. 116th Congress, 1st Session.

[104] G Barber, 'Senators Want Facebook to Put a Price on Your Data. Is That Possible?' (*Wired*, 26 June 2019) https://www.wired.com/story/senators-want-face book-price-data-possible/ accessed December 12, 2020.

[105] S Zuboff, 'It's Not That We've Failed to Rein in Facebook and Google. We've Not Even Tried.' *The Guardian* (2 July 2019) https://www.theguardian.com/ commentisfree/2019/jul/02/facebook-google-data-change-our-behaviour-democracy accessed December 12, 2020.

[106] M Calabrese, 'Battle over the Airwaves: Principles for Spectrum Policy Reform' (2001) New American Foundation Working Paper.

[107] In the broadcast context, this brings us to the contested notion of scarcity. In the social media context, we certainly do not want or expect these platforms to grant widespread public access to these user data aggregations, for a variety of privacy and security reasons.

In this way, both the broadcast spectrum and aggregate user data are somewhat different from traditional public resources, where the guiding logic of the public trustee model is typically to assure public access. This is not the goal in the spectrum and user data contexts. In these contexts, access to a collectively owned resource is inherently limited to a privileged few, which is a key part of what requires these privileged few to operate as public trustees.

Finally, perhaps most important in drawing this analogy between the broadcast spectrum and aggregate user data is re-emphasizing that, within the context of broadcast regulation, this public trustee framework has been deemed sufficient by policymakers and the courts to justify a limited degree of content-based regulation,[108] including regulations directed at dissemination of disinformation (see above). That is, once an entity has been granted access to the public resource (the broadcast spectrum, in this case), this triggers a *quid pro quo,* in which that entity relinquishes some degree of freedom of speech in order to abide by a set of public interest obligations associated with access to that resource.

Transferring this model to the social media context means that those platforms with privileged access to sufficiently large aggregations of user data to be considered a public resource would enter into a similar *quid pro quo* relationship, involving adherence to a set of public interest obligations. These obligations could involve policing/filtering certain types of content and/or amplifying other types of content. The key point here is that, through treating aggregate user data as a public resource, such content-related public interest obligations would be premised on a rational basis that has proven capable of withstanding First Amendment scrutiny.

## 6.    SCOPE AND LIMITATIONS

Given the significant implications of this proposal (in terms of providing a justification for content-based regulation of social media platforms), it is important to consider how the application of this public trustee framework to digital platforms might work. As a first step in this regard, it is important to explicitly lay out the fairly limited scope of what is being proposed here.

First, as much as the broadcast spectrum model has been drawn upon as an analogy, the proposal being put forth here is not intended to – and need not – generate any kind of comparable government-licensing model for digital platforms. Rather, the argument here is that once a firm becomes a user data aggregator/monetizer of sufficient size/scope, the public interest obligations

---

[108]    See e.g., *Red Lion Broadcasting v Federal Communications Commission,* 1969 (n 66).

associated with being a public trustee kick in. Thus, digital platforms would be subject to public interest obligations, but not any kind of associated licensing scheme.

Along related lines, the argument being put forth here is not intended to establish a point of entry for any notion of government ownership of – or access to – the aggregations of user data that fall within the public resource framework being advocated here. Admittedly, there is a very real danger of a slippery slope in this regard, given that government control of a resource is typically central to the public trustee model. For this to work, then, the 'owned by the people' philosophy, espoused in relation to the broadcast spectrum, needs to become much more literal in the aggregate user data context than it has been in the broadcast spectrum context. As much as it is 'owned by the people', the broadcast spectrum is, for all intents and purposes, owned and allocated by the federal government on behalf of the people. This clear delineation would need to be part of any regulations or policies drafted along the lines described above.

Within the context of aggregate user data, 'owned by the people' should be more closely connected to true collective ownership and decision-making. This is because the process of granting access to the public resource in question is a collective decision, contributed to each time an individual agrees to engage with a digital platform. When enough of these individual decisions are made, and the platform's user base reaches a certain size, the aggregation of these individual decisions to grant a platform access to a user's data means that the public trustee governance framework becomes effective – without the government obtaining any kind of privileged position in relation to the data. As was noted previously, the notion of a public resource, and the associated public trust doctrine, are not inherently tied to government ownership of that resource.[109, 110]

In this regard, it is also important to emphasize that application of the public trustee model to digital platforms does not represent *carte blanche* for government regulation of these platforms, just as the public trustee model in US broadcasting has not meant *carte blanche* for government regulation of broadcasting. Instead, what developed in broadcasting was a regulatory framework that, while more extensive than what is applied to other media, still represents fairly limited intrusions into the speech rights of broadcasters; and, according to some interpretations, provides a logical and constitutionally

---

[109]   Patalano 2001 (n 80); Sax 1970 (n 70).
[110]   As Patalano (2001) notes, in Professor Joseph Sax's landmark piece revitalizing the public trust concept, 'Sax originally premised his theory on the ability of citizens to step in and force government action' (n 80) 716.

sound counterweight to the unregulated media sector.[111] We could similarly consider application of the public resource rationale to the data aggregations of social media platforms, and the public interest obligations associated with these aggregations, as a counterweight to the largely unregulated space of the broader Internet, where the regulatory rationale being proposed here would not apply.[112]

In order to thoroughly delineate the limitations of what is being proposed here, it is also important to make clear why the notion of aggregate user data as a public resource applies only to large social platforms and not to advertiser-supported media in general (which all involve the monetization of some form of user data). This is because the model under which traditional ad-supported media have operated and the model under which large social platforms operate are different in a number of fundamental ways.

First, traditional ad-supported media have monetized audience data derived from relatively small samples of media users, who have knowingly volunteered to take part in the measurement process and typically receive compensation for doing so.[113] This is very different from the digital platform model, in which all users must agree to the terms of data extraction in exchange for access to an increasingly necessary communications platform, and certainly nobody is receiving financial compensation in exchange for having their data aggregated.

Second, even when the audience measurement systems for other media involve a census rather than a sample (think, for instance, of traffic audits for web sites), the scope of the user data that can be gathered through such an approach is infinitesimal compared to what can be gathered through large digital platforms, given that this approach involves measuring activity through the prism of the site, rather than through the monitoring of actual users.[114] Monitoring individual sites, and how users engage with them, provides dramatically less data about the users than monitoring users and their behaviour directly as they move across the Internet and engage with platforms such as social media sites and search engines.

Third, the data aggregation for other ad-supported media has traditionally been conducted not by the media outlets themselves, but rather by third-party

---

[111]  See L C Bollinger, *Images of a Free Press* (University of Chicago Press 1991).

[112]  Napoli 2019a (n 2).

[113]  P M Napoli, *Audience Economics: Media Institutions and the Audience Marketplace* (Columbia UP 2003).

[114]  P M Napoli, P J Lavrakas, and M Callegaro, 'Internet and Mobile Audience Ratings Panels' in M Callegaro, R Baker, J Bethlehem, A S Goritz, J A Krosnick and P J Lavrakas (eds), *Online Panel Research: A Data Quality Perspective* (Wiley 2014) 387–407.

measurement firms[115] (Nielsen, comScore, and so on), in a long-standing 'separation of powers' model[116] that seems to have been dismantled in the digital platform context. This model is largely missing from the data aggregation and monetization conducted by social media platforms, for instance.

Fourth, and plainest, the scale and scope of data gathering that can be undertaken by large social platforms dwarfs what can be achieved in almost any other mediated communication context, given the size of user bases and the breadth and depth of information users provide through the various means of interacting with the platforms. On this front, it is important to mention the additional data points that can be reliably imputed from these data when they are being extracted from such a large user base.[117] Other digital media entities, such as Internet Service Providers (ISPs) and web sites cannot come close to matching the breadth and depth of user data that large social media platforms are able to accumulate. Facebook is reported to have over 29 thousand data points on the average user.[118] Only Google, through its cross-platform data gathering (search, email, YouTube, maps, and others) extracts comparable amounts of user data.[119]

Finally, it is important to emphasize that application of the public trustee model to social media platforms as proposed in this chapter is targeted at a select few platforms, and not at aggregators of user data in general. The logic here is that only when platforms reach a certain size/scope in their user data gathering do they cross the threshold into the realm of public trustee. In this way, the approach being put forth here is similar to recent arguments to treat the most dominant digital platforms as 'essential facilities'.[120]

Essentially, only user data aggregations of a to-be-determined size meet the threshold of a public resource. This approach is consistent with calls for a regulatory framework that is targeted at only the largest, most dominant platforms, and that allows smaller and upstart firms to operate without comparable regulatory burdens. In addition, this proposal is directed primarily at those user data aggregators who simultaneously operate as content distributors, given that the proposal's core motivation is to address how content-related platform regulation could operate within the confines of the First Amendment. That being said, one could potentially argue that the notion of user data as a public

---

[115] Nielsen, comScore, etc.
[116] Napoli 2003 (n 113).
[117] Purtova (n 91).
[118] McNamee (n 92).
[119] Ibid.
[120] See e.g., N Guggenberger, 'Essential Platforms' (in press) *Stanford Technology L Rev.*

resource may have broader applicability, such as to the massive aggregations of user data accumulated by large consumer analytics firms.

All of this raises the question of exactly what it should take for a social media platform to qualify as a public trustee of aggregate user data. How many users must a platform have before their user data aggregation triggers the public trustee framework? At what scale does the aggregation of user data meet the criteria of a public resource? As a starting point for thinking about these questions, we can look to current examples in which user-base thresholds have been used as a trigger for the application of a particular regulatory framework. Germany's Network Enforcement Act, for example, applies once a social networking platform reaches a threshold of two million users. As another example, recent legislation introduced in the USA to scale back Section 230 liability immunity is limited to platforms with either 30 million US users or 300 million global users and more than $1.5 billion in global revenue.[121] Ultimately, answering this question is likely to end up being more of a political process than an empirical process, but certainly more work needs to be done to inform the discussion of the exact applicational parameters that are appropriate for this proposal.

A user-base threshold alone may be insufficient, given that some platforms may develop large user bases, but in theory might not gather and monetize user data as a core element of their business model – in which case, classifying them as a public trustee would not be consistent with the logic being put forth here. So, perhaps in addition to a user-base threshold, there would need to be an accompanying threshold that takes into consideration the scope of data gathering being undertaken (in terms, e.g., of the number of data points gathered per user); and/or in terms of the extent to which the monetization of user data is central to the platform's revenue model.

## 7.    CONCLUSION

The primary goal of this chapter has been to consider whether a more prominent federal role in the oversight of social media platforms' efforts to police disinformation could be pursued via drawing upon the public trustee governance model that is utilized within the context of broadcast regulation. Further work in this area is necessary, as is work that delineates the specific federal roles and responsibilities in the realm of addressing disinformation on social media, and that does so in a way that does not send us down the dangerous path of some kind of Orwellian Ministry of Truth (in reality, there is very

---

[121]  Limiting Section 230 Immunity to Good Samaritans Act (2020) (n 15).

little danger of this, in light of the strong – if somewhat more limited – First Amendment protections that broadcasters have enjoyed).

Nonetheless in so moving from theory to practice, the reality is that, at the time of this writing (February, 2021), the reluctantly-departed Trump administration reinforced long-standing reasons for opposing any type of federal intervention in the media sector.[122] Moving forward, then, any regulatory intervention needs to be constructed with this worst case scenario in mind.

At the same time, efforts in this direction need to acknowledge and build upon the fact that the large social media platforms have recently taken what appear to be much more aggressive efforts to operate as socially responsible gatekeepers in relation to harmful content such as disinformation, including more aggressive stances against disinformation originating from political actors, and also removing content containing coronavirus disinformation and QAnon conspiracy theories.[123] From this standpoint, these platforms have, to some extent, adopted a voluntary public trustee governance model akin to what we see in the journalism sector in the USA, where public interest principles have long been central to the professional codes that guide news organizations. However, whether these platforms are doing all that they should, and are enforcing their policies consistently, remains open to debate.[124]

With these considerations in mind, perhaps the best approach for building upon the ideas presented in this chapter would involve the federally man-

---

[122]  P M Napoli, 'Social Media Platforms Genuinely Need Some Form of Regulation' (2020a) *The Hill*, https://thehill.com/opinion/technology/501705-social-media-plat forms-genuinely-need-some-form-of-government-regulation accessed December 12, 2020.

[123]  See e.g.., V Gadde and K Beykpour, 'Additional Steps We're Taking Ahead of the 2020 U.S. Election' (*Twitter Blog*, 9 October 2020) https://blog.twitter.com/en _us/topics/company/2020/2020-election-changes.html accessed December 12, 2020; J Horwitz, 'Facebook Removes Trump's Post About Covid-19, Citing Misinformation Rules' *Wall Street Journal* (6 October 2020) https://www.wsj.com/articles/facebook -removes-trumps-post-about-covid-19-citing-misinformation-rules-11602003910 accessed December 12, 2020; J Shieber, 'YouTube Bans Videos Promoting Conspiracy Theories Like QAnon That Target Individuals' (*TechCrunch*, 15 October 2020) https:// techcrunch.com/2020/10/15/youtube-bans-videos-promoting-conspiracy-theories-like -qanon-that-target-individuals/ accessed December 12, 2020.

[124]  Kari Paul Aten, 'Here are all the steps social media made to combat misinformation. Will it be enough?' (*The Guardian*, 30 October 2020) https://www.theguardian .com/technology/2020/oct/29/here-are-all-the-steps-social-media-made-to-combat -misinformation-will-it-be-enough accessed December 12, 2020; C Tardaguila, 'Without Methodology or Transparency, Facebook and Twitter Become the "Arbiters of Truth"' (15 October 2020) *Poynter* https://www.poynter.org/fact-checking/2020/ without-methodology-or-transparency-facebook-and-twitter-become-the-arbiters-of -the-truth/ accessed December 12, 2020.

dated creation of an independent, multi-stakeholder governance body that oversees and audits content filtering and moderation procedures of dominant social platforms, and that develops and enforces explicit criteria and performance benchmarks related to the algorithmic treatment and policing of harmful content such as disinformation. To some extent, the platforms are already taking their own limited steps in this direction, with actions such as Facebook's recent creation of its Oversight Board,[125] and with some platforms, such as Facebook and Google, relying heavily upon accredited third-party fact-checking organizations.[126]

This move toward a more co-regulatory approach that emphasizes third-party oversight has been endorsed and fleshed out by other analysts of the social media dilemma[127] though such proposals tend not to include disinformation as overtly within the scope of responsibilities, as is being proposed here. Elsewhere,[128] we have proposed adapting the congressionally mandated self-regulatory apparatus that oversees the audience measurement industry in the USA (the Media Rating Council) to the oversight of social media platforms, though with modifications that grant the oversight body more expansive regulatory authority than is currently the case with the Media Rating Council (which lacks enforcement capabilities).

Such an approach keeps direct decisions about the veracity of individual social media posts, or about the accuracy/reliability of individuals or organizations utilizing these platforms, beyond the direct reach of government decision-makers, while at the same time relaxing the also-problematic stranglehold that a small number of platform decision-makers have over the flow of news and information.[129]

It is important to note that even Facebook has expressed a willingness to embrace regulatory frameworks that: (1) require platforms to have certain systems and procedures in place to reduce the availability and spread of

---

[125] N Clegg, 'Welcoming the Oversight Board' (6 May 2020) *Facebook Newsroom* https://about.fb.com/news/2020/05/welcoming-the-oversight-board/ accessed December 12, 2020.

[126] Tardaguila 2020 (n 124).

[127] See e.g., T Wheeler, P Verveer and G Kimmelman, 'New Digital Realities; New Oversight Solutions in the U.S. The Case for a Digital Platform Agency and a New Approach to Regulatory Oversight' (2020) Harvard Shorenstein Center White Paper https://shorensteincenter.org/new-digital-realities-tom-wheeler-phil-verveer-gene -kimmelman/ accessed December 12, 2020.

[128] P M Napoli and A B Napoli, 'What Social Media Platforms Can Learn from Audience Measurement: Lessons in the Self-Regulation of Black Boxes (2019) *24*(12) *First Monday.* http://dx.doi.org/10.5210/fm.v24i12.10124 accessed December 12, 2020.

[129] Tardaguila 2020 (n 124).

harmful content; and (2) require companies to meet specific performance targets for content that violates their policies.[130] The establishment of such systems, procedures, and performance targets places us firmly in the realm of the notion of public interest obligations for digital platforms, an approach that appears to be gaining traction amongst a variety of analysts of the current situation.[131] The growing prominence of this perspective suggests that the contention put forth at the outset of this chapter, namely that the regulatory frameworks developed for traditional media do indeed have some relevance for contemporary digital media challenges, is becoming more widespread. The next step in this work is to outline the specific public interest obligations that should be layered upon the foundation established here, of social media platforms as public trustees.

---

[130] M Bickert, 'Online Content Regulation: Charting a Way Forward' (2020) Facebook White Paper, https://about.fb.com/wp-content/uploads/2020/02/Charting-A-Way-Forward_Online-Content-Regulation-White-Paper-1.pdf accessed December 12, 2020.

[131] See eg, K Kornbluh and E Goodman, 'Safeguarding Digital Democracy: Digital Innovation and Democracy Initiative Roadmap no. 4' (2020) German Marshall Fund https://www.gmfus.org/sites/default/files/Safeguarding%20Democracy%20against%20Disinformation_v7.pdf accessed December 12, 2020; Napoli 2019a (n 2); Samples and Matzoko (n 40); Stigler Committee (n 28); Wheeler, Verveer and Kimmelman (n 127).

# 5.    Artificial intelligence is not a panacea: policing content on social media platforms, three dilemmas and their ethical and legal implications

**Jingrong Tong**

## 1.    INTRODUCTION

The advent and application of artificial intelligence (AI) cannot resolve the dilemmas of policing content on social media sites, which require the updating of ethical and regulatory systems. The birth of the Internet in the 1970s has facilitated the pursuit of free speech. Policing content (user-generated-content) on the Internet, seen as an emblem of censorship and media control, comes into conflict with freedom of speech, a fundamental value of democracy. However, the recent occurrence of tragic, violent events indicates that the world has come to a turning point where a balance needs to be struck between maintaining freedom of expression on the Internet and protecting users and the health of speech in the public domain. Two events of this kind are the 'ethnic cleansing' and exodus of Rohingya Muslims since 2017[1] and the 2018 anti-Muslim riots in Sri Lanka,[2] where the violence may have been fuelled by hate speech on social media.[3] A new reality sinking in is that content moderation may be much

---

[1]    The BBC, 'Myanmar Rohingya: what you need to know about the crisis' *The BBC News* (23 January 2020) www.bbc.co.uk/news/world-asia-41566561 accessed 1 August 2020.

[2]    Zaheena Rasheed and Irfan Cader, 'Sri Lanka on the "brink" amid fresh anti-Muslim violence' *Aljazeera* https://www.aljazeera.com/news/2018/03/sri-lanka -brink-fresh-anti-muslim-violence-180307203031915.html accessed 7 August 2020.

[3]    Steve Stecklow, 'Why Facebook is losing the war on hate speech in Myanmar' *Reuters* https://www.reuters.com/investigates/special-report/myanmar-facebook-hate/ accessed 7 August 2020; Aljazeera, 'Sri Lanka: Facebook apologises for role in 2018 anti-Muslim riots' *Aljazeera* https://www.aljazeera.com/news/2020/05/sri-lanka -facebook-apologises-role-2018-anti-muslim-riots-200513101243101.html accessed 7 August 2020; Anisa Subedar accessed 7 August 2020.

needed for the sake of democratic ideals and the wellbeing of our societies. The urgency to deal with the prevalence of misinformation, disinformation and hate speech, along with worries over predators such as paedophiles preying on children and other victims online, is one of the primary reasons behind the new reality.

As for policing content on the Internet, in authoritarian countries such as China, governments have made it clear – as part of their state-level internet censorship policies – that Internet portals and online intermediaries should shoulder the (legal and regulatory) responsibility for removing (politically) 'inappropriate' content from the Internet. Such content moderation aims to help secure and solidify the rule of governments. By contrast, in democratic contexts, while states usually do not directly interfere in online speech, social media companies such as Facebook and Twitter have become the agents of policing content on their platforms. Their content moderation policies and the implementation of these policies determine the actions to take to tackle inauthentic, harmful and hateful content on their sites. As private businesses with commercial interests, social media firms have to consider their relationship with users and advertisers when designing their policies. Social media firms face practical difficulties caused by the large amount of content sent to their sites, in cleaning up such content entirely and in time. Neither human content moderators nor AI-driven automated algorithms offer perfect solutions for sanitising social media content. Meanwhile, with their content policed, users' rights of freedom of speech may be violated and compromised. All of these – the conflict between free speech and content moderation, the private business nature of social media companies, the expectation for social media firms to shoulder public responsibility, and the practical difficulties and complexity in detecting and removing content, along with the passage of an increasing number of government regulations regulating social media companies – have created dilemmas, prompting a rethink of the responsibilities of social media companies, governments, and users.

This chapter identifies and unpacks three dilemmas relating to (1) public trust, (2) freedom of information, and (3) liability, faced by social media platforms in terms of their policies and practices of content moderation and the implications for ethics and law. These dilemmas reflect the complex relationship between social media platforms, users, and governments. This relationship transforms alongside changes in politics and societies. In light of cleaning up social media content, the chapter contends that states, social media companies, and users should each play their respective role. It would be beneficial to increase collaboration between states and social media firms in tackling problems involving social media content, although both state and corporate powers should be restricted. Social media users also need to share the responsibility for maintaining social media hygiene with awareness of limiting and balancing the powers of states and corporate companies.

## 2.    CONTENT MODERATION AND SOCIAL MEDIA

Content moderation on the Internet – 'the practice of cleaning up digital pollution'[4] – is not a new phenomenon. Indeed, there has been a long history of moderating and sanitising Internet content by online intermediaries – referring to Internet 'service providers that facilitate interactions on the internet between natural and legal persons' like search engines and social media platforms.[5] In authoritarian countries, the state has passed government regulations on the responsibilities of both users and online intermediaries. Take China, for example. The government has hired an enormous army of moderators to cleanse online content by deleting posts that are (politically) inappropriate, in particular those threatening the legitimacy of the ruling party – the Chinese Communist Party (CCP) – and national security. There are also legal and regulatory requirements that Internet intermediaries should remove any (politically) inappropriate content, for which they are legally liable. With their laws and regulations, the Chinese government can decide to remove online materials damaging government legitimacy and prosecute those users who publish such content. During the COVID-19 crisis in 2020, for example, a number of Internet users were arrested across China for publishing 'fake' content on the Internet.[6] Among others, whistleblower Li Wenliang was punished for warning his colleagues in a social media group of the possible outbreak of an infectious disease. In democratic countries, however, content moderation extensively depends on big tech companies' self-regulation, which is complemented by government regulations and laws.[7] These firms have developed their own policies for content moderation.

Content moderation can occur before content is sent to its destination or after content has appeared online.[8] Most social media companies are taking an AI–human hybrid approach to content moderation, which mixes the use of AI and automation tools and human content moderators. Algorithms (supervised

---

[4]    Lisa Parks, 'Dirty data: Content moderation, regulatory outsourcing, and the cleaners' (2019) 73 *Film Quarterly* 11, 11.

[5]    'Internet Intermediaries' (*Council of Europe Portal*) www.coe.int/en/web/ freedom-expression/internet-intermediaries accessed 12 May 2020.

[6]    *The Paper*, www.thepaper.cn/newsDetail_forward_5653965 accessed 29 April 2020.

[7]    Tarleton Gillespie, *Custodians of the Internet: Platforms, Content Moderation, and the Hidden Decisions That Shape Social Media* (Yale University Press 2018).

[8]    Ofcom, *Use of AI in Online Content Moderation* (2019).

machine learning), semi-automated content moderation, or human content moderators have been used to screen, review and remove online content. Algorithms automate batch removal – they normally use computational analysis and techniques such as those of natural language processing (NLP), sentimental analysis or optical character recognition (OCR) skills or rely on a block list to automatically detect and then block, filter or delete certain content.[9] However, the capabilities of algorithms in detecting and removing content are limited. In particular, videos, images and memes pose a great challenge to the automated detection of online content. Instagram, for example, has started to ban content with tags associated with pro-eating disorders; however, their moderation practices, automatically detecting lexical variants in tags, are seen as ineffective due to an increase over time in 'lexical variation'.[10] As a result, human intervention is still necessary, and human content moderators can even play an important role in machine learning semi-automated content moderation. Such human intervention may also happen after AI technologies have performed initial moderation – if some content is uncertain or if content is removed, but users appeal.[11]

Social media platforms such as Facebook, Twitter, and YouTube have hired (human) content moderators to conduct painstaking day-to-day content moderation in this laborious process: by 2018, Facebook had hired 7,500 content moderators.[12] For most of the time, after users report potentially harmful and offensive content to social media platforms, human content moderators review the content manually according to the guidelines they are given, and they will remove it if it qualifies as banned content. The involvement of human content moderators is useful, particularly in cases that involve multimedia content, for example videos or images. However, human content moderators may be unable to cope with content on an enormous scale, which AI and automation tools would work better to handle. For example, after the mass shooting at Christchurch mosques in New Zealand in 2019, YouTube had to use AI

---

[9]    See summary of key AI technologies in the *Use of AI in Online Content Moderation* report (ibid).

[10]    Stevie Chancellor and others, '#thyghgapp: Instagram content moderation and lexical variation in pro-eating disorder communities' (Proceedings of the 19th ACM Conference on Computer-Supported Cooperative Work & Social Computing).

[11]    Cambridge Consultants, https://www.ofcom.org.uk/__data/assets/pdf_file/0028/157249/cambridge-consultants-ai-content-moderation.pdf accessed 15 April 2020.

[12]    Julia Carrie Wong and Olivia Solon, 'Facebook releases content moderation guidelines – rules long kept secret' *The Guardian* https://www.theguardian.com/technology/2018/apr/24/facebook-releases-content-moderation-guidelines-secret-rules accessed 15 April 2020.

software to remove the videos of the shooting uploaded to the site as human moderators could not deal with the flood of videos.[13]

Different social media companies have their in-house policies for controlling content appearing on their sites. A wide spectrum of materials, which are on the list of content moderation and to be reviewed and removed, include disinformation, misinformation, pornography, hate speech, propaganda content that may interfere in political conflicts or elections, content from war zones, content advocating terrorism, cruel content involving the abuse, torture and killing of humans and animals, 'any material that is designed to be shocking, prurient or offensive by nature'.[14] Top banned issues such as sex, violence, terrorism, and hate speech are common across different companies.

These big tech companies are publishing and updating their policies in line with developing realities. Facebook, for example, revised and clarified its community standards on content involving areas such as violence, nudity, hate speech, self-harm and sexual exploitation in 2016[15] and decided to ban 'white nationalism and separatism content' in 2019.[16] Despite these published standards, there are some transparency-related issues surrounding the use of human moderators and AI technologies. Although platforms should be obliged to 'make the moderation visible',[17] most users are unaware of how content moderation works, while human content moderators (as well as AI and automation technologies) remain invisible to the public eye.

In the 2010s, the need to moderate online content became increasingly urgent, in the wake of the prevalence of misinformation, disinformation and hate speech[18] on the Internet in general, and in particular social media

---

[13]   Isobel Asher Hamilton, 'YouTube's human moderators couldn't stem the deluge of Christchurch massacre videos, so YouTube benched them' (*Business Insider*, 18.3.2019)   www.businessinsider.com/youtube-benched-humans-and-used-ai-to-deal -with-christchurch-massacre-2019-3?r=US&IR=T accessed 15 April 2020.

[14]   Sarah T. Roberts, 'Digital refuse: Canadian garbage, commercial content moderation and the global circulation of social media's waste' 10 *Journal of Mobile Media*; Jillian C. York and Ethan Zuckerman, 'Moderating the public sphere' in Rikke Frank Jørgensen (ed), *Human Rights in the Age of Platforms* (The MIT Press 2019).

[15]   Stuart Dredge, 'Facebook clarifies policy on nudity, hate speech and other community standards' *The Guardian* (16 March 2015) www.theguardian.com/technology/ 2015/mar/16/facebook-policy-nudity-hate-speech-standards accessed 20 April 2020.

[16]   Lois Beckett, 'Facebook to ban white nationalism and separatism content' *The Guardian* (27 March 2019) www.theguardian.com/technology/2019/mar/27/facebook -white-nationalism-hate-speech-ban accessed 20 April 2020.

[17]   Gillespie (n 7) 199.

[18]   Minna Ruckenstein and Linda Lisa Maria Turunen, 'Re-humanizing the platform: Content moderators and the logic of care' 22 *New Media & Society* 1026; Giovanni Luca Ciampaglia, 'Fighting fake news: a role for computational social

platforms.[19] Associated with the rise of fake news is the use of political advertising to propagandise by using disinformation or misinformation.[20] Though its impact on elections has not been proved, disinformation or fake news is blamed for having possibly meddled in elections and referenda such as the 2016 US presidential election,[21] the 2016 Brexit referendum[22] and the 2019 UK general election.[23] The UK government had 'judged the Russian state promulgated at least 38 false disinformation narratives around this criminal act', although 'the Government has not seen evidence of successful use of disinformation by foreign actors, including Russia, to influence UK democratic processes'.[24] During the COVID-19 crisis in 2019–20, which has turned out to be an 'infodemic',[25] false statements, ranging from 5G conspiracy theories to bleach-as-a-miracle-cure claims, have been thriving on social media sites.

---

science in the fight against digital misinformation' 1 *Journal of Computational Social Science* 147.

[19]   Kai Wiggins, *Unprecedented Increase Expected in Upcoming FBI Hate Crime Report* (2018) https://www.aaiusa.org/unprecedented_increase_expected_in _upcoming_fbi_hate_crime_report accessed 7 August 2020; Binny Mathew and others, 'Spread of hate speech in online social media' (Proceedings of the 10th ACM conference on web science); Giovanni Luca Ciampaglia, 'Fighting fake news: a role for computational social science in the fight against digital misinformation' 1 *Journal of Computational Social Science* 147.

[20]   Samantha Bradshaw and Philip N Howard, *Challenging Truth and Trust: A Global Inventory of Organized Social Media Manipulation* (2018); Iva Nenadić, 'Unpacking the "European approach" to tackling challenges of disinformation and political manipulation' (2019) 8 *Internet Policy Review*.

[21]   Craig Silverman, 'This analysis shows how viral fake election news stories outperformed real news on Facebook' *BuzzFeedNews* https://www.buzzfeednews.com/ article/craigsilverman/viral-fake-election-news-outperformed-real-news-on-facebook accessed 20 April 2020.

[22]   Pa Mediapoint, Facebook 'fake news' as bad now as during Brexit referendum, ex-Cambridge Analytica employee claims (2020) https://pressgazette.co.uk/ facebook-fake-news-as-bad-now-as-during-brexit-referendum-ex-cambridge-analytica -employee-claims/ accessed 20 April 2020; Matthew Field and Mike Wright, 'Russian trolls sent thousands of pro-Leave messages on day of Brexit referendum, Twitter data reveals' *The Telegraph* https://www.telegraph.co.uk/technology/2018/10/17/russian -iranian-twitter-trolls-sent-10-million-tweets-fake-news/ accessed 20 April 2020.

[23]   *Financial Times*, How fake news is influencing the UK election (2019) www.ft .com/video/85514f6e-7121-4335-8c2b-7029d0652fa0 accessed 20 April 2020; Olivia Goldhill, 'Politicians are embracing disinformation in the UK election' *Quartz* https:// qz.com/1766968/uk-election-politicians-embrace-fake-news-disinformation/ accessed 20 April 2020.

[24]   House of Commons, *Disinformation and 'fake news': Interim Report: Government Response to the Committee's Fifth Report of Session 2017–19* (2018).

[25]   John Zarocostas, 'How to fight an infodemic' 395 *The Lancet* 676; Cristina M. Pulido and others, 'COVID-19 infodemic: More retweets for science-based information on coronavirus than for false information' (2020) *International Sociology* 377.

In addition to fake news, misinformation and disinformation, the wildfire of hate speech spreads widely and rapidly on social media platforms.[26] According to the definition given by the Council of Europe Committee of Ministers, 'hate speech' refers to 'all forms of expression which spread, incite, promote or justify racial hatred, xenophobia, anti-Semitism or other forms of hatred based on intolerance, including: intolerance expressed by aggressive nationalism and ethnocentrism, discrimination and hostility against minorities, migrants and people of immigrant origin'.[27] Hate speech is 'speech that vilifies individuals or groups on the basis of such characteristics as race, sex, ethnicity, religion, and sexual orientation, which (1) constitutes face-to-face vilification, (2) creates a hostile or intimidating environment, or (3) is a kind of group libel'.[28] The Internet, and particularly social media platforms, has provided an ideal space for hate groups and actors to express and circulate hate messages.[29] Online hate speech has great ramifications and could turn into offline violence and actual hate crimes or create a precondition for hate crimes.[30] For this reason, it is necessary to detect and restrict the dissemination of hate speech on the Internet so as to protect users from harmful content. These recent developments – such as fake news, misinformation, disinformation and hate speech – in social media communication generate and justify an urgent need for content moderation, although this could mean restrictions on expression online and have potential repercussions for freedom of speech.

In democratic contexts, for the sake of the fundamental value of free speech, states presumably should not directly interfere in online speech. Social media companies are thus expected to shoulder the responsibility for retaining the health of speech in the public domain, and they are encouraged to self-regulate.[31] In other terms, different social media platforms (are allowed to) adopt their in-house policies and decide their own practices. Over recent years, we have seen the diverse policies and policy adjustments of social media companies. In 2016, both Facebook and Google blocked access by

---

[26] Natalie Alkiviadou, 'Hate speech on social media networks: Towards a regulatory framework?' 28 *Information & Communications Technology Law* 19.
[27] 'Recommendation No. R (97) 20 of the Committee of Ministers to member states on "hate speech"' (30 October 1997).
[28] Susan J. Brison, 'The autonomy defense of free speech' 108 *Ethics and Information Technology* 312, 313.
[29] James Banks, 'Regulating hate speech online' 24 *International Review of Law, Computers & Technology* 233; Binny Mathew and others, 'Spread of hate speech in online social media' (Proceedings of the 10th ACM Conference on Web Science).
[30] Teona Gelashvili, 'Hate Speech on Social Media: Implications of private regulation and governance gaps ' (Lund University 2018).
[31] Article19, *Self-regulation and 'hate speech' on social media platforms* (2018).

fake news sites to their advertising networks.[32] In 2018, Facebook released its content moderation guidelines[33] to increase transparency.[34] In 2019, Twitter announced a ban on all political advertising from its site. This was in contrast to Facebook, which decided to continue to carry political advertising and stop fact-checking political advertisements.[35] Reddit, however, relies on a volunteer moderator system.

Social media companies, which are private businesses, have to consider striking a balance between their commercial interests on the one hand and public duty on the other. Their policies may not be seen as beneficial to the health of online speech and democracies, nor may their content moderation practices be thought to be favorable for society. A prominent example is the aforementioned different policies of Facebook and Twitter on political advertising – one of their main sources of advertising income. In 2019, Facebook and Twitter announced opposite decisions about their content policies. While Twitter decided to prohibit all political advertising from its platform, Facebook, as mentioned above, chose to allow the publication of political advertising and stop fact-checking political advertisements. Their differing decisions have catalysed debates about the rights and obligations of social media platforms. These discussions give rise to questions including: how would the content moderation policies of social media platforms influence public trust in them and freedom of expression in society? And who should bear the legal liability for content published on social media sites? These questions point to three interrelated dilemmas of content moderation faced by social media firms: dilemmas related to freedom of speech, public trust, and liability. The next section of the chapter will explore these three dilemmas in detail.

---

[32]  Kaveh Waddell, 'Facebook and Google won't let fake news sites use their ad networks' *The Atlantic* (15 November 2016) www.theatlantic.com/technology/archive/2016/11/facebook-and-google-wont-let-fake-news-sites-use-their-ads-platforms/507737/ accessed 30 April 2020.
[33]  'Facebook Community Standards (September 2020) www.facebook.com/communitystandards/recentupdates/all_updates accessed 20 April 2020.
[34]  Wong and Solon (n 12).
[35]  Julia Carrie Wong, 'Twitter to ban all political advertising, raising pressure on Facebook' *The Guardian* https://www.theguardian.com/technology/2019/oct/30/twitter-ban-political-advertising-us-election accessed 20 April 2020.

# 3.    THREE DILEMMAS

## 3.1    Freedom of Expression and Public Trust

Closely related, the first and second dilemmas are discussed in this section. To clarify, the first dilemma is associated with freedom of expression, while the second is about public trust. Freedom of speech is one of the fundamental democratic principles, allowing ordinary individuals the right to speak and share their ideas and opinions with the aim of promoting 'a democratic culture'.[36] In the United States (USA), for example, the First Amendment protects online speech from being restricted by government regulations.[37] However, free speech should not be equated with the anarchic autonomy of individuals being able to say anything they wish, nor is exercising freedom of speech identical with encouraging the freedom to harm and hate. Toxic content such as that involving bullying, online stalking and harassment, troll, porn and child sexual exploitation can be materialised to offline crimes and have profound and stark repercussions. All these problems have justified the sanitising of social media content to attain community health and safety, although at the same time users' rights of free speech should be respected and retained as much as possible. The right to disseminate detrimental content such as pornography, hateful statements, Holocaust denial, and false political and commercial statements should be restricted to avoid direct and indirect harm to audiences and third parties.[38] Publishing and propagating harmful content that may ignite or incite discrimination against minority groups, violence, sexual exploitation, terrorism, racism and sectarianism should be limited for the sake of democracy.

Absolute freedom of speech – that is, allowing any content to appear and circulate on social media platforms – would put users and especially those disadvantaged in society at risk, and so will not win trust from users. Removing harmful and hateful content would be one effective solution, *inter alia*, to address the worsening of digital pollution and online preying, bullying and harassment, if it is difficult to identify and remove predators. Good content moderation practices can help polish the corporate brand of social media companies. Being unable to do so would lead to public blame and eventually

---

[36]    Jack M. Balkin, 'Digital speech and democratic culture: A theory of freedom of expression for the information society' 79 *NYU L Rev*.
[37]    John Samples, 'Why the government should not regulate content moderation of social media' 865 *Cato Institute Policy Analysis*.
[38]    Leif Wenar, 'The value of rights' in Joseph Keim Campbell, Michael O'Rourke and David Shier (eds), *Law and Social Justice* (The MIT Press 2005); but there are counter-arguments seeing such content should not be restricted for the sake of intrinsic value of freedom of speech and autonomy (ibid); Brison (n 28) 312.

to loss of public trust. Social media companies such as Twitter[39] and Reddit (in 2018)[40] have already faced criticism from users for permitting racist material to stay on their platforms or being too slow to remove such materials from their sites. In 2018, a survey revealed that Facebook had become the least-trusted big tech company, one important reason for which being its content moderation policies and practices.[41]

Apart from the aforementioned cases of anti-Muslims in Myanmar and Sri Lanka, other cases involving victims of hateful or harmful content have frequently occurred over recent years. In 2017, Molly Russell committed suicide after seeing graphic self-harm content on Instagram, and her father believed Instagram 'helped kill' the 14-year-old.[42] That year, the child protection mechanism of YouTube was reported to have broken down, and YouTube and Facebook failed to remove sexualised child material.[43] In 2019, the AI of Facebook was unable to detect the New Zealand mosque shooting video[44] before it was viewed some 4,000 times.[45] Other social media platforms such as YouTube and Twitter had the same problem of scrambling to remove a live video of the shooting.[46] The same year, TikTok, a Video app, was found to have been failing to remove sexual content targeting children and teenagers

---

[39]    Casey Newton, 'Why Twitter has been slow to ban white nationalists' (*The Verge*, 26 April 2019) www.theverge.com/interface/2019/4/26/18516997/why-doesnt -twitter-ban-nazis-white-nationalism accessed 20 April 2020.

[40]    Nick Statt, 'Reddit CEO says racism is permitted on the platform, and users are up in arms' (*The Verge*, 11 April 2018) www.theverge.com/2018/4/11/17226416/reddit -ceo-steve-huffman-racism-racist-slurs-are-okay accessed 20 April 2020.

[41]    Rani Molla, 'Facebook is the least-trusted major tech company' (*Voxmedia*, 10 April 2018) www.vox.com/2018/4/10/17220060/facebook-trust-major-tech-company accessed 20 April 2020.

[42]    Angus Crawford, 'Molly Russell: Instagram extends self-harm ban to drawings' *The BBC News* (28 October 2019) www.bbc.co.uk/news/technology-50129402 accessed 20 April 2020; Angus Crawford, 'Instagram "helped kill my daughter"' *The BBC News* (22 January 2019) www.bbc.co.uk/news/av/uk-46966009/instagram-helped -kill-my-daughter accessed 20 April 2020.

[43]    Mike Wendling, 'YouTube child protection mechanism "failing"' *The BBC News* (5 August 2017) www.bbc.co.uk/news/blogs-trending-40808177 accessed 20 April 2020; Angus Crawford, 'Facebook failed to remove sexualised images of children' *The BBC News* (7 March 2017) www.bbc.co.uk/news/technology-39187929 accessed 20 April 2020.

[44]    During his attacks, the shooter used Facebook Live to stream his killings in 2019.

[45]    Lauren Feiner, 'Facebook explains why its A.I. didn't detect the New Zealand mosque shooting video before it was viewed 4,000 times' (*The CNBC* 2019) www.cnbc .com/2019/03/21/why-facebooks-ai-didnt-detect-the-new-zealand-mosque-shooting -video.html accessed 20 April 2020.

[46]    Reed Stevenson and Michael Tighe, 'Facebook, YouTube Blindsided by Mosque Shooter's Live Video' *Bloomberg* (15 March 2019) www.bloomberg.com/news/

and other hate speech.[47] These cases have woken the public up to the danger of damaging social media content. Public trust is the trust of an individual or members of a social group, which can be influenced by their personal experience or media representations.[48] The reporting of these cases would lead to an increase in public distrust in social media sites.

Therefore, a complete commitment to absolute freedom of expression would damage public trust in social media companies. Let alone the public, the employees of social media companies may criticise their employers' stance on misinformation or hate speech, as shown in the case of Facebook in 2020 where the Facebook boss was held in contempt by early employees over his attitude toward Trump posts.[49] Big tech companies are trying to meet the expectation to shoulder social responsibility and stop the spread of misinformation and disinformation. During the COVID-19 outbreak, for example, Facebook (temporarily) banned ads and commercial lists selling medical face masks and its Instagram removed misinformation about COVID-19.[50] Google[51] and Twitter[52] also adjusted their policies to handle the same problem. Google forcefully banned virus ads and took down from YouTube videos claiming cures or preventing infection.[53] Social media sites, such as Facebook, Twitter, and Instagram, fact-checked and even removed or hid posts by Donald

---

articles/2019-03-15/facebook-youtube-blind-sided-by-mosque-shooter-s-live-video accessed 20 April 2020.

[47] Marco Silva, 'Video app TikTok fails to remove online predators' *The BBC News* (5 April 2019) www.bbc.co.uk/news/blogs-trending-47813350 accessed 20 April 2020.

[48] Evelien van Der Schee and others, 'Public trust in health care: a comparison of Germany, the Netherlands, and England and Wales' 81 *Health Policy* 56.

[49] Mike Isaac, 'Early Facebook employees disavow Zuckerberg's stance on Trump posts' *The New York Times* https://www.nytimes.com/2020/06/03/technology/facebook-trump-employees-letter.html accessed 10 August 2020.

[50] Kang-Xing Jin, 'Keeping people safe and informed about the Coronavirus' Facebook (19 August 2020) https://about.fb.com/news/2020/04/coronavirus/#limiting-misinfo accessed 15 September 2020.

[51] Jack Webb, 'Google bans face mask adverts to help stop spreading misinformation about coronavirus ' *Evening Standard* https://www.standard.co.uk/tech/google-ban-coronavirus-face-mask-adverts-a4385596.html accessed 20 April 2020.

[52] 'Coronavirus: Staying safe and informed on Twitter' (*Twitter Inc. Blog*, 3 April 2020) https://blog.twitter.com/en_us/topics/company/2020/covid-19.html accessed 20 April 2020.

[53] Mark Bergen and Gerrit De Vynck, 'Google scrubs Coronavirus misinformation on Search, YouTube' *Bloomberg Technology* https://www.bloomberg.com/news/articles/2020-03-10/dr-google-scrubs-coronavirus-misinformation-on-search-youtube accessed 20 April 2020.

Trump for misinformation or hate speech.[54] Of course, the actions of social media companies triggered retaliation from the American President at the time, who, for example, quickly issued an 'Executive Order on Preventing Online Censorship', although this was criticised for misinterpreting Section 230.[55]

While allowing any information to appear online in the exercise of free speech may invite blame and condemnation, at the same time social media companies' content moderation does not guarantee winning over public trust, due to the worry of content moderation impairing freedom of speech – as already noted, one of the fundamental democratic values and principles. Social media companies' content moderation policies have been criticised for practising censorship or being opaque and inconsistent. This is partly because no matter how important, practising content moderation has the potential of undermining the democratic promises of the Internet and the principles of social media companies, as it curbs freedom of expression. This is partly because users do not have much faith in the content moderation systems of social media companies, which lack transparency and consistency.[56]

The Internet in general and social media platforms in particular have the democratic potential of acting as a civic space for members of the public to gather, connect, share information, and express their views. There have been examples in and beyond the West that online communication has played a leveraging role in political events, catalysing and boosting social change. Prominent examples include the events of Sun Zhigang and SARS in 2003

---

[54] Sonam Sheth, 'Instagram hid a photo Donald Trump Jr. posted because it contained "partly false information"' *The Business Insider* https://www.businessinsider.com/instagram-hides-donald-trump-jr-photo-partly-false-information-2020-4?r=US&IR=T 16 August 2020; Alex Hern, 'Twitter hides Donald Trump tweet for "glorifying violence"' *The Guardian* https://www.theguardian.com/technology/2020/may/29/twitter-hides-donald-trump-tweet-glorifying-violence 16 August 2020; Deepa Seetharaman, 'Facebook, Twitter take down video of Trump saying children "almost immune" from Covid-19' *The Wall Street Journal* https://www.wsj.com/articles/facebook-twitter-take-down-video-of-trump-saying-children-almost-immune-from-covid-19-11596674533 accessed 16 August 2020; Shona Ghosh, 'After four years of timidity, Facebook and Twitter are finally taking basic steps to curb Trump's worst instincts' *The Business Insider* https://www.businessinsider.com/facebook-twitter-finally-stood-up-trump-2020-6?r=US&IR=T accessed 16 August 2020.

[55] Anna Wiener, 'Trump, Twitter, Facebook, and the future of online speech' *The New Yorker* https://www.newyorker.com/news/letter-from-silicon-valley/trump-twitter-facebook-and-the-future-of-online-speech accessed 16 August 2020.

[56] H. Tworek and others, *Dispute Resolution and Content Moderation: Fair, Accountable, Independent, Transparent, and Effective* (2020) A working paper of the Transatlantic Working Group on Content Moderation Online and Freedom of Expression.

in China,[57] the 2010 'We are all Khaled Said' campaign in Egypt, the Arab Spring, the 'occupy' movements (both in 2011), and the global #MeToo movement (from 2006 and especially from 2017 onwards). Although social dynamics and tensions played a crucial role in these events, the Internet, supporting and facilitating free speech, offered a boost to their development.

Big Internet companies such as Google (and YouTube), Facebook, and Twitter have embraced and advocated the 'utopian' principle of freedom of expression. For example, freedom of expression is in the code of conduct of Google,[58] while Twitter was defined as 'the free speech wing of the free speech party' by its then manager in 2012.[59] Facebook sees itself as 'a service for more than two billion people to *freely express* themselves across countries and cultures and in dozens of languages' (italics added).[60] Mark Zuckerberg, the CEO of Facebook, defends the site's decision not to fact-check political advertising as a protector of 'free expression'.[61]

Only a fine line differentiates between content moderation and censorship, and content moderation can pose an immense menace to free speech. For example, abiding by a new law adopted by the Turkish parliament in July, 2020, social media companies have to comply with governmental requests to remove content. Adoption of the law is seen as practising censorship by critics, whilst the government sees it as protecting users from fake news and harmful content.[62] Online content moderation has been common practice in authoritarian countries like China with the paramount aim of suppressing dissidents and protecting the rule of the state. In authoritarian contexts, policing online content is a manifestation of censorship as it limits freedom of expression. Even in democratic contexts, in spite of the global imperative to sanitise social

---

[57]  Eunju Chi, 'The Chinese government's responses to use of the Internet' 36 *Asian Perspective* 387.

[58]  'Google code of conduct' (*Alphabet Investor Relations*, last updated 31 July 2018) https://abc.xyz/investor/other/google-code-of-conduct/ accessed 16 August 2020.

[59]  Josh Halliday, 'Twitter's Tony Wang: "We are the free speech wing of the free speech party"' *The Guardian* (22 March 2012) www.theguardian.com/media/2012/mar/22/twitter-tony-wang-free-speech accessed 16 August 2020.

[60]  'Facebook community standards' www.facebook.com/communitystandards/ accessed 16 August 2020.

[61]  Kari Paul, 'Zuckerberg defends Facebook as bastion of "free expression" in speech' *The Guardian* https://www.theguardian.com/technology/2019/oct/17/mark -zuckerberg-facebook-free-expression-speech accessed 16 August 2020.

[62]  See 'Turkey's president cracks down on social media', *The Economist* (6 August 2020) www.economist.com/europe/2020/08/08/turkeys-president-cracks-down-on-so cial-media accessed 12 August 2020.

media content, moderating content on social media platforms by social media companies also has strong implications for freedom of expression.[63]

While content moderation sets up filters and gatekeepers through which content flows and is sieved, concerns arise over political and commercial influences on content moderation, posing a threat to freedom of speech. The political control of authoritarian countries, or societies in transition, is one major force influencing social media companies' content moderation policies and suppressing freedom of speech. Take China for example. Google was severely criticised for removing 'don't be evil' from its founding principles, when it decided to self-censor its content as a compromise to China's great firewall in 2006 after the launch of Google.cn.[64] The move by Google originated from its commercial interest in the massive market in China.[65] Although Google left China in 2010 over the country's censorship, surveillance and crackdowns on dissidents and human rights activists,[66] it sought to return to the country by offering a censored search engine – the Dragonfly, which, however, failed to take off after an internal confrontation from its employees.[67] Facebook was found to have censored and hidden protest-related posts during the Arab Spring, presumably under political pressure by related governments.[68]

Political influence could also involve the influence of ideologies and social values of social media companies which are reflected in their (implementation of) content moderation policies. Facing diverse values and ideologies, social media companies need to decide to support certain ideologies and values over others. Their policies are blamed for being biased. For example, some social groups are protected against hate speech more than others. According to the company's hate speech rules, migrant groups do not receive the same protec-

---

[63]   Jillian C. York and Ethan Zuckerman, 'Moderating the public sphere' in Rikke Frank Jørgensen (ed), *Human Rights in the Age of Platforms* (The MIT Press 2019).

[64]   John Naughton, 'Google's founding principles fall at great firewall of China' *The Guardian* https://www.theguardian.com/business/2006/jan/29/china.theobserver accessed 16 August 2020; James S. O'Rourke, Brynn Harris and Allison Ogilvy, 'Google in China: government censorship and corporate reputation' 28 *Journal of Business Strategy* 12.

[65]   James S. O'Rourke, Brynn Harris and Allison Ogilvy, 'Google in China: government censorship and corporate reputation' 28 *Journal of Business Strategy* 12.

[66]   Christopher R. Hughes, 'Google and the great firewall' 52 *Survival: Global Politics and Strategy* 19; Cynthia Liu, 'Internet censorship as a trade barrier: A look at the WTO consistency of the great firewall in the wake of the China–Google dispute' 42 *Georgetown Journal of International Law* 1199.

[67]   Ryan Gallagher, 'Google's secret China project "effectively ended" after internal confrontation' https://theintercept.com/2018/12/17/google-china-censored-search-engine-2/ accessed 16 August 2020.

[68]   Zeynep Tufekci, *Twitter and Tear Gas: The Power and Fragility of Networked Protest* (Yale University Press 2017).

tion from Facebook against hate speech,[69] and their policies still allow content promoting white nationalism and separatism and advocating the creation of white-only states.[70] During the COVID-19 crisis, in spite of social media companies pledging to deal with misinformation and disinformation, false statements and assertions, such as that by Elon Musk,[71] still stayed online, and related social media companies refused to remove them. British politicians accused social media firms, in particular Facebook, Google and Twitter, of failing to answer questions about how they were handling disinformation in the coronavirus outbreak.[72]

The complexity of related issues and the diverse interests and values of communities and groups have deepened the difficulty of moderating social media content, but, meanwhile, still respecting freedom of expression as much as possible. Some banned topics, such as breastfeeding, are controversial, reflecting different viewpoints. Removing materials on these topics would be in favour of certain groups but annoy others who hold opposite views and thus see this as a violation of their rights of free speech. Protests against Facebook's censorship of breastfeeding photos took place in 2008,[73] 2012[74] and 2015.[75] The situation is similar in terms of political and ideological values. There have been disputes about the ideological implications caused by content moderation by social media companies in democratic contexts. In 2018, for example, the left-wing Southern Poverty Law Center (SPLC)'s (secret) involvement in

---

[69] 'Hate speech against migrants: policy update' *The Guardian* (6 April 2016) www.theguardian.com/news/gallery/2017/may/24/hate-speech-and-anti-migrant-posts -facebooks-rules#img-24 accessed 16 August 2020.

[70] Beckett (n 16); Joseph Cox, *These Are Facebook's Policies for Moderating White Supremacy and Hate* (2018) www.vice.com/en_us/article/mbk7ky/leaked-facebook -neo-nazi-policies-white-supremacy-nationalism-separatism accessed 16 August 2020.

[71] The BBC, 'Coronavirus: Elon Musk "child immunity" tweet will stay online' (2020) www.bbc.com/news/technology-51975377 accessed 16 August 2020.

[72] Jim Waterson, 'Tech firms criticised for "lack of answers" on Covid-19 disin- formation' *The Guardian* https://www.theguardian.com/world/2020/apr/30/tech-firms -criticised-for-lack-of-answers-on-covid-19-disinformation accessed 16 August 2020.

[73] Mark Sweney, 'Mums furious as Facebook removes breastfeeding photos' *The Guardian* (30 December 2008) www.theguardian.com/media/2008/dec/30/facebook -breastfeeding-ban accessed 16 August 2020.

[74] Rowan Davies, 'Let's put Facebook's "no nipples" rule to test with your breastfeeding photos' *The Guardian* (22 February 2012) www.theguardian.com/ commentisfree/2012/feb/22/facebook-no-nipples-rule-breastfeeding accessed 16 Aug- ust 2020.

[75] Sarah Barns, 'Mums post breastfeeding selfies in protest after Facebook removes pic over "nudity" rules' *Express* (25 February 2015) www.express.co.uk/life-style/life/ 560351/Breastfeeding-selfies-brelfies-Facebook-protest accessed 16 August 2020.

YouTube's moderation of hateful content led to complaints by conservative groups claiming bias against them.[76]

Advertising is the lifeline of social media platforms, which are commercial companies after all. However, political advertising has deep political implications, as it can change the mind of voters and reshape the results of elections and referenda. Over recent years, the prevalence of misinformation and disinformation puts social media firms in the public scrutiny of their related policies. Political advertising is one of the worst digital pollution problems in the social media age. In 2019, although political ads could still be directed to audiences according to their other demographics such as age, gender, location and their online exploration history, Google decided not to allow political advertisers to target audiences based on their political affiliations or voting records. This policy is applied to both the Google search engine and YouTube. Google's move is thought to have implications for the coming 2020 US presidential election.[77] As discussed above, Twitter also decided to ban political ads in 2019. However, in spite of criticism and pressure, Facebook, referencing freedom of speech, allows any political advertising, even ads that may contain false political statements aimed at certain audiences specifically and decided not to fact-check political ads.[78] In 2020, Facebook revised its policy by offering users a tool to turn off certain political ads. Overall, social media platforms are criticised for being opaque and lacking 'robust institutional mechanisms' on how to decide the coverage of political advertising on their platform.[79] These influences would shape the content moderation policies of social media companies and determine what kind of content remains showing on social media sites after moderation.

---

[76] Ben Kamisar, 'Conservatives cry foul over controversial group's role in YouTube moderation' *The Hill* https://thehill.com/homenews/campaign/377310-conservatives -cry-foul-over-controversial-groups-role-in-youtube-moderation accessed 16 August 2020; Peter Hasson, 'EXCLUSIVE: YouTube secretly using SPLC to police videos' *Daily Caller* https://dailycaller.com/2018/02/27/google-youtube-southern-poverty-law -center-censorship/ accessed 16 August 2020.

[77] Daisuke Wakabayashi and Shane Goldmacher, 'Google policy change upends online plans for 2020 campaigns' *The New York Times* https://www.nytimes.com/2019/ 11/20/technology/google-political-ads-targeting.html accessed 16 August 2020.

[78] Cecilia Kang and Mike Isaac, 'Defiant Zuckerberg says Facebook won't police political speech' *The New York Times* https://www.nytimes.com/2019/10/17/business/ zuckerberg-facebook-free-speech.html accessed 16 August 2020; Mike Isaac and Cecilia Kang, 'Facebook says it won't back down from allowing lies in political ads' *The New York Times* https://www.nytimes.com/2020/01/09/technology/facebook -political-ads-lies.html accessed 16 August 2020.

[79] Daniel Kreiss and Shannon C. Mcgregor, 'The "arbiters of what ourvoters see": Facebook and Google's struggle with policy, process, and enforcement around political advertising' *Political Communication* 499.

Moderating content means filtering or gatekeeping the content that users send to their destination sites. What content will be banned or removed and what will appear and stay depends on the policies of tech companies as well as how these policies are implemented by algorithms and human content moderators, both of which have biases. Algorithms are often thought of as being neutral and objective; however, they are not always impartial but can have biases as a result of a number of factors.[80] Prominent among other factors are the organisational priorities of companies and afore-discussed commercial or political influences that are embedded in algorithms through design. The design of AI automation technologies, automating enforcement of the policies and guidelines of social media companies, may prioritise certain social groups and values over others. Algorithms may also be manipulated by some malevolent users or influenced by powerful actors such as government officials to serve their respective interests.[81] These factors may also influence human intervention by content moderators, who apply their company's filtering policies and guidelines. In contrast to algorithms, human content moderators' judgements are influenced by their own understanding of social media content and content moderation policies, with their capability of handling content moderation affected by the enormous, overwhelming amounts of data.

Social media companies are pressured to adjust their policies allowing certain content to be carried on their platforms. Their policies – in particular internal guidelines for their moderators such as Facebook's internal guidelines on child abuse to content moderators – and the implementation of these policies, are criticised for being vague, including caveats on actions, and difficult to implement.[82] From users' perspectives, content moderation leaves users feeling confused and frustrated as they have little knowledge of how the systems work, along with implications for limiting freedom of expression. Therefore more transparent information is much needed about the systems and what they are designed for, as it would help engage communities and influence their behaviours in such a way that less content moderation might be needed.[83]

---

[80]  Sasha Costanza-Chock, 'Design justice, A.I., and escape from the matrix of domination' *Journal of Design and Science*; accessed 16 August 2020.

[81]  Nicolas P Suzor and others, 'What do we mean when we talk about transparency? Toward meaningful transparency in commercial content moderation' 13 *International Journal of Communication* 1526.

[82]  'Facebook's internal manual on non-sexual child abuse content' *The Guardian* (21 May 2017) www.theguardian.com/news/gallery/2017/may/21/facebooks-internal -manual-on-non-sexual-child-abuse-content accessed 16 August 2020.

[83]  Sarah Myers West, 'Censored, suspended, shadowbanned: User interpretations of content moderation on social media platforms' (2018) 20 *New Media & Society* 4366.

At the moment, however, secrecy surrounds the work of human content moderators as well as the policies and practices of content moderation.[84]

The capability of social media companies to clean up online content is also limited by technological and language barriers. Although AI automated fact-checking systems that need human participation are thought of as being useful in helping human fact-checkers to conduct their investigation, there is a lack of 'fully automated verification'.[85] In addition, judging by algorithms as to which content is to stay and which to go is proving to be hard, as sometimes context should be considered, as shown in two cases involving live streaming of the shooting of a black man in the USA.[86] In terms of language barriers, terrorist content in Arabic, for example, is difficult for them to detect.[87] Facebook has also struggled to deal with hate speech expressed in Burmese against the Rohingya.[88] These technical difficulties may lead to the (perceived) incompetence of social media companies in content moderation, which would not help improve public trust.

The dilemmas associated with freedom of speech and public trust are thus difficult to solve. Policing content inevitably limits free speech, which is worsened by the influences of political and economic factors, along with the complexity of issues and diversity of values and interests. Inappropriate content moderation would not help, either. Meanwhile, complete free speech on social media would impair the public's faith in social media companies, which would not be successfully restored by practising content moderation. How to strike a balance between defending freedom of speech and protecting the health of speech and how to rebuild public trust are two urgent problems that need to be resolved.

[84] Sarah T Roberts, 'Commercial content moderation: Digital laborers' dirty work' 12 *Media Studies Publications*.

[85] Lucas Graves, 'Understanding the promise and limits of automated fact-checking' (2018).

[86] Kate Klonick, 'Inside the team at Facebook that dealt with the Christchurch shooting' (2019) www.newyorker.com/news/news-desk/inside-the-team-at-facebook -that-dealt-with-the-christchurch-shooting accessed 16 August 2020.

[87] Moustafa Ayad, 'Facebook and YouTube are failing to detect terrorist content in Arabic' (*The Vice* 2019) www.vice.com/en_us/article/59nmyd/facebook-and-youtube -are-failing-to-detect-terrorist-content-in-arabic accessed 16 August 2020.

[88] Steve Stecklow, 'Why Facebook is losing the war on hate speech in Myanmar' *Reuters* https://www.reuters.com/investigates/special-report/myanmar-facebook-hate/ accessed 16 August 2020.

## 3.2    Liability

The third dilemma is about liability. Should social media companies be legally responsible for the materials that appear on their content? The objection against this statement is based on the ground of social media companies being service providers rather than content publishers. Social media firms do not publish content; instead they only offer platforms where people create and consume content. These platforms are supposed to be neutral, innocent, and value-free. Just as we cannot expect a hammer to shoulder the liability for a killing if it was used to kill someone, we cannot blame social media platforms for content published on their platform. If the hammer is innocent, so are social media platforms. And it is the person conducting the killing – or those creating content – who need to be blamed for their behaviour. However, the counterargument of this is if the hammer's owner predicted the killing would happen or noticed something unusual, they should have stopped it from happening. If we apply the same logic, we can argue that social media companies should stay alert as to what their technology – social media platforms – could be used for and try to make its use safe. They would be held accountable if things go wrong, although the main responsibility should still go to the users who create the content.

In countries like China, Internet intermediaries and social media companies are legally liable for the materials held on their servers or platforms, but at the same time users may be arrested or prosecuted for the content they publish on the Internet. In democratic contexts, although related practices differ contextually, the main focus is on social media companies. In the past, between 1996 and 2000, the laws in the USA and the European Union opposed holding online intermediaries responsible for content published by third parties that they did not have knowledge of.[89] However, the case of *Delfi*, in which the European Court of Human Rights judged that Delfi – the online news portal – should be liable for third-party content, suggests changes in the international consensus about the liability of online intermediaries and social media companies.[90]

In the USA, Congress frees social media companies from liability for content appearing on their platforms.[91] However, the wind has changed. In order to prohibit misinformation, a report calls for Congress to hold social media companies accountable for responsibility in terms of allowing and

---

[89]    Lisl Brunner, 'The liability of an online intermediary for third party content: The watchdog becomes the monitor: intermediary liability after Delfi v Estonia' 16 *Human Rights Law Review* 163.

[90]    Ibid.

[91]    Samples (n 37).

facilitating target advertising with their algorithms.[92] Some regulations even specify what to moderate. In 2019, the introduction of a new bill: 'Ending Support for Internet Censorship Act' to the Senate removes immunity given by the Communications Decency Act, which encourages 'providers of interactive computer services to provide content moderation that is politically neutral'.[93] The new bill 'prohibits a large social media company from moderating information on its platform from a politically biased standpoint'.[94]

In the European and Australian contexts, social media firms are blamed for failing to identify, block and remove harmful and hateful content from their platform. Countries like Germany (in 2017),[95] France (in 2019),[96] Australia (in 2019),[97] and the UK[98] have passed laws to penalise social media companies such as Twitter and Facebook for failing to take down hateful and harmful content from their platform. German and French laws even require social media companies to achieve this within 24 hours.

As commercial companies, social media firms' practice of content moderation is more a private, commercial decision, different to governments exercising political power. However, as the platforms and services of social media companies foster an essential part of the public sphere of speech and political action, these platforms and services have social and public importance. Can social media companies (be trusted to) moderate content fairly and in a way that is good for society? As private businesses, social media companies gain profits through providing their platforms for users to access and connect to one another. Users' availing themselves of the service provided by social media companies, the connections and interaction between users, the content they produce and consume and the related data created generate revenues for social

---

[92]   Ranking Digital Rights, 'To stem misinformation online, Congress must address targeted advertising: New RDR report' (2020) https://rankingdigitalrights.org/2020/05/27/to-stem-misinformation-online-congress-must-address-targeted-advertising-new-rdr-report/ accessed 16 August 2020.

[93]   'Ending Support for Internet Censorship Act' (19 June 2019) www.congress.gov/bill/116th-congress/senate-bill/1914 accessed 16 August 2020.

[94]   Ibid.

[95]   Heather Stewart and Alex Hern, 'Social media bosses could be liable for harmful content, leaked UK plan reveals' *The Guardian* https://www.theguardian.com/technology/2019/apr/04/social-media-bosses-could-be-liable-for-harmful-content-leaked-uk-plan-reveals accessed 16 August 2020.

[96]   Agence France-Presse, 'France online hate speech law to force social media sites to act quickly' *The Guardian* (9 July 2019) www.theguardian.com/world/2019/jul/09/france-online-hate-speech-law-social-media accessed 16 August 2020.

[97]   Damien Cave, 'Australia passes law to punish social media companies for violent posts' *The New York Times* (3 April 2019) www.nytimes.com/2019/04/03/world/australia/social-media-law.html accessed 16 August 2020.

[98]   Stewart and Hern (n 95).

media companies. Would they compromise their principles for economic interests?

In 2018, a female child was auctioned for marriage on Facebook. The posts were not taken down before the payments were made and the girl was married. Posts talking about the dowry were still live even after the claimed removal of the posts by Facebook.[99] In this case, Facebook is blamed for earning ad revenues from all users who read, wrote, or engaged with the child bride sale content.[100] In 2020, YouTube was accused of making profits from hosting videos advancing unproven Covid-19 treatments.[101] As these cases have shown, social media companies may compromise the public interest for their private interest. It thus makes sense for governments to regulate the content moderation of social media platforms, clarifying where – and what – liability lies, so as to properly minimise harmful and hateful speech and to secure accepted social values over other extreme ones.[102]

Most government regulations are designed to require social media companies to remove harmful and hateful speech quickly and competently. However, hiring an enormous army of content moderators would be costly. Removing content, blocking users and banning advertisements also have implications for influencing financial incomes. In addition, as discussed above, given the scale of the problem, the available technologies such as AI automation tools may not be good enough to solve the problem. Therefore it may be too harsh if governments impose liability on social media companies rather than adopting other measures such as restricting the origin of content – by regulating the users of social media platforms. For example, the 2017 passage of a German bill to punish social media companies for not removing hate speech from their site within 24 hours was criticised as putting 'too much responsibility for deciding what constitutes unlawful content in the hands of social media providers'.[103]

---

[99]   Bianca Britton, 'Facebook under fire for posts on auction of child bride' *CNN World* (23 November 2018) https://edition.cnn.com/2018/11/20/africa/south-sudan -child-bride-facebook-auction-intl/index.html accessed 16 August 2020.

[100]   Kalev Leetaru, 'Should social media be held responsible for the atrocities and deaths it facilitates?' *Forbes* (23 November 2018) www.forbes.com/sites/kalevleetaru/ 2018/11/23/should-social-media-be-held-responsible-for-the-atrocities-and-deaths-it -facilitates/ accessed 16 August 2020.

[101]   Kari Paul, 'YouTube profits from videos promoting unproven Covid-19 treatments' *The Guardian* (2 April 2020) www.theguardian.com/technology/2020/apr/03/ youtube-coronavirus-treatments-profit-misinformation accessed 16 August 2020.

[102]   Samples (n 37).

[103]   Melissa Eddy and Mark Scott, 'Delete hate speech or pay up, Germany tells social media companies' *The New York Times* (30 June 2017) www.nytimes.com/2017/ 06/30/business/germany-facebook-google-twitter.html accessed 16 August 2020.

The current mentality is to expect social media companies to moderate the content their platforms host, with considerable attention given to the liability of social media platforms.[104] However, this would not entirely solve the related problems and stop them from happening in the first place. Should social media users be more strictly regulated and more cautious about their information dissemination behaviours, less problematic social media content would be published and circulated. Identifying and removing users – in particular online predators – who publish problematic content as well as raising users' awareness of related problems should be a primary task. A burgeoning literature has recognised the promise of law enforcement to limit hate speech and fake news on social media as well as its current limitations and potential for prohibiting freedom of speech.[105] But more attention to regulating users and specifying their liability as well as more effort on the users' end might be needed.

## 4.    ETHICAL AND LEGAL IMPLICATIONS

The three dilemmas discussed above have several ethical and legal implications. First of all, emerging problems surrounding fake news and hate speech suggest that it would be irresponsible to let social media content flow freely and uncontrolled. However, the situation is not purely black and white. In addition to big tech companies shouldering this responsibility, both social media users and states should play their part in improving the situation. With the escalation of hate speech, for example, we have come to a time when social media companies, regulators and users should go beyond the impasse involving competing values between free speech, platform accountability, and the health of speech in the public domain; instead they should work together to establish consensus about how to make and implement policy decisions regarding content moderation.[106]

---

[104] See, e.g., Philip M Napoli, *Social Media and the Public Interest: Media Regulation in the Disinformation Age* (Columbia University Press 2019); Rikke Frank Jørgensen, *Human Rights in the Age of Platforms* (The MIT Press 2019).

[105] Habiburokhman, F Supanto and S Ummul, *The Aspect of Criminal Liability in Law Enforcement for the Prohibition on Hate Speech on Social Media* (Atlantis Press 2019); Victor Claussen, 'Fighting hate speech and fake news: the Network Enforcement Act (NetzDG) in Germany in the context of European legislation' 3 *Rivista Di Diritto Dei Media* 110.

[106] John Bowers and Jonathan Zittrain, 'Answering impossible questions: Content governance in an age of disinformation' 1 *The Harvard Kennedy School (HKS) Misinformation Review* 1.

The second is the importance of transparency. Users are unlikely to have legal protection against content removal.[107] With social media companies becoming the primary gatekeeper of information that social media users receive, it is important to make transparent the criteria for cleaning up content and the application of those criteria. This is partly because being transparent about criteria can help users know what to avoid when they create and disseminate social media content. This is partly because implementation of content moderation policies may be influenced by hidden algorithmic biases, manipulation by malicious or powerful users, and the decisions made by human content moderators about deciding what content to remove and what should stay.[108] This in turn means that content moderation policies and their implementation by human content moderators and algorithms need to be more transparent so that they can be scrutinised. Using either or both means – human content moderators or AI automation technologies – being transparent about how their systems work would win over users' trust as well as allow users to adjust their online behaviour, although this implies self-censorship.

Thirdly, it is important to appreciate practical difficulties and limitations in the content moderation ability of both human content moderators and AI technologies. Therefore, expectations of social media companies' content moderation need to be realistic. The discernment of human content moderators is limited by their own ability and understandings, although these can be complemented by algorithms and AI tools.[109] The limited ability of human content moderators in removing offensive materials and the 'reactive' system – a system where human content moderators review certain content based on complaints reported by users – may mean that before the removal of such content, the harm has already been done. Therefore, an automated detection system is important and more ethical, as by using it, content can be removed before doing any harm.[110] However, the capability of AI technologies to moderate content still needs to be improved. Should AI automation tools be more advanced, accurate and quick, then content moderation would be more efficient.

Fourthly, social media companies cannot be left to do the work unmonitored. Their power needs to be limited and their practices should be scrutinised. This is because the content moderation efforts of social media companies may be

---

[107] Patrik Leerssen, 'Cut out by the middle man: the Free speech implications of social network blocking and banning In The EU' 6 *J Intell Prop Info Tech & Elec Com L* 99.

[108] Suzor and others (n 81).

[109] See Ruckenstein and Turunen (n 18).

[110] Stefanie Ullmann and Marcus Tomalin, 'Quarantining online hate speech: technical and ethical perspectives' 22 *Ethics and Information Technology* 69.

compromised by their commercial interests. As restricted content may easily go viral – as shown in the above-mentioned case of the New Zealand Shooting video – banning and removing certain content may mean losing particular types of users – who may be attractive to advertisers – and therefore advertising revenues. Thus, for social media companies, content moderation may inevitably become an act of balancing its public duty and private, commercial interests. Apart from the problems associated with the limited ability of both humans and machines in picking up problematic content, inappropriate content moderation policies and inappropriately applying these policies may further violate the privacy of users, threaten freedom of expression, and impair the interests of marginalised or disadvantaged social groups and individuals.

Therefore, it is necessary to revise and update regulatory and legal systems to ensure social media companies share their 'corporate social responsibility'[111] and moderate content appropriately. As discussed above, states have started to gain a grip on tech firms' content moderation by designing related regulations. Regulatory systems aimed at social media users may also be needed in addition to regulating social media companies. It is also crucial for users to keep alert to social media firms' content moderation policies and react responsibly, since after all users are the origin of the problems in question.

In terms of regulations, the global reach of social media platforms has brought a challenge. The fact that social media platforms have global reach and social media users are based globally – apart from those countries that have erected firewalls restricting access to social media – suggests that there may be regional variations in the regulations for the content moderation of social media companies. Hate speech laws, for example, have different legal definitions and 'protected characteristics' in different countries.[112]

Accompanying the passage and implementation of regulations may also be a danger of surveillance and censorship. For some scholars,[113] issuing legislation may impose legal censorship, and thus 'the coercive powers of the state' should be withstood, even for the sake of limiting hate speech, given that freedom of speech is a basic condition of political legitimacy. Online censorship in China, for example, largely focuses on sanitising content that is harmful to the regime and the authority of the ruling political party. As the Chinese style of online censorship would be unwelcome in democratic contexts, states' power should be constrained, and big tech companies can be a balancing force

---

[111] Jennifer Grygiel and Nina Brown, 'Are social media companies motivated to be good corporate citizens? Examination of the connection between corporate social responsibility and social media safety' 43 *Telecommunications Policy* 445.

[112] Ullman and Tomalin (n 110).

[113] See, e.g., Ronald Dworkin, 'A new map of censorship' 35 *Index on Censorship* 130.

against state power by offering decentralised space to facilitate freedom of speech. Users can also contribute their part by embracing the right to (responsible) freedom of speech, as shown in above-mentioned cases of using the Internet to facilitate opposing authorities and propelling social change.

Apart from content moderation, we can also explore the possibility of other content-controlling systems, such as a 'quarantining' system,[114] acting as alternative ethical methods for restricting the spread of hateful and harmful speech on social media platforms. In 2018, for example, Reddit announced its quarantine policy with the aim of preventing 'highly offensive or upsetting' content from being accidentally seen by users who may not want to view it.[115] However, users were polarised in their response to the policy, as a result of the influence of their ideological opinions and value systems.[116]

In light of the need to clean up digital pollution, this chapter therefore contends that states, social media companies and even users should play their respective roles in maintaining online content hygiene as well as limiting and balancing state and corporate powers. On the one hand, it would be inappropriate to shield social media companies from taking the responsibility for carrying detrimental content just because of rights of free speech. These firms should shoulder the responsibility for cleansing the content appearing on their platform. On the other hand, they should not be the only ones to rely on. Not only do users need to be regulated and to behave responsibly, but also state regulations are needed to monitor the policies and practices of social media companies, although the power of states should also be limited. There is an urgent need to find a way to balance the responsibilities of social media companies, states, and users as well as to avoid abuse of corporate power, state power or a combination of the two. To solve the problems surrounding policing content on social media, the invention and application of AI is merely one means, but regulatory and societal efforts should be heavily involved as well.

---

114  Ullman and Tomalin (n 110).
115  'Quarantine Subreddits' (*Reddit*, August 2020) www.reddithelp.com/en/cate
gories/rules-reporting/account-and-community-restrictions/quarantined-subreddits Accessed 15 September 2020.
116  Qinlan Shen and Carolyn Rose, 'The discourse of online content moderation: Investigating polarized user responses to changes in Reddit's quarantine policy' (Proceedings of the Third Workshop on Abusive Language Online, January 2019).

# 6. The commercial unfairness of recommender systems on social media

## Catalina Goanta and Gerasimos Spanakis

## 1. INTRODUCTION

In the digital society, the availability of information is both a blessing and a curse. With the rise of personal computing, digitalization and interconnectedness in the past decades, anyone can have access to any information from anywhere around the world. This has not only facilitated an array of public and private practices that use information as a surveillance tool,[1] but it has also led to new approaches of weaponizing information.[2] Particularly on social media, the question of how information spreads is mostly engulfed in the commercial interests of platforms who rely on algorithmic governance in managing information flows,[3] and the adversarial approach taken by their users to game algorithms in the pursuit of their own benefits.

---

[1] Shoshana Zuboff, *The Age of Surveillance Capitalism: The Fight for the Future at the New Frontier of Power* (Public Affairs 2019).

[2] See for instance Lili Levi, 'Real Fake News and Fake Fake News' (2017) 16 *First Amend L Rev* 232; Ari Ezra Waldman, 'The Marketplace of Fake News' (2018) 20 *U Pa J Const L* 845; Marc Jonathan Blitz, 'Lies, Line Drawing, and Deep Fake News' (2018) 71 *Okla L Rev* 59; Russell L Weaver, 'Luncheon Keynote: Fake News: Reflections from History' (2019) 25 *Sw J Int'l L* 1; Donald L Beschle, 'Fake News, Deliberate Lies, and the First Amendment' (2019) 44 *U Dayton L Rev* 209; Rory Van Loo, 'Rise of the Digital Regulator' (2017) 66 *Duke LJ* 1267; Rebecca Tushnet, 'Attention Must Be Paid: Commercial Speech, User-Generated Ads, and the Challenge of Regulation' (2010) 58 *Buff L Rev* 721; Aziz Huq and Tom Ginsburg, 'How to Lose a Constitutional Democracy' (2018) 65 *UCLA L Rev* 78; Kate Klonick, 'The New Governors: The People, Rules, and Processes Governing Online Speech' (2018) 131 *Harv L Rev* 1598; Ellen P Goodman, 'Stealth Marketing and Editorial Integrity' (2006) 85 *Tex L Rev* 83; Erwin Chemerinsky, 'Fake News and Weaponized Defamation and the First Amendment' (2018) 47 *Sw L Rev* 291; Oreste Pollicino, 'Fake News, Internet and Metaphors (to Be Handled Carefully)' (2017) 9 *Italian J Pub L* 1.

[3] See for instance Frank Pasquale, *The Black Box Society: How Secret Algorithms Control Money, Information* (Harvard University Press 2016); Tarleton Gillespie,

As social media platforms diversify content monetization models,[4] more and more peers become engaged in the aspirational work of making content for a living. Brands looking to advertise products (e.g., merchandise) or services (e.g., advertising) rely on content creators (also called influencers) to perform the role of human ads. Amplified by social media platforms, influencers are similar to other categories of peers within the ambit of the gig economy,[5] with the distinction that instead of offering rooms, rides or household tasks, they create and broadcast content. Generally speaking, user-generated content has received a lot of attention as of the early days of the commercial Internet,[6] as people took it to online fora (e.g., gaming) and added a dynamic form of value to existing infrastructures.[7] Yet early into this trend of content democratization, incentives were limited, and it was not until creators started making money out of their content that existing broadcasting platforms saw a surge in their users, both those generating content as well as those consuming it, with new business models and new platforms arising as a result of this shift.

---

Pablo J Boczkowski and Kriste A Foot (eds) *Media Technologies: Essays on communication, materiality and society* (MIT Press 2014).

[4]     Catalina Goanta and Isabelle Wildhaber, 'In the Business of Influence: Contractual Practices and Social Media Content Monetisation' (2019) 4 Schweizerische Zeitschrift für Wirtschafts- und Finanzmarktrecht 346.

[5]     See for instance Irina Domurath, 'Platforms as Contract Partners: Uber and Beyond' (2018) 25(5) *Maastricht Journal of European and Comparative Law* 565; Sofia Ranchordas, 'Peers or Professionals: The P2P-Economy and Competition Law' (2017) 1 *Eur Competition & Reg L Rev* 320; Inara Scott and Elizabeth Brown, 'Redefining and Regulating the New Sharing Economy', (2016–2017) 19 *U Pa J Bus L* 553.

[6]     See for instance Yochai Benkler, 'Overcoming Agoraphobia: Building the Commons of the Digitally Networked Environment' (1998) 11 *Harv J L & Tech* 287; Carmen K Hoyme, 'Freedom of Expression and Interactive Media: Video Games and the First Amendment' (2004) 2 *First Amend L Rev* 377; Jeffrey Kravitz, James Nguyen, Dennis Loomis and Joseph M Gabriel, 'There is Something in the Air: The Legal Implications of Podcasting and User Generated Context' – Loyola Law School's Entertainment and Sports Law Society and the Association of Media and Entertainment Counsel Symposium Series – Tuesday, October 3, 2006 (2006) 27 *Loy LA Ent L Rev* 299; Edward Lee, 'Warming up to User-Generated Content' (2008) 2008 *U Ill L Rev* 1459; Greg Lastowka, 'User-Generated Content and Virtual Worlds' (2008) 10 *Vand J Ent & Tech L* 893; Anthony Ciolli, 'Joe Camel Meets YouTube: Cigarette Advertising Regulations and User-Generated Marketing' (2007) 39 *U Tol L Rev* 121.

[7]     Memes are an example of such value. See Thomas F Cotter, 'Memes and Copyright' (2005) 80 *Tul L Rev* 331; Daniel J Gervais and Daniel J Hyndman, 'Cloud Control: Copyright, Global Memes and Privacy' (2012) 10 *J on Telecomm & High Tech L* 53; Stacey M Lantagne, 'Mutating Internet Memes and the Amplification of Copyright's Authorship Challenges' (2018) 17 *Va Sports & Ent L J* 221.

Influencers build popularity on social media channels and convert it to real-life currency through monetization. Influencer marketing has been the most visible type of monetization addressed in literature so far, because of the advertising issues it gave rise to.[8] Content creators who may own review/commentary channels on YouTube or keep a visual diary of their activities on Instagram, receive money from companies who ask them to advertise their products or services in an often inconspicuous way.[9] The lack of clarity between non-sponsored and sponsored content has raised questions about truth-in-advertising and unfair commercial practices.[10]

However, the legal nature of the economic interaction between social media platforms and content creators who are engaged in monetization has barely received any scholarly attention. In the meanwhile, YouTubers are dealing with issues such as shadow-banning,[11] a practice that entails diverting traffic from some channels and videos on policy grounds, and Instagrammers are increasingly scared of an outright ban from the platform.[12] In growing their online presence, content creators depend on platforms making them

---

[8]    See for instance Laura E Bladow, 'Worth the Click: Why Greater FTC Enforcement Is Needed to Curtail Deceptive Practices in Influencer Marketing' (2018) 59(3) *William & Mary Law Review* 1123; Gonenc Gurkaynak, C Olgu Kama and Burcu Egun, 'Navigating the Uncharted Risks of Covert Advertising in Influencer Marketing' (2018) 39(1) *Business Law Review* 17; Aimee Khuong, 'Complying with the Federal Trade Commission's Disclosure Requirements: What Companies Need to Know When Using Social-Media Platforms as Marketing and Advertising Spaces' (2016) 13(1) *Hastings Business Law Journal* 129.

[9]    For an overview of the business models attributed to influencer marketing, see Goanta and Wildhaber, fn 4.

[10]    Jan Trzaskowski, 'Identifying the Commercial Nature of "Influencer Marketing" on the Internet' (2018) 65 *Scandinavian Studies in Law* 81; Christine Riefa and Laura Clausen, 'Towards Fairness in Digital Influencers' Marketing Practices' (2019) 8 *Journal of European Consumer and Market Law* 64; Sophie C Boerman, Natali Helberger, Guda van Noort and Chris J Hoofnagle, 'Sponsored Blog Content: What Do the Regulations Say: And What Do Bloggers Say' (2018) 9(2) *Journal of Intellectual Property, Information Technology and Electronic Commerce Law* 146.

[11]    The Economist, 'What is "shadowbanning"?' (*The Economist*, 1 August 2018) https://www.economist.com/the-economist-explains/2018/08/01/what-is-shadow banning accessed 28 June 2021; Rebecca Tushnet, 'The Constant Trash Collector: Platforms and the Paradoxes of Content Moderation' (2019) 2019 *Jotwell: J Things We Like* 1, 2; Frank Fagan, 'Systemic Social Media Regulation' (2017–2018) 16 *Duke L & Tech Rev* 393; Joshua A T Fairfield and Christoph Engel, 'Privacy as a Public Good' (2015) 65 *Duke LJ* 385.

[12]    Chelsea Ritschel, 'Instagram Influencer Whose Account Was Deleted Said She Called the Police Because It Felt Like "Murder"' (*The Independent*, 12 April 2019) https://www.independent.co.uk/life-style/instagram-influencer-jessy-taylor-cry-call -police-job-a8868016.html accessed 28 June 2021.

visible, which is done through recommender systems.[13] Whether used in e-commerce,[14] entertainment or social media,[15] just to name a few examples of industries that embrace them, recommender systems are based on the idea of personalizing the information retrieved by or targeting specific Internet users,[16] on the basis of various factors which shape the algorithms that label and disseminate content.

This chapter aims to shed light onto how recommender systems affect content creators. It does so by first looking at how recommender systems work, and how they are applied by social media platforms to the activity of content creators. For this purpose, computer science literature will be consulted. As the insight into the content of proprietary algorithms that generate recommendations on well-known social media platforms is not open to public academic inquiry, a number of assumptions will be made as a starting point for this analysis. Second, the chapter discusses the potential unfair competition issues that arise out of the use of recommender systems in relation to content creators. Third, it reflects on the suitability of existing frameworks on unfair competition in the EU and US to tackle the tensions arising between content creators and social media platforms. While national and state level details may be relevant, this chapter only focuses on EU legislation and US federal-level regulation.

The study innovates existing literature in two ways. It focuses on content creators not as the perpetrators of harms against consumers or citizens, but as the potential victims of social media platforms, thereby providing an illustration of legal issues relating to social media influencers beyond advertising law. Moreover, it revolves around content moderation as an expression of algorithmic governance, with a particular focus on the impact of this governance not

---

[13]  Teresa Rodriguez de las Heras Ballell, 'The Legal Autonomy of Electronic Platforms: A Prior Study to Assess the Need of a Law of Platforms in the EU' (2017) 3 *Italian LJ* 149; Teresa Rodriguez de las Heras Ballell, 'Legal Aspects of Recommender Systems in the Web 2.0: Trust, Liability and Social Networking', in Jose Pazos Arias et al. (eds), *Recommender Systems for the Social Web* (Springer 2012), pp. 43–62; Avi Goldfarb and Catherine Tucker, 'Privacy and Innovation' (2012) 12 *Innovation Pol'y & Econ* 65; Maria Luisa Stasi, 'Social Media Platforms and Content Exposure: How to Restore Users' Control' (2019) 20(1) *Competition and Regulation in Network Industries* 86.

[14]  Christoph Busch, 'Implementing Personalized Law: Personalized Disclosures in Consumer Law and Data Privacy Law' (2019) 86 *U Chi L Rev* 309, 324.

[15]  James G Webster, 'User Information Regimes: How Social Media Shape Patterns of Consumption' (2010) 104 *Nw U L Rev* 593.

[16]  Sarah Eskens, Natali Helberger and Judith Moeller, 'Challenged by News Personalisation: Five Perspectives on the Right to Receive Information' (2017) 9(2) *Journal of Media Law* 259.

on the users-as-audience, but on the users-as-producers, who monetize content as a living.

## 2. RECOMMENDER SYSTEMS AS INFORMATION RETRIEVAL ON SOCIAL MEDIA

Recommender systems are information filtering systems that are supposed to predict a user's preference.[17] Their commercial use stems from the consideration that user profiling leads to the personalization of information,[18] increasing the user enjoyment of a digital service or product.[19] A popular example of recommender systems is reflected by the way in which viewers experience video or music streaming. Using Netflix, Hulu or Spotify streaming services when the user knows what they want to watch/listen to is very straightforward;

---

[17] For a computer science overview of recommender systems, see Shini Renjith et al., 'An Extensive Study on the Evolution of Context-aware Personalized Travel Recommender Systems' (2019) *Information Processing & Management* https://www.sciencedirect.com/science/article/pii/S0306457319300111 accessed 28 November 2021; David Goldberg et al., 'Using Collaborative Filtering to Weave an Information Tapestry' (1992) 35 (12) *Communications of the ACM* 61–70; Luis Terán, Alvin Oti Mensah and Arianna Estorelli, 'A Literature Review for Recommender Systems Techniques Used in Microblogs' (2018) 103 *Expert Systems with Applications* 63; Flora Amato et al., 'SOS: A Multimedia Recommender System for Online Social Networks' (2019) 93 *Future Generation Computer Systems* 914. For a legal overview, see generally Lilian Edwards and Michael Veale, 'Slave to the Algorithm: Why a Right to an Explanation Is Probably Not the Remedy You Are Looking For' (2017–2018) 16 *Duke L & Tech Rev* 18; Nava Tintarev and Judith Masthoff, 'Explaining Recommendations: Design and Evaluation', in Francesco Ricci et al. (eds), *Recommender Systems Handbook* (Springer 2015); Mireille Hildebrandt, 'Defining Profiling: A New Type of Knowledge?', in Mireille Hildebrandt & Serge Gutwirth (eds.), *Profiling the European Citizen* (Springer 2008), p. 17.

[18] Indra Spiecker et al., 'The Regulation of Commercial Profiling – A Comparative Analysis' (2016) 2 *Eur Data Prot L Rev* 535.

[19] Ari Juels, 'Targeted Advertising ... and Privacy Too' (2001) *Topics in Cryptology* 408; Justin P Johnson, 'Targeted Advertising and Advertising Avoidance' (2013) *The RAND Journal of Economics* https://onlinelibrary.wiley.com/doi/full/10.1111/1756 -2171.12014; Simon Gilbody et al., 'Benefits and Harms of Direct to Consumer Advertising: A Systematic Review' (2005) 14(4) *BMJ Quality and Safety* https://qualitysafety.bmj.com/content/14/4/246.short accessed 28 June 2021. Personalization also has negative externalities such as discrimination or radicalization, which are not particularly discussed in this chapter. See for instance Edwards and Veale (fn 17); Danielle Keats Citron, 'Extremist Speech, Compelled Conformity, and Censorship Creep' (2018) 93 *Notre Dame L Rev* 1035; Nabiha Syed, 'Real Talk about Fake News: Towards a Better Theory for Platform Governance' (2017–2018) 127 *Yale LJ F* 337; Evelyn Mary Aswad, 'The Future of Freedom of Expression Online' (2018–2019) 17 *Duke L & Tech Rev* 26.

the same cannot be said when users employ streaming platforms for entertainment, without having a clear goal in terms of what selection to make. In the latter situation, instead of putting the burden of research on the user, platforms attempt to facilitate an enjoyable entertainment experience by trying to predict what the user would like. In order to do so, platforms need to profile the user first, and intelligent agents constantly respond to new input that may enrich the profile. This use of profiling may be perceived as one of the least controversial business purposes for recommender systems, although that finally depends on what the platform does with the data that is used to train the predictive models. In social media:

> the coupling of online social networks with recommender systems created new opportunities for businesses that consider the social influence important for their product marketing, as well as the social networks that want to improve the user experience by personalizing the content that is provided to each user and enabling new connections.[20]

The use of recommender systems by social media platforms raises a world of legal problems, given that the peer content YouTube thrives on cannot be vetted the same way as on Netflix. Or can it?

This section is dedicated to first understanding how social media recommender systems work, and who they may harm. In answering this question, particular attention will be given to content creators, and several trends regarding the professionalization of peer content will be explored.

## 2.1    How Recommender Systems Work

Given the colossal volume of content produced every day on social media, platforms rely on automation in recommending content to their users. This automation poses considerable challenges from three perspectives: scale, freshness and noise.[21] In terms of scale, recommendation algorithms which may perform on a smaller corpus may not work as accurately on a larger scale. Freshness deals with the responsiveness of the recommendation algorithm in balancing recently uploaded content with the latest actions taken by the user, and relation between the time when content is uploaded and noise relates to the

---

[20]  Magdalini Eirinaki, Jerry Gao, Iraklis Varlamis, Konstantinos Tserpes, 'Recommender Systems for Large-Scale Social Networks: A Review of Challenges and Solutions' (2018) 78(1) *Future Generation Computer Systems* 413.

[21]  Paul Covington, Jay Adams and Emre Sargin 'Deep Neural Networks for YouTube Recommendations' (2016) RecSys '16 Proceedings of the 10th ACM Conference on Recommender Systems https://dl.acm.org/citation.cfm?id=2959190 accessed 28 November 2021.

plethora of unobservable external factors which may be invisible to algorithms but still affect user satisfaction.[22] Although specifically identified with respect to YouTube content, these factors extend to other social media platforms as well, and are a clear depiction of the issues faced by these platforms in accurately predicting user preferences.

Recommender systems use a wide array of machine learning methods, with the two most recognizable categories being collaborative filtering and deep neural networks. Collaborative filtering algorithms (e.g., Matrix Factorization) were famously used during the Netflix prize challenge,[23] running between 2006 and 2009.[24] These models display users and items (e.g., videos) in matrices, and attempt to predict a particular user's rating with respect to an item,[25] using information from similar users or items:

> For visualizing the problem, it makes sense to think of the data as a big sparsely filled matrix, with users across the top and movies down the side [...], and each cell in the matrix either contains an observed rating (1–5) for that movie (row) by that user (column), or is blank meaning you don't know. To quantify 'big', sticking with the round numbers, this matrix would have about 8.5 billion entries (number of users times number of movies). Note also that this means you are only given values for one in eighty five of the cells. The rest are all blank.[26]

In addition to Matrix Factorization, another model discussed in literature is the Nearest Neighbors model, which can be used to solve classification problems.[27]

The deep learning alternative to collaborative filtering was proposed by Covington et al. and builds on Google's development of TensorFlow, an open software library commonly used for neural networks. Briefly put, neural networks are machine learning models inspired from the features of biological

---

[22]   Ibid.
[23]   Netflix, 'The Netflix Prize' (*Netflix*, 2009) https://web.archive.org/web/20090924184639/http://www.netflixprize.com/community/viewtopic.php?id=1537 accessed 28 November 2021.
[24]   The competition was not held afterwards due to privacy concerns. See Arvind Narayanan & Vitaly Shmatikov, 'Robust De-anonymization of Large Datasets (How to Break Anonymity of the Netflix Prize Dataset)' (2008) SP '08 Proceedings of the 2008 IEEE Symposium on Security and Privacy 111 https://arxiv.org/abs/cs/0610105 accessed 28 November 2021.
[25]   Yehuda Koren, Robert Bell and Chris Volinsky, 'Matrix Factorization Techniques for Recommender Systems' (2009) 42 (8) *Computer* 30–37.
[26]   Simon Funk, 'Netflix Update: Try This at Home' https://sifter.org/~simon/journal/20061211.html accessed 28 November 2021.
[27]   See for instance Pigi Kouki et al., 'HyPER: A Flexible and Extensible Probabilistic Framework for Hybrid Recommender Systems' (2015) RecSys '15 Proceedings of the 9th ACM Conference on Recommender Systems https://shobeir.github.io/papers/kouki_recsys_2015.pdf accessed 28 November 2021.

neurons, that learn to solve a task from data and can adapt based on this data.[28] In applying deep learning to recommendations on social media, Covington et al. proposed the use of two neural networks: one that generates recommendations, and one that ranks them, making Google 'one of the first companies to deploy production-level deep neural networks for recommender systems'.[29] First, a so-called candidate generation network uses activity history such as demographic statistics, watched videos or search history to generate a few hundred videos which are supposed to broadly predict the user's preferences. Then, the ranking network scores these results using more features.[30] By using this approach, the authors of this seminal paper demonstrated that wider and deeper neural networks decrease the so-called 'per-user loss', namely the 'total amount of mispredicted watch time'.[31]

Due to Google's academic engagement, research such as that by Covington et al.'s offers some transparency into the hardship and solutions involved in social media recommender system theory and practice. However, other platforms are more secretive about how their features are built, and information regarding those aspects can only be pieced together from journalism reports and anecdotal experiences.[32] For instance, Instagram's Recommended posts is:

> a rule-based personal assistant which can focus on broadening users' access to content and switch from chronological feed to algorithmic one based on both topical relevance and personal relevance [...] related to weighted search and data mining, which are two of the prominent natural language processing applications of information retrieval.[33]

---

[28]  See Camron Godbout, 'TensorFlow in a Nutshell – Part One: Basics' (*Medium*, 23 August 2016) https://medium.com/@camrongodbout/tensorflow-in-a-nutshell-part-one-basics-3f4403709c9d accessed 28 November 2021.

[29]  Moin Nadeem, 'How YouTube Recommends Videos' (*Medium*, 7 July 2018) https://towardsdatascience.com/how-YouTube-recommends-videos-b6e003a5ab2f accessed 28 November 2021.

[30]  Ibid.

[31]  Ibid.

[32]  See for instance Josh Constine, 'How Instagram's Algorithm Works' (*TechCrunch*, 1 June 2018) https://techcrunch.com/2018/06/01/how-instagram-feed-works/ accessed 28 June 2021; Sarah Perez, 'Instagram will now Add "Recommended" Posts to your Feed' (*TechCrunch*, 27 December 2017) https://techcrunch.com/2017/12/27/instagram-will-now-add-recommended-posts-to-your-feed/ accessed 28 November 2021.

[33]  See Yajing Hu, 'The Mystery Behind Instagram Recommendation System' (*Georgetown Commons*, 28 January 2019) https://blogs.commons.georgetown.edu/cctp-607-spring2019/2019/01/28/the-mystery-behind-instagram-recommendation-system/ accessed 28 November 2021. See also Margaret A. Boden, *AI: Its Nature and Future* (Oxford University Press 2016), p. 63.

Still, it is unclear how Instagram allocates weights to search terms, and what data mining is used in this respect.

In addition to questions relating to information infrastructure, a lot of governance issues arise in the practice of retrieving data on the basis of user preferences. How often do platforms change recommender systems? What are the pitfalls observed by platform developer teams, and what do platforms do with this information? What is the scientific measure of the pitfalls which are not so easily observable? With his 'Algotransparency' project, former Google employee Guillaume Chaslot aims to show that YouTube algorithms are specifically built with less accuracy, so that users can spend more time on the platform.[34] Unsurprisingly, this view is debated by Google, which argues against the accuracy of the methodology used by Algotransparency.[35]

## 2.2    Harms Caused by Recommender Systems to Content Creators

Going back to the reason why recommender systems are used in practice – they are supposed to help users tailor content according to their needs. In other words, recommender systems personalize information. This personalization, as seen in the prior section, relies on preferences directly or indirectly expressed by users, such as ratings, search history, or demographic profiles. The use of this data has raised serious concerns regarding user privacy,[36] especially given that the de-anonymization of large-scale datasets as those offered by Netflix can be achieved much more easily than previously believed.[37] There may also be a question of dark patterns (whether voluntary or involuntary) surrounding recommender systems, as they may be used to promote illegal or controversial content.[38] On the one hand, platforms may be under a legal obligation to remove illegal content. However, controversial content, found at the edge of their community guidelines, is supposed to increase audience engagement,

---

[34]    Már Másson Maack, '"YouTube recommendations are toxic", says Dev who worked on the Algorithm' (*The Next Web*, June 2019) https://thenextweb.com/google/2019/06/14/YouTube-recommendations-toxic-algorithm-google-ai/ accessed 28 November 2021. See also Algotransparency, 'Daily YouTube Recommendations' (*Algotransparency*, 12 September 2019) https://algotransparency.org/index.html?date=12-09-2019&keyword= accessed 28 November 2021.
[35]    Ibid.
[36]    Arjan Jeckmans et al., 'Privacy in Recommender Systems' in Naeem Ramzan et al. (eds), *Social Media Retrieval* (Springer 2012), p. 236.
[37]    Fn 34.
[38]    See for instance Paul Ohm, 'Manipulation, Dark Patterns, and Evil Nudges' (2019) *Jotwell: J Things We Like* 1.

so platforms may not have a direct interest in removing it, even though their public narrative is to protect public interest.[39]

Yet the impact of recommender systems on the growing number of content creators has remained unexplored from a legal academic perspective. Media reports specifically noted the hardship of small YouTube channels in dealing with automated copyright checks, which led to the termination of their live-streams, as well as 90-day streaming bans,[40] which may be the equivalent of slowly killing a channel off in the long run. For YouTubers who make a living out of streaming, there is also an important short-term implication in that they can no longer count on any source of revenue from the platform for the duration of the streaming ban.

Similarly, in their attempt to tackle fake followers, platforms are downgrading inauthentic followers, likes or comments by helping shut down bot and engagement apps such as Instagress, Social Growth, Archie, InstarocketProX and Boostio.[41] However, platforms like Instagram still show the sponsored ads of some of these platforms that 'masquerade as analytics apps for assisting influencers with tracking the size of their audience'.[42] While the purpose of removing fake accounts and followers may be legitimate, Instagram's actions in tackling this problem are opaque, making it unclear if there are any negative externalities arising from this process, such as impacting the engagement and growth of channels that are mere errors of the models calculating 'fakeness'.

There are currently no scientific metrics developed outside platform infrastructures that facilitate an auditing activity of platform activity. At most, literature in this space – including interdisciplinary literature – has outlined the potential risks posed by the power dynamics behind platform architectures.[43] A considerable reason explaining this status quo is that current information retrieval tasks in recommender system architectures revolve around the use

---

[39]  See for instance Mark Zuckerberg, 'A Blueprint for Content Governance and Enforcement' (*Facebook*, 15 November 2018) https://www.facebook.com/notes/mark-zuckerberg/a-blueprint-for-content-governance-and-enforcement/10156443129621634/ accessed 28 November 2021.

[40]  Richard Priday, 'YouTube's Algorithm is Causing Havoc for Gaming Livestreamers' (*Wired*, 16 May 2018) https://www.wired.co.uk/article/YouTube-streaming-content-id-ban-algorithm accessed 28 November 2021.

[41]  Josh Constine, 'Instagram Kills off Fake Followers, Threatens Accounts that Keep Using Apps to get them' (*Techcrunch*, 19 November 2018)' https://techcrunch.com/2018/11/19/instagram-fake-followers/ accessed 28 November 2021.

[42]  Ibid.

[43]  Snehalkumar Gaikwad et al., 'Boomerang: Rebounding the Consequences of Reputation Feedback on Crowdsourcing Platforms' (2016) Proceedings of the 29th Annual Symposium on User Interface Software and Technology https://dl.acm.org/doi/10.1145/2984511.2984542 accessed 28 November 2021.

of machine-learning processes that are opaque, and not publicly available. Whether the problem is the data used to train classifiers to categorize content, or the deep-learning approaches the explainability of which has been traditionally non-existent, it is at present impossible to reverse engineer or recreate these platform processes. Without the possibility to scientifically benchmark and measure the outputs they create, relating to their governance and implementation, platforms hold a monopoly over the evidence which could be relevant to the quantification of harm. This is why in this chapter, when we speak about harm we refer to assumed harm, and not to approaches that may be useful in gathering practical evidence for it. The most important aspect in this discussion thus becomes the role of platforms as providers of revenue for content creators.[44] As the platform economy moves into new iterations, content monetization makes it increasingly possible for creators to make money by engaging in cultural production.[45] Platforms control user attention, which becomes a currency in relationship with creators. For instance, creators can earn money via ad revenue, where user attention is measured in views, and creators can add advertising to their YouTube channels and are subsequently paid by the platform. Similarly, creators can engage in other business models such as influencer marketing, where they get paid by brands to advertise goods and services depending on the reach and popularity of their content. Given that platforms can algorithmically gatekeep popularity, the main harm this leads to is that creators are at the mercy of the platform's unilateral governance decisions relating to limiting this popularity. A creator who is not able to show brands increasing engagement levels, may be dropped by their sponsors. This leaves creators in a place of vulnerability, where they need to comply with platform policies that can be detrimental to their financial interests, whether due to the fact that unilateral decisions can lead to the limitation of content diffused via recommendations (shadow-banning), or to the total ban of reliance on monetization (e.g., demonetization).[46]

These are actions taken by platforms against their professional users, who may be individuals or companies, depending on their size or business models.[47] From this perspective, a question arises with respect to whether the platform practices may be considered as economic torts against content creators, as they have the potential to harm both consumers and business entities. In answering this question, the next section will first make an outline of unfair competition

---

[44]   See for instance, Michael L Siciliano, *Creative Control: The Ambivalence of Work in the Culture Industries* (Columbia University Press 2021).
[45]   Catalina Goanta and Sofia Ranchordas, *The Regulation of Social Media Influencers* (Edward Elgar 2020).
[46]   Fn 11.
[47]   Fn 10.

in Europe and the United States, and will analyse whether it can be applied to safeguard the interests of content creators.

# 3. UNFAIR COMMERCIAL PRACTICES – A TRANSATLANTIC OVERVIEW

## 3.1 The European Approach

In the European Union, unfair competition rules are brought together in the Unfair Commercial Practices Directive.[48] The UCPD is a maximum harmonization instrument of consumer protection, with the aim of establishing uniform rules on unfair business-to-consumer (B2C) commercial practices in order to support the proper functioning of the internal market and establish a high level of consumer protection.[49] Before the adoption of the UCPD, the

---

[48] Directive 2005/29/EC concerning unfair business-to-consumer commercial practices [2005] OJ L149/22.

[49] See for instance Case C-611/14, *Retten i Glostrup v Canal Digital Danmark A/S*, ECLI:EU:C:2016:800, para. 25; Case C-299/07, *VTB-VAB NV v Total Belgium NV (C-261/07) and Galatea BVBA v Sanoma Magazines Belgium NV*, ECLI:EU:C:2009: 244, para. 52. For an overview of the directive see also Civic Consulting, 'Study on the application of Directive 2005/29/EC on Unfair Commercial Practices in the EU', Part 1 – Synthesis Report, December 2011; Giuseppe Abbamonte, 'The Unfair Commercial Practices Directive: An Example of the New European Consumer Protection Approach' (2006) 12 *Columbia Journal of European Law* 695–712; Georgios Anagnostaras, 'The Unfair Commercial Practices Directive in Context: From Legal Disparity to Legal Complexity?' (2007) 47 *Common Market Law Review* 147–171; Erika Budaite and Cees van Dam, 'The Statutory Frameworks and General Rules on Unfair Commercial Practices in the 25 EU Member States on the Eve of Harmonisation' (2008) *The Yearbook of Consumer Law* 2008 107–139; Hugh Collins, 'EC Regulation of Unfair Commercial Practices', in Hugh Collins, (ed.), *The Forthcoming EC Directive on Unfair Commercial Practices* (Kluwer, 2004), 1–42; Hugh Collins, 'The Unfair Commercial Practices Directive', (2005) 1(4) *European Review of Contract Law* 417–441; Bram Duivenvoorde, *The Consumer Benchmarks in the Unfair Commercial Practices Directive* (Springer 2015); Gerraint Howells, 'Unfair Commercial Practices – Future Directions', in Schulze and Schulte-Nölke (eds), *European Private Law – Current Status and Perspectives* (Sellier 2011), 133–144; Gerraint Howells, Hans-W Micklitz and Thomas Wilhelmsson (eds), *European Fair Trading Law: The Unfair Commercial Practices Directive* (Ashgate Publishing 2006); Hans-W Micklitz, 'Unfair Commercial Practices and Misleading Advertising' in Hans-W Micklitz, Norbert Reich and Peter Rott, *Understanding EU Consumer Law* (Intersentia 2009), 61–117; Cristina Poncibò and Rossella Incardona, 'The Average Consumer, the Unfair Commercial Practices Directive, and the Cognitive Revolution' (2007) 30(1) *Journal of Consumer Policy Issue* 21–38; Peter Shears, 'Overviewing the EU Unfair Commercial Practices Directive: Concentric Circles' (2007) 18 *European Business Law Review* 781–796; Thomas Wilhelmsson, 'Misleading Practices' in Gerraint Howells, Hans-W Micklitz

1984 Misleading Advertising Directive governed the rules against false advertising to consumers.[50] One year after the adoption of the Unfair Commercial
Practices Directive, in 2006, the Misleading and Comparative Advertising
Directive (MCAD) entered into force.[51] The latter, based on minimum harmonization,[52] came to replace the 1984 Directive, and its design sought to protect
traders against the unfair consequences of misleading advertising. The main
difference between the MCA and the UCPD is that the first generally applies
to business-to-business (B2B) transactions,[53] whereas the latter, as mentioned
above, applies to B2C relations.[54] The EU Commission acknowledges that the
UCPD's 'principle-based provisions address a wide range of practices and are
sufficiently broad to catch fast-evolving products, services and sales methods'.[55] The scope of the UCPD is therefore not restricted to the sale of goods,
as the UCPD is equally applicable to services, and therefore digital services
for that matter, regardless of what specific qualification they may have under
national law.[56] Having said this, while a general, principle-based directive such
as the UCPD is not bound to a given industry or sector, questions arise as to

---

and Thomas Wilhelmsson (eds), *European Fair Trading Law: The Unfair Commercial
Practices Directive* (Ashgate Publishing 2006), 49–82; Chris Willett, 'Fairness and
Consumer Decision Making under the Unfair Commercial Practices Directive' (2010)
33 *Journal of Consumer Policy* 247–273.

[50]   Council Directive 84/450/EEC of 10 September 1984 relating to the approximation of the laws, regulations and administrative provisions of the Member States
concerning misleading advertising, OJ 1984, L 250. See also Matthias Leistner,
'Unfair Competition or Consumer Protection' in John Bell and Alan Dashwood (eds)
(2003–2004) 6 *Cambridge Yearbook of European Legal Studies* 153.

[51]   Directive 2006/114/EC of the European Parliament and of the Council of 12
December 2006 concerning misleading and comparative advertising, OJ 2006, L 376
(MCAD).

[52]   Art 7 MCAD.

[53]   The rules on comparative advertising do apply however also to advertising
directed at consumers.

[54]   Art 1 MCAD.

[55]   European Commission, 'Guidance on the Implementation/Application of
Directive 2005/29/EC on Unfair Commercial Practices', SWD(2016) 163 final, at 6.

[56]   According to Art 2(c) corroborated with Art 3(1) UCPD, it does apply to services. See also Case C-357/16, *UAB 'Gelvora' v Valstybinė vartotojų teisių apsaugos
tarnyba*, para. 32. New European rules on digital content may qualify this to be a digital
content contract. See European Commission, 'Proposal for a Directive of the European
Parliament and of the Council on Certain Aspects Concerning Contracts for the Supply
of Digital Content', COM(2015) 634 final. However, until the adoption of such rules,
it is likely that the applicable national qualifications would most likely be service or
innominate contracts.

its suitability for tackling industries that have emerged after its adoption, such as social media.[57]

The structure of the main provisions of the UCPD is laid down as follows. Article 5 sets the general clause according to which a commercial practice is unfair if it satisfies a two-tier test: (i) 'it is contrary to the requirements of professional diligence'; and (ii) 'it materially distorts or is likely to materially distort the economic behaviour with regard to the product of the average consumer whom it reaches or to whom it is addressed, or of the average member of the group when a commercial practice is directed to a particular group of consumers'. In addition, the same Article acknowledges two particular types of commercial practices which may be deemed unfair: (i) misleading practices as set out in Articles 6 and 7; and (ii) aggressive practices as set out in Articles 8 and 9. These two sets of Articles include their own, more specific tests which derogate from the general test in Article 5, although they are set around the same principle – that manipulative commercial practices are prohibited. A black list is annexed to the Directive and contains a total of 31 practices which are in all circumstances considered to be unfair.

## 3.2    The United States Approach

In the United States, absent a unifying regulatory framework that defines unfair competition in terms of unfair commercial practices, this body of rules seems to be about 'courts try[ing] to stop people from playing dirty tricks'.[58] In tracing some of the history of unfair competition law in the US, Chafee makes an overview of cases where plaintiffs were given relief by courts for the loss of the possibility of business other than on the grounds of contractual damages.[59] This is a first group of cases he identified to arise between competitors, bringing together 'a small number of torts of strange sorts'.[60] He additionally identifies trademark infringements and imitations of secondary meaning as second and third groups of cases, and specifies that unfair competition, while mostly used to identify the latter, gradually started including the second cate-

---

[57]  Social media was not an established industry in 2005, when the UCPD was adopted, and its growth to the commercial space it represents today could not have been entirely predicted. This does not affect, however, the material and personal scope of the Directive, see Recital 11 UCPD.

[58]  Zechariah Jr Chafee, 'Unfair Competition' (1940) 7 *Current Legal Thought* 3. See also Harry Nims, *The Law of Unfair Competition and Trademarks* (2d ed. 1921 and later editions) at 17, within the introduction to Chapter 2.

[59]  See for instance Anon., Y. B. 11 H. IV, f. 47, pl. 21 (C. P. 1410); *Ibottson v Peat*, 3 H. & C. 644 (Ex. Ch. 1865); *Tarleton v M'Gawley*, Peake 205 N. P. (1804).

[60]  Chafee, fn 58 at 7.

gory as well.[61] As all competition may be considered a *prima facie* economic tort, there have also been attempts to apply three tort-related conditions to unfair competition:[62] (i) whether the plaintiff suffered legal harm; (ii) whether the plaintiff was responsible for this harm; and (iii) whether the harm was justified. In Chafee's appreciation, unfair competition theoretically meets all these conditions, since (i) all competition is harmful; (ii) this competition is intended by the competitor; and (iii) even though most competition is justified, if it uses 'unfair or socially undesirable methods', then it becomes unjustified.[63]

While the common law doctrine on unfair competition may pose uncertainty with respect to how courts see the body of cases that are considered to pertain to unfair competition,[64] institutional structures were further developed to deal with harms arising out of unfair competition and its impact on consumer protection. In this respect, the Federal Trade Commission (FTC) is authorized 'to gather and compile information concerning, and to investigate from time to time the organization, business, conduct, practices, and management of any person, partnership, or corporation engaged in or whose business affects commerce [...]'.[65] In fulfilling its duties, the FTC has two roles: the role of protecting consumers, as well as that of protecting competition. As a result, the Federal Trade Commission Act prohibits 'unfair or deceptive acts or practices in or affecting commerce'.[66] What is more, according to the US Code, 'unfair methods of competition in or affecting commerce, and unfair or deceptive acts or practices in or affecting commerce, are [...] declared unlawful'.[67] This codification supplements the Supreme Court's interpretation of unfairness in *FTC v Raladam Co.*[68] Unfair or deceptive practices include those practices that fulfil two separate conditions: (i) cause or are likely to cause reasonably

---

[61]   Ibid.

[62]   For these elements in early US doctrine, see Oliver Wendell Holmes, 'Privilege, Malice, and Intent' (1894) 8 *Harvard Law Review* 1–14; John W Wigmore, 'The Tripartite Division of Torts' (1894) 8 *Harvard Law Review* 200.

[63]   Fn 58.

[64]   See also Rudolf Callmann, 'What Is Unfair Competition' (1940) 28 *GEO. L. J.* 585; Tony Bortolin, 'Foundational Objectives of Laws Regarding Trademarks and Unfair Competition' (2017) 107 *Trademark Rep* 980; Sharon K Sandeen, 'The Erie/Sears/Compco Squeeze: Erie's Effects on Unfair Competition and Trade Secret Law' (2018) 52 *Akron L Rev* 423; Harold G Fox, 'A Canadian Trade-Mark Decision' (1945) 35 *Trademark Rep* 124.

[65]   FTC Act Sec. 6(a), 15 USC Sec. 46(a).

[66]   Section 5(a) of the FTC Act.

[67]   15 USC Sec. 45(a)(1).

[68]   283 US 643 (1931). See also Stephen Calkins, 'FTC Unfairness – An Essay' (2000) 46 *Wayne L. Rev* 1935; Larry Saret, 'Unfairness without Deception: Recent Positions of the Federal Trade Commission' (1974) 5 *Loy U Chi L J* 537, 555.

foreseeable injury within the US; or (ii) involve material conduct occurring within the US.[69]

The FTC's first systematic examination of the unfairness doctrine it has legitimacy to enforce occurred in 1964 and dealt with the adoption of the 'Trade Regulation Rule for the Prevention of Unfair or Deceptive Acts or Practices in the Sale of Cigarettes', where it imposed three criteria for a practice to be deemed unfair:[70]

(1)     whether the practice, without necessarily having been previously considered unlawful, offends public policy as it has been established by statutes, the common law, or otherwise – whether in other words, it is within at least the penumbra of some common law, statutory, or otherwise established concept of unfairness;
(2)     whether it is immoral, unethical, oppressive, or unscrupulous;
(3)     whether it causes substantial injury to consumers (or competitors or other businessmen).

In spite of inconsistent applications of this unfairness doctrine, the Supreme Court affirmed the FTC's role in tackling unfair practices in *FTC v. Sperry & Hutchinson Co. (S&H)*, where it held:[71]

[L]egislative and judicial authorities alike convince us that the Federal Trade Commission does not arrogate excessive power to itself if, in measuring a practice against the elusive, but congressionally mandated standard of fairness, it, like a court of equity considers public values beyond simply those enshrined in the letter or encompassed in the spirit of the antitrust laws.

The FTC further developed its unfairness doctrine through truth-in-advertising cases,[72] shaping the practice that '[w]hen advertisers make unsubstantiated claims for products, the FTC has the authority to bring law enforcement actions against them'.[73]

---

[69]     15 USC Sec. 45(a)(4)(a); this also includes unfair methods of competition used in export trade against competitors engaged in export trade, even though the acts constituting such unfair methods are done without the territorial jurisdiction of the United States. Apr. 10, 1918, ch. 50, §4, 40 Stat. 517.

[70]     Teresa M Schwartz, 'Regulating Unfair Practices Under the FTC Act: The Need for a Legal Standard of Unfairness' (1977) 11(1) *Akron Law Review* 1, 4. See also Dorothy Cohen, 'Unfairness in Advertising Revisited' (1982) 46(1) *Journal of Marketing* 73–80.

[71]     US Supreme Court, *FTC v. Sperry & Hutchinson Co.* (S&H) (1972), 244.

[72]     J R H, IV, 'Unfairness in Advertising: Pfizer, Inc.' (1973) 59(2) *Virginia Law Review* 324–54.

[73]     Thomas Pahl, 'Reconsidering Advertising Substantiation Forum and Remedy Policies', 2017 ANA/BAA Marketing Law Conference, 14 November 2017 https://www

As of 1994, however, unfairness became linked to a further test that involves harm specifically relating to consumers themselves:[74]

> The Commission shall have no authority [...] to declare unlawful an act or practice on the grounds that such act or practice is unfair unless the act or practice causes or is likely to cause substantial injury to consumers which is not reasonably avoidable by consumers themselves and not outweighed by countervailing benefits to consumers or to competition. In determining whether an act or practice is unfair, the Commission may consider established public policies as evidence to be considered with all other evidence. Such public policy considerations may not serve as a primary basis for such determination.

With contradictory wording and inconsistent interpretations, the unfairness doctrine used by the FTC remains unclear.[75] This is especially difficult to gauge with respect to its applicability to an industry such as social media, where individual qualities (e.g., consumer) are difficult to pin down, and doctrines such as 'public policy' have not yet been interpreted by courts. More recent FTC complaints seem to acknowledge and attempt to curtail data brokerage and security practices,[76] yet the application of the unfairness doctrine to these instances is based more on deceptiveness than unfairness.[77] In addition,

---

.ftc.gov/system/files/documents/public_statements/1280233/pahl_-_ana_speech_11 -14-17.pdf accessed 28 November 2021.

[74]    15 USC S 45(n) (1999).

[75]    Paul Sobel, 'Unfair Acts or Practices under CUTPA – The Case for Abandoning the Obsolete Cigarette Rule and following Modern FTC Unfairness Policy (2003) 77(2) *Connecticut Bar Journal* 105; Elise M Nelson and Joshua D Wright, 'Judicial Cost–Benefit Analysis Meets Economics: Evidence from State Unfair and Deceptive Trade Practices Laws' (2017) 81(3) *Antitrust Law Journal* 997; Dara J Dionande, 'The Re-Emergence of the Unfairness Doctrine in Federal Trade Commission and State Consumer Protection Cases' (2004) 18 *Antitrust* 53; Maureen K Ohlhausen, 'Weigh the Label, Not the Tractor: What Goes on the Scale in an FTC Unfairness Cost–Benefit Analysis' (2015) 83 *Geo Wash L Rev* 1999.

[76]    Complaint, Nomi Techns., Inc., F.T.C. No. 132 3251 (*FTC*, 3 September 2015) https://www.ftc.gov/enforcement/cases-proceedings/132-3251/nomi-technologies-inc -matter accessed 28 November 2021. See also Cobun Keegan and Calli Schroeder, 'Unpacking Unfairness: The FTC's Evolving Measures of Privacy Harms' (2019) 15 *J L Econ & Po'y* 19, 29; Gautam Hans, 'Privacy Policies, Terms of Service, and FTC Enforcement: Broadening Unfairness Regulation for a New Era' (2012) 19 *Mich Telecomm & Tech L Rev* 163; Timothy E Deal, 'Moving beyond Reasonable: Clarifying the FTC's Use of Its Unfairness Authority in Data Security Enforcement Actions' (2016) 84 *Fordham L Rev* 2227; Dennis D Hirsch, 'That's Unfair – Or Is It: Big Data, Discrimination and the FTC's Unfairness Authority' (2014) 103 *Ky LJ* 345.

[77]    Jennifer L West, 'A Case of Overcorrection: How the FTC's Regulation of Unfair Acts and Practices Is Unfair to Small Businesses' (2017) 58 *Wm & Mary L Rev* 2105, 2106.

the existence of professional or semi-professional users of social media platforms who may not be consumers or competitors but who may be harmed by unfair practices raises further concerns that have yet to be settled.

## 4. SOCIAL MEDIA PLATFORMS AND CONTENT CREATORS: NEW IMPETUS TO EXTEND THE SCOPE OF UNFAIR PRACTICES

So far, this chapter has described both technology (recommender systems) and the law on unfair competition (unfair practices) in the EU and the US. In this section, the discussion shifts to the analysis of the identified regimes to the recommender systems used by social media platforms which may negatively impact content creators. As indicated in section 2.2, it is virtually impossible to obtain the necessary evidence relating to the practical extent to which a creator is affected by the way in which recommender systems are governed. However, it is possible to assume that such harm would reflect the power imbalance between creators and platforms, as the latter gatekeep the popularity (and in some cases even direct monetization) of the former.

In so far as recommender systems are used to curtail the reach of content created by influencers on social media, they deprive creators of business opportunities, or depending on the business model, even of revenue used to support oneself. Of course, a thorough assessment of this loss ought to equally take into account the contractual relationship between the platform and its creators. If a platform prohibits a specific type of behaviour (e.g.. behaviour that encourages self-harm or dangerous activities, very popular on channels that live off prank videos), the platform is contractually entitled to take the remedies it bound its users to when they concluded an agreement and made an account on that platform. However, with questionable content that is on the edge of platform community guidelines, it becomes harder to interpret what remedies ought to come into play,[78] for two main reasons.

First, in fulfilling their content moderation function, social media platforms enjoy a tremendous amount of discretion which they exercise according to internal policies, but which also reacts to various external events that shape public policy. When YouTuber Logan Paul made the video where he was laughing at a man who committed suicide in a Japanese forest, YouTube allegedly removed Paul from the lucrative Google Preferred programme.[79]

---

[78] Paddy Leerssen, 'The Soap Box as a Black Box: Regulating Transparency in Social Media Recommender Systems' (2021) *European Journal of Law and Technology* 11(2).

[79] *BBC News*, 'YouTube punishes Logan Paul over Japan suicide video' (*BBC News*, 11 January 2018) https://www.bbc.com/news/world-asia-42644321 accessed 28 November 2021.

However, given his channel's recovered popularity, it may very well be that this suspension was only temporary. In 2021, Logan Paul is in the top 100 YouTube channels in the US, which also shows that any measures taken may in some situations also have a temporary effect on the reputation and therefore monetization possibilities of a creator.[80] The mere fact that it is not clear what platforms can and actually do when faced with measures against creators whose content they want to control or curtail is a sign of the discretionary use of the power platforms hold over the head of creators.

Second, the evidence relating to how this discretion is exercised is under the full control of the platform.[81] If Instagram removes a user account, that creator no longer has access to any of the analytics which are normally shared by Instagram with its users, even though such analytics are only a sliver of the wealth of information Instagram would have mapped with respect to that profile. This leads to a situation where both within and outside the conflict resolution mechanisms provided for by platforms, the creator will always be in a worse situation, as they will not be able to prove their claims regarding potential harm.

These limitations ought to be kept in mind when dealing with the two jurisdictions outlined above. In the case of the European UCPD, the main legal problem rests in the scope of the Directive, which is only applicable to B2C transactions.[82] Therefore, even before considering any of the tests in the Directive, there is an immediate question of whether the Directive is at all applicable. The answer to this question needs to consider the diversity of content creators: some of them have companies, or are registered freelancers, whereas some do not or are not. More specifically, as consumers are defined as 'any natural person who [...] is acting for purposes which are outside his trade, business, craft or profession',[83] it remains to be seen if individual users who have not taken any measures to set up an additional legal status for their online presence will still be able to fit under this definition, as being a content creator is not a profession or a craft (most content creators start off with close to no video and photo editing skills themselves), and it is counter-intuitive to con-

---

[80]  *Social Blade* www.socialblade.com accessed 28 November 2021.

[81]  Jenna Burrell, 'How the Machine "Thinks": Understanding Opacity in Machine Learning Algorithms' (2016) 3(1) *Big Data & Society*. See also Balasz Bodo et al., 'Tackling the Algorithmic Control Crisis: The Technical, Legal, and Ethical Challenges of Research into Algorithmic Agents' (2018) *Yale Journal of Law and Technology* 19; Margot Kaminski, 'Understanding Transparency in Algorithmic Accountability' in Woodrow Barfield (ed.), *Cambridge Handbook of the Law of Algorithms* (Cambridge University Press 2020).

[82]  Fn 55.

[83]  Art 2(a) UCPD.

sider it a trade or a business, if the individual user has obtained an economic label. This shortcoming is a direct result of the grey area created by the rise of peer-to-peer transactions, which have so far not had any impact on regulatory reform at European level.

Given the scope, it could be argued that mega and micro influencers who have the identity of an economic operator would not be covered by the UCPD. However, considering individual users (e.g., nano influencers without a company or freelance status) as consumers, an argument can be made in that they are protected against unfair commercial practices, as content creators would *be* the consumers. Additionally, there are legal systems that are discussing the application of the UCPD not only to consumers, but also to freelancers (e.g., the Netherlands). This is a broader debate that needs to be had regarding the expansion of the UCPD scope in national implementations, in the light of the emerging types of gig-economies affecting market actors that fall between the consumer and trader categories.

Regarding the actual application of the UCPD, the Annex of the Directive does not include any practices which are in any circumstances considered to be unfair, and which may directly apply to the digital economy. In what follows, we will focus on the next test tier, namely the category of misleading commercial practices. As Micklitz puts it, 'primarily important for the term "misleading" is the distinction between action and omission'.[84] As Community Guidelines do not include any guarantees relating to how recommender systems work, how they are updated, or even whether and how users are notified when updates occur, the application of Article 6 (misleading actions) is questionable. Article 7, however, indicates that commercial practices may be deemed unfair if they omit material information to such an extent that the consumer is manipulated into a decision they would otherwise not have taken. Assuming that creators can be interpreted to fall under the personal scope of the UCPD, the decision in question reflects joining the platform and using it for commercial purposes, to the extent of building a brand. Social media platforms strive to attract as many creators as possible on their platforms: more creators who make content that users enjoy will lead to more users for the platform. However, by not sharing any information with creators regarding the basic governance processes that may affect the reputation of the brand they are trying to create, platforms thus omit to give material information. If YouTube or TikTok clarified the policy considerations behind the implementation of their recommender systems, and those considerations would reveal the level of discretion enjoyed by these platforms in the manipulation of information

---

[84]    Hans-W Micklitz, 'Unfair Commercial Practices and Misleading Advertising', in Norbert Reich et al. (eds) *European Consumer Law* (Intersentia 2014).

flows, creators might chose to interact with them differently, or to not operate in these environments at all. A clear illustration of the frustrations creators already experience in being at the mercy of social media platforms is the trend of building completely independent content websites.[85]

Seeing how content creators seem to predominantly favour this type of legal personhood, the broadening of this applicability could be highly beneficial to them. In so far as unfair commercial practices are deemed to cause the content creator to make transactional decisions they otherwise would not have taken (e.g., using the platform for their commercial activity),[86] and this transactional decision can be expressed as an action or equally as no action (e.g., not being able to access their channel/accounts), it can be considered that content creators may use this legal framework to argue that platform discretion leading to harm is a an unfair commercial practice. This argument is strengthened by the view that professional diligence, the other leg of the general UCPD test, is violated by the discretionary exercise of platform power over its creators.

In the US, while the FTC Act does not limit its scope to B2C relations, Section 5 raises similar concerns as in the EU. Two arguments can be made to support the view that the FTC unfairness doctrine applies to cases of poor algorithmic governance affecting the interests of content creators.[87] On the one hand, it could be argued that the practice of banning or curtailing the economic activity of content creators hurts their audience, which has no way of avoiding such measures. However, in this case, the 'substantial' nature of the injury will be difficult to determine. One estimation of this nature could take into account the way in which followers interact with their favourite content creators, as they form real fan armies that often protect their favourite against other influencers on the Internet. On the other hand, similarly to the analysis of European rules above, the consumers referred to in Section 5 could be content creators themselves, as consumers are considered as natural persons under FTC law,[88] and no additional conditions apply.

---

[85]   'Why Popular YouTubers are Building Their Own Sites' (*BBC News*, 6 March 2021) https://www.bbc.com/news/technology-55349255 accessed 28 November 2021.

[86]   Art 5(2)(b) UCPD.

[87]   So far, the discussions around content creators and the FTC have focused on the consumer harms in influencer marketing. See Laura Bladow, 'Worth the Click: Why Greater FTC Enforcement Is Needed to Curtail Deceptive Practices in Influencer Marketing' (2018) 59(3) *William & Mary Law Review* 1123–[viii]; Sophie Boerman et al., 'Sponsored Blog Content: What do the Regulations Say? And what do Bloggers Say?' (2018) 9 *JIPITEC* 146–159. For further content moderation implications see Daphne Keller and Paddy Leerssen, 'Facts and Where to Find Them: Empirical Research on Internet Platforms and Content Moderation' (SSRN Scholarly Paper 2019) https://papers.ssrn.com/abstract=3504930 accessed 28 November 2021.

[88]   15 USC § 6603(h)(6)(A).

The considerable hurdle, however, would be to link any one of these arguments to the concept of public policy.[89] As data brokers generate new business models at skyrocketing speeds, and US regulators are slow in creating new policies around them, the question of what public policy is when considering the platform restriction of the economic activities of content creators is currently left to academic imagination. Against this background, the FTC already has drafted some concrete plans to bring more legal certainty regarding the application of doctrines around unfair competition to current practices on digital markets.[90] In March 2021, the FTC Acting Chairwoman announced the creation of a new rulemaking group on unfair or deceptive practices and unfair methods of competition, to 'deliver effective deterrence for the novel harms of the digital economy'. None of the current rules and guides directly address the impact of algorithmic decision-making on emerging economic actors, such as content creators,[91] so it will be interesting to follow the scope and interpretations of new rules on unfair competition.

## 5.    CONCLUSION

This chapter aimed to look into recommender systems that curtail the economic activities of content creators and argue that current unfair competition frameworks in the EU and US are a good starting point for the correction of the harms that may arise when social media platforms exercise harmful discretion towards content creators. However, it is also a framework that needs expanding and even updating to current economic activities and actors involved in social media transactions. This expansion is necessary to provide overdue checks and balances to platform powers in the context of content moderation, especially since this topic will only grow in the coming years. As platforms develop new ways of controlling their audiences and exercising their power on market dynamics, it is essential to consider how checks and balances could be placed on this power. The European Commission's Digital Services Act package promises developments in this respect, yet the Digital Services Act itself does not link to the UCPD. From this perspective, it is essential to keep

---

[89]    See for instance Philip M Napoli, 'Social Media and the Public Interest: Governance of News Platforms in the Realm of Individual and Algorithmic Gatekeepers' (2015) 39(9) *Telecommunications Policy* 751–760.

[90]    FTC Press release, 'FTC Acting Chairwoman Slaughter Announces New Rulemaking Group' (*FTC*, 25 March 2021) https://www.ftc.gov/news-events/press-releases/2021/03/ftc-acting-chairwoman-slaughter-announces-new-rulemaking-group accessed 28 November 2021.

[91]    FTC Rules & Guides https://www.ftc.gov/enforcement/rules/rules-and-guides accessed 28 November 2021.

the perspective of what can be achieved with existing rules and doctrines, and unfair trade offers a unique angle to answer this question.

# PART III

Remits and limits of exclusive rights

# 7. Creations caused by humans (or robots)? Artificial intelligence and causation requirements for copyright protection in EU law

**Ole-Andreas Rognstad**

## 1. INTRODUCTION

Copyright is an important cornerstone for the creation of media content. The importance is twofold, in that on the one hand the existence of copyright (and related rights) implies that in many situations consent from right holders is necessary for media corporations in order to make use of content. On the other hand, copyright law is predicated on the notion that protection, and exclusive rights, incentivize production of content. For these reasons, copyright is inevitably also important in the discussion of what role artificial intelligence (AI) plays, and should play, in the media. Unsurprisingly, the relationship between copyright – and intellectual property – on the one hand and artificial intelligence on the other is being discussed in international fora such as the OECD and WIPO,[1] and the question about the copyrightability of AI-generated creations specifically has been subject to much scholarly debate lately.[2]

---

[1] See e.g., OECD Report 'World Corporate Top R&D Investors: Shaping the Future of Technologies and AI' (Publications Office of the European Union 2019) www.oecd.org/sti/world-corporate-top-rd-investors-shaping-future-of-technology-and -of-ai.pdf accessed 1 February 2021 and the WIPO website 'Artificial Intelligence and the IP' https://www.wipo.int/about-ip/en/artificial_intelligence/ accessed 1 February 2021.

[2] It is impossible to enumerate the entire scholarship even in recent years on the subject in this context, so here only a few contributions reflecting different views are mentioned: Annemaria Bridy, 'Coding Creativity: Copyright and the Artificially Intelligent Author' (2012) 5 *Stanford Technology Law Review*, 1–28; James Grimmelmann, 'There's no Such Thing as a Computer Authored Work – and That's a Good Thing' (2016) 39 *Columbia Journal of Law & the Arts*, 403–416; Schlomit Yainsky-Ravid, 'Generating Rembrandt: Artificial Intelligence, Copyright, and

Although views differ as to whether, or to what extent, AI creations *should be* protected by copyright, broad consensus exists in jurisdictions based on human authorship that creations which are not the result of human efforts are not protectable.[3] This raises the question about copyright *causation*, since the implication seems to be that only creations caused by humans can be copyright protected. This contribution will discuss the further implications of this causation requirement in the context of EU law related to the debate about copyright protection for AI-generated output.[4]

The following discussion is based on the presumption that the principle of human authorship also prevails in EU law. Even though the Court of Justice of the European Union (CJEU) has not explicitly ruled on this matter yet,[5] clear indications in legislative material as well as case law suggest that the concepts of work and authorship are dependent on human efforts.[6] The concept of the 'author' is not horizontally defined for all categories of works, but the Computer Software Directive[7] Article 2(1) and the Database Directive[8] Article 4 expressly state that the author must be a natural person. The Infosoc

---

Accountability in the 3A Era – the Human Authors Are Already Here – A New Model' (2017) *Michigan State Law Review*, 659–726; Jani Ihalainen, 'Computer Creativity: Artificial Intelligence and Copyright' (2018) 9 *Journal of Intellectual Property Law & Practice*, 724–728; Jane C Ginsburg and Luke Ali Budiardjo, 'Authors and Machines' (2019) 34 *Berkeley Technology Law Journal*, 343–456; Daniel J Gervais, 'The Machine as Author' (2020) 105 *Iowa Law Review*, 2053–2106; Christian Hartmann and others, *Trends and Developments in Artificial Intelligence. Challenges to the Intellectual Property Rights Framework. Final Report* (European Commission 2020) https://www .ivir.nl/publicaties/download/Trends_and_Developments_in_Artificial_Intelligence-1 .pdf accessed 1 March 2020; Peter Mezei, 'From Leonardo to the Next Rembrandt – The Need for AI-Pessimism in the Age of Algorithms', (2020) 85 UFITA – *Archiv für Medienrecht und Medienwissenschaft* (forthcoming), here cited from the version available at https://papers.ssrn.com/sol3/papers.cfm?abstract_id=3592187 accessed 1 December 2020.

3   See Jane C Ginsburg, 'The Concept of Authorship in Comparative Copyright Law' (2003) 52 *DePaul Law Review*, 1063–1092.

4   Recognizing that similar causation questions may also be raised concerning other IP protection regimes, most notably patent law, see eg Hartmann and others (n 2) 103.

5   That is, several statements in the case law imply that the author is a physical person, e.g., in case C-277/10 *Martin Luksan v Petrus van der L*et EU:C:2012:65, para 78, and case C-572/13 *Hewlett-Packard Belgium SPRL v Reprobel* EU:C:2015:750, paras 44–49.

6   See also Hartmann and others (n 2) 69 et seq.

7   Directive 2009/24/EC of the European Parliament and of the Council on the Legal Protection of Computer Programs [2009] OJ L 111/16.

8   Directive 1996/6/EC of the European Parliament and of the Council on the Legal Protection of Databases, [2009] OJ L 77/20.

Directive[9] does not contain a similar provision, but the Court's elaboration on the concept of a work, also under this Directive, undoubtedly seems to imply human authorship. Thus in case C-469/17 (*Funke Medien*) the CJEU held that a military status report could qualify as a 'work' under this Directive if the author 'was able to make free and creative choices capable of conveying to the reader the originality of the subject matter at issue'.[10] Similar formulations are found in other decisions, for example, case C-683/17 (*Cofemel*) on copyright protection of applied art,[11] and they all closely resemble the Court's earlier findings in case C-145/10 (*Painer*) where a photograph was considered as protected under Article 6 of the Term Directive[12] if the author was able to 'express his creative abilities in the production of the work by making free and creative choices'.[13] In this case the Court also specified that, by making those various choices, the author of a portrait photograph can stamp the work created with his 'personal touch'.[14] It is believed that this is a general consideration in EU copyright law, which also applies beyond the creation of portrait photographs. Although it is not totally excluded that these criteria may apply to machines, in particular the reference to 'personal touch' implies the activity of a human author and not a machine. Adding the fact that machines as such, at least at the present stage, do not even have a legal personality, it is safe to conclude that human agency is a requirement for authorship of works under EU law.

In this situation, the question is *who* – if anyone – is accountable under EU law for output created by means of an AI system? We will here concentrate on creations that may qualify as a 'work' under EU legislation on the premise

---

[9]   Directive 2001/29/EC of the European Parliament and the European Council on the Harmonisation on Certain Aspects of Copyright and Related Rights in the Information Society [2001] OJ L 167/10.

[10]   Case C-469/17 *Funke Medien NRW GmbH v Bundesrepublik Deutschland* EU:C:2019:623, para 23.

[11]   Case C-683/17 *Cofemel – Sociedade de Vestuário SA v G-Star Raw CV* EU:C:2019:721, para 30.

[12]   Directive 2006/116/EC of the European Parliament and the European Council on the Term of Protection of Copyright and Certain Related Rights [2006] OJ L 372/12.

[13]   Case C-145/10 *Eva-Marie Painer v Standard Verlags GmbH et al.* EU:C:2011:798, para 89.

[14]   Ibid., para 92. It is also to be noted that Advocate General Trstenjak in her opinion in the same case explicitly stated that it followed from Art 6 first sentence of the Term Directive that 'only human creations are ... protected, which can also include those for which the person employs a technical aid, such as a camera'. For a discussion about the Advocate Generals' influence on the CJEU case law in copyright cases, see Estelle Derclaye, 'The Multifaceted Influence of Advocates-General on the Court of Justice's Copyright Case Law: Legal Secretaries, Literature and Language' in Eleonora Rosati (ed), The *Routledge Handbook of European Copyright Law* (Routledge 2021) (forthcoming).

already given, namely that this requires human authorship. Accountability in the present context means who is to be credited as an author and consequently has rights to a created work. As stated above, we will here particularly discuss the *causation* problem that arises in the context of AI-generated works. Since AI is used in the process of creating a work, whereas authorship requires human agency, the question is what should be considered as the *cause* of a work created – human agency, the operation of the AI system itself, or both?

Although the discussion will revolve around the causation of human authorship, it should be noted that a causation requirement may also be derived from legal provisions that are not based on human authorship. In some jurisdictions, namely the UK, Ireland, New Zealand, South Africa and India, so-called computer-generated works are also protected by copyright where the author is not a human being.[15] For example, under the UK Copyright Designs and Patent Act (1988) section 9(3), in the case of computer-generated works 'the author shall be taken to be the person by whom the arrangements necessary for the creation of the work are undertaken'.[16] Even though this provision implies that legal persons can also be authors, the requirement that the arrangements be *necessary* is likely to be understood as a causation requirement in that authorship may be claimed only to the extent that creation of the work is caused by arrangements of a natural or a legal person. The fact that AI systems – at least at the present stage – cannot be considered as (legal) persons on their own is a relevant factor in determining whether a person is, or is not, an author of a work. The same seems to apply also to so-called neighbouring rights that are not dependent on human agency, for example the EU Database Sui Generis right (Database Directive Article 7) and Phonogram Producer Rights (e.g. Infosoc Directive Arts 2(c) and 3(2)(b)).

In this chapter, we will concentrate on the human/non-human divide in discussing causation requirements related to AI-generated works in EU law, recognizing that similar problems may also arise with regard to rights that are not dependent on human agency.[17] The intention is to explore the scope of accountability implicit in causation considerations as an instrument for delineating rights in AI-generated output in EU copyright law. The findings will lay a foundation for reflections on whether the current legal situation offers

---

[15] See further Robert C Denicola, '*Ex Machina:* Copyright Protection for Computer-Generated Works' (2016) 69 *Rutgers University Law Review*, 251–287.

[16] See e.g., Lionel Bently and others, *Intellectual Property Law* (5th ed, OUP 2018), 117–118.

[17] See the comparative analysis of various copyright regimes in Petrap Devarapalli, 'Machine Learning to Machine Owning: Redefining the Copyright Ownership from the Perspective of Australian, US, UK and EU Law', (2018) 40 *European Intellectual Property Review*, 722–728, 723–726.

a balanced outcome, but the main purpose is to provide an account of the state of the art in EU copyright law.

## 2.    CAUSATION IN EU COPYRIGHT LAW

Discussions have lately been under way, notably related to US law, about causation requirements hidden in existing copyright doctrines, both particularly connected to AI-generated output as well as on a more general level, though also relevant to AI contexts. As to the former, Gervais proposes a test of 'originality causation' in order '[t]o allow courts to apply the law as it is, and should be'.[18] According to the author, this test 'allows a separation of the protectible creative expression of humans from the nonprotectible expression contained in machine productions'.[19] Burk takes a somewhat broader view and notes that 'concepts of causation, volition and intention ... inform copyright authorship, and that the machine-learning revolution affords us the opportunity to reveal previously hidden assumptions about copyright authorship'.[20]

From a more general viewpoint, Balganesh claims that '[c]ausation has always been an integral part of copyright law's basic entitlement structure, even if only rarely acknowledged as such'.[21] This implies that '[t]he institution's constitutional commitment to authorship – as both a status ('author') and a process ('authoring') – requires paying close attention to the way in which a work is created and then ascribed to an identified human agent'.[22] Balganesh proposes that authorial causation should be considered as a separate requirement of protection in copyright law. This causation requirement consists partly of an epistemic dimension based on factual causation, and partly of some principles of legal causation, meant to evaluate whether human agency 'was normatively sufficient to merit legal characterization as the authorial cause and thereby lead to the status of "author" for the identified agent'.[23] In the following, we will detect possible causation elements inherent in the originality criterion developed in the case law of the CJEU, before discussing whether,

---

[18]   See Gervais (n 2) 2106.

[19]   Ibid., 2100.

[20]   Dan L Burk, 'Thirty-six Views of Copyright Authorship, by Jackson Pollock', (2021) 58 *Houston Law Review* (forthcoming), cited from the version available at https://papers.ssrn.com/sol3/papers.cfm?abstract_id=3570225 accessed 1 December 2020, 1.

[21]   Shyamkrishna Balganesh, 'Causing Copyright' (2017) 117 *Columbia Law Review*, 1–78, 77.

[22]   Ibid.

[23]   Ibid.

and to what extent, the above approaches to causation are helpful to analysis of copyright protection of AI-generated works in EU law.

Returning to the basic requirements for copyright protection in EU law, an originality criterion follows explicitly from three EU Directives. Article 1(3) of the Computer Program Directive states that a 'computer program shall be protected if it is original in the sense that it is the author's own intellectual creation'. In the same vein, under Article 3(1) of the Database Directive, 'databases which by reason of selection or arrangement of their contents, constitute the author's own intellectual creation, shall be protected by copyright'. Finally, Article 6 of the Term Directive contains a similar formulation, in that '[p]hotographs which are original in the sense that they are the author's own intellectual creation shall be protected'. All these provisions underscore that no other criteria are to be applied to determine their eligibility for protection. Outside the scope of the three directives, no statutory originality provisions apply, but the CJEU had already asserted in case C-5/08 (*Infopaq I*) that the term 'work' in Article 2 of the Infosoc Directive implies that 'copyright ... is liable to apply in relation to a subject-matter which is original in the sense that it is its author's own intellectual creation'.[24] In subsequent cases concerning interpretation of the term 'work' in the Infosoc Directive, the Court has confirmed this interpretation and applied a similar formulation,[25] so there is hardly any doubt that the EU originality criterion has general applicability to works of all kinds.

If we look at the various formulations, a causation requirement is implied in phrases such as 'in the sense that it is' and 'constitute [the author's own intellectual creation]'. In other words, all subject matters caused by activities leading to 'the author's own intellectual creation' are protected by copyright. In case C-683/17 (*Cofemel*) the CJEU even expressly specified that the concept of 'work' implies two cumulative conditions: 'First, that ... there exist[s] an original subject matter, in the sense of being the author's own intellectual creation. Second, classification as a work is reserved to the elements that are the expression of such creation.'[26] This implies an additional clarification of the causation requirement implicit in the concept of a 'work' in EU law, as only elements caused by activities leading to 'the author's own intellectual creation' are protected by copyright and thereby relevant to causation assessment.

---

[24]   Case C-5/08 *Infopaq International A/S v Danske Dagblades Forening* EU:C:2009:465, para 37.

[25]   See e.g., joined cases C-403/08 and C-429/08 *Football Association Premier League Ltd. et al v QC Leisure et al and Karen Murphy v Media Protection Services Ltd.* EU:C:2011:631, para 97; case C-310/17 *Levola Hengelo BV v Smilde Foods BV* EU:C:2018:899, para 36; case C-683/17 (*Cofemel*), (n 11) para 29.

[26]   Ibid.

A particular trait from the case law of the CJEU on the concepts of 'work' and 'originality' is that the Court has specified the activities that are relevant to the originality assessment, or put in other words 'the author's own intellectual creation'. Thus, the CJEU has not only concentrated on characterizing the result of creative activity but also on the activity ('process') itself. This became evident in particular from the ruling in *Painer*. Here, the Court emphasized that the originality criterion in the Term Directive Article 6 would be fulfilled if 'the author was able to express his creative abilities in the production of the work by making free and creative choices'. According to the Court:

> the photographer can make free and creative choices in several ways and at various points in its production ... In the preparation phase, the photographer can choose the background, the subject's pose and the lighting. When taking a portrait photograph, she can choose the framing, the angle of view and the atmosphere created. Finally, when selecting the snapshot, the photographer may choose from a variety of developing techniques the one he wishes to adopt or, where appropriate, use computer software.[27]

Although the Court here emphasized the freedom of choices that the photographer enjoys in these situations, it is still quite clear both from the wording of this decision and other decisions[28] that freedom of choice as such is not sufficient in order to create a work – the author must also take advantage of that freedom to make *creative* choices.[29] However, the main point of the *Painer* decision – which is of high relevance to AI-generated works – is to demonstrate that opportunities are a-plenty to make creative choices even in situations where the motive is given and advanced equipment is used in order to create the work.

Combining the observations in *Painer* with the requirement in *Cofemel* that classification as a work is reserved to elements that are the expression of that creation, it is possible to derive an 'originality causation rule' in EU law: elements of a creation that are caused by a (human) author's free and creative choices are protected as a work; the implication, or antithesis, of this rule being that other elements are not protected. For AI-generated works the question is whether these should be considered as caused by free and creative choices made by humans, or whether the operation of an AI system in one way or another breaks the causal link between those choices and the output. Given the diversity of AI systems and their operation, it is not possible to give a clear-cut and general answer to this question. The purpose is rather to sketch out an

---

[27]   Case C-145/10 (*Painer*), (n 13) paras 90 and 91.
[28]   E.g., C-429/17 (*Funke Medien*), (n 10) para 23; case C-833/18 *Brompton Bicycle Ltd. v Chedech/Get2Get* EU:C:2020:461, paras 34 and 35.
[29]   Compare *Bently and others*, (n 16) 101.

approach to the causation analysis implicit in the concepts of work and authorship that may be useful when addressing the question of copyright protection for AI-generated works. One question here is whether causation principles developed in other contexts, notably in tort law, may be helpful in this respect. Discussing this in the following section I will *inter alia* draw on Balganesh's analysis of US law, but with a view to how to formulate an originality causation rule in EU law with applicability to AI-generated works.

## 3.   AN ORIGINALITY CAUSATION RULE IN EU LAW FOR AI-GENERATED WORKS – POINTS OF DEPARTURE

Discussing rights in AI-generated works from a causation perspective inevitably raises the question of the usefulness of drawing on tort law principles in determining the relevant causes. In Balganesh's two-step inquiry model for copyright causation, mentioned above, the first step – creation in fact – is modelled on tort law principles. The first step of the copyrightable-causation requirement 'would look for an epistemic basis to causally relate the work in question to an actor's creative actions'.[30] Here, Balganesh points to the universally applicable 'but-for test' in tort law as a point of departure. This implies that 'the defendant's conduct is a factual cause of the plaintiff's harm if, but for the defendant's conduct, that harm would not have occurred'.[31]

Transcribed into a but-for creation test in copyright law, 'an individual claimant should be treated as having caused the creation of the work—as a matter of authorship—*if, but for that individual's actions, the particular work of expression in question would not have come into existence*'.[32] Phrased as a mere epistemic question, however, it is obvious that the but-for test is over-inclusive and goes too far in order to grab the essence of an originality causation rule in EU law. Many actions that are necessary for the creation of a work, in the sense of but-for that individual's action the particular work of expression would not have come into existence, will not be relevant in order to qualify for authorship. It is quite clear that artists' parents cannot claim copyright to their children's works. We do not even have to mention examples that by analogy in tort law may fall under doctrines of proximate cause to come to this conclusion. Even though it may be obvious that works created under employment or hire contracts would not be created but for the employer's or the principal's undertakings, these persons cannot claim authorship to the work

---

30   See Balganesh (n 21) 53.
31   Ibid., 55.
32   Ibid., 55–56.

under European copyright law, save for computer programs. For the latter, Article 2(3) of the Computer Program Directive decides that:

> [w]here a computer program is created by an employee in the execution of his duties or following the instructions given by his employer, the employer exclusively shall be entitled to exercise all economic rights in the program so created, unless otherwise provided by contract.

Absent a corresponding rule applicable to other types of works, the general rule on authorship will be the opposite: rights vest in the employee(s) as a human author(s), unless otherwise (explicitly or implicitly) provided by contract. In any case, the but-for causation cannot be an argument on its own for the employer (or principal) to claim authorship in a work since it is not the employer, but the employee(s), who will have made the relevant creative choices that result in (cause) the work. Thus, the but-for creation rule as such does not exist in EU copyright law – at least it will have to be linked to the originality criterion.

This is no different with other 'creation in fact' rules modelled on tort law. Due to both the over-inclusiveness and the under-inclusiveness of the but-for rule in tort law, scholars have developed the so-called NESS-test (necessary elements of a sufficient set).[33] According to the NESS test, acts or conditions that are necessary for the occurrence of injury (but-for) as well as those that are independently sufficient for the occurrence of injury and those that are a causally relevant part, will be considered to have caused the injury.[34] Balganesh claims that, applied to copyright causation, 'the NESS test ... fares significantly better than but-for causation', in particular in cases of joint causation (joint works).[35] Balganesh's arguments in terms of the NESS test's capability of solving copyright causation problems go as follows: [Where] two artists work together creating a painting on canvas, ... each contributing various colored shapes and lines to the work during the process, [the but-for test will be under-conclusive, since] it is impossible ... to say if the work of art would have come into being with just one of their contributions in isolation.[36] Here, the NESS test 'produces affirmative answers for both actors' involvement, thereby treating them each as a cause of the consequence under study', Hence, 'the NESS test would ask if each artist's contribution was a necessary

---

[33] Originally, H L A Hart and Tony Honoré, *Causation in the Law* (2nd ed., New York: Oxford University), (1985; 1st ed 1959), 109–119, further developed by Richard W Wright, 'Causation in Tort Law' (1985) 73 *California Law Review* 1735–1828, 1788–1803.

[34] Wright, ibid., 1788–1789.

[35] Balganesh (n 21) 59.

[36] Ibid., 58.

element of the set of actual antecedent conditions that includes both artists' contributions in which that set was sufficient for the creation of the *particular* final work that emerged'.[37] In cases of sequential causation (derivative works), where one artist creates a work and another artist thereafter modifies the first artist's work, both the but-for test and the NESS test seem at first glance to be over-inclusive. Under both tests, both the original author and the author of the derivative work will be considered to have caused the derivative work.

According to Balganesh, '[o]n closer scrutiny ... one realizes that the NESS test tracks copyright law's basic principles about derivative authorship, such as the need to keep the rights in a lawful derivative work distinct from those in the original'.[38] This is so also because in line with Balganesh's two-step model, further scrutiny will take place under the second-step rubric of legal creation. However, his conclusion regarding application of the NESS test to subsequent causation (derivative work) is that 'the significant control over downstream derivatives granted to original authors may derive from the recognition that as a purely epistemic matter, the original author plays crucial role in *causing* the derivative to come into existence'.[39]

Even if one recognizes that the epistemic dimension of copyright causation based on factual causation only represents the first step of the assessment, both the but-for causation and the NESS test *are* over-inclusive in relation to the originality causation requirement in that they fail to take the role of the author's free and creative choices into consideration. This might, under Balganesh's two-step model, to some extent be remedied through one of the three elements of the second step – legal creation – namely, what he calls 'personality conflation'. This principle means:

> focus on copyright law's need to identify and distinguish one author's individual creative choices from those of another (or others) when the works that embody these choices are themselves interrelated. In these situations, even though it might be epistemically defensible to identify one creator (i.e., author) as causally linked to every work that derives from it, one might consider the causal nexus severed when the importance of those individual creative choices is conflated.[40]

The question is still whether starting with the factual causation assessment, even if the more sophisticated NESS test is used, makes the copyright causation analysis more complicated than it has to be. In fact the originality causation requirement (in EU law) is not about factual causation, in the sense that

---

[37]   Ibid., 59.
[38]   Ibid., 60.
[39]   Ibid., 61.
[40]   Ibid., 68–69, with a further exemplification on 69.

copyright is not granted to all persons that have caused creation of the work in an epistemic sense, but to those whose *free and creative choices* have caused the work. Thus, the originality causation test is a legal, more than a factual one, motivated by the fact that only creative, or original contributions, are copyrightable.[41] In other words, to the extent factual causation is relevant, it has to be linked to one – or several – person(s) and their free and creative choices because of the legal requirement of originality. Furthermore, other copyright relevant doctrines endorsed by the CJEU, such as the idea/expression dichotomy, the requirement of sufficient precision and objectivity, and lack of copyright protection for functionality, must also be taken into consideration.

Nevertheless, factual causation will necessarily have to be *part of* the originality assessment in EU law as long as the question is whether the identified work is the *result of* the author's own intellectual creation. Hence, all three – but-for, the necessary elements of a sufficient set of conditions, and proximate causation – may implicitly be relevant factors in determining whether an AI-generated work is caused by human efforts. Nevertheless, the question is whether the originality causation test in EU law can be formulated in a manner that integrates factual and legal causation. Here, the formulation of the CJEU in *Painer*, citing Recital 16 of the Term Directive, that 'an intellectual creation is an author's own if it reflects the author's personality', may serve the function. Given the Court's addendum that this is the case if the author was able to express their creative abilities in production of the work by making free and creative choices,[42] the originality causation requirement may be synthesized as expressing that the free and creative choices of humans have *caused* the work to the extent that those choices *are reflected* in the expression of the work.[43] In these situations, the expression of the work would not be the same but for the

---

[41]   According to Mezei (n 2) 20, 'creativity is not a prerequisite of protection in many countries, including the European Union. To the contrary, originality is generally fixed to authorship and subject matter, both of which are closely connected to humans and human achievements'. The statement is meant to support rejection of the position that machines can be entitled to copyright on the premise that they are 'creative', but is easily misunderstood if not read in this context. To be sure, if the qualification of *human* creativity is a given, then creativity is indeed a prerequisite of protection in EU copyright law, in the sense that the originality criterion is not fulfilled unless the author has made free and creative choices, see the case law cited in (nn 24–25).

[42]   Case C-145/10 (*Painer*) paras 88–89.

[43]   Compare Hartmann and others (n 2) 75, who see the 'requirement of expression' as implying 'a *causal link* between an author's creative act (the exercising of their creative freedom) and the expression thereof in the form of the work produced'. At the same time they note that '[w]hat, however, remains unclear from the Court's case law, is whether and to what extent the original features of the work should (all) be preconceived or premeditated by the author'.

creative choices of the author, the creative choices must be considered as a sufficient set of conditions for the expression, and the expression is a proximate cause of the creative choices. At the same time, the formulation does not rule out the chance that there may be several causes to the expression as the work is only protected *to the extent* that free and creative choices are reflected in the work. How this is to be handled in the context of AI-generated works will be discussed in the next section when discussing the impact of unforeseeable and random factors.

Turning to AI-generated works, it is a given that irrespective of the diversity of technology labelled as AI,[44] the output is governed by human efforts, and that a multitude of free and creative (human) choices are made in the process. As one author has put it, '"training" a model to learn a task involves careful human effort to formulate the problem, acquire appropriate data, and test different formulations'.[45] Nevertheless, the notion that the '"designer" of "fully generated machines", in the sense that "their outputs … flow from the creative contributions of the machines" …, are the authors of the resulting works, even if someone other than the machine's designer operates the machine',[46] seems too simplistic. The same goes for the distinction between 'fully generated machines' and 'partial generated machines', implying that in the former case the outputs flow from the creative contributions of the 'designers', while in the latter the 'outputs [reflect] the creative contributions of *both* the designer and the user' of the machine.[47] If limiting ourselves to AI systems based on advanced machine learning, several stages are involved in the machine-learning process: problem definition, data collection, data cleaning, summary statistics review, model (algorithm) selection, model training, and feature selection.[48] These stages *may* be carried out by the same persons or entities, but the tasks may also be allocated to different persons and entities.

---

[44] Noting that 'AI is a diffuse term that corresponds to a web of human actors and computational processes interacting in complex ways', cf Ziv Epstein and others, 'Who Gets Credit for AI-Generated Art?', (2020) 23 *iScience*, 101515, with reference to Nick Seaver, 'Algorithms as Culture. Some Tactics for the Ethnography of Algorithmic Studies', (2017) *Big Data and Society*.

[45] Aaron Hertzmann, 'Can Computers Create Art?', (2018) 7 Arts, https://doi.org/10.3390/arts7020018 accessed 1 March 2021, 12.

[46] Ginsburg and Budiardjo (2019), (n 2) 439.

[47] Ibid.

[48] Following the description in David Lehr and Paul Ohm, 'Playing with the Data. What Legal Scholars Should Know about Machine Learning', (2017) 51 *University of California, Davis Law Review*, 653–717. See also Josef Drexl and others, 'Technical Aspects of Artificial Intelligence: An Understanding from an Intellectual Property Law Perspective', (2019) Max Planck Institute for Innovation and Competition Research Paper No. 19-13.

Thus, the design of the model (algorithm) may be separated from data collection and training of the model, and so on, in the same manner as the 'designer' may be separated from the 'user'.

Hence, problems related to situations where the designer and the user have not collaborated on the output, each contributing insufficiently to the final result in order to claim copyright,[49] may equally be raised in regard to the design process as such. Since the originality causation requirement presupposes an assessment of whether the creative choices undertaken are reflected in the output, a general statement that the 'designer' is the author of 'fully generated machines' is too sweeping to stand scrutiny. One will have to assess the causal links between the various creative choices involved in the machine-learning process and the expression in order to determine the copyright status of the output. The result of these assessments may be that certain features of the output are protected by copyright, while others are not.[50] This is no different from other creative processes, implying that the final result includes unprotected ideas and unoriginal traits. The question that will be discussed in the following is what role the operation of the machine is likely to play in assessment of the causal links between free and creative (human) choices and the output of machine-learning processes. Given the diversity of such processes the question is discussed at a general level with a view to analysing the application of originality causation related to AI-generated works in EU copyright law.

The central problem here is the so-called 'black box' features of machine-learning systems, that is, the features that make it impossible to predict the outcome of such systems and to even explain precisely why the AI system generated a concrete output based on a given input.[51] Here, we have to keep in mind that the predictability and 'explainability of machine learning vary depending on the complexity of a model and the training techniques used'.[52] The problem usually arises with regard to deep neural networks.[53] In the following, we will nevertheless discuss the relevance of lack of foresee-

---

[49]    See Ginsburg and Budiardjo (n 2) 440 et seq.

[50]    See e.g., Jean-Marc Deltorn and Ralph Macrez, 'Authorship in the Age of Machine Learning and Artificial Intelligence', (2018) *Center for International Intellectual Property Studies Research Paper* No. 10, 1–25, 21–22, on the possibility of acquiring copyright to the setting of one or two parameters of an AI-generated musical work.

[51]    See Hertzmann (n 45) '[AI systems] are not always predictable, and the results are often surprising and delightful'.

[52]    See Drexl and others (n 48) 11.

[53]    Ibid., defining deep neural networks as 'complex architecture, composed of a high number of layers' (12). A different kind of definition is 'a type of artificial intelligence that uses algorithms ... based on the way the human brain operates', see e.g.,

ability and randomness for the originality causation assessment in EU law, in light of the discussion about copyrightability of the output of AI systems.

## 4.     THE BREAKING OF THE CAUSAL LINK BETWEEN CREATION AND EXPRESSION – THE RELEVANCE OF UNFORESEEABILITY AND RANDOMNESS OF THE RESULTS

Indeterminacy is held to be part of the copyright picture, in that originality and authorship do not require that the author is able to foresee every aspect of the outcome of their creative efforts. The works of the American painter Jackson Pollock are often used as an example.[54] Exercising his 'painting dripping technique':

> Pollock could not, as he flung paint at his canvas, control every detail of the work that emerged, Pollock's painting seems to have involved a give-and take between accident and deliberation; in part he 'discovered' the work as it progressed and adjusted his intentions accordingly.[55]

Or:

> Jackson Pollock could not have anticipated the precise trajectory and landing points of the paints, even though his splatter painting process was, despite appearances, highly controlled; yet copyright law would not doubt his authorship of his occasionally aleatory output.[56]

Grounding this view and the assertion that copyright law tolerates some degree of randomness in the originality causation requirement in EU law,[57] copyright protection for Pollock's works will be granted because his controlled splatter-painting process is the result of his free and creative choices that are reflected in the painting. The fact that Pollock was unable to foresee every aspect of the outcome is irrelevant in this setting. The planned, controlled

---

https://dictionary.cambridge.org/dictionary/english/deep-learning accessed 1 March 2020. That definition is illustrative as long as it is not taken too literally.

[54]   See e.g., Alan R Durham, 'The Random Muse: Authorship and Indeterminacy', (2002) 44 *William and Mary Law Review* 569–642; Burk (n 20); Ginsburg and Budiardjo (n 2) 363–364, with further references. See also, from an art and design perspective, Kenny Verbeek, *Randomness as a Generative Principle in Art and Architecture*, Thesis (S.M.) – Massachusetts Institute of Technology, Dept. of Architecture (2006).

[55]   Durham (n 54) 601.

[56]   Ginsburg and Budiardjo (n 2) 363.

[57]   Compare Ginsburg and Budiardjo, ibid., stating that 'copyright law would not doubt his authorship of his occasionally aleatory output'.

and at the same time intuitive process involved in his method of painting implied a multitude of creative choices that were all reflected in the final result. Stated in other words, no incidents or circumstances intervened in the process between his free and creative choices other than natural forces and physical phenomena. In such situations randomness or lack of foreseeability with regard to the final result will not be a bar to the author's copyright since the basic requirements – creativity and reflection in expression – are fulfilled.

Here it is suggested that discussion of the role that randomness plays in the copyright picture will have to relate to two different stages. The first stage is the creativity stage and the requirement that the author has to perform free and creative choices. To what extent are the choices to be considered as free and creative if the author does not know what they are doing? This touches upon the discussion about authorial intent and to what extent intent is an implicit requirement for copyright protection.[58] In EU law, the CJEU has not yet had the opportunity to rule in the matter, but it has been suggested that 'general authorial intent' is sufficient, that is, 'that the author has a general conception of the work before it is expressed, while leaving room for unintended expressive features'.[59] The latter part of this observation refers to the second stage – the (causal) link between free and creative choices and expression. In my opinion the better view, or perhaps only a different way of phrasing the same but in an analytically clearer setting, is to distinguish between the two stages, and accept that intent may be relevant for the first but not the second. Hence, in assessing whether the alleged author has undertaken free and creative choices, intent to create a work may at least be a relevant factor.[60] In contrast, intent is not an element in assessing whether creative choices are reflected in expression of the work (the causation assessment). This means that randomness is accepted at the second stage, implying that the author does not have to predict the outcome of their creative choices, but that there is less room for accepting randomness at the first stage in determining whether the author has performed free and creative choices in the first place.

The relationship between the two stages may be further illustrated by another popular tale much referred to in AI and copyright discussions,[61]

---

[58]   See Burk (n 20) 5 with references to David Nimmer, 'Copyright in the Dead Sea Scrolls: Authorship and Originality' (2001) 38 *Houston Law Review,* 1–218, 209–210 and Christopher Buccafusco, 'A Theory of Copyright Authorship' (2016) 102 *Virginia Law Review,* 1229–1285.

[59]   See Hartmann and others (n 2) 75, with reference to Burk (n 20) and Ginsburg and Budiardo (n 2) 363.

[60]   Compare Burk, ibid.

[61]   See e.g., Andrés Guadamuz, 'The Monkey Selfie: Copyright Lessons for Originality in Photographs and Internet Jurisdiction' (2016) 5 *Internet Policy Review.*

namely the 'monkey selfie' story.[62] There are different versions of the story,[63] but the one implying that photographer David Slater did not have copyright to the photographs that the macaque Naruto took of itself with Slater's camera obviously ignores Slater's free and creative choices.[64] Slater's own version of the incidents is different, in that he had 'put [his] camera on a tripod with a very wide angle lens settings configured such as predictive autofocus, motorwind, even a flashgun, to give [himself] a chance of a facial close up if [the monkeys] were to approach again for a play'. Thus, Slater had everything prepared for the photo of the monkeys (macaques), but since they showed signs of nervousness, he 'moved away, and bingo, they moved in, fingering the toy. Pressing the buttons and fingering the lens'.[65] In preparing the photo, Slater seemed in his own version to have made several free and creative choices according to the *Painer* formula of the CJEU. Nevertheless, even in this version Slater lost control of the photographic process when he let the macaques take over. Thus, neither the motif nor the camera angle was caused by Slater's free and creative choices. This could have been different if Slater had intended this scenario, but it would have required at least a plan with regard to the macaques' behaviour. In the situation that occurred, the fact that copyright law does not require that the author could foresee the result is irrelevant as lack of foreseeability was a result of events other than the author's free and creative choices. In other words, there was a break in the causal link between the creative choices and the final expression. However, this does not exclude Slater's authorship of the picture, but originality is limited to traits covered by his free and creative choices, and does not include traits caused by the monkeys. That affects the scope of protection and infringement assessments correspondingly.

The situation here is different from the fictitious scenario drawn by Ginsburg and Budiardjo, where 'Slater positions his camera in the jungle with all the chosen settings, pushes a button that releases the shutter at timed intervals, leaves the scene', and later 'Slater's camera captures some other denizen of the wildlife preserve unexpectedly attacking and eating Naruto'.[66] As the authors point out, the resulting image would be very different from the image 'Slater' thought he would capture.[67] Nevertheless, in this situation the photographer's free and creative choices cover all features of the image, including the camera

---

[62] See US Court of Appeals for the 9th Circuit, *Naruto v Slater*, 888 F.3d 418 (2018).

[63] See Ginsburg and Budiardjo (n 2) 364–365.

[64] See also ibid.

[65] See http://www.djsphotography.co.uk/original_story.html accessed 3 December 2020.

[66] Ginsburg and Budiardjo (n 2) 373.

[67] Ibid.

angle and the motif. Since 'Slater' in this scenario determined both the angle and the time intervals of shutter release, he took account of the fact that the photograph would reflect the scene at the time of release. Here, in contrast to what seemed to be the 'real scenario' in the monkey selfie case according to the photographer himself, in the fictitious scenario described above, no events other than the photographer's free and creative choices affected the taking of the photograph. In this situation, lack of predictability of the final outcome will not influence the scope of protection, since the free and creative choices of the photographer are reflected in the expression. That was only partly the case in 'the real scenario'.

Turning to AI-generated works, although the process is normally far more complex, it is possible to draw some analogies from the monkey selfie situation. To be sure, normally a multitude of free and creative choices are carried out by humans in AI-generated work processes. For example, the innovation director of the already famous Next Rembrandt project has explained the following about the process leading to the AI-generated painting inspired by Rembrandt:

> In terms of design choices, it was a fairly complex process. We started the design journey by gathering the complete collection of images of all 346 Rembrandt paintings. We used high-resolution scans provided by TU Delft and the Mauritshuis Museum, but we also used images from other sources. This meant that the resolution across all of the images was inconsistent. To solve this problem, the team used a Deep Neural Network algorithm to upscale the images, increasing the resolution by 300% and reducing visual noise. After gathering all the data, we had to determine the subject of our 3D painting, by analysing who it was Rembrandt painted. After classifying over 400 faces, the data concluded that the subject should be around 30 to 40 years old, male, wearing black clothing, a hat and facing the right. The next task was to develop software that could understand Rembrandt, based on his use of geometry, composition and painting materials. Together with Microsoft, we started to analyse specific features such as eyes, nose, mouth and ears, by mapping 67 landmarks per face.[68]

This explanation makes it evident that a multitude of creative choices (by humans) are made during the design phase of this project. On the other hand, it is also clear even from the explanation by the innovation director, and not least the fact that on the basis of the 6000 facial landmarks that were used to classify the features, that the computer learned how to create a Rembrandt face

---

[68] Interview with innovation director Emmanuel Flores, J Walter Thompson Amsterdam, in 'The Next Rembrandt: bringing the Old Master back to life. Case study: behind the scenes of digital design' https://medium.com/@DutchDigital/the-next -rembrandt-bring ing-the-old-master-back-to-life-35dfb1653597 accessed 3 December 2020.

based on these typicalities. Although human efforts are the condition *sine qua non* for creation of the painting, a plausible question is *to what extent* the *free and creative choices* of the humans involved *are reflected* in the final painting. The 'black box' features of machine-learning systems are not irrelevant in this context.[69] In contrast to the 'Pollock situation' and the fictitious monkey selfie scenario, not only the result but also *the process* leading to the result is unpredictable for the designers.[70] Thus, it is possible to claim – with a certain analogy from the 'real monkey selfie case' – that the machine intervenes in the creative process in a way leading to the result that the free and creative choices of humans are not fully, but only partly, reflected in the final expression.[71] This implies that with AI-generated – or assisted – works, there is a need to analyse *what* features of the expression reflect the free and creative choices of the human authors. The answer is not necessarily denial of authorship altogether, but may nevertheless have an impact on the scope of protection of the work.

Consequently the argument is that an originality causation approach to AI-generated works, at least at this stage of technological development,

---

[69] See, however, the discussion about the explainability of algorithms in Lehr and Ohm (n 48) and the elaboration on the 'black box problem' in Sandra Fink Hedrick, 'I "Think", Therefore I Create: Claiming Copyright in the Outputs of Algorithms' (2019) 8 *NYU Journal of Intellectual Property and Entertainment Law*, the latter also pointing out that explainability only will increase in the future.

[70] Compare Hertzmann (n 45) 12–13, about the unpredictability of AI systems, as he points out that 'the same could be said for the way watercolor flows on the page. There is no plausible sense in which current systems reflect "true" artificial intelligence: there is always a human behind the artwork'. The difference is, however, that the unforeseeability of watercolours relates to the result of the process but not the process leading to the result.

[71] Compare Ginsburg and Budiardjo (n 2) 402 et seq. on the so-called 'amanuensis doctrine' in US law implying that '[w]hen those amanuenses act as "faithful agents" – operating under the broad control of and within the scope of the authority delegated by the author-principal – copyright law is content to ignore the contributions of the amanuenses and instead recognize the principal-creator as the sole author' even though the 'the amanuensis may exercise *some* creative autonomy and may apply her expertise to the task at hand'. This view is grounded in US case law requiring that 'the agent-amanuensis becomes an author in her own right only if she embarks upon a "frolic on her own" acting "entirely without" the influence of the principal-author'. Here, it is held that this doctrine is not compatible with EU law, since it provides for sole authorship even though a different person has executed free and creative choices. In other words, authorship is also granted to elements that are not *caused* by the principal author herself. The analogy to AI-generated works is that when the machine acts in the place of the amanuensis, under the 'designer's' control, it certainly does not embark upon 'a frolic of its own', but may nevertheless intervene in a way that implies that the expression cannot be ascribed to the 'designer's' own free and creative choices. Consequently, the designer's copyright cannot comprise traits that are caused by the machine in such situations.

implies that the relevant question is often not, and indeed not solely, *whether* there is (human) authorship to such works, but if so *what* is protected in the work.[72] However, the approach that 'courts should identify machine-made choices and exclude them in determining whether a production is original',[73] seems like a detour. This is in particular the case since 'machine-made choices' are non-copyrightable causes of the final output. There may be several non-copyrightable causes of the final product, and it does not seem necessary to identify every single one of them. What is important is to identify the free and creative choices made by *humans* and to ask whether, and to what extent, those choices are reflected in the final output. Only to the extent they do will there exist a copyrightable 'work' in accordance with the qualifications set by the CJEU.

This also implies that the output may be unprotected, namely in situations where no free and creative choices of humans are reflected in the expression.[74] As indicated above, such situations may occur not only in the context of 'partially generative machines', where neither the 'designer' nor the user's contributions are sufficient to meet the originality causation criteria,[75] because in situations of 'fully generative machines', separate contributions may also be insufficient to fulfil the originality causation criteria. Although rules on joint authorship are not explicitly harmonized at the EU level, it is possible to claim that the originality causation requirement only will be fulfilled where two or more contributors whose separate contributions are not sufficient to meet the requirement collaborate on the result in order to jointly represent free and creative choices reflected in the expression. This will be in line with domestic law in European countries, where collaboration is a normal requirement for joint authorship.

---

[72] Answering the questions raised in Bob L.T. Sturm and others, 'Artificial Intelligence and Music; Open Questions of Copyright Law and Engineering in Praxis' (2019) 8 *Arts*, 115; doi:10.3390, concerning 'the folkrnn project', which 'has built and trained several music AI models on data produced from tens of thousands of transcriptions of folk music available online ... resulting [in] models [that] are able to generate novel transcriptions that exhibit many characteristics similar to the original data': Q(1) 'Should a person who uses material generated by folkrnn models in the composition process specify where it came from, i.e., that it was not entirely their own creation?' A(1): Yes, that is at least necessary in order to identify the rights pertaining to the composition; Q(2): 'Should music created in such ways, with the "input of AI", be considered inferior to music created without?' A(2): Not to any further extent than other pieces of music containing non-protected elements or elements derived from others (derivative works).

[73] Gervais (n 2) 2100.

[74] Compare Ginsburg and Budiardjo (n 2) 439 et seq.

[75] Ibid., 440.

## 5.    CONCLUSION

When discussing copyright and authorship of AI-generated output, it may be useful to identify causation requirements hidden in the current copyright rules. In EU law this requirement is implicit in formulations such as 'in the sense that [the work] is the author's own intellectual creation' or '[the work] constitutes the author's own intellectual creation'. Linking these formulations to the CJEU's originality test, the originality causation requirement in EU law implies that copyright to AI-generated output may be granted to the extent that free and creative choices of humans *are reflected* in the expression of the work. This may be considered as a legal causation test, where factual causation is expressed through the requirement of 'reflection' of free and creative choices in the final expression. While this does not exclude authorship to expressions that the author(s) were not able to foresee, free and creative choices are not reflected in the expression to the extent that expression is caused by other factors or events. Intervention by a machine may be one such factor. This does not exclude the copyrightability of AI-generated works altogether at the current stage of technological development, but may have an impact on the scope of protection. This is no different from other situations where the final expression contains protected as well as non-protected elements. Nevertheless, the copyrightability assessment may be challenging in certain cases. Whether such challenges imply a need for revision of current copyright rules is a different question, which is not sought to be answered here. However, it is far from obvious, and the best advice at this stage may be to wait and see. In the meantime analytical tools such as causation tests may be useful in solving problems under the current regime.

# 8. Artificial intelligence and intellectual property rights: the quest or plea for artificial intelligence as a legal subject

## Rosa Maria Ballardini and Robert van den Hoven van Genderen

## 1. INTRODUCTION: ARTIFICIAL INTELLIGENCE A POTENTIAL LEGAL SUBJECT IN INTELLECTUAL PROPERTY RIGHTS?

Even today, artificial intelligence (AI) can create a vast number of physical and intangible systems. Multiple parties point out how AI will play an active role as an actor in our future society. In diverse fields, tasks and jobs traditionally the work of natural persons will be performed by these non-human entities. Companies are already training machine learning algorithms to help develop film trailers; media content producers are using AI software to improve the speed and efficiency of the media production process; and entertainment providers are even using AI to recommend personalized content based on data from user activity and behaviour. These automated activities have vast financial and legal consequences. While all kinds of products are manufactured by robots, from cars, to food, to art and music, one might wonder what the role of human participation in these processes actually is. In the field of intellectual property rights (IPR), this question pops up both in relation to entitlements, ownership, and requirements for protection of the innovations automatically generated by AI and in relation to infringement by these entities of third-party IPR. In this regard, a key question relates to the legal nature of these non-human actors.

Notably, AI does not yet have a clear legal foundation in our society. But 'the times they are a-changin'.[1] Indeed, the aspect of human participation is an important point for discussion of the legal positioning of AI applications:

---

[1] Bob Dylan, 8 March 1965.

the less meaningful human control becomes, the greater the need to regulate AI entities *per se*. By placing our analysis in the specific context of the entertainment and media industries, and in the legal framework of intellectual property (IP) law, this chapter investigates the need for regulating AI actors as legal subjects. The chapter begins with an overview of some of the major pressures that AI is posing to the IP system. It then takes a critical look at the feasibility of recognizing AI entities as legal persons, both for IPR purposes and in general, as well as the possible need to create a new *sui generis* legal subjectivity for independently functioning AI entities and systems. This is followed by an analysis of the possible repercussions of a new *sui generis* legal entity for AI in the context of AI-generated innovations protectable by IPR. In particular, we discuss the concept of a new *sui generis* legal entity for AI which is based on different levels of autonomy. The chapter concludes that if an AI entity is completely autonomous in the creation of works or inventions it would be sensible to let these fruits of AI labour fall into the public domain, even if AI is granted *sui generis* legal personhood. In other words, we embrace the line of thinking according to which only natural persons should be eligible for authorship or inventorship in IP law. This notwithstanding, however, the different layers or groupings based on the various degrees of AI autonomy, as we propose in our concept of *sui generis* legal personhood for AI, could help in taking decisions when facing the difficult question: have humans contributed 'enough' to deserve IPR? Moreover, giving AI *sui generis* legal status could be useful in terms of liability and accountability issues, particularly relevant in the context of IPR infringement cases caused by AI.

## 2.     LEGAL POSITIONING OF DIFFERENT TYPES OF ARTIFICIAL INTELLIGENCE – SOME STARTING POINTS

What is artificial intelligence? There are numerous descriptions but, to keep it simple, it could be defined as a system or entity that processes data, compares, analyses and makes decisions in a wide sense.[2] Commonly a distinction is drawn between 'weak' AI, 'strong' AI, and 'General and Super' AI. Weak AI (also called narrow AI) is not weak as such. In fact, weak AI can have a high intelligence potential but is directed to perform one task and achieve one result.

---

[2]     Based on the definition of 'codebots': 'Artificial Intelligence is a branch of computer science that endeavours to replicate or simulate human intelligence in a machine, so machines can perform tasks that typically require human intelligence. Some programmable functions of AI systems include planning, learning, reasoning, problem solving, and decision making'. See: https://codebots.com/artificial-intelligence/the-3 -types-of-ai-is-the-third-even-possible accessed 28 June 2021.

It is not intended to copy, or even be comparable with, human intelligence. In short: Weak AI will perform a certain task with a certain result. The use of weak AI is completely controlled by natural persons. Weak AI is already being integrated into production processes in the automobile industry, food processing, and logistics. These applications can be considered comparable to advanced automation. Weak AI is based on humanly controlled data sets that will be used for repetitive and relatively simple automated tasks. Even Deep Blue, the chess program that beat world chess champion Gary Kasparov in 1997 (May 1997, New York sixth match), is considered 'weak' AI.[3] Still, AI technologies are projected to boost corporate profitability in 16 industries across 12 economies by an average of 38 per cent by 2035.[4] Those applications are completely dependent on human performance and do not need a legal qualification beyond being an instrument or object.

In contrast, strong (or high level) AI is more complicated and, based on the machine learning – or even self-learning – capability of the underlying algorithm, can perform numerous and diverse intelligent tasks based on self-learning ability (HLAI). These applications are already developed and can be more complicated in the sense of legal qualification when creating results with legal consequences on uncontrolled or independent activities. With 'strong' AI systems, the moment of human intervention has shifted from the input phase to the output phase, now that only the desired outcomes are selected. An example of more autonomous AI is Google's Deep Dream. This is a visualization tool that uses neural networks to create unique, bizarre and disturbing images. Google's Deep Dream refers to a system that imitates the human brain and produces surreal landscapes based on it. It is the neural networks that make the choices, not the programmers. The programmers feed the system with a random photo, which the neural network then analyses and makes its own choices about what it wants to keep. This results in an unpredictable outcome, which is the direct result of the decisions made by the neural network.[5]

If and when rational and cognitive, creative and emotional intelligence coincide, and self-learning is made possible, then so-called 'general' AI (GAI) will be in existence. GAI combines the above-mentioned capabilities with human-

---

[3]    'Kasparov vs. Deep Blue | The Match That Changed History' at: https://www .chess.com/article/view/deep-blue-kasparov-chess accessed 28 June 2021.

[4]    Accenture, 'How AI boosts industry profits and innovation' (21 June 2017).

[5]    Andres Guadamuz, 'AI and copyright', *WIPO Magazine*, May 2017, available at: https://www.wipo.int/wipo_magazine/en/2017/05/article_0003.html. See also the recent example of the Ai-darobot at: https://www.ai-darobot.com/welcometotheai damovement both accessed 28 June 2021.

oid intelligence performance levels and capabilities, such as understanding and performing creativity, emotion, morality, and so on.

Strong AI and certainly general AI are a promise of the (near) future. The main difference is that machine learning and self-learning are based on data-sets which are at most partly human controlled and will result in products and services where the processing of data by the underlying algorithms is not trans-parent, controlled or understood by human intelligence. Entities and systems functioning on strong and general AI can be considered to acquire legal personhood because they function completely autonomously and will certainly perform tasks with legal effect. It is indicative that this future requirement was, amongst others, considered seriously in a European Parliament resolution considering civil liability, according to which it would be important to create:

> a specific legal status for robots in the long run, so that at least the most sophisticated autonomous robots could be established as having the status of electronic persons responsible for making good any damage they may cause, and possibly applying electronic personality to cases where robots make autonomous decisions or other-wise interact with third parties independently.[6]

Because autonomy will vary in the application of AI-driven systems, legal capability and liability doctrines and schemes also do not necessarily fit within existing doctrines. That does not mean that AI entities need to have the same legal status as natural persons or even the existing framework for artificial legal persons. As with actual artificial persons, also with AI: their legal status will depend on their functionality in society.

## 3.    AI-GENERATED WORKS AND INVENTIONS – THE IPR CHALLENGE

### 3.1    AI in Media-creation and Innovation

As noted, multiple parties have pointed out how AI will play an active role as an actor in our future society. In the media field, companies are already train-ing machine learning algorithms to help develop film trailers,[7] while media

---

6    European Parliament resolution of 16 February 2017 with recommendations to the Commission on Civil Law Rules on Robotics ((2015/2103(INL) (2018/C 252/25)) and Digital Agenda for the EU: https://www.europarl.europa.eu/factsheets/en/sheet/64/digital-agenda-for-europe accessed 28 June 2021.

7    Netflix is investing in technology to automate movie and television trailers, an executive said on a July earnings call. The technology could help Netflix lower the cost of creating trailers while adding personalization for its subscribers. See *CBS News*, 19 Aug. 2019.

content producers are using AI software to improve the speed and efficiency of the media production process,[8] and entertainment providers are even using AI to recommend personalized content based on data from user activity and behaviour.[9] AI is already used massively in the entertainment industry, and as an instrument in the gaming industry and the cinematographic world.[10] AI programs create possibilities in gaming by giving different outcomes dependent on the storyline one chooses. These actions will be personalized by AI dependent on data from user activity and behaviour and even by their activities on other platforms or relevant interests. The purpose of AI in games is decision-making, perceptions, and prediction. In other words, in video games, AI is used to generate intelligent behaviours primarily in non-player characters (NPCs), often simulating humanoid intelligence.

Indeed, several activities that used to be the creation and innovation of natural persons, such as performing stunts and even creating dialogues, seem to be taken over by intelligent programs. These examples show that, even today, AI is already having a significant impact on the creation, production, and distribution of economic and cultural goods and services. On the one hand, it is clear that several of these creations and innovations could be economically valuable, and thus could attract the interest of various actors in the innovation value chain to control them via the use of exclusive rights such as IPR. At the same time, however, one cannot help but wonder what the role of human participation in these kinds of processes actually is. It is precisely this level

---

[8] Research by TechEmergence found that the majority of AI use cases in media and entertainment appear to fall into three major categories: (1) marketing and advertising: companies are training machine-learning algorithms to help develop film trailers and design advertisements; (2) personalization of user experience: entertainment providers are using machine learning to recommend personalized content based on data from user activity and behaviour; (3) search optimization: media content producers are using AI software to improve the speed and efficiency of the media production process and the ability to organize visual assets. See https://www.cio.com/article/3308996/making-magic-in-media-and-entertainment-with-artificial-intelligence.html accessed 28 June 2021.

[9] Ibid.

[10] Due to, e.g., multiplayer global gaming, AI is the driving motor for modern gaming industry as well as scientific gaming applications:

> Player experience modeling (PEM) is the study and use of AI techniques for the construction of computational models of experience of players. PEM places an AI umbrella to the multidisciplinary intersection of the fields of user (player) modeling, affective computing, experimental psychology and human-computer interaction.

See Georgios N Yannakakis, 'Game AI Revisited', Center for Computer Games ResearchIT University of Copenhagen (2012), at https://dl.acm.org/doi/pdf/10.1145/2212908.2212954 accessed 28 June 2021.

of 'autonomicity' that disturbs key features of our modern IPR system. If the contribution of the human element is so minimal to the innovation involved, should humans still have some degree of control via exclusive rights like IPR regardless? If not, what should be the destiny of AI-generated innovation?

## 3.2 AI-generated Works Meet IPR: Challenges or Opportunities?

Issues related to the inter-relation between IP and AI have been already thoroughly discussed at the EU level, as well as internationally.[11] Amongst the most controversial topics presented in these political,[12] legislative and academic discussions, are issues related to inventorship, authorship and ownership of AI-generated innovations,[13] the interpretation of key IP requirements such as the requirement of originality in copyright and the requirements of inventive step and disclosure in patent law for AI-generated outputs,[14] as well as issues related to IPR infringements by AI agents.[15] In terms of inventorship, authorship and ownership of AI-generated innovations, the key questions revolve

---

[11]   See European Parliament resolution of 16 February 2017 (n 6).

[12]   See, e.g., Maria Iglesias, Sharon Shamuilia and Amanda Anderberg, 'Intellectual Property and Artificial Intelligence – A literature review', EUR 30017 EN, Publications Office of the European Union, Luxembourg, 2019, ISBN 978-92-76-14178-5, doi:10 .2760/2517, JRC119102. Available at: https://publications.jrc.ec.europa.eu/repository/ bitstream/JRC119102/intellectual_property_and_artificial_intelligence_jrc_template _final.pdf accessed 28 June 2021.

[13]   Rosa Maria Ballardini, Kan He and Teemu Roos, 'AI Generated Content: Authorship and Inventorship in the Age of Artificial Intelligence', in T Pihlajarinne, J Vesala and O Honkila (eds) Online Distribution of Content in the EU (Edward Elgar Publishing 2019); Anette Alén-Savikko, Rosa Maria Ballardini and Taina Pihlajarinne, 'Tekoälyn tuotokset ja omaperäisyysvaatimus – kohti koneorientoitunutta tekijänoikeutta?', *Lakimies* 7–8/2018, s.975–995; Tanya Aplin and Giulia Pasqualetto, 'Artificial Intelligence and Copyright Protection', in Rosa Maria Ballardini (ed, author), Olli Pitkänen (ed, author) and Petri Kuoppamäki (ed), *Regulating Industrial Internet through IPR, Data Protection and Competition Law* (Kluwer Law Int. 2019); Guadamuz (n 5); Jane Ginsburg, 'People not Machines: Authorship and what it Means in the Berne Convention', (2018) 49(2) *International Review of Intellectual Property and Competition Law* 131–135.

[14]   William Samore, 'Artificial Intelligence and the Patent System: Can a New Tool Render a Once Patentable Idea Obvious?' in B Woodrow et al. (eds) *Research Handbook on the Law of Artificial Intelligence* (Edward Elgar Publishing 2018); Guadamuz (n 5); Alén-Savikko, Ballardini, and Pihlajarinne (n 13).

[15]   Juha Vesala and Rosa Maria Ballardini, Chapter 6: 'AI and IPR Infringement: a Case Study on Training and Using Neural Networks', in Rosa Maria Ballardini, Olli Pitkänen and Petri Kuoppamäki (eds), *Regulating Industrial Internet through IPR, Data Protection and Competition Law* (Kluwer Law International 2019).

around whether and to what extent it is legally and theoretically justified to extend IP entitlements and IP ownership to non-human-generated innovations.

In the field of copyright, authors have always been the starting point and centre of any discussion. Copyright entitlement is usually justified based on John Locke's labour theory, according to which the intellectual labour of the author, mixed with other resources, justifies the author's right over the fruit of their labours.[16] Moreover, Hegel's personality theory claims that a work belongs to or reflects the personality of its creator.[17] Although utilitarian theory starts with the welfare of the public and society as a whole, the fact that copyright is considered as an incentive for authors to create cannot be denied.[18] From the perspective of European law, international copyright treaties to which the EU is a party,[19] EU legislation[20] and cases from the Court of Justice of European Union (CJEU), as well as national laws and cases, all tend to interpret the concept of 'author' as a natural person, with very limited openings towards authorship by legal persons. At the same time, however, although the main EU copyright Directives offer some harmonized definition of 'author', there is as yet no uniform or common understanding of the concept in EU copyright law: on the one hand, the Directives define 'author' only for specific types of works, while, on the other, there is still no clear answer as to whether a legal person can be regarded as an 'author'. At the same time, this issue should also be interpreted and understood in line with the concept of originality: a *conditio sine qua non* for copyright protection. In this regard, an important issue that AI-generated works raise is the fundamental question whether a non-human author can ever be able to produce an 'original' work of

---

[16]    John Locke, *The Second Treatise of Civil Government* (1690). Available at https://rintintin.colorado.edu/~vancecd/phil215/Locke.pdf accessed 28 June 2021.

[17]    Acton, 3 *The Encyclopedia of Philosophy*, Georg Wilhelm Friedrich Hegel, 442 (1967 ed).

[18]    See William Landes and Richard Posner, *The Economic Structure of Intellectual Property Law* (Harvard University Press 2003), 294–402.

[19]    See, e.g., Berne Convention for the Protection of Literary and Artistic Works as amended on 28 September 1979, WIPO Copyright Treaty (WCT) and Agreement on Trade-Related Aspects of Intellectual Property Rights (TRIPs).

[20]    See, e.g., Directive 2009/24/EC of the European Parliament and of the Council of 23 April 2009 on the legal protection of computer programs [2009]OJ L111; Directive 96/9/EC of the European Parliament and of the Council of 11 March 1996 on the legal protection of databases [1996] OJ L 77/20; Directive 2006/115/EC of the European Parliament and of the Council of 12 December 2006 on rental right and lending right and on certain rights related to copyright in the field of intellectual property [2006] OJ L 376; Directive 93/83/EEC of the European Parliament and of the Council of 27 September 1993 on the coordination of certain rules concerning copyright and rights related to copyright applicable to satellite broadcasting and cable retransmission [1993] OJ L 248.

art as understood under current doctrine. In particular, the numerous decisions of the CJEU interpreting originality seem to stick to the romantic concept of the author as a natural person. This can be deduced *inter alia* from the emphasis placed on the interpretation of originality as reflecting authors' 'own intellectual creation', 'personal touch' and 'personality'.[21]

As for patents, their main accepted justification is that, unless protection is provided, an inventor who is trying to cover the costs of R&D might face challenges when a new product is ready to be commercialized due to the ability of others to copy it. Because competitors are able to copy without having to bear R&D costs, the price of the product might drop and the inventor might not be able to cover the costs incurred. Ultimately, this might disincentivize development of further inventions.[22] Patents are also conceived positively in respect to secrecy because they allow disclosure of information: the inventor discloses information about the invention in exchange for being granted a temporary limited monopoly.[23] Indeed, a balance needs to be sought regarding protecting IP investment in order to promote innovation and creativity, that is, between providing incentives and guaranteeing access. In this same narrative it is the figure of the inventor as a natural person that is predominant as the 'type' of inventor that needs to be incentivized via IPR. Even though the multi-level system of national and regional European patent laws leaves open the possibility for legal (instead of natural) persons to act as owners of patent rights,[24] for a patent application to be valid, an inventor (generally understood as a natural person only) needs to be named. This interpretation has also lately been endorsed in the first EPO cases where an AI system was designated as the inventor in the DABUS patent applications. Both patent applications indicated 'DABUS' as the inventor. DABUS was described as 'a type of connectionist artificial intelligence'.[25] The applicant stated that they had acquired the right to the European patent from a non-human inventor as its successor in title, arguing that as the owner of the machine, the applicant was assigned any IPR created by this machine. The EPO considered that according to the interpre-

---

[21]  See, e.g., Case C-5/08 *Infopaq International A/S v Danske Dagblades Forening* [2009]ECLI:EU:C:2009:465; Joined Cases C-403/08 and C-429/08 *Football Association Premier League Ltd et al v QC Leisure et al* [2011] ECLI:EU:C:2011:631; Case C-145/10 *Eva-Maria Painer v Standard Verlages GmbH et al.* [2013]ECLI:EU: C:2013:138; Case C-604/10 *Football Detaco Ltd et al. v Yahoo! et al.* [2012]ECLI:EU: C:2012:115.

[22]  Landes and Posner (n 18), 294–402.

[23]  Ibid.

[24]  See, e.g., Convention on the Grant of European Patents of 5 October 1973 (European Patent Convention) Arts 60 and 62; EPC Implementing regulations, Rule 19 (2); Guidelines for Examinations (2017), G.VII.3.

[25]  See EP 18 275 163 and EP 18 275 174.

tation of European patent law the inventor designated in a European patent *must be a natural person* (emphasis added). The Office further noted that the understanding of the term inventor as a natural person appears to be an internationally applicable standard. The EPO also added that the designation of an inventor is linked to legal consequences, such as 'to ensure that the designated inventor is the legitimate one and that he or she can benefit from rights linked to this status'. The Office concluded that to exercise these rights, 'the inventor must have a legal personality'. And because AI systems or machines do not enjoy legal personality, they cannot be inventors.[26] At the same time, whether a legal person can be an inventor or whether a legal person can currently also be an inventor is not so clear from the wording of the relevant provisions and their interpretations. Generally, however, it seems that the tendency is to conceive inventors only as human beings (even though patent ownership can clearly also be held by legal persons).[27] Finally, it should be stressed that, as with copyright, in the patent framework the idea of an inventor being a natural person is interlinked with certain patentability requirements, in this case especially the requirement of inventiveness, as determined by the 'contribution to the inventive concept'. Inventiveness is usually understood as the act of the (natural) person that has creatively contributed to the subject matter of the patent in view of the entire content of the patent application, including description and drawings.[28]

Another important discussion point concerning AI and IPR relates to the issue of IPR infringements caused by AI. On the one hand, the question involves the fact that the uncertain issue of data ownership arises, as AI can produce creative works or inventive inventions by learning from data with AI techniques, such as machine learning.[29] On the other, the issue revolves around

---

[26]   See https://register.epo.org/application?documentId=E4B63SD62191498&number=EP18275163&lng=en&npl=false  and  https://register.epo.org/application?documentId=E4B63OBI2076498&number=EP18275174&lng=en&npl=false  both  accessed 28 June 2021.

[27]   See, e.g., the opinions expressed on this matter in 'Inventorship of multinational inventorship' (2015) AIPPI. Available at: http://aippi.org/library/?publication_title=inventorship+of+multinational+inventions&=&publication_categories%5B%5D=7&start_date_range=&end_date_range and 'Inventorship of inventions made using Artificial Intelligence' (2020) AIPPI: https://static1.squarespace.com/static/56cad60dc6fc08941fb64e07/t/5e425fa9c10f9011f52cf737/1581408175113/Q272-SGL-P-2020+Inventorship+of+inventions+made+using+AI.PDF  both  accessed  28 June 2021.

[28]   See, e.g., BGH decision X ZR 70/11 of 22 January 2013; BGH decision X ZR 53/08 of 17 May 2011 – *Atemgasdrucksteuerung*; BRG GRUR 1979 – 540 (541) – *Biedermeiermanschetten*; BRG GRUR 1978 – *Motorkettensäge*; BRG GRUR 1966 – *Spanplatten*.

[29]   Vesala and Ballardini (n 15).

who is liable in the case of IPR infringement caused by AI agents. Infringement liability (either direct or indirect) clearly requires legal status as a prerequisite. As AI does not enjoy such status, the question then is: who is the infringer? In the case of direct infringement, for instance, it could be argued that the direct infringer would be the developer of the AI system, or of the programme(r), or the data feeder. But what if, for instance, the AI program, as originally developed, was not able to infringe? Or what if the AI program was not capable of infringing until used by the operator for a significant amount of time? Or if the AI program required significant training before it was able to actually infringe? Similar questions might arise in relation to indirect infringement liability. In addition, interesting questions might arise in respect of where the infringer is based and where the infringement takes place (e.g., in the cloud?), as well as how one pleads and proves infringement.[30]

All in all, it is evident that the current IPR framework might be shaken by the rise of AI technology. As often happens with new disruptive technological advances, the question boils down to whether this is just business as usual – and eventually our legal framework will adapt and cope with the challenge – or whether, instead, this is a rather special occasion where a radical change is needed. Here, we take the untracked road and explore whether and how a radical change like assigning legal status to non-human AI agents could help in addressing some of the challenges raised by AI in the IPR framework.

## 4.      AI AND LEGAL PERSONS

### 4.1      Persons and Nonpersons in Law – Some Key Issues

Law is generally defined as a body of norms that regulates the relationships between legal entities, or between such entities and 'things' not having legal capacity (that is, nonpersons). According to Tuori, this divide between persons and nonpersons is a part of the 'deep structure of law' that is shared by all Western legal systems.[31] Legal personality (or legal personhood) is a prerequisite to legal capacity, which has traditionally been defined as the ability to exercise one's own rights and duties.[32] In other words, legal personhood is given to actors within that society to perform legal acts having legal effect. In our legal system, natural persons – and to a lesser extent, artificial legal persons – are primarily the main actors in our legal system.[33]

---

[30]    See also Iglesias, Shamuilia and Anderberg (n 12).

[31]    See Kaarlo Tuori, *Critical Legal Positivism* (Ashgate 2002), 147–197.

[32]    Visa A J Kurki, *A Theory of Legal Personhood* (OUP Oxford 2019).

[33]    For an overview of the main differences between natural and legal persons see Kent Greenfield, *Corporations Are People Too: (And They Should Act Like It)* (Yale

Legal personhood is not engraved in stone. Instead, the scope of these conceptions is variable. The need for legal action and the scope of legal concepts is defined by the social and political system and is dependent on time, culture, and often even geographical circumstances. Luckily, law is flexible, and rules are defined by the societal requirement of a particular historical and cultural society. Legal personhood is given to actors within that society to perform legal tasks having legal effect. Legal persons have the legal capacity to perform legal transactions, buying, selling, inheriting, and the like. The scope of legal capacity depends on the role and function of the legal person in the particular society and its legal system. The range of legal capacity is adapted to the function of the legal person.[34] Even within natural personhood, differences occur in actual legal capacity, for instance in the case of children and persons under guardianship. Moreover, historically the capacity of natural persons has varied from having no rights based on sex or race to full legal capacity. In some countries, differences based on sex or race still exist.[35] Additionally, the legal capacity of artificial legal persons has changed over time and still varies in different legal systems. For instance, in the US the claim for fundamental rights such as due process and equal treatment were already recognized in 1886.[36] All this indicates that a new concept for a legal person is far from unthinkable.

Technological developments are rapidly moving in the direction of AI programs embodied in many types of physical entities and a variety of robotic systems in more or less anthropomorphic shapes that can perform a variety of tasks, often with legal effect.[37] AI applications can be simply considered as products, instruments and systems to be used by humans without any significant legal status. But the inclination is towards a sliding scale. As we have seen, there is often no clear separation between the different manifes-

---

University Press 2018), at https://www.jstor.org/stable/j.ctv6hp3qr.7 accessed 28 June 2021.

[34]  For a comprehensive description of legal personhood see Kurki (n 32).

[35]  For instance in Saudi Arabia, women need male guardianship for all (legal) actions. See: https://www.hrw.org/report/2016/07/16/boxed/women-and-saudi-arabias -male-guardianship-system     and:     https://www.hrw.org/world-report/2020/country -chapters/saudi-arabia both accessed 28 June 2021.

[36]  Claims to due process and equal protection are recognized in the United States for companies. See Landmark Briefs and Arguments of the Supreme Court of the United States, ed Gerhard Casper et al., Vol 452, 2014, 296. For further general development of the concept of legal entities see Henry Hansmann, Reinier Kraakman and Richard Squire, 'Law and the Rise of the Firm', *Harvard Law Review*, March 2006, 1333–1403.

[37]  Robert van den Hoven van Genderen, 'Legal Personhood in the Age of Artificially Intelligent Robots', in Ugo Pagallo (ed), *Research Handbook on the Law on Artificial Intelligence* (Edward Elgar Publishing 2018), 213–250.

tations of AI-driven innovations. However, AI applications are increasingly developing in a more human-independent direction, especially in relation to strong or general AI. The fact that human control is weakening – perhaps even vanishing – for AI-driven entities and systems is creating an opportunity and perhaps even a need to create a novelty in terms of legal status in the sense of responsibility, legal capacity, accountability, and liability.[38] In other words, the case of IPR and AI-generated innovations is indeed but one out of many such situations where the legal status of AI could be important.

## 4.2    AI as a Legal Person – Introducing a New *Sui Generis* Legal Status

As noted, in 2016 the European Parliament initiated a progressive proposal, leading to a resolution, to consider legal status as 'electronic persons' for various forms of autonomous AI entities.[39]

As AI develops, obvious differences will appear in terms of autonomy between systems resulting in a variety of legal requirements dependent, among others, on a social need to have AI perform tasks as more or less autonomous acts. However, generally speaking, for legal analysis and classification of the legal personhood status of an AI, it is necessary to look at:

1. the embodiment or nature of the system;
2. the degree of autonomy shown by the system;
3. the function of the AI robot;
4. the environment it operates in; and
5. the interaction between human and robot.[40]

Examples of *sui generis* types of legal personhood for AI have already started to appear in some jurisdictions. For instance, Sophia, a social humanoid robot developed by Hong Kong-based company Hanson Robotics in collaboration with Google's parent company Alphabet and SingularityNET, is a semi-autonomous legal entity, which, however is still owned as a 'thing' by Hanson, even though she received citizenship in Saudi Arabia and Bangladesh in 2018.[41] In Dubai the first 'Robocops' have officially been added to the Dubai

---

[38] Brussels, 19.2.2020 COM(2020) 64 final.
[39] European Parliament resolution (n 6).
[40] Andrea Bertolini, 'Robots as Products: The Case for a Realistic Analysis of Robotic Applications and Liability Rules' (2013) 5(2) *Law, Innovation and Technology* 219.
[41] See: https://www.arabnews.com/node/1183166/saudi-arabia accessed 28 June 2021.

police force.[42] Autonomous entities have also been given analogue legal positions in some companies. In October 2016, a Finnish OMX-listed company, Tieto, appointed Alicia T, an AI expert system, as a member of the leadership team of its new data-driven business unit. According to Tieto's website, Alicia T will not only become a fully-fledged member of the management team, but also possesses the capacity to cast votes: 'AI will help the management team to become truly data-driven and will assist the team in seeking innovative ways to pursue the significant opportunities of the data-driven world'.[43] However, none of these structures have to date fully endorsed a holistic comprehensive vision of assigning legal personhood to AI. Nor is there general legal acceptance by scholars or the legal profession in general of the legal independent status of (semi) autonomous AI entities.[44] Additionally, the mentioned resolution the harmonized solution provided for by the European Parliament died prematurely through the hesitant reaction of the European Commission.[45]

A step forward could be taken by creating innovative *sui generis* types of legal status framework, meaning a unique legal conception, differing from the existing legal framework conceptions for legal personhood that could be structured around the following three main pillars:

1.  *Trust:* Acceptance by other legal entities by creating trust and reliability for other legal entities and natural persons to integrate into economic, social and legal interactions.
2.  *Consensus:* To create legal consensus for legal acts, deeds with legal effect and legal competence.

---

[42]  A robotic policeman which can help identify wanted criminals and collect evidence has joined Dubai's police force and will patrol busy areas in the city, as part of a government programme aimed at replacing some human crime-fighters with machines. See: https://www.arabnews.pk/node/1108286/science-technology accessed 28 June 2021.

[43]  See Ugo Pagallo, 'Vital, Sophia, and Co. – The Quest for the Legal Personhood of Robots, Information', 10 September 2018, 3, at: https://res.mdpi.com/d_attachment/information/information-09-00230/article_deploy/information-09-00230.pdf accessed 28 June 2021.

[44]  Even a protest against the legal personhood of AI entities in an open letter to the EU Commission by expert scholars in their protest letter against legal personhood for electronic persons, 2018. See Open Letter to the European Commission. Artificial Intelligence and Robotics (05.04.2018), at:https://g8fip1kplyr33r3krz5b97d1-wpengine.netdna-ssl.com/wp-content/uploads/2018/04/RoboticsOpenLetter.pdf accessed 28 June 2021.

[45]  See: On Artificial Intelligence – A European approach to excellence and trust, Brussels, 19.2.2020 COM(2020) 65 final.

3. *Certified:* To be confirmed and accepted there is a need for legal certification by verified authorities and a publicly available register of the legal status of the different artificial actors.

Certainly, if a *sui generis* status dependent on the variety of autonomy of the AI entity is created, it will be complicated to connect the AI capacity of, for example, creating works or inventions. This idea is not a *'rara avis'* in the legal system. As previously mentioned, in the current system the role of both natural and artificial persons is also based on their functioning in society, and the need and degree of need to regulate their rights and obligations. In the context of AI *sui generis* legal personhood and IPR, this discourse entails addressing issues such as what degree of legal personhood that does not yet exist in positive law is necessary in order to recognize AI as creator of works or inventor of inventions, as well as what gradation of legal embodiment is needed, or desirable, taking into account the variability of AI systems and robotics.

Compared to the existing legal personhood models, the difference with this *sui generis* structure would be that AI status should be explicitly specified for its designated function. This system would consist in a categorization of AI, dependent on the functionality of the specific AI entity or system. It is doubtful whether there is additional value in giving rights that are comparable with general human rights or even the rights and obligations of current artificial persons. However, the human factor should not be underestimated. The more a robot is indistinguishable from a natural person, the more human society will be inclined to treat it as such. As stated by Giger et al: 'Human preferences for anthropocentric interactions are frequently presented as the reason underlying the humanization of robots'.[46] This could lead to humanized rights for robots too.

Instead, a more rational solution is to provide legal status for AI based on its function. Imagine the difference between a weak intelligence system to perform simple tasks in comparison with a highly complex autonomous strong AI entity. The first AI system does not need legal status but the second entity could function as an independent actor in society needing legal status to perform tasks with legal effect. If not dependent on the actions and control of another legal person it will be advisable to create an independent legal status based on the function of the entity. There must be clarity as to the status of autonomy for the AI entity, as well as (in the context of IPR) in the creation of the work or invention concerned. Therefore, it is clear that this difference in legal status is to be connected to legal capacity and has to be available for

---

[46]   Jean-Christophe Giger, Nuno Piçarra, Patricia Alves-Oliveira, Raquel Oliveira and Patricia Arriaga, 'Humanization of Robots: Is it Really Such a Good Idea?' (2019) 1 *Human Behavior and Emerging Technologies* 112.

other actors to see what legal capacity is connected to the status of AI. The best solution could then be to create a public register where the AI entity's legal capacity is categorized and made available to the public, as is also the case with officers of companies in legal registers of companies. By consulting these public registers any actor would then know what legal consequences could be the result of engaging with that entity.

A common question that arises among lawyers is what to do with this *sui generis* status concerning questions of accountability and liability. If AI has an autonomous legal status to create legal effects in its activities, will it also be accountable and liable for its actions? It should also be noted that this *sui generis* solution of giving legal status to AI entities is not the same as giving a status concerning accountability and liability to AI. First of all, there is a difference between accountability and liability: while liability means being legally bound to or obligated by law, accountability concerns the notion that someone is answerable for their behaviour in a broader sense. Second, even though there are many different types of accountability and liability in different legal disciplines, a common basic principle is that one can be considered accountable in the sense of responsibility – and therefore be a party that can be connected in a responsible sense to the most prominent causal relation between an action and its consequences – but cannot be considered liable by reason of circumstances or by law.[47] On the other hand, liability considers the legal consequences in the sense of the position of the party, meaning responsibility for damages or other legal consequences for the action or position. For instance, a representative of a company who commits an act with negative (legal) consequences in the execution of their company function will be held liable and not the company, even though the representative is functioning in their legal capacity as representative of the company and is recognized in that legal capacity.[48] Another example is so-called risk liability where the owner of a vehicle, animal, or parent of a child is liable for damage without any causality to the damage on the part of the owner of the vehicle or parent of the minor. Even within the accountability concept, persons who can be held accountable still do not suffer the consequences in the same way as in criminal law a natural person or legal person can be held accountable but not receive punishment.

---

[47]   As an example, we can refer to circumstances as a crisis (like the one caused by Covid-19) where local authorities limit fundamental rights, or allow killing by a soldier in wartime. Those persons will be accountable but not liable as would be different under 'normal' circumstances.

[48]   Art 6:172 Dutch Civil Code: Liability for faults (tortious acts) of a representative states that 'If a representative, in the exercise of his powers, granted to him under the authorisation of representation, commits a fault which causes damage to a third party, then also the represented principle is liable towards this third person.'

Liability law regulates the frictions that will develop in a complex society. Indeed, the development from an agricultural society to a complex automated society also creates new legal questions concerning liability. In an agricultural society liability and accountability merged. People were accountable for their actions and liable for the damage caused by their actions. However, liability law, as most other law areas, mirrors the complexity of the society – the more complex a society develops, the more it requires rules on accountability and liability. In a recent European Commission document concerning emerging digital technologies, liability is defined as: '[t]he responsibility of one party for harm or damage caused to another party, which may be a cause for compensation, financially or otherwise, by the former to the latter'.[49] The current liability rules in most European countries are based on wrongful intent (malice, fraud) (dolus), guilt (culpa), laws and societal conceptions of what is acceptable and what is unacceptable.[50] Clearly, these rules will evolve in the context of AI. It is also imaginable that liability will be divided between different actors based on their involvement and possibility of exercising control. Concerning the use of AI and underlying algorithms, this could refer to the manufacturer, owner, programmer, or (human) supervisor. The legal status of AI is and will be dependent on its autonomy. If it exists or consists of a complexity of different 'building bricks', not being an independent autonomous entity, it will still be classified as a product, in the EU falling within the ambit of, for example, the Product Liability Directive.[51] But also in this case the situation is not always clear in terms of outcome concerning the further development and change of the basic algorithm of the AI product. As stated by the Commission:

> There may be also situations in the future where the outcomes of the AI systems cannot be fully determined in advance. In such a situation, the risk assessment performed before placing the product on the market may no longer reflect the use, functioning or behaviour of the product. In these cases, insofar as the intended use, initially foreseen by the manufacturer, is modified.[52]

This would result in the absence of liability of the developer or manufacturer. A strict liability system or qualitative liability like this will not be based on

---

[49] 'Liability for emerging digital technologies', {COM(2018) 237 final}.

[50] Based on the roman legal concepts of Gaius and others codified in Codex Justinianus.

[51] Council Directive 85/374/EEC of 25 July 1985 on the approximation of the laws, regulations and administrative provisions of the Member States concerning liability for defective products. See also 'Liability for emerging digital technologies', {COM(2018) 237 final}.

[52] 'Report on the safety and liability implications of Artificial Intelligence, the Internet of Things and robotics', Brussels, 19.2.2020 COM(2020) 64 final, 7.

fault or culpability of a party, but on the specific role and function, that is, the specification of this role of the entity will be shared based on its societal relevance. This liability concept could, for instance, be supported by a general insurance system that could cover damage caused by independently functioning AI systems or entities.

Still it will be quite difficult to establish a watertight doctrine and derived liability system when the independence of the actions of an AI-driven system is not clear. For instance, the programmer of the underlying algorithm cannot be held liable for the self-learning capability of the system. As made clear by Omri Rachum-Twaig:

> lack of personhood and agency, and the impossibility of foreseeing and explaining certain behaviors the robots exhibit, are two key factors that substantially disrupt current tort doctrines in the context of AI-based robots. For example, products liability doctrines (as well as other tort doctrines) are commonly restricted to physical injuries and damage to property and cannot necessarily account for other types of damages such as privacy violations, pure economic harm, denial of critical services, and the like.[53]

Similarly, the European Commission also recognizes liability problems by the effects of lack of human agency: 'Combined with self-learning and autonomy, the behaviour of these technologies may be difficult to predict. This could raise questions regarding liability, in situations where the damage caused by a machine operating with a certain degree of autonomy cannot be linked to a defect or a human wrongdoing'.[54]

So, one can imagine that extrapolation of this line of reasoning concerning determination of the uncertainty of liability could result in finding a solution in the specification of a *sui generis* kind of legal competence that could create more clarity in terms of defining an acceptable liability doctrine for AI and AI-generated products and services depending on the autonomy of the AI actor and the involvement of the human actor. It is interesting to see, though, that the European Commission still wants to connect the liability question to the

---

[53]  Omri Rachum-Twaig, 'Liability for Artificial-Intelligence-Based Robots', blog, The Federmann Cyber Security Research Center – Cyber Law Program, University of Jerusalem, at: https://csrcl.huji.ac.il/blog/Liability-for-Artificial-Intelligence-Based -Robots accessed 28 June 2021.

[54]  Liability for emerging digital technologies. Accompanying the document Communication from the Commission to the European Parliament, the European Council, the Council, the European Economic and Social Committee and the Committee of the Regions Artificial intelligence for Europe, Brussels, 25.4.2018 SWD(2018) 137 final.

old doctrine of culpa by trying to find a connection with the 'fault' of the AI system.[55]

## 5.  AI AS A LEGAL PERSON – REFLECTIONS ON THE IPR SYSTEM

The (future) role of AI in creating works and inventions is undeniable. As we have presented, both the current copyright and patent systems are strongly connected to the author or the inventor as a natural person, as are the ways in which major requirements such as originality and inventiveness are interpreted. Indeed, the creator and inventor must have legal competence in the sense of legal personhood. On the one hand, even though most interpretations have thus far shown a tendency to stick to authors/inventors as natural persons only, the system might also seem to leave open possibilities for other persons, such as artificial persons, to become authors or inventors as well. Indeed, it is indisputable that IPR can be owned by artificial persons. Should AI be granted a *sui generis* type of legal status as above described, then what would be the consequences in the specific context of AI-generated works and inventions protectable by IPR? In this regard the questions to address are at least as follows:

1. From the point of view of protection: is there a need to incentivize via IPR developments of non-human-produced innovations? In our specific context this question boils down to whether a system that forbids AI-generated works or inventions (also in the hypothetical case that AI would have legal status) is or is not optimal to foster innovation and creativity.
2. From the point of view of infringement: is there a need to assign some sort of better accountability and liability framework to AI systems in order to enable IP holders to better retain control of their innovation? If so, how?

In the *sui generis* model for AI legal personhood presented above, the idea would be to achieve clarity in the status of autonomy for the AI entity and categorize AI innovations on that basis. In the case of IPR issues related to question (1) (that is, protection) we argue that non-humans cannot be authors/ inventors and that creations or inventions produced by non-humans cannot –

---

[55]   'It will need to be assessed whether challenges of the new technologies to the existing frameworks could also cause legal uncertainty as to how existing laws would apply (e.g., how the concept of fault would apply to damage caused by AI)'. Report on the safety and liability implications of Artificial Intelligence, the Internet of Things and robotics, Brussels, 19.2.2020 COM(2020) 64 final, 13.

and should not – be eligible for IPR. This reasoning embraces the emerging body of literature that supports the idea that, on the one hand, only human beings should be entitled to qualify as authors or inventors,[56] while on the other hand creativity, originality and inventiveness should be interpreted from an anthropocentric perspective only.[57] Indeed, the core issue relates to whether and to what extent there is any reason at all for granting IPR to some natural person that is behind the arrangements of the innovation concerned, even in the case where the AI-generated innovation was not originally foreseen by the human. From the point of view of IP theories, especially economic theories, it is quite clear that the complexity of developing AI systems, which requires considerable upfront investment in R&D, justifies IPR for AI in order to recoup those costs (and thus incentivize further investment and technological development). However, such IPR should be directed to the AI machine *per se*, not to innovations generated by the AI entity. As far as such innovations have been produced autonomously and do not involve (sufficient) human contribution in the form of humans' own intellectual creation or contribution to the inventive concept, IPR to the humans behind development of the innovation[58] should not be granted.[59] As stated by Franzosi and De Sanctis in relation to copyright:

> When an AI system participates in the creative process or even autonomously creates a work, it is no longer possible to trace an author in the classic sense of the word, since the umbilical cord which traditionally links man to his creation is irreparably cut.[60]

This anthropocentric approach is reflected in many elements of the IP systems, for instance, (1) in the theoretical justifications of IPR, (2) in the concepts of author, inventor, originality and inventiveness, (3) in the fact that moral and

---

[56]  See, e.g., the 'monkey selfie disputes' where the judge declared that a monkey is not an author within the meaning of the US Copyright Act, as non-humans are not capable of producing original works of art under the meaning of copyright law, at https://www.telegraph.co.uk/technology/news/11015672/Wikipedia-refuses-to-delete -photo-as-monkey-owns-it.html and https://assets.documentcloud.org/documents/ 2700588/Gov-Uscourts-Cand-291324-45-0.pdf) accessed 28 June 2021; and the EPO decision in the field of patents (n 20).

[57]  Guadamuz (n 5); Aplin and Pasqualetto (n 13); and Ginsburg (n 13).

[58]  Or, as phrased by some ad hoc pieces of legislation such as in the UK, 'the person by whom the arrangements necessary for the creation of the work are undertaken' see Copyright, Designs and Patents Act 1988, s 9(3).

[59]  Ballardini, He and Roos (n 13).

[60]  Mario Franzosi and Giustino De Sanctis, 'Moral Rights and New Technology: Are Copyright and Patents Converging?' (1995) 17(2) *European Intellectual Property Review* 63, 65.

economic rights are granted, (4) in the *post mortem auctoris* calculation of terms in copyright. However, an additional point should be highlighted in this discourse: humans should also not be entitled to authorship, inventorship, or ownership claims over innovations where their contribution is not sufficient and lacks human creativity. The different layers or groupings based on the various degrees of AI autonomy as proposed by the aforementioned *sui generis* legal personhood for AI would help in taking decisions when facing the difficult question of: have humans contributed 'enough' to deserve IPR? Should the answer be negative, then the most suitable alternative would be for such innovations to fall into the public domain. However, this solution leaves open for future debate whether for example *sui generis*, related rights or unfair competition law tools might instead be suitable avenues for protection of AI-generated innovations. In this discourse, the question would still be: why, from a utilitarian or economic standpoint, is a separate, specific right needed for AI innovations? In sum, though, while it is not advisable that non-humans such as AI systems should qualify for IPR authorship or inventorship, the above-presented *sui generis* proposition for AI legal personhood could anyways help with answering question (1), as this would make it easier to decide when human intervention is sufficient for IPR purposes. Should the need arise at some point in time, and market failure (thus the need to provide IPR for AI-generated innovations) be identified, possible alternative solutions could be to connect IPR to investment. For example, should the AI entity be privately financed by another legal person, be it a company or natural persons, one could decide to give the IP rights to that investor. This would also be a deviation from the majority of contemporary IP tools where the creative and inventive aspect is considered the most important connection to protection. Connecting to investment would instead be more comparable with the legal system for *sui generis* database rights in Europe, although not the most fortunate example of regulation in the EU.[61]

Instead, concerning the questions in point (2) above (i.e., infringement), the proposed *sui generis* AI legal personhood could be more helpful. Civil liability could arise in cases where causality links the actor that exploits IPR-protected innovations, and damage. Whether this is a legal person, be it a natural person, an artificial person, or a *sui generis* AI person, this is a matter that would need to be determined in a legal process, ultimately by a judge or appointed arbitrator. Generally speaking, the complexity of accountability and liability issues

---

[61] See Alen-Saviikko, Ballardini and Pihlajarinne (n 13). See also Taina Pihlajarinne and Rosa Maria Ballardini, 'Paving the Way for the Environment – Channeling "Strong" Sustainability into the European IP System', (2020) 42 *European Intellectual Property Review*, 239.

with AI infringement situations can be illustrated by the following research questions from a study at Utrecht University:

1.  What are the limits to liability in the main areas of the law, given the intended objectives and functions, the institutional context and the legal and extra-legal arguments for determining those limits?
2.  Are those limits adequate, and if not, where should they lie given what society wants to achieve with liability and accountability when it comes to redress, influencing behaviour and standard-setting?

To answer these questions a specific study on the different status of AI could be most relevant. Liability and accountability could be framed on the basis of specific *sui generis* insurance schemes connected to the special legal status of AI applications. As far as it is not clear (or not economically feasible) to look for a liable party as, for instance, with autonomous cars, in the case of infringement of IPR by an autonomous AI system one could rely on a system of risk liability provided by common risk funds, financed by the AI industry and insurance companies on the basis of compulsory insurance systems.[62] A well-known example of the latter in almost every state is traffic (user) insurance that has been made compulsory by law, commonly in national traffic law.[63] The user of any motor vehicle has to be insured against any damage that comes from using the vehicle. For example the UK Road Traffic Act states that the user will not be liable if they prove that the vehicle was not theirs or was not in their possession under a lease or employer's contract. In the Netherlands Motor Vehicle Liability Insurance Act legal liability is compulsorily insured for the driver.[64] The interesting part is that if the cause of damage is not clear or the damaging party is not identified then damage may be compensated by the Damage Compensation Body guarantee fund (*'waarborgfonds'*).[65] This could be an acceptable model for securing damages caused by an AI entity as well. If it is clear that there is a responsible party for, for instance, infringing IPR (or any other damage) using AI or even the programmer of the algorithm, then the natural or legal person in charge of or responsible for the damaging

---

[62]  Ivo Giesen and François G H Kristen, 'Liability, Responsibility and Accountability: Crossing Borders', Utrecht Centre for Accountability and Liability Law (UCALL), (2014) 10(3) *Utrecht Law Review* 1.

[63]  See, e.g., UK Road Traffic Act 1988, s 143 Users of motor vehicles to be insured F2.

[64]  Wet aansprakelijkheidsverzekering motorrijtuigen (WAM).

[65]  Art 27k. 2. WAM states that: '1. Our Minister of Justice and Our Minister of Finance designate a legal person with full legal capacity as the Damage Compensation Body, which has the task of compensating damage to injured parties in the cases referred to in Article 27o'.

activity will be the responsible and liable party. Still the AI entity would be insured on the basis of a possible EU AI liability Regulation. If there is no attributable control or accountability, or if the accountable party cannot be identified, a Damage Compensation fund – that could be created for example by the government and financed by insurance companies and the AI industry – would compensate the damage.

## 6.   CONCLUSIONS

As stated above, the European Parliament (EP) has addressed the role of robots as electronic personalities.[66] According to the EP's draft report, the question of the legal status of robots is an issue that will arise in the future. The draft considered whether the legal status of robots was to be compared with the legal conception of natural persons, legal persons, animals or objects. It clearly concluded that robots should be considered neither as natural persons nor as animals. However, it was decided that for the time being AI and robots are to be considered as objects, although their degree of autonomy might change this consideration in the future. The resolution adopted by the EP omitted this reflection but highlighted what responsibilities for research and development of robots and artificial intelligence should be defined at EU level. The Commission has since taken the view that liability could be realized, for example, through new, more flexible, insurance mechanisms. Situations may also arise in the future where the outcomes of AI systems cannot be fully determined in advance. In such a situation, the risk assessment performed before placing the product on the market may no longer reflect the use, functioning or behaviour of the product. In these cases, insofar as the intended use, initially foreseen by the manufacturer, is modified, this could result in a kind of 'flexible insurance policy', based on a fixed-frequency risk assessment.[67] Besides the risk assessment performed before placing a product on the market, a new risk assessment procedure could be put in place where the product is subject to important changes during its lifetime, for example different product functions not foreseen by the manufacturer in the initial risk assessment. This should focus on the safety impact caused by the AI entity's autonomous behaviour throughout the product lifetime. The risk assessment should be performed by

---

[66]   European Commission, Artificial Intelligence for Europe. COM(2018) 237 final, 2018; European Commission, Liability for Emerging Digital Technologies. Commission Staff Working Document SWD(2018) 137 final, 2018.

[67]   See: Report from the Commission to the European Parliament, the Council and the European Economic and Social Committee Report on the safety and liability implications of Artificial Intelligence, the Internet of Things and robotics, Brussels, 19.2.2020 COM(2020) 64 final, 7.

the appropriate economic operator. In addition, the relevant Union pieces of legislation could include reinforced requirements for manufacturers on instructions and warnings for users.

Hence, the subject of debate is a question of the grounds on which a non-human being like an AI entity can be a legal person and, at the same time, responsible for its actions without fully re-establishing responsibility and punishment. The behaviour of animals is the responsibility of the person who owns the animal, and the ultimate punishment is the killing of the animal, namely interference with human property, which may be punished by the owner. In the case of a robot, it could be seizure of the robot, which may result in its destruction or reprogramming. However, it is not the form of punishment that matters, but the fact that the object is legislated through separate regulation for both rights and punishment. However, autonomous robots are currently an object where all responsibility is channelled to humans. The place of robots and other AI entities in this continuum will change as they achieve greater autonomy, ethical abilities and moral sophistication. How such change is to be considered in the legal system will depend on the purpose and function of such AI in the society involved.

Considering the IP position of an autonomous AI actor as a creator of works or inventions independent from human control, AI is indeed the source of innovation. Because no author or inventor is identifiable as a human, and still no protection of the investment of a party amounts to a ground for protection, the best solution is that within the *sui generis* concept of an autonomous AI entity, the IP created falls into the public domain. Instead, in cases where the AI entity is an IP infringer, when no other party can be identified as such, the *sui generis* legal status herein envisioned for AI would enable developing a multi-layered system of insurance to cover damage caused.

In general, in creating anthropomorphic robots with general AI characteristics, the chance to consider them as legal subjects, instead of objects, would ultimately pave the way for robots to obtain rights and personhood and even to own objects and hold rights. Whether this could be embodied in an extended *sui generis* status or through adaptation of the existing positive law framework is an issue that we leave for further research. Ultimately, the definite solution will be dependent on legislators and policymakers, and the applicability of Moore's law on AI leading to entropy or a utopian legal solution.

# 9. The European copyright system as a suitable incentive for AI-based journalism?

**Taina Pihlajarinne, Alexander Thesleff, Leo Leppänen and Sini Valmari**

## 1. INTRODUCTION

News automation was already under way in the 1980s with mainly low-context, data-driven types of news such as weather reports.[1] But with the recent paradigm-defying advent of artificial intelligence, an increasing amount of news is expected to be produced by 'algorithmic journalism' in the future. Some estimate that by 2030 a large majority of news items will be written by machines.[2] In the field of automated text generation, the list of current examples includes different styles of text, from reporting and summarising

[1]   Laurent Bourbeau and others, 'Bilingual Generation of Weather Forecasts in an Operations Environment' (1990) 3 COLING *Papers presented to the 13th International Conference on Computational Linguistics.*

[2]   Noam Lemelshtrich Latar, *Robot Journalism: Can Human Journalism Survive?* (World Scientific 2018), ch 3; Jane Wakefield, 'Intelligent Machines: The Jobs Robots Will Steal First' (*BBC News*, 13 September 2015) https://www.bbc.com/news/technology-33327659 accessed 9 October 2021. However, Linden, for instance, has emphasised the fact that creative journalistic jobs might not be under great risk due to the strong capacity of journalistic work for adaptation and mitigating for new technology. Carl-Gustav Linden, 'Decades of Automation in the Newsroom: Why Are There Still So Many Jobs in Journalism?' (2017) 5(2) *Digital Journalism* 123, 136.

scientific results,[3] to literary works such as poems,[4] novels,[5] magazines[6] and books[7] on diverse topics written by artificial intelligence technologies or 'AI'. The quality of artificially generated works is increasing rapidly and we are starting to see works that are virtually indistinguishable from those created by humans.[8]

From the viewpoint of copyright law, these AI works, also sometimes labelled 'emergent works', are problematic to say the least. On the one hand, the investment required to develop the necessary technologies to facilitate autonomous news creation is substantial, calling for legal protection of their

---

[3]    Springer has published a book on lithium-ion batteries, written by AI, utilising the summarisation method. Beta Writer, *Lithium-Ion Batteries: A Machine-Generated Summary of Current Research* (Springer 2019) https://link.springer.com/book/10 .1007/978-3-030-16800-1 accessed 9 October 2021; Matthew Griffin, 'World's First Book Written Entirely by an AI Is a Real Thriller' (*Fanatical Futurist*, 11 June 2019) https://www.fanaticalfuturist.com/2019/06/worlds-first-book-written-entirely-by-an-ai -is-a-real-thriller/ accessed 9 October 2021.

[4]    Robot Newman, *The Art of Artificial Poetry: I Wrote This in Three Hours* (inde-pendently published, Amazon 2019) https://www.amazon.com/Art-Artificial-Poetry -Wrote-Three-ebook/dp/B07TN3SP12; Yisela Alvarez Trentini, 'Computer Generated Poetry Will Knock Your Socks Off' (*Medium*, 21 March 2017) https://yisela.medi um.com/computer-generated-poetry-will-knock-your-socks-off-763c815a1b52; Isobel Hamilton, 'Researchers Built an AI Capable of Writing Poetry That's Equal Parts Woeful and Impressive' (*Mashable*, 27 April 2018) https://mashable.com/2018/04/27/ poetry-writing-ai/?europe=true.

[5]    Aditya Vivek Thota and Soumya Kundu, 'Interesting Novels Written by Artificial Intelligence: How Good and Comprehensible Are They?' (The Research Nest, *Medium*, 2 August 2020) https://medium.com/the-research-nest/interesting-novels-written-by -artificial-intelligence-d407e330fe07; On '1 The Road', the novel written by AI, see Thomas Hornigold, 'The First Novel Written by AI Is Here—and It's as Weird as You'd Expect It to Be' (*SinglarityHub*, 25 October 2018) https://singularityhub.com/ 2018/10/25/ai-wrote-a-road-trip-novel-is-it-a-good-read/.

[6]    Montag https://www.montag.xyz/ accessed 27 October 2020; Beebom, 'Montag is a New Magazine Written Entirely by AI' (14 August 2019) https://beebom.com/ magazine-written-by-ai/; CuratedAI, A Literary Magazine Written by Machines, For People (2017) http://curatedai.com/ accessed 28 October 2020.

[7]    INSEAD Professor Philip Parker actively utilises artificial intelligence in book writing. Bianca Bosker, 'Philip Parker's Trick for Authoring Over 1 Million Books: Don't Write' (*HuffPost*, 11 February 2013) https://www.huffpost.com/entry/philip -parker-books_n_2648820?guccounter=1; Noam Cohen, 'He Wrote 200,000 Books (but Computers Did Some of the Work)' (*The New York Times*, 14 April 2008) https:// www.nytimes.com/2008/04/14/business/media/14link.html.

[8]    These works pass the so-called 'Turing test', which is widely considered as an indication of a computer's ability to imitate the more intricate forms of human cogni-tion. See e.g., Nils Köbis and Luca D Mossink, 'Artificial Intelligence Versus Maya Angelou: Experimental Evidence That People Cannot Differentiate AI-Generated From Human-Written Poetry' (2021) 114 *Computers in Human Behavior*, article 106553.

output from free-riding. On the other hand, the potential lack of direct creative effort by an identifiable (human) author *by definition* excludes the possibility of clear-cut copyright protection, since – according to historically undisputed anthropocentric copyright doctrines – only works created by natural persons enjoy copyright protection.

As AI applications and the quality of their output evolve even further, it becomes increasingly relevant to evaluate their protection and the suitability of the incentives that the existing legal framework offers.[9] Authorship issues relating to AI, especially from the causal link point of view, have been assessed in Chapter 7 by Ole-Andreas Rognstad. So for its part, this chapter focuses instead on mapping out the protection of AI news in general and on the need to revise the current legal status and the feasibility of doing so.

## 2.     EXAMINING THE EXISTING COPYRIGHT FRAMEWORK

### 2.1     Justification of Copyright: Incentive-based Theories

As the research question of this chapter delves into the suitability of copyright as an incentive for the deployment of AI in creative industries, a natural starting point is an overview of incentive-based justification theories behind copyright.

Despite differences in emphasis, both the continental 'author's right' tradition, and the common law copyright tradition have assigned a central role to so-called utilitarian arguments when defining the ultimate basis for justification of modern copyright.[10] Utilitarian theories argue that the market failure that would result from the low cost of copying works contrasted with the high cost of creating them is best rectified by granting authors exclusive economic rights to their works.[11] The economic rights of copyright law – the exclusive right to control a work by reproducing it and by making it available to the

---

[9]     M Iglesias Portela, S Shamuilia and A Anderberg, 'Intellectual Property and Artificial Intelligence: A Literature Review' (Luxembourg, Publications Office of the European Union 2019).

[10]     Utilitarian justification arguments are quite convincing and perhaps the most widely used, but other justification arguments, which carry less relevance towards AI works, do have rightful support. For example, natural rights arguments mostly focus on protection of the *personality* of the author and 'fair reward'-based theories presuppose a human agent as well.

[11]     See e.g., William M Landes and Richard A Posner, *The Economic Structure of Intellectual Property Law* (Belknap Press and Harvard University Press 2003), 37–41.

public – are thus seen as incentives both necessary and best suited for authors to undertake their creations.

An important feature of incentive-based utilitarian theory is an emphasis on the common good of the public. It endeavours to maximise production and dissemination of cultural objects such as news articles, while at the same time minimising the restrictions and costs to the public that wishes to use and consume these works. According to utilitarian theories, exclusive and injunctive copyright is a necessary evil that ensures production of vital cultural and informational goods.[12]

As the digital age has slowly shifted the significance of copyright towards 'entrepreneurial works' such as online broadcasts, non-authorial photographs and even databases, the incentives are arguably being directed increasingly towards monetary investment in technological advancement rather than towards the time, energy and craftsmanship of the 'romantic' author.[13] As discussed below in section 4.3, the tendency of the EU legislator seems to follow this trend, one of the latest signs of which is the introduction of the press publishers' right in the DSM Directive.

Despite the investment-centric shift, however, it is quite self-evident that an AI algorithm capable of creating works (or content resembling works) does not in itself need any financial incentives in order to create and continue creating works. Robots do not need to make a living. The one who does is the developer of the initial technology or the algorithm, or the user of the technology. The *human* need for incentives can be seen (with of course the Lockean view of natural rights) as the basis on which the key concepts of copyright are built. These key concepts are the boundaries and prerequisites of copyright, and the incentivising effect that copyright provides is only available to works and creators that fit within them.

## 2.2    Originality and Authorship

When assessing AI-generated content through the lens of the current copyright regime, it is crucial to outline their standing vis-à-vis the key concepts of *originality* and *authorship*.

---

[12]    About these type of arguments, see e.g., Adrian Brown, 'Can Utilitarianism Accommodate Moral Rights?' (1995) 2 *UCL Jurisprudence Rev* 16.

[13]    See e.g., Tuomas Mylly, Juha Lavapuro and Marko Karo, 'Johdanto: Tekemisen Vapaus' in Tuomas Mylly, Juha Lavapuro and Marko Karo (eds) *Tekemisen Vapaus: Luovuuden Ehdot ja Tekijänoikeus* (Gaudeamus 2007) 11.

The CJEU has created a practice of assessing *originality*, in which it has stated repeatedly that a work must be the 'author's own intellectual creation'.[14] While the CJEU has considered that each category of works must be assessed under the above-mentioned criterion, it should be noted that the originality requirement for written works has traditionally been relatively easily met. Considering for example the *Infopaq* ruling,[15] where an extract consisting of 11 words was found to be copyrightable if it is considered as an author's own intellectual creation, the vast majority of news articles, notwithstanding the relative simplicity of the literary content, will be sufficiently *original* in order to be afforded copyright protection. When assessing the following example of an article published in *The Guardian* we can quite easily determine that, on the surface level, it satisfies this – relatively speaking low – requirement of originality:

> Australian political parties declared donations worth $16.7m in the 2017–18 financial year, according to the latest figures from the Australian Electoral Commission. This amount is lower than usual, with donations averaging $25.2m a year over the past 11 years. The largest donation overall, $2.3m, was made by Vapold Pty Ltd to the Liberal party. The party with the most donations was the Liberal party, which declared $7.6m, followed by the Labor party with $7.1m. The Labor party also declared $33.2m in 'other receipts', which includes money received from investments, but also includes money from party fundraisers where people pay for event tickets in lieu of donations.[16]

In this specific case, however, the article was generated by an automated news reporting system, which brings us to the second concept: the question of authorship. Separating originality from authorship is admittedly somewhat theoretical, in view of the considerable overlap between them ('*author's* own intellectual creation'), but in the case of AI works there is justifiably newfound interest in the *creativity* aspect of originality (reminiscent of the German notion of '*Schöpfungshöhe*'). In other words, while acknowledging that the *Infopaq* test of originality does necessitate authorship,[17] an examination of

---

[14]   Case C-5/08 *Infopaq Int'l A/S v Danske Dagblades Forening* [16 July 2009] ECR I-06569; Case C-393/09 *BSA*. Case C-403/08 and Case C-429/08 *FAPL*, Case C-145/10 *Painer*, Case C-604/10 *Football Dataco*, Case C-406/10 *SAS*, Case C-683/17 *Cofemel*.

[15]   *Infopaq*, ibid.

[16]   ReporterMate, 'Political Donations Plunge to $16.7m – Down From Average $25m a Year' (*The Guardian*, 31 January 2019). https://www.theguardian.com/australia-news/2019/feb/01/political-donations-plunge-to-167m-down-from-average-25m-a-year accessed 28 June 2021.

[17]   See also Christian Handig, 'The Copyright Term "Work" – European Harmonisation at an Unknown Level' (2009) 40(6) *International Review of Intellectual Property and Competition Law* 665.

*Artificial intelligence and the media*

originality should, according to some viewpoints,[18] accentuate evaluation of the output's features and disregard the philosophical problem of whether a robot can exhibit 'intellectual' or 'creative' behaviour.

The concept of the *author* is not defined in most European copyright statutes or even in the Berne Convention. Nevertheless, the doctrine requiring *human* authorship can be viewed as being an inherent part of copyright in the Western world. Many articles of the Berne Convention quite self-evidently imply that copyright protection is afforded to natural persons only.[19] In the USA, the well-cited *Monkey Selfie* case also shows this clearly to be true there as well, as a federal court refused to grant protection to photographs made by a black macaque.[20] Additionally, the moral right side of copyright (*right of attribution, right of integrity*), which is more prevalent in the continental author's right tradition, specifically aims to protect the *personality* of the author,[21] a quality that is overly foreign to others than humans.

AI used as a tool (similarly to e.g., spellcheck functions and thesaurus tools in text processing software) aiding the *human* creative process is therefore very differently viewed from autonomous AI that essentially operates with no, or at most a notably indirect, causal link connecting a source of human originality (or creativity) to the end product. Analysis by Ole-Andreas Rognstad in Chapter 7 demonstrates how complicated the assessment of causation is in the case of AI and utilisation of causation tests may be feasible.[22]

---

[18] See e.g., Stephane Sejourne (rapporteur): European Parliament's report on intellectual property rights for the development of artificial intelligence technologies (2020/2015(INI)), p. 13:

> the general trend with regard to [originality] is towards an objective concept of relative novelty, making it possible to distinguish a protected work from works already created. AI-generated creation and 'traditional' creation still have in common the aim of expanding cultural heritage, even if the creation takes place by means of a different act. [...] [W]e seem to be moving towards an acknowledgement that an AI-generated creation could be deemed to constitute a work of art on the basis of the creative result rather than the creative process.

[19] For instance, the term of protection is counted from the death of an author (art 7 and art 7 bis). Additionally, the art 6 bis includes rules on utilisation of moral rights after the death of the author.

[20] *Naruto and others v David John Slater and others*, 888 F.3d 418 (2018). Péter Mezei, 'From Leonardo to the Next Rembrandt – The Need for AI-Pessimism in the Age of Algorithms' (2020), 13 https://papers.ssrn.com/sol3/papers.cfm?abstract_id= 3592187.

[21] For a summary, see Lionel Bently and Brad Sherman, *Intellectual Property Law* (4th edn, OUP 2014), 36–38. For more on Hegelian justification and personality theory, see Justin Hughes, 'The Philosophy of Intellectual Property' (1988) 77 *The Georgetown Law Journal* 287, 330–350.

[22] See Ole-Andreas Rognstad, Chapter 7.

When AI is used as a tool, the user of the tool might be considered as the author in most cases if the creative choices made by the user are decisive. However, sometimes the programmer of the tool can be assessed as the author if the operation of the tool, that is, the AI algorithm, is distinctly predetermined and a clear causal link exists between the work and the programmer's creative choices. The programmer is also quite naturally entitled to the copyright in the underlying program code itself as a literary work. But when autonomous AI applications generate works without significant direct contributions from either the programmer[23] or the user of the system (i.e., the person pressing the 'start' button), we will face instances of 'authorless' works that according to current legal status will fall into the public domain.[24] The line between 'tool' and 'autonomous agent' will be met by courts and legal praxis in the forefront of the rise of creative AI industries on a case-by-case basis as AI will start slowly approaching and even crossing this line.

All in all, the intertwined fundamental concepts of originality and authorship are, as of now, insurmountable obstacles for fully autonomous AI works to be protected through copyright.

## 2.3    Related Rights

Despite the above, some forms of protection within the broad meaning of copyright might still be available for automatically generated content even if the requirements of originality and human authorship are not fulfilled. For example, the *sui generis* database right does not necessitate originality – only substantial investment. According to recital 41 of the Database Directive, the maker of a database is the person who takes the initiative and the risk of investing. The database maker can be a natural person or legal entity.[25]

The controversial press publishers' right adopted by DSM Directive article 15 will be an additional form of potentially applicable related rights protection. Publishers of press publications will be the right holders. However, there are no special requirements in the Directive as to how and by whom press publi-

---

[23]    The word 'programmer' is used as a hypernym here – in the real world, usually a large group of people contributes to the development of a program. Furthermore, the initial copyright holder will in many cases be the employer as per the Software directive 2009/24 art 2.3.

[24]    About this development in general, see, e.g., Woodrow Barfield, 'Towards a Law of Artificial Intelligence' in Woodrow Barfield and Ugo Pagallo (eds), *Research Handbook on the Law of Artificial Intelligence* (Edward Elgar 2018) 2, 15–17; Mirelle Hildebrandt, *Smart Technologies and the End(s) of Law* (Edward Elgar 2016), 35–36.

[25]    See e.g., Estelle Derclaye, 'The Database Directive' in Irini Stamatoudi and Paul Torremans (eds), *EU Copyright Law. A Commentary* (Edward Elgar Publishing 2014), 325.

cations should have been created. This new right will provide press publishers with a short – two-year – protection for online use. Even though no originality is needed, the right does not cover use of very short extracts.

In order to evaluate how compatible the current copyright system is as an incentive with artificially generated news content, we will next take a closer look at how AI is used in newsrooms in practice today and in the near future.

## 3. ARTIFICIAL INTELLIGENCE IN NEWS PRODUCTION – A CLOSER LOOK

### 3.1    Rule-based AI and Machine Learning

It is notoriously difficult to precisely define AI. However, a useful proposal by Russel and Norvig describes AI as the study of agents that perceive an environment and then perform actions based on what they perceive.[26] In other words, AI is about systems that adapt their behaviour based on the different inputs they receive. On a broad level, and essential to the research questions of this chapter, two main branches of AI differ on *how* they know what actions to take following observation of the initial input.[27]

The first branch consists of systems that are based on rules and heuristics dictated by humans, also sometimes known as 'Good Old-Fashioned AI'. In these kinds of systems some human actor, while building the system, has explicitly constructed a ruleset that governs the actions of the system. As an example, a financial institution might use a rule-based AI system to automatically screen loan applications in situations where a combination of the applicant's assets, income and previous loans fail to reach a prerequisite level. These thresholds would be determined by humans, perhaps by interviewing experts, and programmed into the AI system by programmers. The system then simply applies these rules to any new applications it is presented with.

The second branch, and the one that perhaps better fits the current colloquial meaning of AI, consists of systems that learn. In machine learning, a human author defines only a larger framework and then provides the system with examples of what action it should take when presented with certain input. A machine learning algorithm then attempts to learn (within the limits of the human-provided framework) an internal model that minimises the difference between the actions it would take given an input, and the action defined as

---

[26]    Stuart J Russel and Peter Norvig, *Artificial Intelligence: A Modern Approach* (4th edn, Pearson 2020) vii–viii.

[27]    This description of AI is simplified, as the breadth of the field is too complex to completely discuss in this context. For a more complex description, we refer to text books such as *Artificial Intelligence: A Modern Approach* by Russel and Norvig (n 26).

'correct' in the training data. Continuing with the loan application analogy, a human might define that a decision on whether to instantly reject a loan application is based on some combination of assets, income and existing loans. The machine learning algorithm would start with a random model that is then applied to a loan application resulting in a determination of whether to reject or pass the application. The model's decision is then compared to that produced previously by a human. If the decisions are different, the model is slightly tweaked to better align with the human decision. As it is presented with a large amount of training data produced previously by humans, the machine-learning algorithm gradually modifies this internal model so that its actions follow human actions as closely as possible. Once this training is complete, the model obtained can be used to screen applications where the correct action to take is not previously known.

Importantly, in both branches the actions of the system can in some way be traced back to human actors. In the case of rule-based AI systems, the human actors involved are those that defined the rules the system should follow. In the case of machine learning, the final model is learned from examples set by humans, and is limited by a framework defined by the human programmer. However, the end result might eventually be something that is not predictable by the human actors behind the preparatory efforts.

## 3.2    News Generated from Raw Data vs. Pre-existing Texts

As discussed above, AI systems can be used to produce news from some underlying data, such as the statistics produced by various national statistical agencies. In the last half-decade, systems for automated text generation have been introduced in increasingly complex news domains. For example, Associated Press has been using a rule-based automated solution to produce news stories about corporate earnings reports since 2014.[28] *The Los Angeles Times* has used automation to write news reports about homicides and earthquakes since at least 2013.[29] Since then, various AI systems have been used to

---

[28]    Paul Colford, 'A Leap Forward in Quarterly Earnings Stories' (*The Associated Press*, 30 June 2014) https://blog.ap.org/announcements/a-leap-forward-in-quarterly -earnings-stories accessed 15 January 2021.

[29]    *Los Angeles Times* news automation related to homicides and earthquakes. Sarah Marshall, 'Robot Reporters: A Look at the Computers Writing the News' (*journalism.co.uk*, 12 March 2013) https://www.journalism.co.uk/news/robot-reporters-how -computers-are-writing-la-times-articles/s2/a552359/ accessed 28 June 2021.

produce news articles about elections,[30] sports[31] and other domains such as real estate.[32] The use of news automation has been well established in at least the larger newsrooms for years.[33]

While the technical details of these systems are often trade secrets, available public information indicates that these systems are commonly technical successors of the early weather report-producing systems. In other words, they are commonly based on human-produced text 'templates' which are then combined and filled with data from the system input by automation.[34] These templates are snippets of text, ranging in length from individual sentences to paragraphs, with slots that are filled from the system input by the automation. A crude analogy is provided by considering a combination of a choose-your-own-adventure book and a mad-libs word game. As such, the

---

[30]  Chris Fox, 'General Election 2019: How Computers Wrote BBC Election Result Stories' (*BBC*, 13 December 2019) https://www.bbc.com/news/technology -50779761 accessed 28 June 2021; Tamedia Switzerland example: France24, 'Robo-Journalism Gains Traction in Shifting Media Landscape' (*Washington (AFP)*, 10 March 2019) https://www.france24.com/en/20190310-robo-journalism -gains-traction-shifting-media-landscape accessed 28 June 2021; L Leppänen, M Munezero, M Granroth-Wilding and H Toivonen, 'Data-Driven News Generation for Automated Journalism' [2017] *Proceedings of the 10th International Conference on Natural Language Generation* 188; Suomen Lehdistö, 'Ohjelmistot Tekivät Tuhansia Vaaliuutisia Ilman Isoja Kömmähdyksiä' (13 April 2017) https://suomenlehdisto .fi/ohjelmistot-tekivat-tuhansia-vaaliuutisia-ilman-isoja-kommahdyksia/ accessed 28 June 2021; Kati Rantala, 'Voitto-Robotti Urakoi Uutisia Joka Kunnan Tuloksesta Presidentinvaaleissa – Satoja Juttuja Silmänräpäyksessä' (*YLE*, 28 January 2018) https://yle.fi/uutiset/3-10043742 accessed 28 June 2021.
[31]  MittMedia http://unitedrobots.ai/about-united-robots accessed 28 June 2021, United Robots provides automated editorial services to a majority of Swedish local media groups, including MittMedia, Gota Media, NTM, Stampen Lokala Medier, Hallpressen, Norran, Sörmlands Media and Skånskan/Norra Skåne. Clients also include Sweden's largest news site Aftonbladet (Schibsted) and HSS Media in Finland. AI-powered smart news assistant Voitto. YLE, 'The First of Its Kind in the World: Yle Newswatch's Smart Voitto Assistant Shows Recommendations Directly on the Lock Screen' (12 October 2018) https://yle.fi/aihe/artikkeli/2018/10/12/the-first-of-its-kind -in-the-world-yle-newswatchs-smart-voitto-assistant-shows accessed 28 June 2021; STT, 'News Robotics at STT: Completed, Current and Upcoming Projects' https://stt .fi/en/product/news-robotics/ accessed 15 January 2021.
[32]  Tal Montal and Zvi Reich, 'I, Robot. You, Journalist. Who Is the Author? Authorship, Bylines and Full Disclosure in Automated Journalism' (2017) 5(7) *Digital Journalism* 829.
[33]  Alexander Fanta, 'Putting Europe's Robots on the Map: Automated Journalism in News Agencies' (Reuters Institute Fellowship Paper, University of Oxford 2017).
[34]  Stefanie Sirén-Heikel, Leo Leppänen, Carl-Gustav Lindén and Asta Bäck, 'Unboxing News Automation: Exploring Imagined Affordances of Automation in News Journalism' (2019) 1(1) *Nordic Journal of Media Studies* 47.

human element is still strongly present in both the templates themselves and the rules that govern how they are combined and used in the larger document.

Such template-based approaches are, however, increasingly difficult to employ as the complexity of the news domain increases. In addition, these kinds of approaches are costly to implement and hard to reuse,[35] while also presenting difficulties for producing varied and fluent textual output. As a consequence, recent years have seen increasing academic interest in machine-learning methods.[36] As discussed above, these systems observe (tens to hundreds of) thousands of examples of training data as pairs of training samples of the form 'given this input data, you should produce this output text' and attempt to learn a model that mimics the human process that constructed the 'gold standard' outputs present in the training data. While we have seen promising advances in these technologies, they are not yet well established in real-world newsrooms.[37]

In addition to using AI to write news 'from scratch', it is possible to use artificial intelligence to produce news content based on other content. Perhaps the most obvious use of AI technologies in this manner is presented by auto-mated *translation*,[38] which enables a newsroom to produce a story in a single language and then use automation to translate it for publication in other languages. Ongoing research efforts into several research areas could provide tools for even more complex AI applications in journalism.

Automated *summarisation* is the task of taking some relatively long text and automatically producing from it a shorter summary. Such summaries can be produced from either individual articles or clusters consisting of multiple source texts. These summaries can be either extractive, that is, consisting of snippets of text lifted from the original document, or abstractive, that is,

---

[35]   Linden (n 2).

[36]   For an example of applying neural methods to generating news text, see Ratish Puduppully, Li Dong and Mirella Lapata, 'Data-to-Text Generation With Content Selection and Planning' (2019) 33(01) *Proceedings of the AAAI Conference on Artificial Intelligence* 6908.

[37]   While details of newsrooms' activities are scarce due to secrecy, available evidence indicates that non-neural methods are still the norm. See, e.g., Sirén-Heikel and others (n 34), where none of the interviewed media representatives employed neural methods. At the same time, newsrooms are exhibiting some interest in neural methods, even if the early results are far from perfect https://stt.fi/scoopmaticin-opit/ accessed 28 June 2021.

[38]   STT, 'Nordic Breaking News: STT's News Wire Automatically Translated Into English and Swedish' https://stt.fi/en/product/nordic-breaking-news/ accessed 2 November 2020.

producing completely new sentences.[39] Other systems attempt to *rephrase text* while retaining the original meaning of the input document.[40] Such systems, if they were to become increasingly robust, would allow masking of the reuse of other newsrooms' content, potentially in completely automated fashion.

A more benign version of the above is, for example, text *simplification*. The goal of text simplification is to transform a text so that it is simpler and understandable by wider audiences such as children and language learners. Simple text is also potentially easier to translate using machine translation. Similarly, machine-learning methods are being investigated for modifying the *style* of a document, that is, rewriting a text in the style of another text. While progress is slow, similar approaches have achieved impressive results with images, for example producing variants of paintings in other painters' styles.[41] Such methods provide tools for increased personalisation of news.

### 3.3     Other Notions on the Prolificacy and Capability of AI Technologies

Closely related to the distinction between rule-based AI and machine learning is the distinction between 'narrow' or 'weak' AI and 'general' or 'strong' AI. Behind this distinction is the observation that while present-day AI methods are able to perform extremely well in specific tasks, they lack the ability to 'learn to solve new problems that they didn't know about at the time of their creation'.[42] AI experts largely agree that AI capable of achieving every task better and more cheaply than human workers is still at least decades away.[43]

At the moment, the user's contribution is still significant, but AI technologies are able to (and often do) notably impact the end results. However, as AI journalism evolves even further, eventually the creative decisions made by

---

[39]   Wafaa S El-Kassas, Cherif R Salama, Ahmed A Rafea and Hoda K. Mohamed, 'Automatic Text Summarization: A Comprehensive Survey' (2021) 165 *Expert Systems with Applications,* article 113679.

[40]   Jonathan Mallinson, Rico Sennrich and Mirella Lapata, 'Paraphrasing Revisited With Neural Machine Translation' (2017) 1 (Long Papers) *Proceedings of the 15th Conference of the European Chapter of the Association for Computational Linguistics* 881.

[41]   DeepArt, 'Turn Your Photos Into Art. Repaint Your Picture in the Style of Your Favourite Artist' https://deepart.io/ accessed 28 October 2020.

[42]   Ben Goertzel and Cassio Pennachin (eds), *Artificial General Intelligence* (Springer Science & Business Media 2007), VI.

[43]   Katja Grace and others, 'When Will AI Exceed Human Performance? Evidence From AI Experts' (2018) 62 *Journal of Artificial Intelligence Research* 729.

AI will probably not have a clear, direct link to human activities, and the end result may not be dependent on the user's guidance.[44]

In the above sections, we have described several news automation techniques, working from both raw data and previously written texts. It is notable here that the use of such automated methods makes the concept of a 'news article' significantly more fuzzy than previously. Automation can be used to produce thousands of variations of a single article with minor content differences. For example, automation can be used to augment a news story about some national phenomenon such as housing prices with content specific to the user's locale. Similarly, the results of a sports game might be reported using slightly different language, aiming slightly modified stories to the fans of the winning team, the fans of the losing team, and neutral fans. In addition, automated methods using text as input, such as translation and text simplification, can be used to produce article variants aimed at various demographics, such as non-native speakers, younger readers, and so on.

## 4. AI-BASED NEWS PRODUCTION AND COPYRIGHT – A FUNCTIONING MISFIT?

### 4.1 The Compatibility of Current Doctrines

When looking at how well the incentives provided by the copyright system meet the realities of AI journalism, we first need to conclude that – as we observed through examination of different kinds of AI technology used in newsrooms – the majority of *rule-based* AI journalism seems to fit within the existing legal paradigm. As long as primarily rule-based AI technologies are used in a tool-like manner in newsrooms, the framework of copyright law seems to mostly be well applicable. As a result of sufficient human intervention in the creative process, the threshold of originality can be passed. In this case, the beneficiaries of the incentives provided by copyright can be, rather traditionally, both journalists (and the news publishers employing said journalists), as well as developers of AI tools, as long as the end results themselves reach a level of originality. With this notion, the problem clears up in part – traditional copyright is still available for the majority of AI-generated (or more precisely, AI-assisted) news today.

The question that remains therefore focuses on works created by autonomous AI that utilises advanced machine learning. Incentives provided by copyright law for their creation mainly stem from related rights. It seems

---

[44] About this development in general, see for instance Barfield (n 24) and Hildebrandt (n 24).

that the above-discussed new press publishers' right does not require human authorship and therefore protected subject-matter could, as far as we can see, include news generated with the assistance of AI. Despite many uncertainties – discussed by Juha Vesala in Chapter 10 – the press publishers' right could protect AI-generated news. Technically speaking, the *sui generis* database right might also protect AI generated news content since it does not necessitate a human author or originality.[45]

The press publishers' right can generally be criticised as creating too strong a protection, and ultimately failing to genuinely solve the problem it set out to solve, namely the power imbalance between online platforms and news publishers.[46] However, it can be said to have a somewhat favourable incentivising effect in the development and adoption of news-generating AI technologies via exclusive rights protection, even though the protection is nowhere near as robust as proper copyright. Of course, this might lead to an unbalanced situation between different types of AI-generated works: for instance, music created by AI without a sufficient link to human acts is not protected, no matter how creatively commendable it is, while at the same time, in practical terms all AI-created news enjoys this new short-term protection. This is not to say that said imbalance should necessarily be corrected by even further new regulation.

Another feature of copyright law, when considering the system as a whole, can be seen as a potential, though possibly undesirable, incentive for use of AI technologies in news production. Namely, allowing alterations of works by others, when combined with a highly competent AI application, enables an almost endless amount of possibly exploitable variations from existing texts. From a copyright standpoint, if AI is utilised to produce news from existing texts that are copyrighted by others, the outcomes must be assessed case by case from a *derivative work* perspective. Therefore, the crucial question is: how creative are the efforts employed in the alterations, and how independent is the outcome in comparison with the underlying work?

First, it is possible that an alteration infringes the rights to the original work if the new version does not demonstrate sufficient creativity in the alterations as demanded for assessability as a new original work, but instead parts that can be considered as expressions of the intellectual creation have been copied.

---

[45] The database right might be available to e.g., interactive data-oriented news articles that might have an index or a catalogue of data accessible by the reader.

[46] See, e.g., Taina Pihlajarinne and Juha Vesala, 'Proposed Rights of Press Publishers: A Workable Solution?' (2018) 13(3) *Journal of Intellectual Property Law & Practice* 220. However, Höppner, for instance, argues that the new related right is justified in addressing market failures in the area of the online press. Thomas Höppner, 'EU Copyright Reform: The Case for a Publisher's Right' (2018) (1) *Intellectual Property Quarterly* 1.

Secondly, it is also possible that the alteration is copyrightable as a derivative work due to some discernible creative efforts but without prejudice to the rights in the original work. A third possibility is that the result is considered to be independent to a transformative degree, foregoing the connection to the underlying work in the copyright sense.

Thus, the methods mentioned of automatic summarisation, translation, localisation, personalisation, and some forms of simplification performed by AI can result in derivative works that could be copyrightable by a human author in varying degrees. Translations are usually protected as such, but rights are without prejudice to rights in the original work.[47] Summaries could be protected in the same manner. In the case of a freely composed and rephrased summary, however, an independent, "transformative" news article will probably be created. On the other hand, a summary that uses only word-for-word fragments of the original article is likely viewed as a copyright infringement of the original work if it is unauthorised.

Methods such as automated rephrasing might be problematic in terms of traditional copyright doctrines. It is a fundamental starting point that copyright is intended to protect creative expression, not ideas.[48] If an automated system changes expressions but only utilises the idea behind the article, there is no copyright infringement under traditional doctrines. The result, however, is dependent on overall assessment: are elements demonstrating expression of the intellectual creation of their author being reproduced or is it considered as a new original work due to the alterations? Has the original structure of the text remained similar despite the alterations?

In all the situations mentioned, where derivative works are created solely by AI without a sufficient link to human creative effort, no copyright protection will be afforded according to the current anthropocentric regime. However, as with original works, the press publishers' right might be applicable even without a human author.

All in all, the current copyright system seems to be *partially* suitable as an incentive for AI-driven news production. When considering the somewhat

---

[47]   According to art 2 (3) of the Berne Convention such works as translations 'shall be protected as original works without prejudice to the copyright in the original work'. Berne Convention for the Protection of Literary and Artistic Works (9 September 1886, as revised 14 July 1967) 828 UNTS 221 (Berne Convention); about copyright for machine-generated translations, see Anniina Huttunen and Anna Ronkainen, 'Translation Technology and Copyright' [2012] 3 *Nordiskt Immateriellt Rättsskydd* 330.
[48]   Copyright protection extends to expressions, not ideas as such. See WIPO Copyright Treaty (adopted 20 December 1996, entered into force 6 March 2002) 2186 UNTS 121 (WCT). Idea-expression dichotomy, see e.g., Edward Samuels, 'The Idea-Expression Dichotomy in Copyright Law' (1989) 56 *Tennessee L Rev* 321.

futuristic *fully* autonomous machine learning-based composition of texts, legal incentives are restricted to the above-outlined related rights. Since the protection they might offer is not particularly robust, there seems to be room for the question: should the law be amended in pursuit of more substantial protection of non-human creative content?

## 4.2    Arguments For and Against Reforms

Above, when discussing the utilitarian justification theory of copyright, we pointed out that there is no need to financially incentivise machines. Additionally, the programmers responsible for algorithms might have intellectual property rights to the applications as such. One might still suggest that, in addition, programmers could be even more incentivised to develop useful autonomous creative AI applications, were they afforded some form of exclusive rights to the resulting new emergent works. This indirect incentive – the exclusive right to the 'offspring' of their primary work – might increase innovation in the creative AI field even further. Similarly, there might be a need to incentivise journalists and publishing houses to utilise such tools in a creative way. No conclusive economic studies showing this have been carried out to the knowledge of the authors of this chapter, but these claims could *prima facie* have some merit.

Furthermore, there is some room for arguments and suggestions for a more encompassing copyright system. These arguments in turn emphasise the apparent imbalance of protection that results from the perhaps seemingly arbitrary requirement of human authorship – after all the end result of AI is potentially of very high creative quality though facilitating autonomous AI-driven content creation does require considerable temporal and monetary investment. In today's world we are faced with methods of creation that were unimaginable at the time when the general principles of intellectual property law were first established; so should copyright doctrines not simply be revised rather than just passively allowing these new kinds of works to fall into the public domain? Extension of protection could be seen as warding off a culture of theft and exploitation.[49] These viewpoints are grounded on the prevention of free-riding, one of the core functions of IPR protection, as well as on the standpoint that the added value achieved through a creative process should be protected irrespective of the technology employed.

---

[49]    For instance Celine Melanie A Dee, 'Examining Copyright Protection of AI Generated Art' (2018) 1(1) *Delphi – Interdisciplinary Review of Emerging Technologies* 31, 36.

Arguments that support a more comprehensive system of incentives, that is, protection of AI-generated works, also tend to be supplemented by the concern that the current system encourages concealing a work's origins if it is created by AI.[50] To briefly touch upon this, it seems that this line of thinking assumes that in the 'normal' case it is somehow visible or otherwise easy for a user to assess whether a particular work is copyrighted or not. This is certainly not the case: assessment of originality, for instance, is not simple, not to mention the factor of who is the right holder and whether or not the term for protection has expired. Secondly, development of digital licensing models and possibilities created by blockchain in supervising copyright and utilisation of works might also increase visibility concerning origin and authorship issues, including whether a work is created by human hand or AI. Thirdly, as explained by Anette Alén-Savikko in Chapter 2, due to the transparency requirement in the media sector, a news producer should in any case disclose and explain how their news is produced, including utilisation of AI. Therefore, this does not seem to be a great problem in the media sector.

Many suggestions have been presented on how this 'incentive gap' of unco-pyrightable AI-works should be bridged. These often start with how we could rethink the ownership of copyright and its governance, such as through structures where AI could be seen as an independent legal entity with legal rights and responsibilities. Others suggest that authorship and ownership interests of artificially generated content could be jointly acknowledged and the output subsequently compulsorily licensed through Creative Commons licences. The 'humans behind the machine' approach, where the person by whom the arrangements necessary for creation of the work are undertaken will be the author, has also been seen as a potential solution.[51] Most popular perhaps have

---

[50]  WIPO, 'WIPO Conversation on Intellectual Property (IP) and Artificial Intelligence (AI)' (Revised issues paper on intellectual property policy and artificial intelligence, 2nd session, 21 May 2020), Issue 7 Authorship and ownership, para 23(viii) https://www.wipo.int/edocs/mdocs/mdocs/en/wipo_ip_ai_2_ge_20/wipo_ip_ai_2_ge_20_1_rev.pdf accessed 15 January 2021. For further conversation on AI issues across IP rights see WIPO, 'The WIPO Conversation on Intellectual Property and Artificial Intelligence' https://www.wipo.int/about-ip/en/artificial_intelligence/conversation.html accessed 15 January 2021.

[51]  This model is already utilised to some extent. For instance, in the UK there are specific rules on computer-generated works. According to Copyright, Designs and Patents Act 1988 (CDPA), s 9(3) in the case of a literary, dramatic, musical or artistic work which is computer-generated, the author will be taken to be the person by whom the arrangements necessary for creation of the work are undertaken. See, e.g., Ryan Abbott, 'Artificial Intelligence, Big Data and Intellectual Property: Protecting Computer Generated Works in the United Kingdom' in Tanya Aplin (ed), *Research Handbook on Intellectual Property and Digital Technologies* (Edward Elgar 2020).

been proposals for creating a completely new related right for these emergent works or AI works. These proposals generally favour a short period of protection and the quite natural exclusion of moral rights.[52]

However, arguments against any additional new forms of protection revisions of existing doctrines are perhaps even more compelling than those supporting them. First of all, utilisation of highly developed AI applications might reduce the marginal costs of creative work to near zero, which might lead to the conclusion that we do not need copyright for these works.[53] Additionally, in accordance with the principle of *optimal* incentives within utilitarian justification theories, we must not start with the question how to maximally incentivise creation of works, but rather with how to appropriately incentivise creation of works without crippling the normal use and consumption of cultural objects in society through overprotection. Following the logic of utilitarian models, the *lowest effective* approach should be adopted.[54]

Before considering the need to incentivise an activity through legislative reform, any extra-judicial incentives should be evaluated. As we are observing the current explosion in AI innovations, it is clear that the developers of AI technology are not exactly starved of incentives for creative work completed by AI. It should be emphasised that the driving forces promoting advances in AI research are not necessarily immediate returns on investments or extreme tailor-made forms of IP protection, but rather general scientific curiosity, and the cutting edge of what is possible in IT, data processing and computer science.

The investments made towards AI-based journalism are undeniably worthwhile from a more business-minded view. First, and rather self-evidently,

---

For a suggestion of an AI work made for hire model, where AI is seen as a creative employee or contractor, see Shlomit Yanisky-Ravid, 'Generating Rembrandt: Artificial Intelligence, Copyright, and Accountability in the 3A Era – The Human-Like Authors are Already Here – A New Model' 2017) *Michigan State L Rev* 659, awarded for the 2017 Visionary Article in Intellectual Property Law, available at https://digitalcommons.law.msu.edu/lr/vol2017/iss4/1 accessed 28 June 2021.

[52]   See, e.g., Dee (n 49) 36–37.

[53]   See Jeremy A Cubert and Richard G A Bone, 'The Law of Intellectual Property Created by Artificial Intelligence' in Woodrow Barfield and Ugo Pagallo (eds), *Research Handbook on the Law of Artificial Intelligence* (Edward Elgar 2018) 411, 426–27.

[54]   Optimal incentives are generally thought to be those that minimise social cost. See e.g., Jeffrey Harrison, 'A Positive Externalities Approach To Copyright Law: Theory And Application' (2005) 13(1) *J Intell Prop L* 1. R. Hurt and R. Schuchman actually favour less costly alternatives to the copyright's temporary monopoly such as literary prizes and rewards, private patronage and government support in form of, e.g., tax reliefs. Robert Hurt and Robert Schuchman, 'The Economic Rationale Of Copyright' (1966) 56(1/2) *The American Economic Review* 421, 424–425, 432.

considerable possibilities exist for reducing labour costs in news automation, as within any industry. Secondly, the spread of news is extremely fast due to modern information technology, so that publishing speed is an enormous competitive advantage. In the world of digital journalism with a short lifespan, competition is very much focused on generating advertising income through breaking news headlines.[55] This means that even if fully artificially generated news content were to remain unprotected it would still likely be utilised in the future in the race to break the news first. And, as stated above, if someone else is first, AI-generated alterations, translations and the equivalent derivatives – provided that no infringements are committed in the process – are a possibly legitimate use of information provided by others. Even if the resulting derivative works would not be copyright protectable due to non-human authorship, they would still be a means for generating content in the fast-paced world of news.

The most convincing argument against any legislative reforms, however, is presented in the next section.

## 4.3     Direction of European Copyright Law: The Problem of Uncontrolled Expansion and Mistargeted Protection

When trying to predict the future shifts in European copyright law as it tries to accommodate the inevitable fully autonomous creative artificial agents, we have to take a look into the general direction of EU copyright. As copyright is clearly an internal market matter, the European Union has been carrying out copyright harmonisation from the early 1990s. Harmonisation includes 15 directives, not all of them purely copyright directives but directives that (also) affect copyright. One part of harmonisation efforts has been an endeavour to seek a 'high level of protection of intellectual property' due, among others, to the growth and competitiveness of European industry-related reasons.[56]

---

[55]   Will Slauter, 'Taking the Long View: The Business of News and the Limits of Copyright' (2019) 6(2) *Critical Analysis of Law: An International & Interdisciplinary L Rev* 262; Joanne Lipman, 'OPINION: Tech Overlords Google and Facebook Have Used Monopoly to Rob Journalism of Its Revenue' (*USA TODAY*, 11 June 2019) https://eu.usatoday.com/story/opinion/2019/06/11/google-facebook-antitrust -monopoly-advertising-journalism-revenue-streams-column/1414562001/ accessed 28 June 2021; Megan Graham, 'To Show How Easy It Is for Plagiarized News Sites to Get Ad Revenue, I Made My Own' (*CNBC*, 17 May 2020) https://www.cnbc.com/2020/ 05/17/broken-internet-ad-system-makes-it-easy-to-earn-money-with-plagiarism.html accessed 28 June 2021.

[56]   See recital 4 InfoSoc Directive.

Protection has often exceeded the minimum protection offered by the Berne Convention and the level offered before by many of the Member States.[57]

Many parts of this development have been widely criticised due to the tendency to overprotection. For instance, the InfoSoc directive and *sui generis* database protection has been claimed to be a failure,[58] and the DSM directive was created amid intensive lobbying by right holders on the one hand and criticism by academics on the other hand.[59] Every new directive has meant a new layer to EU copyright regulation, adding its complexity and fragmentation in terms of the rationale, subject-matter and scope of protection.[60] However, while

---

[57] As Hugenholtz explains, to some extent this might have been inevitable since upscaling the level of protection is in practice much easier than its downscaling. See Bernt Hugenholtz, 'The Dynamics of Harmonisation of Copyright at the European Level' in Christophe Geiger (ed), *Constructing European Intellectual Property. Achievements and Perspectives* (Edward Elgar 2013).

[58] First Evaluation of Directive 96/9/EC on the Legal Protection of Databases [online]. Brussels: Commission of the European Communities 2005; Final report: A study prepared for the European Commission DG Communications Networks, Content & Technology: Study in Support of the Evaluation of the Database Directive, 140–141; Lucie Guibault, Guido Westkamp and Thomas Rieber-Mohn, 'Study on the Implementation and Effect in Member States' Laws of Directive 2001/29/EC on the Harmonisation of Certain Aspects of Copyright and Related Rights in the Information Society', 165–169; Robin Elizabeth Herr, *Is the Sui Generis Right a Failed Experiment: A Legal and Theoretical Exploration of How to Regulate Unoriginal Database Contents and Possible Suggestions for Reform* (DJØF Publishing 2008), 201–202.

[59] A Q&A published by the European Parliament stated that: 'The directive has been the subject of intense campaigning. Some statistics inside the European Parliament show that MEPs have rarely or never been subject to a similar degree of lobbying before (through telephone calls, emails etc.)' See European Parliament, 'Questions and Answers on Issues About the Digital Copyright Directive' (1 November 2019), available at https://www.europarl.europa.eu/news/en/press-room/20190111IPR23225/questions-and-answers-on-issues-about-the-digital-copyright-directive accessed 28 June 2021. From the academics' perspective, open letters and academic statements criticising the DSM were signed by more than 200 scholars, see e.g., Copyright Reform: Open Letter from European Research Centres, available at https://www.create.ac.uk/wp-content/uploads/2017/02/OpenLetter_EU_Copyright_Reform_24_02_2017.pdf accessed 28 June 2021; Statement from EU Academics on Proposed Press Publishers' Right, available at https://www.ivir.nl/publicaties/download/Academics_Against_Press_Publishers_Right.pdf accessed 28 June 2021.

[60] Pihlajarinne, Vesala and Honkkila, 'Conclusions' in Pihlajarinne, Vesala and Honkkila (eds), *Online Distribution of Content in the EU* (Edward Elgar 2019). Regarding the DSM directive specifically, in chapter 2 of the same book, Kivistö notes that 'there are few, if any, generic rules or provisions that are meant to or could be applicable beyond their immediate context as imposed in the [DSM] directive. [...] All this points to the conclusion that it is difficult to accept the DSM Directive as a serious attempt to counteract fragmentation.' Martti Kivistö, 'The DSM Directive: A Package

the Commission has favoured strong and fragmented protection, the CJEU has recently started to place greater stress on the need for a fair balance.[61] The continuous adoption of such measures as *sui generis* database protection and press publishers' rights has weakened the fundamental idea that protection for creative investment – investments that are clearly connected to creativity – should be the main issue in IPR.[62] In addition, *sui generis* database protection, for instance, has proved itself mistargeted, being applicable only to traditional databases.[63] Further, one could ask whether the neighbouring right for all photographs should somehow follow technical development: the changed level of effort and skills needed for taking photographs. We can compare the roots of the photographer's rights and today's society where taking photographs is easy, cheap and fast for everybody.[64] This situation is further complicated by AI appliances taking photographs.[65] Member States' legislation also includes such forms of related rights protection that might not be in line with the needs of a modern, digitalised society.[66]

---

(Too) Full of Policies' in Pihlajarinne, Vesala and Honkkila (eds), *Online Distribution of Content in the EU* (Edward Elgar 2019), 24.

[61]   See, e.g., the following CJEU cases. Joined Cases C-403/08 *Football Association Premier League Ltd and others v QC Leisure and others* and C-429/08 *Karen Murphy v Media Protection Services Ltd* [GC] EU:C:2011:631 [2011] ECR I-09083; C-201/13 *Johan Deckmyn and Vrijheidsfonds VZW v Helena Vandersteen and Others* [GC] EU:C:2014:2132 [2014]; C-516/17 *Spiegel Online GmbH v Volker Beck* [GC] EU:C:2019:625 [2019]. The approach adopted by the CJEU means more flexibility in the level of weighing and balancing and in giving room for fundamental rights.

[62]   See Taina Pihlajarinne, Rosa Maria Ballardini, 'Owning Data via Intellectual Property Rights: Reality or Chiemera?' in Rosa Maria Ballardini, *Regulating Industrial Internet through IPR, Data Protection and Competition Law* (Kluwer 2019).

[63]   Ibid.

[64]   It is estimated that the number of photographs taken annually is well over 1 *trillion*. See e.g., Stephen Heyman, 'Photos, Photos Everywhere' (*The New York Times*, 29 July 2015) and Caroline Cakebread, 'People Will Take 1.2 Trillion Digital Photos This Year – Thanks to Smartphones' (*Business Insider*, 1 September 2017). When considering CCTV cameras and other various extremely automated photographic processes, it does seem quite unnecessary to protect every single photograph via related rights provisions. See for instance Olli Pitkänen, 'Mitä lähioikeus suojaa?' (2017) 115(5) *Lakimies* 580.

[65]   In 2017 Google released their Google Clips camera: a wearable hands-free photographic device that determined independently of the user when to capture images or video. An AI algorithm was used to recognise social interactions and other highlights of the user's day. Google Clips has since been discontinued. See Google Clips Help, 'What is Google Clips?' https://support.google.com/googleclips/answer/7545440?hl=en accessed 15 January 2021. Quite naturally, questions about the ownership of the photographs and videos taken were raised.

[66]   'Press report protection' in the Nordics is an example of an outdated relic when considering today's modern information flow. According to section 50 of the Finnish

All in all, while copyright harmonisation clearly has its benefits from the single market perspective, the system includes many overprotective parts or parts where legitimate interests are not in line with the scope of rights. For some parts, these elements are results of technological and economic development – and for other parts, the adopted legislative elements have been overreactions to technological and economic development. It is also typical that they include fragmented, narrow-scoped elements that might correct some specific problem for the time being, but these kinds of rules are not necessarily easily reconciled with technological development in the end.

As the EU legislator will be seriously confronted with new developments of AI-created works, it is possible or even probable that we will be continuing on the same path. This would mean a risk of overprotection of either developers or users of AI, as well as further increasing fragmentation of the copyright framework by adopting, for instance, new related rights.

## 5.    CONCLUSIONS: CAN WE STRIKE A BALANCE WITHOUT OVER-CORRECTING?

Even if an imbalance of incentives or an 'incentive gap' might seem to arise when categorically not affording copyright protection to artificially created works when an AI system is operating autonomously, the authors of this chapter find further regulation aiming to amend such apparent issues uncalled for. This mainly stems from the view articulated in the previous section: fragmented and potentially uncontrolled expansion of protection is generally undesirable. The current system of incentives of AI works might not in some cases be optimally proportional to the investment required for their creation, but extension of protection might be more risky than tolerating some potential gaps in incentive mechanisms provided by intellectual property. From the utilitarian perspective, we should carefully assess the impact on society of any new rights, not taking it for granted that adding new IPRs is the most suitable remedy for new problems.[67] Incentives should also be assessed as a whole, and in fact, efficiency benefits such as increased output of news and reallocation of human resources might serve as sufficient incentive for news producer houses to invest, utilise and develop AI in news production. From the journalists'

---

Copyright Act, a press report supplied by a correspondent (by virtue of a contract) abroad may not be made available to the public without the consent of its recipient until 12 hours have elapsed from its being made public.

[67]    Ole-Andreas Rognstad, *Property Aspects of Intellectual Property* (CUP 2018) 77–78.

side, while automation could represent an actual risk of fewer jobs,[68] at the same time automation support in news gathering, production and delivery could be seen as advancing and improving the working environment.[69] On the other hand, the possible applicability of the new press publishers' right for AI-created news might reject claims on the incentive gap. Nevertheless, it could mean overprotection, especially in the case of relatively simple news with a low degree of creativity.

In general, utilisation of AI creates new problems that might not be resolvable by traditional copyright doctrines. Despite the fact that copyright structures and concepts would be in dire need of adaptation to the digital and AI revolution, some of the current building blocks of copyright such as the requirement of a human author and the idea/expression dichotomy, should be left untouched or at least the feasibility of amendments should be assessed very carefully.

While arguing that overprotection and fragmentation should be avoided and AI creations without sufficient link to human creativity should, at least in the current situation, fall into the public domain (the press publishers' right notwithstanding), the capability of AI in terms of creating unlimited possibilities for alterations on the basis of existing works, might on the other hand challenge current doctrines. As for translations, simplifications, localisation, personalisation and summarisation of news written by others, the first impression might be that no specific problems seem to emerge, that these issues could be tackled by traditional doctrines relating to derivative works. However, a general question arises from the endless possibilities for creating new versions, possibly by only pressing a button. In this kind of situation, the costs of creating a work would be very low. Is it feasible that all these versions (that are created highly efficiently and quickly with a short economic period for utilisation) would potentially enjoy protection? In the case of sufficient links to human creative work, the author's right might last 70 years after the death of the programmer or the journalist. Even a related right with short-term protection might be economically non-feasible.

A second issue is that AI-based rephrasing methods and other similar methods that might extensively use the idea behind the news while using

---

68   On Microsoft layouts in May 2020, see Jim Waterson, 'Microsoft Sacks Journalists to Replace Them With Robots: Users of the Homepages of the MSN Website and Edge Browser Will Now See News Stories Generated by AI' (*The Guardian*, 30 May 2020) https://www.theguardian.com/technology/2020/may/30/microsoft-sacks-journalists-to-replace-them-with-robots accessed 28 June 2021.

69   Aljosha Karim Schapals and Colin Porlezza, 'Assistance or Resistance? Evaluating the Intersection of Automated Journalism and Journalistic Role Conceptions' (2020) 8(3) *Media and Communication* 16.

decidedly different expressions and structures might raise the question whether it is justified to assess them as independent works. The question arises whether following current doctrines is feasible from an incentive point of view, as this could be considered as some kind of free-riding on previous creative work by others. In a traditional environment, taking an article written by somebody else and using it as a basis for a new one by changing the expressions is possible as well, and the same question arises whether this kind of utilisation is a copyright infringement. However, the difference might lie in the level of how systematic the utilisation is and the level of effort that the utilisation demands. Automated systems make it possible to systematically utilise others' work in commerce with a very low level of effort demanded by the user. While copyright doctrines might need a general update by taking into account, for instance, whether utilisation means free-riding on the right holder's investment, how systematic the utilisation is, and whether exploitation occurs in a commercial context,[70] it is clear that the idea/expression dichotomy should remain untouched as a fundamental principle in copyright. This is crucial from the freedom of speech and creativity perspectives. However, automatic modification could in some cases be assessed as an act of unfair competition. Therefore, the possibility of free-riding does not seem to be a problem.

When assessing overall incentives, the potential of AI to bring competitive advantages in news production – combined with a possibility to apply the short-term press publishers' right in AI-created news – should be considered as sufficient without the need for legislative interference. As such, the possibility of exclusive rights for endless possibilities of variations and personalisation of news articles maybe only by pressing a button might easily lead to over-protection. In general, EU policymakers' reactions to AI include a risk of further fragmentation of copyright, and the specific features and interests of AI utilisation in journalistic work include a risk of additional contribution to this development.

---

[70] Pihlajarinne has argued that copyright doctrines should be reformed by taking into account whether exploitation of a copyrighted work affects or is liable to affect legitimate copyright interests, or is in accordance with honest practice followed in a particular sector of the creative industry. In this assessment, for instance, the following issues could be taken into account: does exploitation of a work mean free-riding on the investments of the author or right holder; does exploitation of a work occur in a commercial or private context and, specifically, does the utiliser of the work compete with the right holder; is the work exploited with the purpose of creating new and innovative business models; and how systematic is the exploitation of the work? See Taina Pihlajarinne, 'Should We Bury the Concept of Reproduction – Towards Principle-Based Assessment in Copyright Law?' (2017) 48(8) *Intl Rev of Intellectual Property and Competition Law* 953.

All in all, copyright law should be perceived as a dynamic area of law having the ability to adapt to continuous societal and technological development, but at the same time, it should maintain its fundamental core and identity. Many of the problems connected with AI copyright seem in fact rather to be issues of competition and free-riding, and thus contingent on further research, they might be better tackled by unfair competition law.

# 10. Press publishers' right and artificial intelligence

## Juha Vesala

## 1.  INTRODUCTION

Artificial intelligence (AI) plays an increasing role in the production of journalistic content.[1] Simple news articles such as sports or financial news can already be automatically generated, and various technologies be used to facilitate journalistic work and production of news content.[2]

However, despite the growing significance of AI, its implications were not examined when the press publishers' related right in the Directive on copyright in the Digital Single Market (2019/790) (DSM Directive) was drafted.[3] Regardless, the question how the right should be applied to AI-based news production is becoming relevant as situations are starting to arise where questions about the copyright status of such activities need to be examined.[4] Moreover, in order for the press publishers' right to succeed in its goal of promoting investment in journalistic and editorial investment, the impact of AI on the operating conditions of news production needs to be taken into account

---

[1]  Recent technological advances suggest new applications for producing natural language could also emerge. For examples on authoring text, see e.g., https://www.gwern.net/GPT-3 accessed 1 March 2021.

[2]  See e.g., examples mentioned in Iglesias Portela Maria, Shamuilia Sheron and Amanda Anderberg, Intellectual Property and Artificial Intelligence – A Literature Review EUR 30017 EN (2019), 12–13 and for a general overview https://en.m.wikipedia.org/wiki/Automated_journalism accessed 1 March 2021.

[3]  While text and data mining are considered in the DSM Directive (Arts 3 and 4), AI can extend much further than text and data mining (TDM) entail and the exceptions only address one aspect of AI technologies and one copyright aspect of exceptions to the reproduction right.

[4]  E.g., the question whether a news article authored by AI qualifies for copyright protection has already arisen in China. Decision of the Nanshan District People's Court (2019) Yue 0305 Min Chu No. 14010 (24 November 2019) (finding that an AI-generated article was protected and infringed).

when applying the right to news content, whether produced conventionally or with AI.

This chapter examines the application of the press publishers' related right to AI-based news production. It proceeds as follows. First, the chapter examines the hallmarks of the press publishers' right – the conditions for protection and protection granted in terms of exclusive rights and their limitations (Section 2). Second, the chapter analyses the conditions under which news content produced with AI could meet the conditions for protection of press publications and qualify for protection under the right (Section 3). Third, the chapter examines issues raised by infringement of other press publishers' related right in AI-based news production (Section 4). Lastly, the chapter presents concluding remarks (Section 5).

## 2.   PRESS PUBLISHER'S RELATED RIGHT: CRITERIA FOR PROTECTION AND RIGHTS GRANTED

### 2.1   Press Publishers' Related Right

The press publisher's related right was adopted as part of the DSM Directive in 2019. The right was proposed by the European Commission in order to provide protection to press publishers against unauthorized reuse of their news content in online services, such as news aggregators, media monitoring services and social media, as well as to improve the bargaining position of press publishers vis-à-vis firms using content.[5]

The press publishers' right, due to be implemented by Member States in June 2021, protects 'press publications' by providing publishers with the exclusive right to reproduce and make available press publications to the public online by information society services for two calendar years following publication.[6] In this way, the right enables press publishers to oppose unauthorized online use of their news content. This ability goes beyond copyright protection of

---

[5]   COM(2016) 593 final, 3 'This proposal provides for a new right for press publishers aiming at facilitating online licensing of their publications, the recoupment of their investment and the enforcement of their rights.' Whether the right will achieve these objectives is far from clear. See e.g., Taina Pihlajarinne and Juha Vesala, 'Proposed Right of Press Publishers: A Workable Solution?' (2018) *Journal of Intellectual Property Law & Practice* 220. Regardless of whether or not that is the case for the final Directive, the focus in this chapter is on how the Directive should be transposed in national legislation and ultimately applied by courts in a manner that succeeds in its objectives as relates to the use of AI in the press sector.

[6]   See below Sections 2.2 and 2.3.

works because it extends to extracts not containing copyright-protected elements.[7] Protection also enables press publishers to require information society services providers (ISSPs) using press publications online to strike licensing agreements for reuse of content.

Since applying the press publishers' right to AI-generated content raises thorny questions about interpretation of certain elements in the general conditions for protection, the key features of the right are laid out below and some of the problematic issues are pointed out.

## 2.2    Object and Conditions for Protection

The object of protection of the press publishers' right is 'press publications'. The concept refers to subject matter that meets the following criteria:

(1)   a *collection* composed
(2)   *mainly of literary works of a journalistic nature*, but which can also include other works or other subject matter, and which:
(3)   constitutes *an individual item within a periodical or regularly updated publication under a single title*, such as a newspaper or a general or special interest magazine;
(4)   has the *purpose of providing the general public with information related to news or other topics;* and
(5)   is *published in any media under the initiative, editorial responsibility and control of a service provider.*[8]

The complex definition of the object of and conditions for protection features diverse aspects. Not only does the subject matter need to meet certain qualitative requirements (such as type and purpose, status under other rights) but it also needs to be published under certain conditions (e.g., subject to editorial control) and in a certain way (for instance, as a collection in a regularly updated publication under a single title). As discussed below, many of these conditions are not defined in the Directive and their application to AI-based news generation exposes ambiguities as to interpretation issues that are also relevant for conventionally produced news content.

---

[7]   C-5/08 *Infopaq International A/S v Danske Dagblades Forening* EU:C:2009: 465, paras 47–48.
[8]   Art 2(4) DSM Directive.

## 2.3     Exclusive Rights and their Limitations

Publishers of press publications have the exclusive right to reproduce and make available to the public press publications as regards online use of press publications by ISSPs.[9] However, the act of linking does not infringe exclusive rights.[10] Nor do private or non-commercial uses by individual users.[11]

While the exclusive rights of publishers are stated in the Directive to be the same as for works and certain related rights under the InfoSoc Directive,[12] it is not possible to use their standards when assessing alleged infringement. This is because the conditions and object of protection of the right differ from those applicable to works and other related rights. For this reason, for instance, it is not possible to rely on conditions of originality when evaluating infringement of the press publishers' right, but infringement needs to be assessed in a way unique to the press publishers' right.

Two particular issues arise in terms of evaluating infringement of the press publishers' right. First, as regards the extent of use constituting infringement, the Directive makes clear that use of a press publication as a whole, or articles contained in it or parts of it may infringe the right.[13] However, the Directive does not determine how extensive excerpts do so and how this is to be evaluated. The substantive conditions of protection provide little guidance on how lengthy excerpts infringe the right since there is no reference to the degree of infringing use (e.g., substantiality of reproduction) or a condition of protection such as originality that could be used to determine whether part of a press publication is reused in an infringing manner. Nevertheless, it is explicitly stated in the Directive that the use of individual words or very short extracts is not infringing.[14] Very short extracts are to be understood in a way that ensures that investment by and incentives for press publishers are not threatened even by aggregation of small extracts.[15] Arguably, the capability of the extent and nature of reuse affecting investment is also relevant when assessing alleged infringement concerning longer extracts.

---

[9]     Art 15(1), first sentence DSM Directive, referring to Arts 2 and 3(2) of Dir 2001/29/EC of the European Parliament and of the Council of 22 May 2001 on the harmonisation of certain aspects of copyright and related rights in the information society (below 'InfoSoc Directive').

[10]     Art 15(1), third sentence DSM Directive.

[11]     Art 15(1), second sentence DSM Directive.

[12]     Art 15(1), first sentence DSM Directive; Recital 57 DSM Directive.

[13]     Rec 58 DSM Directive.

[14]     Art 15(1) fourth sentence DSM Directive. While that excludes infringement, it does not follow that very short excerpts would automatically infringe.

[15]     Rec 58 DSM Directive.

Second, it is not clear if or to what extent the exclusive rights cover non-literal infringement, that is, unauthorized reuse of press publications in modified form, for example reproduced with different wording.[16] Arguably, infringement other than non-literal infringement is not excluded in the Directive and, for instance, protection of 'part' of a press publication can be understood to cover reuse of aspects of a press publication in other than the exact same form. However, as noted above, few of the conditions of protection provide substantive standards that would help in delineating the breadth of protection since they do not refer to protected aspects of content that would help pinpoint the elements that qualify for protection in terms of the exact form, expressions, structure, or substance. The best tool in this regard would also be to consider whether reuse in non-identical form is liable to harm incentives to produce news.[17] In any event, a Recital of the Directive explicitly states that facts are not protected,[18] which at least makes clear that protection does not cover facts as such.

Exclusive rights are subject to certain required and optional exceptions and limitations in the DSM Directive, the InfoSoc Directive, and others.[19] Additionally, exclusive rights cannot be invoked against a rightholder whose work or subject matter is incorporated in a press publication (or certain authorized users).[20] Moreover, authors whose works are incorporated in press publications are entitled to an appropriate share of revenues that publishers receive from use of press publications by ISSPs.[21]

Finally, the right is protected for the two calendar years following publication and is automatically granted to publishers established in an EU Member State and whose registered office, central administration, or principal place of business is seated within the Union.[22]

---

[16]  Elżbieta Czarny-Drożdżejko, 'The Subject-Matter of Press Publishers' Related Rights Under Directive 2019/790 on Copyright and Related Rights in the Digital Single Market' (2020) 51 *International Review of Intellectual Property and Competition Law* 633.

[17]  Rec 58 DSM Directive.

[18]  Rec 57 DSM Directive.

[19]  Arts 3–6 and 15(3) DSM Directive.

[20]  Art 15(2) DSM Directive.

[21]  Art 15(5) DSM Directive.

[22]  Art 15(4) and Rec 55 DSM Directive.

3.   PROTECTION OF AI-GENERATED NEWS
     CONTENT BY THE PRESS PUBLISHERS'
     RELATED RIGHT

Although AI is gaining an increasingly important role in content production, the DSM Directive and its preparatory works contain little consideration of the impact of AI on press publishing or other areas of content production. In any event, the objective of the press publishers' right to improve industry conditions for journalism[23] calls for application of the right to AI-based news production in a way that is consistent with those policy objectives.

Meeting that aim raises two immediate questions: (1) whether and how the right should protect AI-generated content; and (2) how infringement of the right in AI-based news production should be adjudged. This section focuses on the question whether and under what conditions AI-generated news content would benefit from protection under the press publishers' right, whereas infringement issues that AI-based news production faces are the subject of the section that follows thereafter.

As a premise for discussion, the general conditions of protection for the press publishers' right do not in any way exclude protection from AI-generated content as such. No reference is made in the conditions for protection or otherwise that, for instance, a natural person is required to produce the subject matter or to be the initial rightholder. However, the conditions for protection contain elements that can limit and condition the protection available for AI-produced news content (or certain business models) as well as giving rise to implicit requirements on news content that can or cannot be produced when using AI if protection under the right is sought, as discussed below.

### 3.1   Publication of Collections Regularly Under a Single Title

In order for the press publishers' right to confer protection on AI-generated content, there first of all needs to be a collection of certain types of materials incorporating the AI-generated content.[24] Moreover, the collections need to constitute an individual item, published periodically or as a regularly updated publication under a single title.[25]

Since such a collection existing as and constituting a regularly published item under a single title is a practical arrangement, this can be accomplished

---

[23]   Rec 54 DSM Directive.
[24]   Art 2(4) first sentence DSM Directive. It is not clear how many components constitute a collection. Czarny-Drożdżejko (n 16), 624.
[25]   Art 2(4)(a) DSM Directive.

by bundling content and publishing it in the required manner also when AI-generated content is concerned. However, some of the requirements can question the applicability of protection to certain business models involving AI-generated news materials on grounds relating to the required form of publication.

First, if an AI-based content creator only produces news content for another organization to publish, but does not publish that content itself, the question arises whether the producer of the content gains press publishers' rights to the content. Crucially, protection under the right is not granted to the creator or producer of news content, but to the press publisher that publishes the content in accordance with the requirements of the Directive.[26] While the Directive does not clarify what publishing or being a press publisher entails, the controlling factor seems to be under whose initiative, control and editorial responsibility publication takes place.[27] For this reason, if publication does not take place under this kind of editorial oversight by the content producer – for example, by the producer or its customer – the content producer would not be deemed to be the press publisher nor would the content produced meet the conditions for protection. In this situation, the producer would lack exclusive rights to the content and thus (absent legal title) be potentially hampered in licensing it to customers.

However, if publication of content by the customer of the content producer takes place under the control, initiative and responsibility of the content producer – for example, if editorial tasks are also carried out by the producer – the content producer would seem capable of being a press publisher and gaining protection as to the content.[28] Whether content publication takes place under the initiative, control and responsibility of the organization supplying edited content may, though, raise legal and factual issues where the customer exercises ultimate control and initiative and bears primary responsibility for publication.[29]

Second, when wholly personalized news content is concerned, it is not clear if pieces of content only produced and made available to individual users can be considered as 'publications' that have been appropriately 'published'. If

---

[26]  Rec 54 DSM Directive.

[27]  Art 2(4)(c) DSM Directive. This is consistent with the objective of recognizing investment in these activities. Rec 55 DSM Directive. See on the substantive contents of these requirements Section 3.3 below.

[28]  In this regard, a comparison to a press agency is appropriate: according to Rec 55 they can be regarded as press publishers when they publish press publications as required in the Directive.

[29]  This could preclude content supplier protection or allow protection to both the content supplier and the subsequent publisher.

individualized articles are not also made publicly available (for several users), they might not be 'published' in the manner required for protection to arise but might constitute private communication or a personal service, not a 'press publication'.[30] Overall, the examples in the Directive represent the form of the conventional mass media.[31]

Accordingly, business models based on only licensing AI-created news content to others and offering fully personalized content to users might not be eligible for protection under the press publishers' right, or protection may require additional arrangements in order to meet the requirement of publishing the content in the required form and manner by the content producer itself or another organization.

## 3.2    Collections of Mainly Literary Works: Dependency on Other Protection

### 3.2.1    Of mainly literary works

A further requirement for protection under the press publishers' right is that the collection needs to mainly consist of literary works of a journalistic nature.[32] Focusing here on whether 'literary works' are concerned ('journalistic nature' is examined below), it is clear in EU copyright law that news articles and other types of news content can be protected as literary works as long as they are their authors' independent creations.[33] For example, protection as a work can subsist in the 'form, the manner in which the subject is presented and the linguistic expression'.[34] To be clear, press publications can be published in any media, for example as audio, and thus need not be published in textual form in order to qualify for protection.[35]

If a collection consists only or mainly of AI-generated content, the question whether the contents qualify as literary works becomes decisive for availabil-

---

[30]    Moreover, another condition of protection requires that publications are intended to inform the 'general public'. Art 2(4)(c) DSM Directive. This may also limit the possibilities of protection if the circle of intended recipients of AI-produced news content is very narrow.

[31]    Rec 56 DSM Directive (newspapers, magazines, websites, blogs).

[32]    Art 2(4) first sentence DSM Directive. See on application of 'mainly' and 'literary works' Czarny-Drożdżejko (n 16).

[33]    C-683/17 *Cofemel — Sociedade de Vestuário SA v G-Star Raw CV* EU:C:2019:721, para 29 (*Cofemel*).

[34]    C-5/08 *Infopaq International A/S v Danske Dagblades Forening* EU:C:2009:465, para 44. However, protection does not extend to mere items of press information. Art 2(8) Berne Convention for the Protection of Literary and Artistic Works (as amended on 28 September 1979).

[35]    Art 2(4)(c) DSM Directive.

ity of protection under the press publishers' right. Determining whether a literary work is concerned depends on the characteristics of the materials produced – if they feature expressions or other elements that meet the above-mentioned requirements for copyright protection. This puts considerable weight on the broader copyright question whether or under what circumstances AI-produced content can be protected as works,[36] since protection under the press publishers' right also depends on the answer to the question whether AI-produced content forms the main body of a collection of news. Undoubtedly, for instance, when natural persons have made the creative choices and AI is only used as a tool in production of news content, the outputs created can obtain copyright protection as literary works and hence also under the press publishers' right.[37] However, it can also be argued that copyright protection cannot protect automatically generated content where human involvement is absent since the law presupposes a natural person as author.[38] If for any such reason the main body of a collection of news items lacks protection as literary works, the collection as a whole cannot obtain protection as a press publication.

It should be recalled, though, that this requirement of a collection mainly consisting of literary works can be met by those authored by natural persons. Thus when AI-generated content forms only a minor part of a collection mainly consisting of literary works produced by human journalists, the condition can be satisfied regardless of whether the AI-generated content is protected as literary works. For this reason, it is not necessary that AI-generated content itself constitutes literary works, as the content is capable of receiving protection as

---

[36]   See e.g., Tanya Aplin and Giulia Pasqaletto, 'Artificial Intelligence and Copyright Protection' in Rosa Maria Ballardini, Petri Kuoppamäki and Olli Pitkänen (eds), *Regulating Industrial Internet Through IPR, Data Protection and Competition Law* (Wolters Kluwer 2019); Rosa Ballardini, Kan He and Teemu Roos, 'AI-generated Content: Authorship and Inventorship in the Age of Artificial Intelligence' in Taina Pihlajarinne, Juha Vesala and Olli Honkkila (eds), *Online Distribution of Content in the EU* (Edward Elgar 2019).

[37]   See for an overview e.g., Portela et al. (n 2), 13–14; UK IPO, 'Artificial intelligence call for views: copyright and related rights' (2020) https://www.gov .uk/government/consultations/artificial-intelligence-and-intellectual-property-call-for -views/artificial-intelligence-call-for-views-copyright-and-related-rights  accessed  1 March 2021; Christian Hartmann and others, 'Trends and Developments in Artificial Intelligence – Challenges to the Intellectual Property Rights Framework' (European Commission 2020) https://ec.europa.eu/newsroom/dae/document.cfm?doc_id=71915 accessed 1 March 2021.

[38]   See e.g., Ballardini, He and Roos (n 36); Hartmann and others (n 37), 76. Indeed, the above cited CJEU cases determine the conditions for protection for works so that they need to reflect the author's personality and be an expression of their choices. See e.g., *Cofemel* (n 33) para 30.

part of a press publication that otherwise qualifies for protection.[39] However, even then the status of the non-main components of the collection under copyright and other laws can be relevant for their protection under the press publishers' right, as discussed next.

### 3.2.2 That can include other works and subject matter

A press publication obtaining protection under the press publishers' right is defined, as noted above, as consisting of a collection of mainly literary works (of a journalistic nature) but can also include other works and subject matter. Consequently, where a collection consists mainly of literary works of a journalistic nature, other works and subject matter included in that collection – even when they do not qualify as literary works – can also benefit from protection of the press publication. Thus, AI-generated content that constitutes any kind of work (literary, artistic or other) or is protected by a related right, can qualify for protection as part of a press publication.[40] For instance, AI-produced content that constitutes an artistic work, such as an image, benefits from the protection that the press publication as a whole is entitled to. Materials produced with AI that do not constitute works can also be protected by related rights, such as phonograms, or the *sui generis* database right (e.g., raw data refined with AI so as to meet conditions of protection) and on that basis qualify for protection under the press publishers' right.[41]

However, it is not entirely clear whether protection under the press publishers' right applies to AI-generated (or, for that matter, otherwise produced)

---

[39] This option would, however, limit the proportion that a press collection can include AI-generated content not protectable as literary works: if their share is too large, the entire collection may fail to qualify for protection as it would no longer consist of mainly literary works of a journalistic nature. Interestingly, then, including non-protected AI-generated content could even endanger protection of the whole collection (including human-authored literary works) under the press publishers' right if the literary works no longer constituted its main body.

[40] An implication from other protection applying is that it can limit the press publisher's exercise of its right against the authors or certain authorized users as well as that it gives rise to an obligation for the press publisher to compensate appropriately those authors whose works are incorporated in a press publication used by an ISSP. Art 5(2) and (5) DSM Directive. E.g., an author under copyright law may be an employee of the publisher or of the organization that developed the AI application – someone different from the press publisher. Thus, the publisher may need to provide appropriate compensation for the authors of AI-generated works and be limited in its ability to invoke the right against authors and their authorized users (e.g., other customers).

[41] E.g., Hartmann and others (n 37), 91–94 consider that AI-generated content could benefit from protection under certain related rights.

content that is not protected as works or by other related rights.[42] This is because the Directive is ambiguous as to whether otherwise unprotected subject matter qualifies for protection as part of a press publication or whether the unprotected subject matter does not belong at all to a collection that qualifies.[43]

One reading of the passage 'a collection composed mainly of literary works of a journalistic nature, *but which can also include other works or other subject matter*' (emphasis added)[44] is that the entire collection qualifies for protection, as long as it mainly consists of literary works of a journalistic nature – regardless of whether or not the other parts constitute works or otherwise protected subject matter.[45] That would be the literal interpretation of the first sentence – the definition that a collection which is mainly composed of literary works would be met independently of what the non-main components are (the second sentence, separated by a comma, merely acting as a clarifying addition to the first sentence, not a limitation to it).[46] Under this construction, all AI-generated news content (such as entirely mechanical news reports lacking any originality) would enjoy protection when placed in an otherwise qualified collection, regardless of whether otherwise protected by copyright or related rights.

However, the latter part of the definition 'can contain other works and subject matter' can also be understood so that a collection constituting a press publication solely consists of the enumerated types of protected subject matter and thus that other (unprotected) elements do not belong to the protected press publication at all. This would follow if 'subject matter' is understood to refer only to protected subject matter and 'can' as only permitting inclusion of the listed types of materials in a press publication. This reading would mean that only content protected as a work or by other rights would benefit from protection under the press publishers' right. Under this interpretation, the press publishers' right would not provide protection to otherwise unprotected AI-generated content, even if published in a collection otherwise meeting the requirements of a press publication.

---

[42]   Czarny-Drożdżejko (n 16), 632, noting additionally that even the different language versions of the Directive differ on this matter.

[43]   Ibid.

[44]   Art 2(4) first sentence DSM Directive.

[45]   Christophe Geiger, Oleksandr Bulayenko and Giancarlo Frosio, 'The Introduction of a Neighbouring Right for Press Publisher at EU Level: The Unneeded (and Unwanted) Reform' (2017) 39 *EIPR*, 202–210, 209.

[46]   Another indication that speaks in favour of this interpretation is that Art 15(2) DSM Directive is structured in a way that is premised on only otherwise protected subject matter benefiting from the protection offered by the press publishers' right. Namely, only rightholders and certain of their authorized users are shielded from the exclusive rights of press publishers.

The provisions concerning the press publishers' right or other parts of the Directive do not provide a clear answer to the above question about the constituents of the press publication. In some parts of the Directive 'subject matter' seems to be used in reference to protected subject matter (given the context and effect of the provisions)[47] but in others reference is made to 'protected subject matter'.[48] Moreover, a Recital of the Directive mentions as examples of other subject matter photographs and videos – types of materials that are not necessarily protected by copyright or related rights throughout the EU.[49] These factors seem to suggest that otherwise unprotected subject matter is not excluded from protection as part of a press publication. This would also be consistent with the fact that out-of-term subject matter is explicitly excluded from protection under the right[50] – there would be little reason to so provide unless protection applied to the no-longer protected subject matter to begin with. Moreover, in any event unprotected parts of protected subject matter contained in press publications would still qualify for protection (e.g., excerpts of works containing no original expression) under the press publishers' right.

However, it is noteworthy that several Member States only refer to works and other protected subject matter as the elements that a press publication can contain.[51] If that proposed or already enacted language means that exclusively literary works, other works and other protected subject matter can be protected as parts of a press publication, then news items not receiving other protection would not form parts of a press publication and hence not be subject to protection as part of one. While certainly a possible reading of the Directive as noted above, this interpretation would nonetheless raise various concerns. First, if protection is conditioned on whether content is otherwise protected subject matter, then diverging standards of protection for press publications in the EU would result. This is because related rights protection varies significantly across Member States[52] and, as a consequence, different conditions of protection would apply to press publications in Member States depending

---

[47] See e.g., Arts 3–6 DSM Directive.

[48] See e.g., Arts 2(6), 17 and 22 DSM Directive.

[49] Rec 56 DSM Directive.

[50] Art 15(2) DSM Directive.

[51] See e.g., German Discussion Proposal (15 January 2020), § 87f(1) (works and subject matter protected under the German Copyright Act); French Intellectual Property Code, Art L218-1 (works and other protected subject matter); the Implementation Proposal in the Netherlands, Arts 1(2)(p) and 7(b) (referring to certain types of protected subject matter).

[52] Although the EU copyright *acquis* provides for and recognizes certain related rights, it does not in doing so preclude other related rights protection in the Member States.

on whether or not the content is protected by national related rights.[53] For example, in some Member States non-original photos would be covered by the additional protection that the press publishers' right provides, whereas in others not. Second, the scope of protection for unprotected elements would also depend on how the boundaries of works or other protected subject matter are understood (e.g., whether they comprise parts of a literary work or are self-standing). For instance, whether an AI-created headline, illustration or summary lacking other protection would enjoy protection under the press publishers' right would depend on whether it is considered as part of a literary work that an article constitutes.

Third, given the legal uncertainty relating to whether or under what circumstances protection as works would apply to AI-generated content, excluding protection under press publishers' right of unprotected subject matter could endanger incentives to invest in AI-based news production as that could preclude any protection due for them. In this regard, it should be noted that the conditions of protection for works and other related rights do not vet whether investments into editorial efforts have been made of the types that are sought to be promoted by the press publishers' right. In particular, status under copyright and related rights is not an appropriate screen for whether investments encouraged by the press publishers' right have been made.[54]

These risks can be avoided by interpreting the conditions of protection so that collections mainly consisting of literary works of a journalistic nature can include otherwise non-protected elements. This approach, as argued below, also allows the presence of investments that the press publishers' right seeks to protect and the need for protection of such investments to be more accurately gauged under the other conditions of protection as well as to be taken into account in assessing infringement.[55] The conditions of protection examined

---

[53]  If protected subject matter is understood to encompass legal protection beyond copyright and related rights, even greater discrepancies among Member States would result. E.g., protected subject matter could be understood to include content subject to contractual, technical or access protection under national or EU legislation. As for press content, that is a tangible question since much of press content online is subject to access controls allowing access only by authorized users (e.g., subscribers access to the content).

[54]  In particular, the absence of creative, original expression in journalistic content does not exclude (or vice versa, indicate) investment in acquisition and analysis of facts, and in the editorial work underlying publications.

[55]  One problematic consequence of allowing protection of non-protected elements as parts of a press publication is that it creates a situation where the press publisher can invoke rights against the creators of unprotected content and its other authorized users. This is because Art 15(2) DSM Directive only excludes application of the press publishers' right vis-à-vis the rightholders of works and other subject-matter contained in

next are the central tools in doing precisely that and thereby directing incentives and protection at journalistic and editorial investment, not all kinds of content production.

## 3.3    Editorial, Journalistic and Informative Features: Accountability for AI Applications?

Whereas the conditions for protection examined above primarily relate to the form of publication and status of the contents of a collection of news materials under other rights, the Directive lays down central conditions of protection that concern the nature of the contents, how they are produced, and how they are published. After all, the right seeks to contribute to the financial and organizational contributions that publishers make in production of press publications in order to ultimately promote availability of reliable information and quality journalism,[56] whereas protection is not available for content production that lacks this kind of editorial involvement.[57] These are examined next, starting from editorial requirements concerning publication then proceeding to conditions relating to the journalistic nature of works in a press publication and the informative purpose required from protected press publications.

### 3.3.1    Initiative and control
A key condition of protection for press publications is that in order for protection to apply, the press publication needs to be published under the initiative, control and editorial responsibility of a service provider, such as a publisher.[58]

---

press publications – those not deemed to be rightholders due to non-existence of protected subject matter could thus not benefit from the provision. To overcome the issues this would create, the rightholders under Art 15(2) DSM Directive could be understood as referring to the person controlling the content included in a press publication regardless of whether they benefit from protection under copyright law. Otherwise, press publishers would be able to incorporate unprotected content created by others in press publications (even without permission) and invoke the right against its creator and users authorized by the creator (e.g., customers of the content producer). Moreover, often the producer of content or its authorized user may be able to avoid reproducing a press publication published by the press publisher by only exploiting the original, unprotected content.

[56]    Rec 54 and 55 DSM Directive.
[57]    Rec 56 DSM Directive.
[58]    Art 2(4)(c) DSM Directive. For an overview see e.g., Czarny-Drożdżejko (n 16), 639–640. See on the difficulty of drawing distinctions between editorial and other tasks Mireille M M van Eechoud, 'A Publisher's Intellectual Property Right. Implications for Freedom of Expression, Authors and Open Content Policies' (OpenForum Europe 2017) https://www.openforumeurope.org/wp-content/uploads/2017/01/OFE-Academic -Paper-Implications-of-publishers-right_FINAL.pdf accessed 1 March 2021, 35.

Under whose remit these editorial tasks are carried out is also significant in determining as a press publisher is the initial rightholder.[59]

As with any type of news content, AI-produced content can be published in a way that meets the requirements of control and initiative on the basis of the practical and organizational arrangements by which publication takes place. For example, production of AI-generated content could occur at the initiative of an editor (for instance, based on the actions of an editor selecting a topic and setting parameters for the content), and be reviewed by an editor before publication, with control being maintained over published content by the service provider (for instance, an editor deciding when and how content is published). This requirement does not as such seem to constitute an obstacle to AI-generated content receiving protection under the right.

However, meeting the requirements is not obvious if AI is used in a significantly independent manner to produce and publish news content, with limited involvement of natural persons such as editors in the process. In particular, it might be technically challenging to automate the required editorial tasks to the required degree since the contents of publications may not be sufficiently foreseeable where AI-based content production is concerned. This may arise, for example, due to the data sources used, such as websites, the behaviour of users affecting the content, and the very nature of certain AI technologies not being entirely explainable.[60] For these reasons, unless the initial technical design of the services is such that it secures full control and initiative, oversight by natural persons may be required as part of the publishing process, for example review before publication and oversight afterwards. Consequently, business models based on full automation of news production and publication may face challenges in qualifying for protection under the right, or their activities need to be structured conservatively enough in order for the outputs produced

---

[59]  Art 5(1) DSM Directive (referring to the exclusive rights of press publishers). Although the Directive does not determine which organization is deemed to be the press publisher, its Recitals suggest that it would be the one making the organizational and financial contributions to publishing press publications. Recs 54 and 55 DSM Directive. However, as noted above, it is also possible that one organization carries out the editorial duties and responsibilities and another publishes the content (with or without additional editorial efforts). This creates a potential issue where, e.g., an organization produces news content with AI and engages in editorial tasks but provides the content for other organizations to publish – the outcome may be that neither, both, or only one is regarded as the press publisher regarding the content concerned.

[60]  See on the challenges e.g., Claude Castelluccia and Daniel Le Métayer, 'Understanding Algorithmic Decision-making: Opportunities and Challenges' (European Parliamentary Research Service 2019) https://www.europarl.europa.eu/RegData/etudes/STUD/2019/624261/EPRS_STU(2019)624261_EN.pdf accessed 1 March 2021, iii.

to be sufficiently predictable so as to meet the standards set by the service provider. For example, predictable articles based on sports results or weather forecasts based on logical rules and known input data can certainly meet these requirements.

### 3.3.2    Editorial responsibility

Protection further requires that publication takes place under the editorial responsibility of a service provider. Yet the DSM Directive does not define what types of responsibility (for instance, what types of legal liability associated with publications) need to be borne by press publishers to meet this requirement, or to what extent (e.g., fully or to some degree) and if responsibility also requires certain types of obligations (e.g., publication of rectifications or retraction of publications), or refers to the rights and freedoms of the service provider.[61]

While there appear not to be fundamental obstacles to meeting this requirement, satisfying it can in some situations raise doubts when automated, AI-based publication is concerned. For example, it would not appear compatible with this requirement if the AI operator organized its activities in a way that seeks to skirt responsibility for published news content or argued that it does not bear liability for the unlawful or illegal activities of AI.[62] For example, technical designs and other arrangements that seek to avoid liability by the publisher for AI-generated publications on the basis of safe harbours (such as the e-commerce Directive[63]) could be argued to preclude protection of news content as press publications. In fact, some AI companies seem to be using a model in which they host content that their users post but which has been

---

[61]    As a point of reference, 'editorial responsibility' under the Audiovisual Media Services Directive (2010/13/EU), Art 1(a)(i) is defined to mean: 'the exercise of effective control both over the selection of the programmes and over their organisation either in a chronological schedule, in the case of television broadcasts, or in a catalogue, in the case of on-demand audiovisual media services. Editorial responsibility does not necessarily imply any legal liability under national law for the content or the services provided', although Member States can further specify the contents of editorial responsibility according to Rec 25. Since the above definition relates to very different kinds of context, it might not be directly transferrable to the press publishers' right and, e.g., the references to initiative and control would seem to overlap the above definition. One reflection of the requirement in the AVMSD can be thought to be that press publishers need to have their registered office, central administration or principal place of business within the EU. Rec 55 DSM Directive.

[62]    Thomas Höppner, Martin Kretschmer and Raquel Xalabarder, 'CREATe Public Lectures on the Proposed EU Right for Press Publishers' (2017) 39 *EIPR* 607–622, 610, linking editorial responsibility generally with legal liability of publishers.

[63]    Dir 2000/31 on certain legal aspects of information society services [2000] OJ L178/7.

created with the companies' AI tools at the initiative of the user – something that could be claimed to prevent the company from being liable for content produced using its tools.[64]

### 3.3.3    Journalistic nature

The fact that press publications need to mainly consist of literary works of a *journalistic nature* requires that the content of press publication in its main part is of 'a journalistic nature'.[65] This might not only require a certain kind and substance of subject matter (for instance, topics, subject matter and style are of a journalistic character), but may also require that the content and the underlying activities comply with certain journalistic principles going beyond the contents of the works, such as being based on sufficiently verifiable facts, appropriate attribution, protecting sources, and the like.[66] If AI-generated content forms the main body of a press publication based on which protection is claimed, protection under the right requires that the AI-generated content meets those requirements. This raises fundamental questions as to what a 'journalistic nature' means and to what extent that nature can be met when using only or primarily AI.[67] Unfortunately, neither the Directive nor its preparatory works illuminate how the concept should be understood and applied.

It should be noted, though, that AI-generated content need not be of a journalistic nature if the press publication mainly consists of otherwise produced literary works of that nature. Moreover, even if AI-generated content were the main body of the collection claimed as a press publication, AI-produced content could also be subject to elaboration and control by journalists who lend it a journalistic nature, or the AI-based news generation could in advance be designed in a way that does not at least violate journalistic principles, such as ensuring that only factually verified inputs are used in generating news content.

---

[64]    Under Art 14 e-Commerce Directive.
[65]    Art 2(4) first sentence DSM Directive. The intention is to limit press publications 'so that it only covers journalistic publications' and exclude from protection 'activity that is not carried out under the initiative, editorial responsibility and control of a service provider'. Rec 56 DSM Directive. Although what 'journalistic' means has been considered by the CJEU and by national legislators in other areas of law, it is unclear how 'journalistic nature' is to be assessed as regards the press publishers' right. Czarny-Drożdżejko (n 16), 628–631.
[66]    Ibid., 631.
[67]    Defining 'journalism' has not been easy. See e.g., Lionel Bently and Hercel Smith 'Call for Views: Modernising the European Copyright Framework' (University of Cambridge 2016), https://microsites.bournemouth.ac.uk/cippm/files/2017/01/IPO ModernisingIPProfResponsePressPublishers.pdf accessed 1 March 2021, 9–10.

### 3.3.4    Informative purpose

Protection further requires that the purpose of the press publication is to inform the general public about news or other topics.[68] Encouraging availability of reliable information is a core objective of the right.[69] For this reason, the contents of press publications arguably need to meet certain criteria relating to their type (for instance, having the purpose of reporting on news or other topics) and informative nature.[70] This could exclude protection for AI-generated content whose contents lack any factual content or basis as in those circumstances the purpose of the content cannot be to inform the general public. For instance, publication of 'fake news' generated with AI rather seeking to disinform the public would fail to qualify for protection on this ground. Similarly, press publications whose purpose is entirely only to entertain, such as magazines only featuring fictional contents, could also fail to have the purpose required for protection.

Unlike the requirement for literary works to be of a journalistic nature, the requirement of informative purpose applies to the whole collection constituting a press publication – therefore AI-generated content included in a press publication (not only the literary works contained in it) is also relevant when determining the purpose of publication as a whole.

### 3.3.5    Journalistic, editorial and informative requirements as tools for directing incentives and encouraging AI accountability

The above conditions of protection impose various editorial, journalistic and informative requirements relating to the substance of press publications, how they are produced, and how they are published. They highlight the fact that the related right to press publications is granted to press publishers, not the creators of news content, and seeks to promote quality journalism and availability of reliable information.[71] For AI-based press publication the conditions may impose significant technical challenges since achieving the potentially applicable editorial and journalistic standards with AI alone seems hard, at least beyond those of merely creating news content. For this reason protection of AI-generated content as press publications may often require further oversight

---

[68]   Art 2(4)(b) DSM Directive. For a broader discussion see e.g., Czarny-Drożdżejko (n 16), 637–639 (distinguishing, e.g., entertainment purpose from informational purpose).

[69]   Rec 55 DSM Directive.

[70]   A key justification for the EU adopting the right is specifically to protect contributions by publishers that 'foster the availability of reliable information'. Rec 54 DSM Directive.

[71]   Recs 54–56 DSM Directive.

by natural persons or careful editorial and journalistic choices when designing automated content production systems.

While directed at editorial and journalistic matters, the conditions also encourage AI trustworthiness.[72] First, if AI is used in producing and publishing content, responsibility needs to be borne by the service provider for the activity and control and initiative exercised sufficiently in order for the contents produced to be protected under the rights. This encourages human oversight over AI applications and compliance in their design with the law as well as ethical requirements relating to news publishing (e.g., due to the required journalistic nature and editorial responsibility) that may extend beyond the legal duties of the publisher. Second, the requirements of literary works being of a journalistic nature and press publications being intended to inform the public may also require that AI solutions are otherwise fair in terms of their intended use and design.[73] However, the implications are weak in that no obligations are imposed on press publishers, only preconditions for obtaining protection under the right (without which a publisher using AI may be fully content).

### 3.4 Protection Against Infringement of Press Publications Containing AI-generated Content

If AI-generated content meets the conditions for protection outlined above, the publisher can exercise its exclusive rights against the making available and reproduction of press publications taking place online by ISSPs.[74] For example, a press publisher could object to a news aggregator publishing excerpts from AI-generated news content protected by the right.

---

[72] See on the concept High-Level Expert Group on Artificial Intelligence, 'Ethics Guidelines for Trustworthy AI' (European Commission 2019) https://ec.europa.eu/digital-single-market/en/news/ethics-guidelines-trustworthy-ai accessed 1 March 2021.

[73] However, the conditions of protection do not seem to give rise to any requirement relating to transparency of AI imposed by the conditions of protection – it does not appear that information on the design and operation of AI (e.g., the technologies and data used) would need to be divulged in order to gain protection. An exception could be where, e.g., the journalistic nature of literary works has been questioned and needs to be defended by the press publisher explaining how the AI meets the requirement.

[74] Although some provisions relating to exclusive rights to press publications refer to 'authors' – potentially implying a natural person – the provisions do not preclude protection from AI-generated content where there is no author since they only provide for certain benefits that authors enjoy in relation to publishers. If AI-produced content constitutes works, its author, e.g., would be entitled to appropriate compensation for the use of the works by ISSPs (Art 15(5) DSM Directive) as well as to be shielded from action by the holder of the press publishers' right against the author (Art 15(2) DSM Directive).

Although exclusive rights (reproduction and making available to the public) are the same regardless of whether AI-generated content is concerned or not, the fact that AI has been used to generate the contents of a press publication can be relevant when assessing its alleged infringement. This is because, when considering whether extracts from press publications infringe the right or not, a relevant factor is whether that is capable of harming incentives to invest in creation, at least when short or very short extracts are concerned (and arguably also otherwise as noted above).[75]

In particular, it could be argued by alleged infringers that the impact on incentives for AI-generated news creation of republishing extracts is not harmful due to AI being used to produce the content. That may be the case in some situations, but not necessarily in all. First, it could be argued that when news articles are automatically produced (for instance, financial news) at low cost per news item, their reuse cannot threaten investment and consequently that a finding of infringement is not warranted. However, the investments and costs that are required to produce news content with AI may still be significant especially initially, for example due to costs associated with technical development, design of the news production service, and acquisition of required data. Moreover, some of these investments fall under the types of investments which the press publishers' right seeks to promote, especially when they relate to journalistic and editorial aspects. If these costs are taken into account, investment and costs attributable to news articles produced are not necessarily trivial any more, and can be threatened by unauthorized reuse.

Second, it could be claimed that the business models associated with AI-based news production are not vulnerable to copying or other kinds of reuse of content. For instance, when the value of AI-based news generation to consumers lies in the service it provides (such as convenience and personalization), third parties may not be able to effectively copy the service or at least copying does not necessarily harm the prospects of the service if the valuable aspects cannot be replicated by merely copying the content (for instance, personalization of content). However, other business models involving AI can undoubtedly be harmed by unauthorized copying of news content. For example, if the business model is based on publishing AI-produced news articles, incentives to produce articles could be harmed as a result of reduced advertising, subscription, or licensing revenue if reuse cannot be objected to.

Accordingly, at least in borderline cases of infringement such as short extracts, it can be relevant whether or not content has been produced with AI as it can be significant for whether or not reuse of extracts is capable of harming

---

[75]   Rec 58 DSM Directive.

investment and incentives.[76] For instance, if reuse cannot undermine incentives to produce content, it could be concluded that a 'very short extract' is concerned and that the right is not infringed.[77] However, categorical conclusions as to the need for protection or its absence are not justified but need to be considered in the specific circumstances of the alleged infringement, in assessing which of the extent and nature of reuse, the existence of relevant investments, and their vulnerability to reuse are relevant factors.

## 4.    INFRINGEMENT BY AI-BASED NEWS PRODUCTION OF OTHERS' PRESS PUBLISHERS' RIGHT

When considering the implications of the press publishers' right on AI-based news production, an equally if not even more relevant consideration is potential infringement of others' press publications in AI-based news generation. Namely, if AI-generated content includes excerpts from other publishers' news content protected by the press publishers' right, their publication online may infringe the right.

From the perspective of AI-based news production and publishing, an infringement of the press publishers' right can pose a serious challenge since publication of the content online may result in infringement of others' press publishers' right. While this is a risk that other rights pose, too, the new right exacerbates this concern as even short excerpts – containing no obvious sign of creative expression or other hallmarks suggesting protection – could infringe the press publishers' right of third parties.[78] This can make it difficult for AI-based news producers to operate in a way that does not infringe others' press publishers' rights, which would undermine the objectives of the right to contribute to journalistic efforts by hindering technological progress and uptake of AI technologies.

---

[76]    Although the expression 'short extract' limits what can be regarded as a very short extract (e.g., extracts of dozens of pages of news content might in absolute terms not be very short), it might be possible to evaluate this also on qualitative and relative terms (e.g., an extract of 20 pages from a collection of news content of thousands of pages in total may in relative terms be short). In any event, 'short' would have little meaning in the context of photos or other images, requiring such other assessment criteria. Moreover, it is possible to conclude no infringement even in the case of an extract lengthier than 'very short'. Nowhere in the Directive is it stated that any longer extract than 'very short' or of individual words automatically infringes (only that those do not infringe): assessment of infringement needs to be carried out in any event, as is the case when assessing where other related rights are infringed (e.g., phonograms).

[77]    Art 15(1) fourth sentence DSM Directive.

[78]    Art 15(1) DSM Directive.

In order for infringement risks not to unnecessarily undermine the quality and provision of AI-based news content and associated services, responsible use of AI-based news production could be supported by applying EU copyright rules in ways that recognize the technological challenges involved and their effects on investment, as argued next.

## 4.1    Avoiding Infringing Excerpts

In order to avoid infringement, AI-based news generation could, first, be sought to be designed in a way that avoids inclusion of infringing extracts in any contents subsequently published online.[79] This could be achieved only by using sources of data that do not contain any press publications. However, that can be difficult since press publications may be contained in all kinds of information sources; for example, on the web or social media news materials may be posted by users as well as press publishers themselves. Additionally, limiting AI-based news reporting to firmly managed information sources would constrain the topics that could be covered by using AI in news production. This would curtail the ability of AI to deliver on its promises to expand the scope of reporting and to be used to analyse large pools of data.

Another possibility to avoid infringement would be to avoid reproducing excerpts exceeding a certain length in publications. That would not appear technically impossible where written text is concerned since comparisons could be drawn between the sources and outputs produced to screen out identical excerpts exceeding a certain length. However, since clarity is lacking as to how short excerpts avoid infringement and that can also depend on the circumstances, avoiding infringement may require all extracts longer than 'individual words' to be removed from the content produced.[80] Doing so could also filter out ordinary language, expressions and even names of persons and places, for instance if three-word excerpts are used as a limit. Although reproduction of 'very short extracts' would not infringe either, assessing whether an

---

[79]    An additional consideration is avoiding internal reproduction of press publication that could take place when collecting data and processing the press publishers' right of others. However, since the press publishers' right only concerns online uses by ISSPs, it seems possible to avoid any reproduction taking place 'online' by carrying out these activities offline (e.g., on an internal server). However, this does not apply to subject matter protected as works and by other related rights since their protection is not limited to online uses and, thus, their internal reproduction during these processes can also infringe. These activities may benefit from copyright exceptions, such as those examined below (e.g., reporting on current events) or the TDM exception examined below in Section 4.2.

[80]    See above Section 3.4 on assessing infringement, in which the capability of reuse harming investment is a relevant factor.

extract is indeed 'very short' may require evaluation of how significant a risk to investment the given reuse is and thus could be challenging to achieve in an automated manner.

To avoid infringement issues creating an unjustified obstacle to using AI in news production, the Directive could be interpreted in a way that reduces infringement risks where the objectives of the right are not threatened. This could be the case particularly when an AI-based news producer undertakes such effective measures to avoid and limit infringement as are reasonable. For instance, occasional and accidental inclusion of short excerpts from others' press publications does not endanger investment by press publishers; consequently, courts could conclude that no infringement takes place in those situations. For example, this could be the case if an AI-based news service is designed to scour various sources for data, not specifically websites of news publishers, and press publications are sometimes included in them and repro-duced in AI-generated news content. By contrast, intentional and systematic inclusion of excerpts in AI-generated news content can undoubtedly under-mine investment by press publishers and thus justify a finding of infringement of a press publishers' right. For instance, if an AI-based news service is primarily using publications of other press publishers (such as news websites) as a data source press and extracts from them are repeatedly and intentionally reproduced in the content produced, harm to investment in the original news production would be possible and a finding of infringement warranted.

An interesting issue raised by advances in AI technology relates to the fact that it is becoming technologically possible to automatically summarize the contents of written text by using AI, so that the resulting output contains no direct excerpts from the source. On the one hand, this can significantly reduce the risk of infringing others' rights as direct extracts can be avoided. However, on the other, this kind of reuse can still undermine the investment and incen-tives that the right seeks to promote as news content phrased differently may act as a substitute for the original article. An example would be a service by one of the major internet services that summarizes news articles for its users instead of constituting a news aggregator.[81]

This raises the question whether non-literal infringement of the right is possible, which, as argued above, is possible but unclear as to assessment

---

[81]  E.g., Facebook has been reported as developing this kind of service. Alison DeNisco Rayome, 'Facebook AI tool called TLDR would summarize news articles, report says' *CNET* (16 December 2020) https://www.cnet.com/news/facebook-creating -an-ai-tool-called-tldr-that-summarizes-news-articles-report-says/ accessed 1 March 2021. To be clear, there is no indication of plans to use TLDR without authorization of press publishers, but similar technologies may be available to others who could choose to do so.

and scope.[82] While reuse of facts from other press publications clearly would not infringe,[83] drawing the line between facts and other contents of a press publication (such as the combination and relationships of facts presented in them, their analysis, and structure and manner of presentation) can be hard. For instance, presenting several facts and illustrating the links between them may venture beyond mere reproduction of facts to also replicating the analysis contained in a news article and thus potentially constitute non-literal infringement. Arguably, absent explicit legal standards in the Directive, when such reuse of the contents beyond just the facts is concerned, the capability of reuse harming the investments made originally would be the central factor when assessing alleged non-literal infringement of a press publication. Similarly, as noted above in relation to literal infringement, intentional and systematic free-riding on the contents of others' press publications could support a finding of infringement due to its capability of harming incentives and investment. For instance, systematic AI-based summarization in an online service of press publishers' press publications can significantly harm the incentives of press publishers and warrant a finding of non-literal infringement.[84] As an opposite example, AI-based generation of content in which only individual facts, such as individual sports results, are extracted from the source materials, but with no further content, and presented in a completely different form and manner of expression (for instance, as analysis of numerous sports events) would not seem capable of infringing the press publishers' right even in a non-literal manner but, rather, to constitute independent creation of wholly new value.

---

[82]   In determining how large extracts and what types of reuse infringe the press publishers' right, a comparison could be made to other related rights. As regards phonograms, the legislative context and purpose are relevant as to these questions. C-476/17 *Pelham GmbH and Others v Ralf Hütter and Florian Schneider-Esleben* EU:C:2019: 624, paras 29–30 and 43–47 (*Pelham*). Infringement is avoided where the phonogram has been modified to the extent of becoming unrecognizable or no substantial part is used. Ibid., paras 37–39 and 47. Similarly, when applying the press publishers' right the context and objective of the right are relevant when considering reuse in modified form. In particular, where non-literal uses cannot undermine investment in press publishing, finding reuse infringing would not be appropriate given the objectives of the right.

[83]   Rec 57 DSM Directive.

[84]   An issue from the press publishers' right perspective is that AI-based content creation is increasingly possible on users' devices. For instance, when news summarization tasks are carried out by an application on a user's mobile phone, the press publishers' right may be of no avail since no reproduction or making available by the provider of the app might take place online by an ISSP (to which the exclusive rights are limited).

## 4.2    Reliance on Copyright Exceptions

Another way for AI-based news producers to avoid infringement is to design and organize their activities in such a way as to meet the requirements of a copyright exception that authorizes reproduction and making available of press publications. That is a more comprehensive way to address infringement risks since it also helps avoid infringement of other rights that the source materials may include (such as copyright-protected works) as well as infringement in the internal processes of producing content, whereas avoiding infringing excerpts of press publications in outputs produced resolves just one facet of copyright risks.

In EU copyright law, only a few exceptions may meaningfully cover the publication of news content produced with AI which Member States are allowed (but not required) to implement.[85] In particular, where a Member State has adopted an exception falling under Article 5(3)(c) InfoSoc Directive concerning reporting on current events[86] or (d) pertaining to quotations of the InfoSoc Directive to the press publishers right, publication of AI-generated content could avoid infringement even if publications include third party press publications.[87]

---

[85]    EU copyright legislation exclusively lists the permissions that are allowed for Member States and freedom of the press and information do not authorize derogation from the exclusive rights beyond them. C-516/17 *Spiegel Online GmbH v Volker Beck* EU:C:2019:625, para 49 (*Spiegel Online*).

[86]    Art 5(3)(c) InfoSoc Directive contains a second limb that allows the press to reproduce and communicate to the public articles, broadcasts and other subject matter pertaining to current economic, political or religious topics, to the extent required by the purpose, unless such use has been reserved by the rightholder and subject to indication of source and author. This exception can also justify AI generation of news content where the press publications used relate to the topics mentioned and are current. However, only 'the press' is entitled to the benefit of the exception – raising the question which organizations and activities qualify and if an organization engaging in AI-based content production qualifies as 'press'. Moreover, the possibility of rightholders reserving use may limit the ability to do so, especially when online sources, such as websites, are concerned that often subject access to various conditions only allowing specific uses. See on the exception e.g., Michel M Walter and Silke von Lewinsky (eds), *European Copyright Law: A Commentary* (OUP 2010), § 11.5.54–57. According to a report, there is considerable divergence in the scope and conditions that Member States provide for exceptions under Art 5(3)(c) InfoSoc Directive, including who may benefit from the exception, for what purposes and acts, and in relation to what materials. Guido Westkamp, 'The Implementation of Directive 2001/29/EC in the Member States' (2007), Part II, 40–43 http://bat8.inria.fr/~lang/orphan/documents/europe/ivir/InfoSoc_Study_2007.pdf accessed 1 March 2021.

[87]    The exceptions seek to favour the exercise of freedom of expression and freedom of the press. C-469/17 *Funke Medien NRW GmbH v Bundesrepublik Deutschland* EU:C:2019:623, para 60 (*Funke Medien*).

Although these exceptions may thus authorize reuse of press publications, they do have elements and conditions that limit the kinds of AI-based news solutions that can benefit from the exceptions. First, the exceptions only authorize certain types of activities: reporting on current events (indicating more than just noting an event and requiring that it is of interest at the time[88]) or quotations for purposes such as criticism or review (although not limited to those purposes but also covering similar ones[89]). Second, both exceptions require that sources be indicated appropriately (unless impossible)[90] and the use of quotations needs to be in accordance with fair dealing and reporting on current events to be justified by the informative purpose. Third, the quotation exception only applies to subject matter made lawfully available to the public.[91]

These conditions limit the kinds of source materials that can be reproduced in AI-generated news content, what kinds of outputs they can be used to produce (to report on current events or in some form of dialogue with quoted materials), and to what extent and how their use can take place. In particular, not all types of AI-based news production or all news content produced with AI is able to benefit from the exceptions since not all constitute reporting or quotation of the kind permitted by the exceptions. For example, AI news production applications geared towards news aggregation or news monitoring might not qualify since they lack the additional analysis or engagement with the topics and source materials required by the exceptions.

Moreover, even when AI-based news production activities in principle would be capable of benefiting from the exceptions, some of the additional requirements may be at least challenging to implement in an automated manner. First, reporting on current events (beyond just noting them) as well as criticism, review or otherwise entering in a dialogue with the sources in the case of quotations would seem to require quite advanced analysis of the source

---

[88] *Spiegel Online* (n 85) paras 66–67.
[89] *Funke Medien* (n 87) para 43. Other accepted purposes include quotations:
... for the purposes of illustrating an assertion, of defending an opinion or of allowing an intellectual comparison between that work and the assertions of that user, since the user of a protected work wishing to rely on the quotation exception must therefore have the intention of entering into 'dialogue' with that work ... .
(*Pelham* (n 82) para 71)
In other words, there needs to be a link between the quoted material and the own reflections presented. Tatiana Eleni Synodinou, 'Reflections on the CJEU Judgment in *Spiegel Online*' 2020 42 *EIPR* 129–134, 133.
[90] E.g., indication of the source instead of author has been considered sufficient in specific circumstances. C-145/10 *Eva-Maria Painer v Standard Verlags GmbH and Others* EU:C:2011:798, paras 147–149 (*Painer*).
[91] That can be based also, e.g., on an exception to copyright. *Spiegel Online* (n 85) para 89.

materials and other capabilities. It is not clear how well these requirements can be met by only using AI at the current stage of technological progress.[92]

Second, determining to what extent reuse is allowed (for instance, length of permitted quotation) for a given purpose may require abstract balancing of interests as well as understanding the contents of the reused materials. This, too, could be challenging to implement using AI.

Third, while mentioning the sources used (e.g., URL addresses) might not be impossible technically, automatically listing the authors as well may not be simple as authors are not necessarily indicated in machine-readable or otherwise easily extractable form in the source materials. However, this kind of technical impossibility could be argued to suffice for impossibility as referred to under the exceptions and it would be sufficient that the source (for instance, a URL) is properly mentioned.[93] A reference to the source would allow the authors to be identified and thus the interests underlying the requirement to mention the authors to be secured.

Fourth, additional complexity is added by the requirement that when applying the exception, all circumstances need to be taken into account and fundamental rights adhered to.[94] It would seem difficult to implement these requirements in automated systems as proportionality and other assessments would need to be carried out with respect to the fundamental rights affected and as consideration of information beyond that contained in the source materials would be required.

Finally, a practical challenge is that AI-based news production would need to be designed in different ways for different Member States. This is because reliance on the exceptions examined above requires that the applicable national legislation provides for the exception – something that many EU

---

[92] As a comparison, mere presentation of excerpts was not considered as a quotation of the type (not used as illustration or comment) or as the kind of use by the press (no obstacle to obtaining authorization on short notice when reporting news) meeting requirements for the exceptions. See e.g., Decision of Belgian Court of Appeal (5 May 2011) http://www.copiepresse.be/pdf/Copiepresse5mai2011.pdf accessed 1 March 2021. On the other hand, publication in a structured form of materials and in conjunction with an introductory note has been deemed sufficient to constitute 'reporting' by the CJEU. *Funke Medien* (n 87) para 75, while Art 5(3)(c) InfoSoc Directive alternatively authorizes the press to reproduce and make available published articles without a similar degree of reporting or engagement with sources, that is provided rightholders have not expressly reserved the right and is limited to activities by 'the press'. See note 86.

[93] As a comparison, see *Painer* (n 90) paras 147–149.

[94] *Funke Medien* (n 87) para. 76. Additionally, the three-step-test may need to be considered when applying the exceptions, which requires consideration of the impact of the exception on normal exploitation of the subject-matter concerned and the legitimate interests of the rightholders. Art 5(5) InfoSoc Directive.

Member States do in the case of these exceptions – [95] but not necessarily in the maximal scope that EU law allows. For this reason, different legal standards can apply in different Member States (e.g., no exception or a narrower national exception) in which case the publications offered to users in different Member States would need to be differentiated in accordance with the breadth of the exceptions.

Accordingly, while AI-based news content production can benefit from the exceptions in EU copyright law examined above, not all such activities can benefit from those exceptions and at least technical challenges are faced in meeting the requirements of the exceptions. Problematically, it is exactly the potentially exempted press activities that seem difficult to automate due to their advanced intellectual nature (e.g., criticism). To some extent the challenges raised by technical difficulties could be alleviated under current legal tests by lowering the threshold for satisfying the conditions, for instance as regards indicating authors. Moreover, the extent of permitted use, its accordance with fair dealing and recognition of all circumstances and fundamental rights could be assessed at the level of the entire AI-based service instead of each incidence of reproduction and communication to the public. For example, courts could deem that the design and activities of an AI-based news service overall meet the requirements of an exception (e.g., a quotation), even if in some cases excessively lengthy excerpts are reproduced or other requirements are not met.

Finally, there are other exceptions and legal arguments that in some situations can be relevant for AI-based news publishing.[96] In particular, Member

---

[95]   The Berne Convention requires that quotations are permissible. Art 10(1) Berne Convention for the Protection of Literary and Artistic Works (as amended on September 28, 1979). Therefore, such exceptions should exist in most countries in the world at least in some form, including in EU countries. However, it does not automatically follow that EU countries also adopt an exception on press publications.

[96]   Although the mandatory TDM exceptions may seem suitable in this context, they do not enable publication of AI-created news content that contains extracts falling under exclusive rights since the exceptions do not apply to the making available right at all or reproduction associated with publication of AI-generated news. The TDM exceptions in Arts 3 and 4 DSM Directive do not apply to making available press publications at all, only reproduction required for the purposes of TDM the definition of which may exclude the purpose of content creation. See Art 2(2) DSM Directive ('any automated analytical technique aimed at analysing text and data in digital form in order to generate information which includes but is not limited to patterns, trends and correlations'). Also, e.g., the exception for caricature, parody or pastiche in Art 5(3)(k) would rarely apply to AI-based news generation except for perhaps some special cases if 'news' is understood to be mostly of a factual, journalistic nature. In particular, parody should evoke the original work. C-201/13 *Johan Deckmyn and Vrijheidsfonds VZW v Helena Vandersteen and Others* EU:C:2014:2132, para 33. Further, instead of a copyright

States are permitted to provide for an exception on 'incidental inclusion of a work or other subject-matter in other material'.[97] Where inclusion of excerpts from others' press publications in AI-produced content is not intentional, the exception could apply and by its nature be suitable for enabling AI-based news production.[98] As argued above, unintentional inclusion of excerpts would not warrant condemnation as infringing the press publishers' right to the extent that it is not liable to harm investment (as could be presumed to be the case) and the same would even more justify application of the exception when additional societal value is created by the activity – for example, press reporting. However, the exception is of limited applicability at the EU level since it has not been widely adopted in national legislation of the EU Member States,[99] and when it has been, it sometimes occurs in a quite restrictive form.[100]

### 4.3    Alleviating Infringement Risks and Requiring AI Accountability

Infringement risks may limit the ability to offer news content produced with AI since any use of uncontrolled sources of data as sources entails the risk of infringement of the press publishers' right (as well as other rights under copyright law), as explained above. While there are wide-ranging possibilities for AI-based news production to minimize risks, the legal uncertainty relating to assessment of infringement and application of the exceptions to AI-based news production may still undermine the ability to offer AI-based news content and limit the quality and scope of the services offered. Due to residual copyright infringement risks that automation cannot tackle and because human involvement would be too impractical or expensive, AI-based news producers may need to limit the data sources used and design the services in a way that reduces both the breadth and quality of coverage. This would not

---

exception, AI-based content production could be designed to avoid at least direct copyright infringement, e.g., by taking place only on the user's device at user initiative, or by benefiting from a liability exception (e.g., one for hosting under Art 14 e-Commerce Directive 2000/31).

[97]   Art 5(3)(i) InfoSoc Directive.

[98]   Walter and Lewinsky (n 86) § 11.5.64 (arguing inclusion cannot be based on choice and the included material should be insignificant).

[99]   E.g., the study 'Copyright Law in the EU: Salient Features of Copyright Law across the EU Member States' (European Parlamentary Research Service 2019) https://www.europarl.europa.eu/thinktank/en/document.html?reference=EPRS_STU %282018%29625126 accessed 1 March 2021, refers to implementing provisions only in some national laws examined and even then with qualifications about, e.g., the significance of the materials included or the type of the materials involved.

[100]  See e.g., Decision of the German Federal Supreme Court (I ZR 177/13 17 November 2014: *Möbelkatalog*).

be an outcome consistent with the very objectives of the press publishers' right, although the overall impact on the press sector depends on how significant a role AI-based or AI-assisted news production gains in the industry. Nevertheless, where these uncertainties can be alleviated without undermining other means of press publishing, courts should do so, for instance in the ways discussed above when assessing infringement and applicability of exceptions, acknowledging the absence of negative effects or harm to other interests that are protected by conditions that are only technically difficult to comply with.

It is also possible to secure ethical, trustworthy use of AI when considering the requirements that the rights of others impose on the technological design and use of AI-based news production. Respect for the rights of others (copyright and related rights) is required in order to avoid infringement (a form of 'lawful AI') and the permitted reuse of others' content pursuant to copyright exceptions is subject to requirements of fairness, proportionality and acceptable purpose (ethical and robust AI). Additionally, the requirement that the source is indicated when relying on certain exceptions improves transparency as to the sources of data used to generate news. These levers are stronger than the incentives arising from the conditions for protection of press publications since the remedies and other consequences of infringement of others' rights leave less room for choice to AI-based news producers due to their mandatory nature and severe consequences (such as an injunction requiring infringing activities to cease).

## 5. CONCLUSIONS

This chapter examined the applicability of the press publishers' right to AI-based news production from the perspectives of protection and infringement. As regards protection of AI-generated news content, it was concluded that such content can be protected under the right when included in a qualifying collection of materials consisting mainly of literary works of a journalistic nature – either human- or AI-authored. However, it is not clear if protection of a press publication covers content that is not also protected by copyright or related rights. This places considerable significance on the question under what conditions AI-generated content is protected as works or by other related rights since that can also determine if protection under the press publishers' right is available for AI-produced news content. To avoid the risks that the absence of protection for AI-generated news content creates as well as fragmentation of conditions and objects of protection in the EU, it would be warranted not to require all constituents of press publications to be otherwise protected subject matter.

Protection further requires that a press publication is published under the initiative, control and editorial responsibility of a service provider. Although not a fundamental obstacle, this may exclude protection from automated AI-based news production and publication unless sufficient technical or practical arrangements are employed to exercise sufficient initiative and control over the process. For instance, this could be the case if content produced is only licensed to others for publication, without exercising editorial oversight, or if the arrangements fail to secure sufficient control. Moreover, protection could also be precluded on grounds of lacking editorial responsibility if the AI-based activity is arranged in a way that seeks to avoid liability for publications. The requirements that press publications consist mainly of literary works of a journalistic nature and that press publications have the purpose of informing the general public also set demands as to the type of content amenable to protection, the factual accuracy of AI-generated content, and compliance with journalistic principles. These complex and demanding requirements could be hard to meet in a completely automated manner using only AI to carry out publication activities.

The chapter also examined the risk that infringement of the press publishers' right may pose to developing and offering AI-based news services. Since publication of even short extracts can infringe the right, avoiding infringement may require careful design of AI to avoid infringing reuse or to meet the requirements of an exception to copyright. However, assessment of infringement and the conditions of exceptions are subject to considerable legal uncertainty as well as technical challenges in complying with them. These risks could be alleviated by assessing infringement and interpreting the exceptions in ways that absolve the activity where AI publication is not capable of harming investment and the AI application is designed in a way that seeks to comply with the requirements (or at least addressing their underlying interests) to an extent that is technically realistic. Otherwise, the press publishers' right may at least partially undermine the very conditions of the press sector it seeks to improve.

The above observations have palpable implications for AI-based news production. In particular, protection under the press publishers' right may not be available for some business models (such as certain personalized services) or when content is published without the content producer complying with the required editorial demands (for instance, fully automated publication lacking editorial oversight or licensing of content not subject to editorial control over subsequent publication). Additionally, the potential infringement of others' press publishers' rights (and other rights) requires design of AI-based press activities in a way that either avoids infringement or falls under a copyright exception, as explained above. Overall, both avoiding infringement and gaining protection involve such complex legal demands that even when content production could be fully automated, it might be challenging to implement other required aspects (e.g., certain tasks of an editorial and journalistic nature) only using AI technologies – significant involvement of natural persons may thus in practice be required.

Finally, the chapter identified aspects of AI trustworthiness that the press publishers' right and associated rules give rise to. In particular, the conditions of protection encourage compliance with certain journalistic and editorial principles and acceptance of responsibility for publications. Avoiding infringement of others' rights requires that the rights of others are respected and that others' protected content is only used for an acceptable purpose and in a fair and proportionate manner, and by transparently disclosing the source information used. These aspects of the copyright regime influence the design and use of AI news production and publishing in various ways consistent with trustworthy AI.

# 11. Access to data for training algorithms in machine learning: copyright law and 'right-stacking'

## Inger B. Ørstavik

## 1.    INTRODUCTION

One effect of the digital revolution in the media industry is the employment of automated digital tools in the gathering, production and presentation of journalistic news and information services. While representing challenges on its own, artificial intelligence (AI) and its tools are valuable in tackling the challenges that digitalization also represents for journalism. Digitalization entails an information overload, as all content from every source is available instantly in digital format. Further, news production and distribution is becoming more pluralistic, moving away from traditional media and into social media channels without a legally responsible editor. Many media houses use AI systems to assist journalists in handling the massive amount of information readily available, by tracking down breaking news or by assisting in research, for instance by highlighting information deviating from a norm for evaluation by a human reporter.[1] The first 'robot reporters' can provide brief notices of companies' financial reports or minor league sporting events.[2] AI's ability to handle bulk reading also enables automated tools for fact checking and

---

[1]    See Corinna Underwood, 'Automated Journalism – AI Applications at New York Times, Reuters, and Other Media Giants', 2019, https://emerj.com/ai-sector-overviews/automated-journalism-applications/, accessed 3 December 2020.

[2]    See Jaclyn Peiser, 'The Rise of the Robot Reporter', 5 February 2019, *New York Times*, https://www.nytimes.com/2019/02/05/business/media/artificial-intelligence-journalism-robots.html, accessed 2 November 2020; David Caswell and Konstantin Dörr, 'Automating Complex News Stories by Capturing News Events as Data', Journalism Practice, 2019, 951–955, DOI:10.1080/17512786.2019.1643251; Javier Díaz-Noci, 'Artificial Intelligence Systems-Aided News and Copyright: Assessing Legal Implications for Journalism Practices', Future Internet 2020, 85; doi: 10.3390/fi12050085.

efficient and reliable corroboration of information.[3] Finally, most large news publishers use algorithms to support differentiated homepages and advertising to their readers.

Automated techniques applying AI are developed using machine learning techniques. Machine learning (ML) is an overall description of a process where computer systems are able to learn and adapt without following explicit instructions, by using algorithms and statistical models to analyse and draw inferences from patterns in data in order to make predictions or decisions without being explicitly programmed to do so.[4] An algorithm is a set of mathematical instructions or rules to a computer that will help it calculate an answer to a problem.[5] In automated systems, algorithms are trained upon massive amounts of data to optimize their problem-solving when applied to new data in the 'real' world. To develop services related to the news industry and journalism, training data can consist of journalistic articles, notices, reports, social media posts, tweets and similar.

This chapter discusses the role of copyright law in balancing the interests of authors and of owners of collections of protected works against the interests of AI developers and service providers, also considering the public interest in development and use of AI. By framing the discussion in the news services industry, public interests on both sides can be highlighted, making the findings applicable across industries. On the one hand, there is a need to promote development of automated tools to ensure information integrity.[6] The problem is extrapolated in the buzzword 'fake news':[7] verification of information and translucency in presentation of information is threatened as news and information production and distribution become more pluralistic. Furthermore, social media has the potential to exponentially magnify the impact of false or misleading information. There is an overt public interest in having a public

---

[3]  Richard Fletcher et al., 'Building the "Truthmeter": Training Algorithms to Help Journalists Assess the Credibility of Social Media Sources', *Converg. Int. J. Res. New Media Technol.*, 2020, 19–34, at 20–21, doi.org/10.1177/1354856517714955.

[4]  See e.g., https://en.wikipedia.org/wiki/Machine_learning.

[5]  Drexl, Hilty et al., 'Technical Aspects of Artificial Intelligence: An Understanding from an Intellectual Property Law Perspective', Version 1.0, October 2019, available at: https://ssrn.com/abstract=3465577, 4 (Drexl, Hilty et al.).

[6]  Fletcher et al. (n 3), 19–20.

[7]  The term no longer carries a specific meaning, but its connotations are illustrative. See Edson Tandoc, Zheng Wei Lim and Richard Ling 'Defining "Fake News"', *Digital Journalism*, 2017, 1–17. Available at: https://www.tandfonline.com/doi/full/10.1080/21670811.2017.1360143, accessed 2 December 2020. See also Margi Murphy, 'Government Bans Phrase "fake news"', *The Telegraph* 23 October 2018, available at https://www.telegraph.co.uk/technology/2018/10/22/government-bans-phrase-fake-news/, accessed 2 December 2020.

discourse that is informed, not misinformed. On the other hand, AI systems, including well-trained algorithms, can be extremely valuable and overtake traditional media consumption based on human reading. To sustain human journalistic and edited content production, the law should ensure that authors and publishers are awarded a fair share of such earnings.

While the above-mentioned public interests concern the application of AI, that is, operation of the services employing AI, a more nuanced approach is necessary with regard to development of AI and copyright law. Focus in this chapter is on the use of works and collections of works in connection with training of algorithms to develop AI. An information service, such as an automated service offering summaries of news stories, 'reads' news articles when operating. Development of the service, however, is likely to involve use of other works or collections of works, upon which the algorithm involved has 'trained' to enhance its functionality. The balancing of interests between right holders and developers is not necessarily the same at the development stage as at the operating stage, and nor are the public interests involved. There is also a discrepancy between the development stage and the operating stage, as a training corpus may be used to train different algorithms, and one algorithm may be used to develop different services. The analysis here focuses on the development stage, that is, the training of an algorithm, but will also take into account the application of AI in a service, to pave the way for a discussion on how the interests at these different stages can be aligned.

Legal problems pertaining to the use by AI of copyrighted works have been subject to scrutiny in literature, as regards whether copyright protection is available for AI-produced works,[8] and whether authors' rights over their works could also extend to output produced by AI.[9] Furthermore, text and data mining techniques (TDM) have been subject to analysis.[10] While clearly overlapping, there are differences between TDM and ML that should be discussed. The literature offers very little concrete analysis of the application of EU copyright law to training of algorithms as part of ML. Under US law, ML

---

[8]   See Pamela Samuelson, 'Allocating Ownership Rights in Computer-Generated Works', 47 *U Pitt L Rev* 1185, 1226–28 1986; Bruce E Boyden, 'Emergent Works', 39 *Colum JL & Arts* 377 (2016); Pratap Devarapalli, 'Machine Learning to Machine Owning: Redefining the Copyright Ownership from the Perspective of Australian, US, UK and EU Law, *EIPR* 40(11), 722–728 (2018); Bob L T Sturm et al., 'Artificial Intelligence and Music: Open Questions of Copyright Law and Engineering Praxis', *Arts* 2019, 8, 115; doi:10.3390/arts8030115.

[9]   See Mirko Degli Esposti et al., 'The Use of Copyrighted Works by AI Systems: Art Works in the Data Mill', 11 *European Journal of Risk Regulation*, 51–69 (2020), doi:10.1017/err.2019.56 (Esposti et al.), and Ole-Andreas Rognstad in Chapter 7 in this volume.

[10]   See section 4.1 below and references there.

is considered under the fair use doctrine; thus US law does not provide direct guidance for European law. The contribution of this chapter is a discussion of the room for training algorithms in ML in EU copyright law, including the new DSM Directive.

The chapter starts with a presentation of ML and algorithms in section 2. Here, it will also be made clear how and why a copyright law analysis must differentiate between development of AI and application of AI-based services. In section 3, the question is first whether the process of training an algorithm infringes the right of reproduction to individual works under Article 2 InfoSoc Directive.[11] Training an algorithm, however, requires access to a large amount of data. The discussion is restricted to training models where the algorithm trains on a centralized collection of data, a training corpus. As training does not involve transfer of any of the data, only the right of reproduction is discussed in relation to individual works. Compiling and preparing a training corpus, as well as using it to train an algorithm, may infringe rights in collections of data, that is, database rights under the Database directive[12] and the new publisher's right in Article 15 DSM Directive.[13] This is discussed in sections 3.2 and 3.3.

Section 4 turns to interpretation of the exceptions from exclusive rights, and their application to ML. Focus is on the new exception for commercial TDM in Article 4 DSM Directive. Section 4.2 asks whether the exception for temporary digital copying of copyrighted works in Article 5(1) InfoSoc Directive could supplement the exception for TDM.

In section 5, the discussion returns to the balance struck between the interests of right holders and AI developers, bringing together the policy arguments from the earlier sections, in particular whether a case can be made for maintaining an approach to copyright as a control instrument to ensure freedom of information. The economic rationales behind database and press publishers' rights better support control with ML, but do not give sufficient basis for controlling the societal impacts of services employing AI.

---

[11]  Directive 2001/29/EC of the European Parliament and of the Council of 22 May 2001 on the harmonisation of certain aspects of copyright and related rights in the information society.

[12]  Directive 96/9/EC of the European Parliament and of the Council of 11 March 1996 on the legal protection of databases.

[13]  Directive (EU) 2019/790 of the European Parliament and of the Council of 17 April 2019 on copyright and related rights in the Digital Single Market.

## 2.      MACHINE LEARNING AND ALGORITHMS

This section takes a peek into the 'black box' of ML to concretize how AI systems are developed and what training an algorithm means in practice.[14] Most AI services in use in the news industry today rely on *supervised machine learning*, where an algorithm is trained based on a pre-defined set of training data and on given examples. By using regression and classification techniques, the algorithm learns to make consistent predictions when applied to new data. More sophisticated machine learning processes exist. *Unsupervised learning* relies on unlabelled – that is, unstructured – data. The model is trained to identify similarities, parallels or differences in data, mainly using clustering techniques. The training process requires less human participation, as the training data do not have to be labelled and structured, but interpretation of the output requires more human involvement.[15] *Reinforcement learning* relies on evaluation of the results provided by the system. The system relies on algorithms to classify and define results. The newest learning methods are *neural networks*, where the system gives its own feedback for further learning, based on a pre-determined algorithm, thereby 'learning' without human assistance.[16] In this chapter, focus is on supervised learning, but as the research question relates to the process of training and not the output of the algorithm after training, the conclusions can apply similarly to other learning methods.

Very briefly, machine learning consists of three stages: the development and programming of a model architecture; the training process where a model is developed based on a training algorithm and training data; and finally the model is applied to new data.[17] In the first phase, the programmers define the problem that the algorithm will predict or evaluate. The algorithm can be chosen among standard algorithms available in online libraries or developed individually for the project. The criteria that the algorithm will apply to evaluate results must be defined. The purpose of what is here termed the 'AI system' or 'service' might differ from what the algorithm measures. The service might

---

[14]   This section relies on the extensive and qualified discussions in David Lehr and Paul Ohm, 'Playing with the Data: What Legal Scholars Should Learn About Machine Learning', 51 *UC Davis L Rev* 653, 655–717 (2017); Thomas Margoni, 'Artificial Intelligence, Machine Learning and EU Copyright Law: Who Owns AI?' CREATe Working Paper 2018/12, DOI: 10.5281/zenodo.2001763 (Margoni); Mauritz Kop, 'Machine Learning and EU Data Sharing Practices', Stanford-Vienna Transatlantic Technology Law Forum, 1/2020, 7 (Kop), and Drexl, Hilty et al. (n 5).

[15]   Definitions from Drexl, Hilty et al. (n 5), 8.

[16]   See Andres Guadamuz, 'Do Androids Dream of Electric Copyright? Comparative Analysis of Originality in Artificial Intelligence Generated Works', *Intellectual Property Quarterly*, 169 at 171 (2017).

[17]   Drexl, Hilty et al. (n 5).

be an automatic personalization of the display of articles in an online news-paper, but the algorithm will measure the particular reader's historical reading habits to make predictions for future reading interest.

For the training stage, a corpus of training data must be collected. There must be a sufficient amount of data, the data must be representative, that is, giving variables measurement validity, and it must be generalizable, that is, give a basis for the algorithm to make the 'right' decisions when running on new data. Here, I assume that the training data consists of natural language texts, such as articles, comments, posts, tweets, and so on. I also assume that these texts are protected by copyright. However, other materials may be included, such as dictionaries, data, databases and other works such as music, pictures, and the like.[18]

In a *centralized learning method*, the training data is collected as a corpus, and either downloaded to a local server, or access is secured for the software to run on a corpus of data remotely stored. Pre-processing activities prepare the data for the statistical analysis that the training of the algorithm really amounts to. Texts are automatically converted to a format that the system can read: plain text or similar. The data is 'cleaned', correcting missing values, sorting out incorrect data and outliers that would obstruct generalizability. To define examples and classifications for supervised learning, metadata is added to label the text. These annotations define the text using the types of classifications that the algorithm will use as predefinitions for right or wrong answers in its training.

In the training process, the algorithm 'learns' abstract probabilistic characteristics from the training data, which it will use to predict learned labels on unseen data.[19] The labels can be names, part-of-language tags, sentiment or meaning tags, and so on. The 'learned' information is stored in a separate file, which once accumulated becomes the 'trained model'. After training, the algorithm can run without access to the training data. The algorithm runs back and forth on the data, testing a large number of 'hypothesis' rules to enhance its function in a non-linear process of tuning, assessment and evaluation. Those rules that prove correct based on the training data will be included in the final algorithm. The point is to enhance the function of the algorithm by minimizing the number of wrong predictions.

In a *decentralized learning model*, the algorithm is distributed to multiple decentralized devices, connected over the internet. The algorithm runs on

---

[18]   The findings here will be relevant to other kinds of works, although supplemental analysis is needed to include the particularities of each type of work. See e.g., Sturm et al. (n 8).

[19]   Margoni (n 14), 2.

the materials stored on local devices, and uploads the 'learned' information to a central server, where all the training information from all the devices collectively makes up the trained algorithm. Decentralized learning methods do not require compilation of a training data corpus.[20] These models may involve transfer of data from the training materials and might raise questions with regard to the right to communication to the public in Article 3 InfoSoc Directive. This is not discussed further here, but could be the subject of further research.

A machine learning model can be either static – that is, training is completed before the model is actually applied – or it can be dynamic – that is, training never ends, as the output of the system when applied continues to modify and optimize the system. A dynamic model requires constant feedback on the correctness of the output of the algorithm when applied.[21] An algorithm that displays articles on a web page based on readers' preferences is typically learning constantly. In dynamic algorithms, the learning process cannot be clearly discerned from the AI service.

ML uses very similar techniques as in TDM, which can be defined as computerized processes aimed at extracting and elaborating information from large digital data sets, extracting new knowledge, in particular by identifying correlations and trends.[22] TDM also involves a preparation phase where data are collected and prepared for automated analysis, and information is extracted by running an algorithm on the data. In a final recombination phase, the extracted data are arranged to visualise results.[23] In ML, the information extracted when running the algorithm on the data is incorporated into the algorithm, and the trained algorithm can be used for various purposes. Section 4.1 discusses whether these differences have legal implications.

The next section analyses exclusive rights to materials and collections that might need clearance to facilitate ML, starting with copyright in the individual materials (3.1) and then rights in collections of works (3.2 and 3.3).

---

[20]   See Kop (n 14) with further references.

[21]   Drexl, Hilty et al. (n 5), 6.

[22]   Maurizio Borghi and Stavroula Karapapa. *Copyright and Mass Digitization*, OUP 2013, 47. DOI:10.1093/acprof:oso/9780199664559.003.0003; Max Planck Position Statement, 1, available at https://papers.ssrn.com/sol3/papers.cfm?abstract_id =2900110, accessed 3 December 2020.

[23]   Romain Meys, 'Data Mining Under the Directive on Copyright and Related Rights in the Digital Single Market: Are European Database Protection Rules Still Threatening the Development of Artificial Intelligence?' *GRUR Int.*, 457 (2020), doi: 10.1093/grurint/ikaa046 (Meys).

# 3. EXCLUSIVE RIGHTS IN TRAINING MATERIALS

## 3.1 The Right of Reproduction, Article 2 Infosoc Directive

The wording of Article 2 InfoSoc Directive reserves for the copyright holder 'temporary or permanent reproduction by any means and in any form, in whole or in part'. The acts covered by this right of reproduction are construed broadly.[24] The CJEU applies a formal and technical approach, extending the right to every act of reproduction, 'however transient or irrelevant it may be from an economic perspective'.[25] This includes intermediate digital copies in the RAM memory of the computer, as well as other digital copies regardless of whether they are accessible by a human reader, such as cache memory, even if such copies may be intrinsic to (lawfully) accessing a work by computer, such as online browsing.[26]

The question is whether training an algorithm entails copying of training materials that infringe the right of reproduction. For centralized machine learning models, compiling the training data either by uploading it to a platform or by downloading it to a local server, results in copies of the materials. These copies are likely to have a permanent character in the sense of the Infosoc Directive, even if the corpus is deleted after completion of the training process.[27] Furthermore, pre-processing the training corpus could entail acts of reproduction.[28] Materials created for human reading, such as pdf-files, have to be converted to machine-readable formats, thereby creating a copy of the materials.[29] 'Cleaning' the training data by sorting out outliers or irregular data could also include copying. Preliminary data processing may employ crawlers, but these will also 'read' materials by creating temporary copies in the cache memory of the computer. Adding metadata and annotations to the materi-

---

[24]   Rec (21) InfoSoc Directive.

[25]   Michel M Walter and Silke von Lewinsky, *European Copyright Law*, OUP, 2010, 968.

[26]   Ibid.

[27]   Art 5(1) InfoSoc Directive, discussed below, section 4.2. See Maarten Truyens and Patrick van Eecke, 'Legal Aspects of Text Mining', *Computer Law and Security Review*, 153–170, at 162 (2014).

[28]   Christophe Geiger et al., 'Text and Data Mining in the Proposed Copyright Reform: Making the EU Ready for an Age of Big Data? Legal Analysis and Policy Recommendations', *IIC*, 814–44, (2018) https://doi.org/10.1007/s40319-018-0722-2, at 818 (Geiger et al. 2018).

[29]   See Jean-Paul Trialle, 'Study on the Legal Framework of Text and Data Mining' (TDM), EC Commission, 2014, 32, available at https://op.europa.eu/en/publication -detail/-/publication/074ddf78-01e9-4a1d-9895-65290705e2a5/language-en, accessed 3 December 2020 (Triaille).

als – that is, supervising the algorithm – could also include such temporary copying.[30] Thus, it seems quite clear that compilation of a training corpus in a centralised learning model would entail several acts of reproduction infringing Article 2 InfoSoc Directive.

Whether the actual 'learning' process – where the algorithm is running on the data – infringes the right of reproduction could be questioned. The algorithm can go back and forth between the data, as it is 'testing' and modifying its 'rules'. The information extracted is factual information that when aggregated gives statistical information about correlations, trends, differences, and the like in the training data. This information is stored in a separate file. When included in the final algorithm it takes the form of 'rules' based on statistics, and the original works are not recognizable. The stored information is not likely to include sufficient parts of the training materials to infringe the right of reproduction. In the literature, some doubt has been expressed as to whether an algorithm, when running on the materials, makes relevant copies of the materials.[31] But, as even cache memory copies are considered reproductions under Article 2 InfoSoc Directive, most analytic techniques, including crawling, will entail copying, even if no human-readable copies are made.[32] Cache memory copying is intrinsic to the way a machine 'reads'. It therefore seems likely that training an algorithm infringes the right of reproduction.[33]

This very broad and formal construction of the right of reproduction has been criticized for going beyond the fundamentals of copyright, in particular the incentive and remuneration rationale for exclusive rights, which does not include use of a work to gather information as opposed to use of the work 'as a work'.[34] Seeing that copyright protects free speech to spread original ideas and enlightened communication between humans, acts of reproduction that do not impact this author–audience nexus should also fall outside the scope of

---

[30]   Esposti et al. (n 9), 15.

[31]   Meys (n 23), 460 and Geiger et al. (n 28).

[32]   CJEU case C-360/13, *Meltwater*, ECLI:EU:C:2014:1195. See also Rossana Ducato and Alain Strowel, 'Limitations to Text and Data Mining and Consumer Empowerment: Making the Case for a Right to "machine legibility"', *IIC*, 50(6), 649–684, 658 (2019) (Ducato and Strowel).

[33]   Christoph Geiger et al., 'Text and Data Mining: Articles 3 and 4 of the Directive 2019/790/EU', CEIPI Studies Research Paper No. 2019-08, https://ssrn.com/abstract= 3470653 at 8 (Geiger et al. 2020). The author's right is infringed if so much of the work is copied that it includes subject matter that is 'original in the sense that it is its author's own intellectual creation', case C-05/08, *Infosoc I*, para 37, ECLI:EU:C:2009:465.

[34]   See in general P Bernt Hugenholtz (ed), *Copyright Reconstructed: Rethinking Copyright's Economic Rights in a Time of Highly Dynamic Technological and Economic Change*, Alphen aan den Rijn, 2018. For TDM, see Ducati and Strowel (n 32), 667–668.

copyright.[35] Following this argument, training algorithms with the objective of developing new services should not infringe copyright, as ML make use of the facts and information extracted from works, but not their creative expression.[36] This is not to say that access to copyright-protected works should be free and without restrictions for the purposes of ML. Clearly financial interests are involved in ML, and well-trained algorithms are extremely valuable, as is evidenced by large content service providers such as Netflix and Amazon. The value of the service can be traced back to access to the works in a training corpus. This value, however, does not relate to individual works, but to the fact that the training corpus consists of a large number of works. This is an economic value rather associated with collections of works (databases) than with individual creative works, and probably better managed through database rights or the new press publishers' right.[37] Furthermore, requiring individual consent from right holders for all copying in the processes of ML is likely to be prohibitive to the development of AI-based services. Copyright risks being used to block the spread of information, thus working against the original aim of copyright.[38] On the other hand, the output of ML can be used for any purpose, and individual authors may feel strongly opposed to their works being used to develop services such as pre-emptive policing where individuals are sought out for surveillance if the algorithm finds them likely to commit crimes based on their social media postings.[39] As discussed below, a possible way to safeguard the interests of individual authors would be to require database owners to allow authors to opt out of including their works in ML licensing, and to require consent from database owners or press publishers for ML. A topic for further research would be to consider how individual authors interests could be protected by limited 'digital ideal rights' when full exclusive economic rights are not warranted.

With the introduction of exceptions for text and data mining in the DSM Directive Articles 3 and 4, there is a presumption that an exception is also

---

[35]  Alain Strowel, 'Reconstructing the Reproduction and Communication to the Public Rights: How to Align Copyright with its Fundamentals' (Strowel), in Hugenholtz (n 34), 206–209.

[36]  Lemley, Mark A and Casey, Bryan, Fair Learning (January 30, 2020). Available at SSRN: https://ssrn.com/abstract=3528447 or http://dx.doi.org/10.2139/ssrn.3528447, at 152, accessed 3 December 2020 (Lemley and Casey).

[37]  Analysis of economic arguments in Joost Poort, 'Borderlines of Copyright Protection: An Economic Analysis', in Hugenholtz (n 34) (Poort).

[38]  Strowel (n 35), 226–228.

[39]  See e.g., the description of the AI system GPT2 in Alex Hern, 'New AI Fake Text Generator may be too Dangerous to Release, say Creators', *The Guardian*, 14 February 2019, available at https://www.theguardian.com/technology/2019/feb/14/elon-musk-backed-ai-writes-convincing-news-fiction, accessed 3 December 2020.

needed, and discussion of whether ML is copying relevant to copyright seems closed, at least for the time being.[40] For all practical purposes, the question is whether the process of training an algorithm can benefit from any of the exceptions to exclusive rights. The EU lawmaker has confirmed its approach to copyright as broad and all-encompassing exclusive rights. In addition, individual copyrights are supplemented with rights-protecting investment in collections of works, such as database rights and the new publisher's right in Article 15(1) DSM Directive. This layered system of rights poses additional challenges with regard to ML. The only practical approach to gaining access to the amount of works necessary for ML is through intermediaries, typically publishing houses or other entities holding libraries of relevant works. In sections 3.2 and 3.3, the discussion turns to database rights and the new publishers' right.

## 3.2    Database Rights

A set of training data must contain a large amount of materials, and it is not practical to collect these individually. Collections of works may be subject to database rights.[41] A database may be protectable by copyright – Article 5 Database Directive if the choice of materials or their structuring in the database demonstrates originality.[42] Copyright to the database is only likely to be infringed if the whole database is downloaded for incorporation in a centralized training corpus, as only then will the structure of the database also be reproduced.[43] Hence, the question is whether running an algorithm on a database infringes the *sui generis* database right in Article 7(1) of the Database Directive, protecting databases for which 'obtaining, verification or presentation of the contents' requires 'a substantial investment'. I discuss only the right of extraction, as the right to 're-utilization' in Article 7(2)(b) is not likely to be infringed in centralized ML models.

The right of extraction is related to the right of reproduction and defined in Article 7(2)(a) as 'the permanent or temporary transfer of all or a substantial part of the contents of a database to another medium by any means or in any form'.[44] It also covers the 'repeated and systematic' extraction of insubstantial parts of the database.[45] The CJEU has emphasized the economic interests

---

[40]    See Rec (8) DSM Directive and Geiger et al. 2018 (n 28).
[41]    A database is 'a collection of independent works, data or other materials arranged in a systematic or methodical way and individually accessible by electronic or other means', Art 1(2), Database Directive.
[42]    Art 3(1) Database Directive.
[43]    See Triaille (n 29), 34–35.
[44]    Rec (44).
[45]    Art 7(5).

of the *sui generis* right holder in protecting their investment, finding it less relevant whether copies are technically being made and transferred to another medium.[46] Whereas searching the database may entail digitally copying contents, this does not infringe the extraction right if the consultation is lawful.[47] The *sui generis* right is infringed if the investment in making the database is harmed, which it is if the right holder is deprived of revenue which should have enabled them to redeem the cost of investment.[48]

Applied to ML and training algorithms, it seems likely that downloading the whole or a substantial part of the database to compile a centralized training data corpus would infringe the right of extraction. A labelled, annotated training data set can itself be awarded data base rights, as this type of investment is what the *sui generis* right is meant to protect.[49]

Under the *sui generis* right, the question whether actual training of the algorithm infringes the right, does not hinge on whether the algorithm makes temporary copies of materials in the cache memory of the computer or otherwise copies materials, but whether the right holder's investment is harmed. ML makes use of the economic value associated with works being part of a large collection of works. This is exactly the investment in the database that the *sui generis* right protects, and it therefore appears difficult to find arguments supporting a finding that ML should not require a licence.[50] On the other hand, ML is not an activity that could be described as 'parasitical competing' activities.[51] ML rather reveals new knowledge and facilitates new and innovative services. However, when activities appropriate the value inherent in the database, the CJEU has emphasized that it is legitimate for the database holder to reserve a fee in consideration for use of the database.[52]

Even if the concrete ML model did not exploit the database by repeatedly extracting insubstantial parts contrary to Article 7(5), it is doubtful whether ML could be considered as 'normal exploitation' of a database under Article 8(2) if not explicitly included in a licence.[53] The criterion is undetermined, but

---

[46]   CJEU case C-304/07, *Directmedia*, paras 33 and 35, ECLI:EU:C:2008:552.

[47]   CJEU case C-203/02, *William Hill*, para 54, ECLI:EU:C:2004:695; case C-304/07, *Directmedia*, para 51, ECLI:EU:C:2008:552.

[48]   Rec (49) and CJEU case C-203/02, *William Hill*, para 51, ECLI:EU:C:2004:695; case C-202/12, *Innoweb*, para 37, ECLI:EU:C:2013:850.

[49]   See Kop (n 14), 7.

[50]   See CJEU case C-490/14, *Verlag Esterbauer*, para 16, ECLI:EU:C:2015:735; C-202/12, *Innoweb*, para 46–48, ECLI:EU:C:2013:850. See Lemley and Casey (n 36), 127; Geiger et al. 2018 (n 28), 823–824.

[51]   Rec (42) Database Directive; CJEU case C-203/02, *William Hill*, para 47, ECLI: EU:C:2004:695.

[52]   CJEU case C-203/02, *William Hill*, para 57, ECLI:EU:C:2004:695.

[53]   Rec (24). See also Geiger et al. 2020 (n 33), 15–16.

as discussed above, if the use harms the investment in the database, then the *sui generis* right is likely to be infringed.[54] TDM techniques have been considered in literature as going beyond 'normal' exploitation of a database, although this might depend on a concrete assessment of what use the database was meant for, and what techniques are employed, that is, bulk reading, crawling, scraping or other machine-enabled analysis.[55] In conclusion, the exception for 'normal' use in Article 8(2) does not provide sufficient legal certainty as a basis for ML.

### 3.3    Press Publishers' Right

The DSM directive Article 15 introduces a new press publishers' right that has been heavily criticized.[56] Under Article 15(1), press publishers are granted full exclusive rights as in Article 2 and 3(2) InfoSoc Directive, but only against 'the online use of their press publications by information society service providers', and only for a period of two years from publication.[57] An information society service is 'any service normally provided for remuneration, at a distance, by electronic means and at the individual request of a recipient of services', that is, any service provided individually over the internet.[58] Due to the short duration of the right and its restricted scope to information society service providers, it will most likely only restrict dynamic ML, for example, use by news aggregation services of continuously improving and self-learning algorithms in their service. In these instances, the new right may provide an

---

[54]   See also Estelle Derclaye, 'The Database Directive', in Irini Stamatoudi and Paul Torremans (eds), *EU Copyright Law*, Edward Elgar, Cheltenham, 2014, 111.

[55]   Irini Stamatoudi, 'Text and Data Mining', in Irini Stamatoudi (ed), *New Developments in EU and International Copyright Law*, Wolters Kluwer 2016, 278; Geiger et al. 2018 (n 28), 823–824.

[56]   The criticism concerns the paradox of ensuring a free press and free access to information by introducing yet another exclusive right, see Rec (54) DSM Directive. See e.g., Lionel Bentley et al., 'Strengthening the Position of Press Publishers and Authors and Performers in the Copyright Directive', study for DG IPOL, 2017, available    at    https://www.europarl.europa.eu/RegData/etudes/STUD/2017/596810/IPOL _STU%282017%29596810_EN.pdf, accessed 30 November 2020; Lionel Bentley et al., 'Response to Article 11 of the Proposal for a Directive on Copyright in the Digital Single Market, entitled "Protection of press publications concerning digital uses" on behalf of thirty-seven professors and leading scholars of Intellectual Property, Information Law and Digital Economy', 2016, https://www.cipil.law.cam.ac.uk/press/ news/2016/12/cambridge-academics-respond-call-views-european-commissions-draft -legislation, accessed 3 December 2020.

[57]   Art 15(4).

[58]   Directive (EU) 2015/1535 of the European Parliament and of the Council of 9 September 2015 laying down a procedure for the provision of information in the field of technical regulations and of rules on Information Society services Art 1 (1) (b).

opportunity for centralized consent for AI services, but is not likely to have a separable impact on ML and training of algorithms.

If protected materials are used in centralized ML within the two-year exclusivity period, then interpretation of the right raises some questions. First, the exclusive right does not extend to facts.[59] However, as the right is a full exclusive right of reproduction, it includes any temporary machine-generated copying. Thus, an exception might still be necessary to allow machine access to the data. Second, the protected subject matter is the publications contained, but in determining how much content can be reproduced without infringement the decisive factor is whether the investments by publishers in production of the content are undermined.[60] Only reproductions of individual words or short extracts can be lawful, for which purpose the exceptions in Article 5(1) InfoSoc Directive apply *mutatis mutandis*.[61] This combination of the different rationales from individual copyright and database rights that differ from the rationale behind the press publishers' right is somewhat of a paradox. The Preamble uses the practical term 'use' of publications to explain the scope of the right.[62] This could possibly signal a step away from the formalistic approach of the CJEU in interpreting the right of reproduction in Article 2(2) InfoSoc Directive, but the reference to the exceptions in Article 5(1) InfoSoc Directive probably leaves it with the CJEU to interpret whether ML infringes the press publishers' right. Finally, as individual or collective copyrights and database rights[63] are not affected by the new publishers' right,[64] the obstacles to obtaining authorization for ML are hardly overcome with the introduction of the press publishers' right.

---

[59] Rec (57) DSM Directive.

[60] Rec (58) DSM Directive.

[61] Art 15(3).

[62] Rec (58) DSM Directive.

[63] Many press publishers will also have *sui generis* database rights in their online publications, see Lionel Bentley et al., 'Strengthening the Position of Press Publishers and Authors and Performers in the Copyright Directive', study for DG IPOL (n 56), 23.

[64] See Art 15(2).

## 4.    ARE THE EXCEPTIONS TO EXCLUSIVE RIGHTS SUFFICIENT TO FACILITATE MACHINE LEARNING?

### 4.1    The Exceptions for Text and Data Mining in the DSM Directive

#### 4.1.1    Definition

The DSM Directive also introduced new exceptions to exclusive rights for TDM. The first question is whether the definition of TDM could also cover machine learning, that is, training algorithms. The DSM Directive Article 2(2) defines TDM as 'any automated analytical technique aimed at analysing text and data in digital form in order to generate information which includes but is not limited to patterns, trends and correlations'. The definition does not limit the type of digital data or the tools involved.[65] An algorithm can be an automated analytical technique, and it analyses text and data in digital form. When training an algorithm, the algorithm extracts trends and correlations from the training data patterns, in the same way as a TDM process.[66] The difference is that in TDM the purpose is to present the extracted information, whereas in ML the algorithm adds the new information to its set of 'rules' in an automated process, enhancing its ability to make accurate predictions when presented with new data. Use of the information generated, however, is not part of the definition of TDM in the Directive. As the Directive points to how TDM techniques are used for developing new technologies, many ML models are likely to fall within the definition of TDM.[67]

The question in the following is whether the exceptions for TDM in the DSM Directive could apply to training of algorithms in ML. Under Article 4(1), the Member States must provide for 'an exception or limitation' to copyright, database rights and the press publishers' right, 'for reproductions and extractions of lawfully accessible works and other subject matter for the purposes of text and data mining'. Contrary to the limited exception for scientific research done by public interest research organizations,[68] the exception in Article 4 is available to commercial developers of AI.[69] Some interpretative questions are discussed in the following.

---

[65]   Meys (n 23), 464.
[66]   See discussion in Triaille (n 29), 9.
[67]   Rec (18), see also Meys (n 23), 464–465.
[68]   Art 3.
[69]   Rec (10), (12) and (13). Some public broadcasting institutions can be 'cultural heritage institutions' that are eligible for exception under Art 2(3). However, as they are not likely to offer large text work datasets online, they are not further discussed here. The original proposal only included the exception for research purposes in Art 3, and

### 4.1.2    Application of the 'three-step test'

Article 7(2) DSM Directive prescribes that the three-step test in Article 5(5) InfoSoc Directive shall apply for the exceptions for TDM. Accordingly, the exception in Article 4 DSM Directive may only apply to special cases which do not conflict with normal exploitation of the work and do not unreasonably prejudice the legitimate interests of the right holder. The first question is whether the public interest in developing services to secure a free press and information integrity may be balanced against the interests of right holders through application of the three-step test.

The CJEU has repeatedly stated that the exceptions from copyright must be interpreted strictly.[70] However, interpretation of the conditions for exception must 'enable the effectiveness of the exception thereby established to be safeguarded and permit observance of the exception's purpose'.[71] Possibly, recent case law under Article 5(1) InfoSoc Directive may indicate a broader weighing of interests with the basis in Article 5(5).[72] The purpose of the exception for temporary digital copying in Article 5(1) Infosoc Directive, is to 'allow and ensure the development and operation of new technologies', and for this purpose to become effective, it must be interpreted in a way that 'safeguards a fair balance between the rights and interests of rights holders and of users of protected works who wish to avail themselves of those technologies'.[73] This points to a concrete balancing between the general interest of copyright holders and the narrow interests of users in availing themselves of new technologies in their use of works.

In *Infopaq I* and *Premier League,* the CJEU merely said that the conditions in Article 5(1) InfoSoc Directive must be construed with regard to the three-step test in Article 5(5), but it did not discuss the three-step test

---

was heavily criticized for not facilitating commercial services protecting public interests, such as fact checking in journalism. See Geiger et al. 2018 (n 28), 834, Meys (n 23), 466; Rec (18) DSM Directive.

[70]    CJEU case C-05/08, *Infopaq I,* para 56, ECLI:EU:C:2009:465; case C-302/10, *Infopaq II,* para 27, ECLI:EU:C:2012:16; case C-360/13, *Meltwater,* para 23, ECLI: EU:C:2014:1195.

[71]    CJEU case C-403/08, *Premier League,* para 163, ECLI:EU:C:2011:631.

[72]    Taina Pihlajarinne, 'Copyright Exceptions and Limitations – is the Principle of Narrow Interpretation Gradually Fading Away?', NIR – Nordiskt Immateriellt Rättsskydd, 2020, 117–122, at 121; P Bernt Hugenholtz, 'Flexible Copyright: Can the EU Author's Rights Accommodate Fair Use?', in Ruth L Okediji, *Copyright Law in an Age of Limitations and Exceptions,* CUP, 2017, 275–291, at 286.

[73]    CJEU case C-403/08, *Premier League,* para 164, ECLI:EU:C:2011:631; case C-360/13, *Meltwater,* para 24, ECLI:EU:C:2014:1195. See also Rec (31) InfoSoc Directive.

288 Artificial intelligence and the media

separately, perhaps not reading independent normative content into it.[74] In *Meltwater*, however, the CJEU balanced the interests of right holders against the interests of users both under Article 5(1) and under Article 5(5). The Court cited its statements in *Premier League*, pointing to the narrow balancing of interests under Article 5(1).[75] The Court then went on to consider the three-step test in Article 5(5) independently. This should theoretically further narrow the scope of the exception in Article 5(1), as further conditions must be fulfilled for the exception to apply. However, and especially when seen in connection with the more abstract statements about the interpretation of Article 5(5) in *Spiegel Online,* the Court appears to open up for a broader balancing of interests that also includes public interests. First, the *Meltwater* case indicates a more user-oriented approach where the interests of internet users, availing themselves of the right to information in the online media, must be safeguarded.[76] Specifically, they must be able to trust that the publishers of websites have fulfilled their obligation to obtain sufficient consent from the individual right holders, so that it is not necessary for internet users to obtain further authorization.[77] Second, in *Spiegel Online*, the CJEU characterizes the rights of online media users as fundamental rights, enshrined in the EU Charter of Fundamental Rights Article 11.[78] The fair balance to be struck between right holders and users of works is elevated to balancing two fundamental rights: Copyright as enshrined in Article 17(2) of the Charter, on the one hand, and freedom of information on the other.[79] As observed by Pihlajarinne, this development could possibly give more room for societal needs and a less stringent property-right approach, anchored in the three-step test in Article 5(5).[80] While development of AI can clearly serve the public interest in access to information and information integrity, a disconnect exists between developers and the

---

[74] CJEU case C-05/08, *Infopaq I*, para 56, ECLI:EU:C:2009:465; CJEU case C-403/08, *Premier League*, para 181, ECLI:EU:C:2011:631. See Annette Kur et al., *European Intellectual Property Law*, second edn, Edward Elgar, Cheltenham, 2019, 384.

[75] CJEU case C-360/13, *Meltwater*, para 24, ECLI:EU:C:2014:1195.

[76] See also CJEU case C-403/08, *Premier League*, para 179, ECLI:EU:C:2011: 631; Justine Pila and Paul Torremans, *European Intellectual Property Law*, second edn, OUP, 2019, 311, show how the national court in the Meltwater case came to the same conclusion, but based on the author-oriented argument that it would be better to seek a single, higher licence fee from Meltwater than to seek many small fees from end users.

[77] CJEU case C-360/13, *Meltwater*, paras 57–59, ECLI:EU:C:2014:1195.

[78] CJEU in case C-516/17, *Spiegel Online*, paras 54 and 57, ECLI:EU:C:2019:625.

[79] CJEU in case C-516/17, *Spiegel Online*, para 58, ECLI:EU:C:2019:625.

[80] See Pihlajarinne (n 72), 122; Rec (3) DSM Directive; Geiger et al. 2018 (n 28), 282.

public interest as AI can also be used for other purposes. Under the current copyright law regime, it is not clear whether the need to control use of AI will be considered when applying exceptions to exclusive rights, or whether such control will be left to other law and regulation.

Secondly, it is not clear how the three-step test can be applied when the same subject matter is protected by several different exclusive rights. The exception for TDM in Article 4 DSM Directive applies to copyright to works and databases as well as the *sui generis* right and the press publishers' right. The three-step test as construed by the CJEU does not apply to the *sui generis* right to databases.[81] For TDM and ML, the exception in Article 4, might answer a need for a better balancing of interests in delineating the scope of the *sui generis* right.[82] However, it is very difficult to see how a balance of interests may be struck with any kind of legal certainty between AI developers also representing public interests on the one side and several holders of different rights based on different purposes on the other. Adding new rights and exceptions does not improve this.

### 4.1.3    Scope of the exception

The scope of the exception in Article 4 DSM Directive is wide, but its interpretation is not entirely clear. First, the extractions and reproductions may be retained 'for as long as is necessary for the purposes of text and data mining'.[83] The wording indicates that more permanent copying might be included than under the exception for temporary reproductions in Article 5(1) InfoSoc Directive. However, it is not clear to what extent downloading of materials is included, and if so, how long the materials might be retained. While downloading is the practical way to compile a centralized training corpus, it also facilitates further use of the training materials. It may be costly to compile, prepare and annotate a training corpus, and it might be attractive to reuse it to train other algorithms or to license it. Licensing or selling a training corpus will likely go beyond normal exploitation of works and prejudice the interests of database or press publishers' right holders.[84] It is questionable whether a developer may reuse the corpus for training other algorithms.

---

[81]    The wording of the relevant Art 8(2) in the Database Directive differs from Art 5(5) InfoSoc Directive.

[82]    In this direction Meys (n 23), 469; DG CONNECT, 'Study in support of the evaluation of Directive 96/9/EC on the legal protection of databases', 2018, 25, https://op.europa.eu/en/publication-detail/-/publication/5e9c7a51-597c-11e8-ab41 -01aa75ed71a1, accessed 30 November 2020.

[83]    Art 4(2).

[84]    See Art 5(5) Infosoc Directive and the discussion in sections 3.2 and 3.3.

Secondly, right holders may expressly reserve against use of their works in ML.[85] Recognizing that materials to be used in TDM or in ML are likely to be obtained using automated tools, the reserve must be made by 'machine-readable means' for content made available to the public online.[86] All right holders may reserve, including authors of individual works. With the absolute wording of Article 4(3), a reserve by one author will prevent a developer from running the algorithm on that work. As training data are likely to be collected or accessed through intermediaries who might have database or press publishers' rights, these individual reserves may pose challenges to developers in ensuring that training data are representative and generalizable. For the reasons discussed above in section 3.1, the better solution might have been to make the exception mandatory for copyright in individual works, but allowing database right holders and press publishers a right to reserve.[87]

### 4.1.4    The condition of lawful access

It follows from Article 4(1) that the user must have lawful access to materials to benefit from the exception. Lawful access can be based on a licence, and in that case the new exception gives publishers and database owners an incentive to distinguish prices for licensing for TDM or ML purposes and other uses.[88] The exception also applies to content that has been made available to the public online without reservation for TDM.[89]

A final question is whether 'lawful access' should be construed to mean the same as 'lawful use' in Article 5(1) InfoSoc Directive. Under that article, a use is lawful if it is either authorized by the right holder or falls outside the scope of the exclusive right of the author.[90] The CJEU has applied the exception in Article 5(1) to services that have as their output excerpts of the works so small that they do not reproduce the 'expression of the intellectual creation of the author'.[91] While this could be as little as 11 consecutive words, the problem with both TDM and ML and training algorithms is that while the techniques may make (temporary) copies of whole works, the output of the techniques does not reproduce any part of the works. The direct output of training an algo-

---

[85]   Art 4(3) DSM Directive.
[86]   Art 4(3) and Rec (18).
[87]   Similar Lemley and Casey (n 36) 130 with regard to US law.
[88]   Geiger et al. 2018 (n 28), 83.
[89]   Preamble (18) DSM Directive.
[90]   See CJEU case C-302/10, *Infopaq II*, para 42, ECLI:EU:C:2012:16, and case C-403/08, *Premier League*, para 168, ECLI:EU:C:2011:631 and Preamble (33) InfoSoc Directive.
[91]   CJEU case C-05/08, *Infopaq I*, para 39, ECLI:EU:C:2009:465; InfoSoc Directive Art 3(1).

rithm is an enhanced and trained algorithm. Using a trained algorithm in an AI-assisted service for fact checking might also not reproduce any part of any works. Hence, for the exception in Article 4(3) to have practical relevance for TDM and ML, the condition of lawful access should be construed narrowly, thus not including the output of the technique.

## 4.2 The Exception for Temporary Reproductions, Article 5(1) Infosoc Directive

The exception for TDM in the DSM Directive entails a presumption not only that TDM (and ML) techniques infringe copyright, but also that the exception for temporary digital reproductions in Article 5(1) InfoSoc Directive is insufficient to cover TDM techniques and ML.[92] While discussion of the scope of the exception is now less potent, it remains open whether the exception in Article 5(1) could supplement the exception for TDM or benefit aspects of ML that are not covered by the TDM exception.[93]

A concrete analysis of the ML model is necessary to determine whether the exception in Article 5(1) could apply.[94] Only selected questions are discussed here. First, as the algorithm is running on training data, the computer will make temporary copies of the materials in its cache memory. Mostly, these copies are automatically deleted when the cache memory is full.[95] Only the information required to optimise the algorithm is stored in a separate file, later to become the trained algorithm. It seems likely that cache memory copies are considered transient, temporary, and to be an integral and essential part of a technological process, regardless of whether on-screen copies are made that would be readable by humans.[96] It will not prevent application of the exception that the process contains multiple steps where a copy is made,[97] as when the algorithm runs back and forth on the materials, or that human intervention is involved.[98]

Apart from compiling training data,[99] the exception in Article 5(1) could cover the individual steps of training an algorithm. The question of its applica-

---

92  See Rec (18) DSM Directive. See Meys (n 23), 465.
93  Rec (9) DSM Directive.
94  See Margoni (n 14), 19.
95  Automatic deletion would be necessary for Art 5(1) to apply, see CJEU case C-05/08, *Infopaq I*, paras 37 and 62, ECLI:EU:C:2009:465.
96  In this direction CJEU case C-360/13, *Meltwater*, ECLI:EU:C:2014:1195.
97  See CJEU case C-05/08, *Infopaq I*, para 65, ECLI:EU:C:2009:465.
98  CJEU case C-302/10, *Infopaq II*, para 22, ECLI:EU:C:2012:16.
99  Downloading or uploading a training data set will likely require permanent copying in the sense of Art 5(1) InfoSoc Directive. See also Triaille (n 29), 48.

tion is conceptual, but can be tied to the condition that the act of reproduction must not have 'independent economic significance'. Training an algorithm that will present articles on a personalized front page, or perform a fact check will have as its output a trained algorithm which is not likely to contain a reproduction of the training materials. Hence, the overarching purpose of ML can be argued to fall outside the scope of the right of reproduction.[100] However, ML is based on the algorithm 'reading', thereby intrinsically copying, huge amounts of works. In *Infopaq II*, the CJEU found that temporary copies can have 'economic significance' if the copies can be exploited for gain, or if temporary copies transform the object of lawful use or if they facilitate other use.[101] The *Infopaq* cases concerned a service that included temporarily copying works, but where the output of the service was to present clients with short – and lawful – excerpts of the works. Applied to development of AI through ML, a differentiation should be drawn between training the algorithm and performing a service based on a trained algorithm. ML models based on static training, that is, where training is completed before the algorithm is used on new materials, may be seen as separate acts of exploitation of the works in the training corpus. As this exploitation is not accessory to otherwise lawful use, it would be likely to require the authorization of the authors.[102] This would also be the reason for excluding TDM from the exception under Article 5(1).[103]

For services based on trained algorithms, such as performing a fact check, or bulk reading to sort out information to consider reporting, the output of the service could be the primary act, to which the temporary copying involved in machine 'reading' can be accessory. If the output of the service is lawful by consent or because it falls outside the scope of copyright, the conditions for exception in Article 5(1) can be considered in the same way as in the *Infopaq*, *Meltwater* and *Spiegel Online* cases. Following this reasoning, a service including an algorithm that continuously learns – a dynamic learning model – could benefit from the exception if the output of the service, such as display of articles on a personalized front page, would be considered lawful.

---

[100] See Strowel (n 35), 213, 225 and Maurizio Borghi and Stavroula Karapapa, *Copyright and Mass Digitization*. OUP, 2013, 58–60 and ch 2, DOI:10.1093/acprof: oso/9780199664559.003.0003.

[101] CJEU case C-302/10, *Infopaq II*, paras 52 and 53, ECLI:EU:C:2012:16; case C-403/08, *Premier League*, para 175, ECLI:EU:C:2011:631; Ole-Andreas Rognstad, *Opphavsrett*, second edn. Oslo, 2019, 192.

[102] See also Ducati and Strowel (n 32), 660–661. Same conclusion, but with some uncertainty, Geiger et al. 2018 (n 28), 821–822.

[103] Irini Stamatoudi, "Text and Data Mining", in Irini Stamatoudi (ed), (n 54), 251–282.

## 5.    CONCLUSIONS: A MISSED OPPORTUNITY FOR A BALANCED APPROACH TO MACHINE LEARNING AND COPYRIGHT LAW

Under the current EU legal regime, a differentiation is needed between operating online services and developing services. Services that rely on AI, and inherently trained algorithms, may operate on copyright-protected works as long as their output does not contain infringing reproductions of those works. Case law from the CJEU indicates that these services can be considered under Article 5(1) InfoSoc Directive. Looking only at the application of AI in online services, copyright seems fairly well adapted to striking a balance between the interests of right holders, both individual authors and owners of collections of works, and the interests of service providers. Although services employ AI, the situation does not significantly differ from other use of protected works in a digital market.

The development of new AI systems by off-line machine learning techniques, however, is dependent on consent from right holders in materials used to train algorithms, regardless of their output. In this regard, the DSM Directive represents a missed opportunity to balance the interests of right holders and users in relation to big data-related innovation. Although the exception for TDM in Article 4 DSM Directive likely covers ML and training of algorithms, the EU lawmaker has continued on its path of expanding exclusive rights towards any new uses of content. It is questionable whether the current regime will further the ambition for the EU to become a global leader in innovation in the data economy, for which development of AI is essential,[104] especially compared to the USA, where ML as a main rule is considered fair use of copyrighted works.[105]

First, problems with expanding copyright in individual works with regard to uses not related to the creative expression of a work have not been resolved for development of AI. To allow individual authors to oppose use of their works to

---

[104] See White Paper on Artificial Intelligence – A European approach to excellence and trust, COM(2020) 65 final, https://ec.europa.eu/info/publications/white-paper-artificial-intelligence-european-approach-excellence-and-trust_en, accessed 4 December 2020. See also Christian Handke et al., 'Is Europe Falling Behind in Data Mining? Copyright's Impact on Data Mining in Academic Research', in B Schmidt and M Dobreva (eds), 'New Avenues for Electronic Publishing in the Age of Infinite Collections and Citizen Science: Scale, Openness and Trust', Proceedings of the 19th International Conference on Electronic Publishing, 2015, 120–130, doi:10.3233/978-1-61499-562-3-120.

[105] See, e.g., Esposti et al. (n 9), Lemley and Casey (n 36) and James Grimmelmann, 'Copyright for Literate Robots', *Iowa Law Review*, (101), 657–682 (2016).

train AI when those works are included in a collection or database, cannot be explained by the economic incentive system of copyright.[106] If the developer has lawful access to the works no market failure needs to be resolved by extending the exclusive rights of individual authors to the downstream market for AI systems.[107] It is also highly unlikely that individual authors' right to reserve would result in payment.[108] To train an algorithm, it is necessary to have access to so many works that individual payment is both practically impossible as well as prohibitively expensive. For an AI system in operation – that is, the service employing a trained algorithm – it is relevant to ask whether it reproduces such content from works it has 'read' or been trained upon, so that the creative expression of the author is infringed. Using copyright-protected works to train algorithms is a use of those works as information, where the value of access to the works may be ascribed to the collection and whether the collection is representative, complete and generalizable, features that are unrelated to the individual works. This 'added' value is related to the collection, and as such forms part of the incentive system for database rights or publishers' rights.[109] Economic arguments therefore support rules that strike a fair balance between database right holders and publishers and developers of AI when using the collection to train their algorithms, but with regard to the authors of individual works, the exception would have been more effective if mandatory.

Second, it is questionable whether the balance struck with the new exception for TDM – if applicable to ML – is fair. As automated processing of huge amounts of data becomes easier and has infinite future use cases, the income potential from big data-related services is likely to exponentially increase the value of data and content collections. Reluctance by publishers and database owners can be expected in terms of opening their repositories to be included in training corpora for commercial ML, and pricing may be prohibitive for start-ups and innovators.[110] It would have been a possibility to open up for compulsory licensing for ML to develop services serving the public interest, such as journalistic tools for fact checking, or securing information integrity, to avoid so-called 'fake news'-related issues. However, it is difficult to use one application of an AI service as justification for a mandatory exception or compulsory licence for the process of ML. As discussed above, an algorithm after training might be used to develop multiple services serving even opposing objectives, so the justification for ML will only cover ML for the purpose

---

[106]   Poort (n 37), 330.
[107]   Ibid.
[108]   Margoni (n 14), 20.
[109]   Poort (n 37), 330.
[110]   See also Geiger et al. 2020 (n 33), discussing how the right to opt out could discriminate against small businesses and start-ups in access to data.

of developing that one service. Furthermore, a balancing of interests based on a public interest justification for the application of the service must cover both the interests of collective right holders in training materials for the algorithm in the development phase, as well as the interests of individual right holders in works used in running the (trained) service. To what extent these interests are interfered with will depend on the individual characteristics of the ML process and the service. Thus, it is difficult to make out a clear scope for a public interest justification that provides legal certainty both for right holders and for AI developers.

Finally, regulation of TDM and ML in EU copyright law may be seen as a further step in developing copyright law as a system for balancing access to and control of uses of online available content in general, gradually moving away from the traditional functionality of copyright law; namely, as an incentive for creative efforts. Exclusive rights have been gradually expanded, but focus within copyright law remains narrow, limited to the economic interests of right holders. It is questionable whether the public interests concerned with development of AI, and training of algorithms can be sufficiently safeguarded within this system. Overlapping rights and many and complicated exceptions create legal uncertainty.[111] The option to reserve against ML activities and the narrow focus on economic interests may pose risks to data transparency and integrity, as well as making it more difficult to ensure that datasets are complete, representative and generalizable and free of human bias that might pose a risk for secure use of AI. It would probably better serve the public interest – in particular to promote transparency – to base control of the use of AI on the use of the service online or in the market, but not through privately enforced rights at the development stage.

---

[111]  Geiger et al. 2018 (n 28), 836.

# Conclusions on *Artificial Intelligence and the Media*

## Taina Pihlajarinne and Anette Alén-Savikko

In the light of the contributions of this volume, we can conclude that, in the field of automated media, AI is not something outside our everyday lives or something science-fictional – it is operational and governance tools that affect our experiences and world views. Whether it is a question of biased data or invisible algorithmic tools, they end up changing the world for better or worse. Accountability, for its part, is about tackling those issues in a way that restores or establishes a balance for the better. For example, when technical operations lead to opacity, the answer is to reduce that opacity. Or we can look back on traditional models in hope of finding a cure for the dissemination of disinformation. But it matters how all this is achieved: we need to rethink the basics and find the right questions. Only this will enable informed law and policy which then may incentivise accountable utilisation of AI and reduce at least some of the negative societal impacts. This will take us one step closer to our goal in becoming a sustainable democratic society.

While some questions relating to the accountable utilisation of AI cross many areas (such as general liability issues), the contributions in this volume demonstrate that context-specific problems in the media sector are in dire need of examination and re-evaluation. For its part, the media – and especially journalism – have a specific role in society as a source of reliable information and as a venue for diverse views and opinions. The media caters for many tastes in entertainment and cultural content. However, it very prominently follows economic logic or is at least under substantial demands for efficiency. These roles and frameworks are then reflected in the potential benefits and risks of AI. The usual story is that the benefits of AI in the media sector include more effective journalistic work and more room left for the creative efforts of journalists as well as improved filtering systems for content containing material harmful for a democratic society such as hate speech. However, the other side of the coin is that the same technology involves risks such as boosting bias by utilising data without careful analysis and precautions or by perpetuating unfair practices. Automated media and creation of media content need a carefully balanced system of rights and responsibilities, including a system of incentives. Policymakers are in a difficult position in tailoring such a system for the media sector.

Even though automation and diverse AI applications are already widely utilised in many types of media practices, it becomes clear from many contributions in this volume that in some regards AI is still at the stage of future expectations and potential uses rather than an actor or factor that would already have revolutionised the media sector. As illustrated by most authors, if not all of them, a need for human control – or lack of it if technology becomes more advanced – is a key feature from the perspective of the legal issues discussed in this volume. Furthermore, the reactions of policymakers relating to adaptations of law towards this independent 'actorship' of AI will have a crucial impact on the incentives and possibilities for accountable utilisation of AI.

Indeed, incentivising accountable utilisation of AI in the media implies multiple measures. One crucial element is the basic knowhow of AI that both media professionals and the public should acquire or possess. For instance, Leiser highlights the risks for journalistic integrity and for society at large caused by utilisation of biased training data in journalistic endeavours. The consequences can be unexpected and very serious, ranging from discrimination and other infringements of civil liberties to economic and social losses. We can safely conclude that knowledge of AI all the way from development to production and consumption is a basic requirement for accountable use of AI in the media.

Secondly, as Napoli and Graf point out, we should not be blind to continuity or structural issues in automated media, especially when it comes to social media. It is a question of evolution rather than revolution in terms of new technology: solutions may therefore draw from the past even if tailored for the future, while digitalisation should not turn our gaze away from incumbency. Indeed, it may create new imbalances as Goanta and Spanakis show. The key is – as stated above – to rethink the basics and find the right questions. This means, for example, rethinking the concept of public resources and regulation in their benefit. Similarly, as Päivi Korpisaari concludes, AI further blurs the lines between journalism and other types of media activity. For this reason, concepts used in legal instruments, such as 'journalistic purpose', become even more difficult to interpret and apply. Accountable utilisation of AI from a data privacy perspective would mean that the concept is not interpreted too broadly in order to preserve the legitimacy of the exception. However, Korpisaari also advises not to give the utilised technology too much emphasis. Indeed, the EU proposal also aims for a 'future-proof' model and relies on principles.[1] Even if

---

[1]    Commission, 'Proposal for a Regulation of the European Parliament and of the Council laying down rules on artificial intelligence (Artificial Intelligence Act)

AI has its peculiarities, we can safely conclude that these issues of continuity are crucial with regard to the 'balance' that both this volume and the EU proposal for an Artificial Intelligence Act[2] aim to promote.

As noted in the Introduction, this volume offers both complementary and critical perspectives in comparison to the EU proposal. For example, the proposal includes (specifically tailored) transparency obligations[3] which at first sight appear to be much in line with those discussed by Alén-Savikko in this volume in the context of automated media. Moreover, it is worth mentioning that, in this context, content manipulation is discussed in the EU proposal as a particularly distressing method for disinformation powered by AI and therefore calling for an obligation to disclose the fact that automation is involved.[4] However, it seems that transparency is being transformed into a legal obligation without much hesitation – or indeed, the caution and cross-disciplinary insights advised by Alén-Savikko. With regard to future expectations, AI has great potential to promote legal and ethical practices in the media sector. AI might be able to 'self-certify' or it may be designed for compliance of various legal and ethical requirements – as pointed out by both Alén-Savikko and Vesala. Moreover, as Tong states, AI tools – unlike people – might eventually be able to remove hate speech or other types of hostile content from social media platforms even before such content causes damage. However, this is not a reality yet, as Tong explains, due to the stage of technological development. With this in mind, we should not be expecting too much too soon, but should rather acknowledge and share our own responsibility for content on social media. These issues relate to caution, research-based solutions, and our own actions, which are also crucial in terms of the increasing 'actorship' of AI.

Finally, then, we need to address the question of appropriate incentives in the media sector disrupted by the increasingly independent AI. Traditionally, legal tools have included IP rights, copyright and related rights in particular. For his part, Rognstad emphasises the importance of utilising analytical tools such as a causation test developed for the current copyright framework. These kinds of tools might promote predictability in a situation where it might be too risky, timely, or costly to revise copyright rules and where the future of AI remains an open question. This approach seems to be in line with the views of Pihlajarinne, Thesleff, Leppänen, and Valmari. According to them, promptly implemented extensions to exclusive rights should be avoided – also

---

and amending certain Union legislative acts COM (2021) 206 final (21 April 2021) 3
https://eur-lex.europa.eu/legal-content/EN/ALL/?uri=CELEX:52021PC0206 accessed
16 May 2021.
[2]   Ibid.
[3]   Ibid., 14–15.
[4]   Ibid.

in terms of challenges for current doctrines and incentives caused by unlimited possibilities for alterations of journalistic works (e.g., rephrasing methods, translations, simplifications, localisation, personalisation, and summarisation methods). For his part, Vesala takes a look at a relatively new right in the field of media and concludes that it has consequences for the way media practices powered by AI are designed – all the way to favouring less independent forms of AI.

When it comes to AI, availability of data is another crucial question for incentives, and the current system might not create balanced outcomes in this regard. As demonstrated by Ørstavik, the current exclusive rights regime around data might hinder the development of AI and training of algorithms, which in turn creates risks for data transparency and integrity as well as for the quality of datasets. These issues take us back to issues of transparency and bias already discussed in other contexts by Leiser and Alén-Savikko respectively. To avoid these risks, Ørstavik recommends that control of the use of AI would be based elsewhere than in privately enforced rights at the development stage. Then again, from a viewpoint of possible legal personhood status for AI, Ballardini and van den Hoven van Genderen note that *sui generis* legal status for AI would enable developing a multi-layered system of insurance to cover damage caused in an infringement situation.

All in all, we need research-based knowledge. We also need to recognise both the role of the human(s) and the machine(s) involved – the portions depend on each case of application and use. We need to return to the basics and address questions of private and public, journalism, and so forth. Moreover, no ready-made solutions are fit for all situations where rights and responsibilities need rethinking.

We sincerely hope that the contributions in this volume function as elements in establishing a balanced solution – whether in terms of legal and policy solutions or ethical ones. The authors have ventured into unknown territory during peculiar times of global emergency. Our warmest thanks to all authors for their amazing efforts.

# Index

access to data for training algorithms, *see* training data
access to information, as a fundamental right 66–7
accountability 4
    conditions of press publishers' right protection and 257–8
    legal personality for AI 206–7, 209, 211–13
    requirement of AI accountability 269, 271
    transparency and 36–9, 41–3, 45, 51, 56, 58
accountable content 59
accountable journalism 53–4, 59
ad revenue 158
advertiser-supported media 117–18
aggregate user data 108, 109–22
    as public resource 110–22
    scope and limitations of the public trustee model 115–19
agricultural society 207
AI–human hybrid content moderation 125–6
AI impact assessment 30
algorithmic auditing 51, 58
algorithmic journalism
    development of 33–6
    self-regulation in Finland 53–6, 57
    transparency in 48–60
algorithmic transparency 49, 51
algorithms 12
    access to data for training algorithms, *see* training data
    content moderation on social media 125–6, 139, 140
    machine learning and 276–8
Algotransparency 156
Alicia T 204

alterations of others' works 225–6, 228–9, 237–8
amanuensis doctrine 189
Angwin, J. 101
*Animal Defenders International v The United Kingdom* 74
anti-Muslim riots 123
antitrust enforcement 99–100
Arab Spring 136
Arabic, terrorist content in 140
artificial intelligence (AI)
    AI impact assessment 30
    evolution and revolution in the AI era 1–2
    in fact-checking 17–21
    legal personality 6, 192–3, 203–14, 299
    legal positioning of different types 193–5
    in media creation and innovation 195–7
    in news production 14–17, 18, 55–6, 57–8, 222–7
    regulating AI in the EU 21–5
    understanding AI systems 10–14
Associated Press 15, 223
Association for Technology and Internet 78
Australia 142
Austria 78
authorial intent 186
authoritarian countries 124, 125, 135–6, 141
authorship
    AI-generated works and IPR 197–9, 210–11
    copyright law 173–5, 176, 218–21, 231
        AI-generated works 179–85, 191